Communications
in Computer and Information Science 1151

Commenced Publication in 2007
Founding and Former Series Editors:
Phoebe Chen, Alfredo Cuzzocrea, Xiaoyong Du, Orhun Kara, Ting Liu,
Krishna M. Sivalingam, Dominik Ślęzak, Takashi Washio, Xiaokang Yang,
and Junsong Yuan

Editorial Board Members

More information about this series at http://www.springer.com/series/7899

Moisés Torres · Jaime Klapp (Eds.)

Supercomputing

10th International Conference on Supercomputing in Mexico, ISUM 2019
Monterrey, Mexico, March 25–29, 2019
Revised Selected Papers

 Springer

Editors
Moisés Torres 🆔
Sociedad Mexicana de Supercomputo
Guadalajara, Jalisco, Mexico

Jaime Klapp 🆔
Instituto Nacional de Investigaciones
Nucleares
La Marquesa, Estado de México, Mexico

ISSN 1865-0929   ISSN 1865-0937   (electronic)
Communications in Computer and Information Science
ISBN 978-3-030-38042-7   ISBN 978-3-030-38043-4   (eBook)
https://doi.org/10.1007/978-3-030-38043-4

This Springer imprint is published by the registered company Springer Nature Switzerland AG
The registered company address is: Gewerbestrasse 11, 6330 Cham, Switzerland

Preface

High Performance Computing (HPC) or Supercomputing have the power to contribute in an important way to the research and development of a country and to improve and reform many industrial sectors. Researchers at universities and engineers in diverse industries, have come to depend on the power of these machines to compute high volumes of data for finding the results they are looking for. Complex calculations in many cases require high volumes of data that would have taken hours, days, and sometimes weeks or months to process two to three decades ago. But now a days with the processing power that HPC machines manage, we are able to move faster with our results to save time, money, and often sometimes lives. On the other hand, we can now perform numerical simulations with a much higher resolution that is translated into producing results which better reproduce the physical world in which we live.

As an example of an HPC initiative that could boost the development of an industry in a country, we mention that the Mexican government and the European Union (EU) decided to collaborate to improve their energy industries, which provided an opportunity for EU HPC researchers to team up with Mexican colleagues. The aim? To provide solutions for the oil and gas industry, improve wind energy performance, and solve issues of combustion efficiency for transportation systems. Recently launched in Barcelona (June 2019), ENERXICO, a new project jointly funded by the EU and the Mexican government, brought together 15 institutions in an academic-industry collaboration to solve real-world engineering problems. It focused on scaling in wind energy, oil/gas exploration and reservoir modeling, and biofuels for transportation. In parallel, to power these applications, the project will work on achieving scalable, energy-efficient simulations for the exascale era. The project is led by the Instituto Nacional de Investigaciones Nucleares of México (ININ) and the Barcelona Supercomputer Centre of Spain (BSC). The other institutions that collaborated in the project are: Petróleos Mexicanos (PEMEX-PEP), Universidad Autónoma Metropolitana, Universidad Nacional Autónoma de México, Centro de Investigación y de Estudios Avanzados del Instituto Politécnico Nacional, Instituto Mexicano del Petróleo, Instituto Politécnico Nacional, Tecnische Universität München, Université Grenoble Alpes, Centro de Investigaciones Energéticas, Medioambientales y Tecnologías, Repsol, Iberdrola, Bull Atos, and Universitat Politécnica de Valencia. We hope that following the ENERXICO project, new HPC large scale initiatives will be carried out in Mexico.

This 10th International Supercomputing Conference in Mexico fosters the continuous growth of HPC in Mexico and Latin America, gathering the supercomputing communities to share their latest research works.

It is worth noting that Mexico has significant experience in the uses of supercomputers, which began in 1991, when UNAM installed a Cray YMP. Afterwards, Mexico appeared in the Top 500 supercomputing list several times: the case of the oil industry (Top 83, Top 84, and Top 85 in the list of November 2003). A few years later, UNAM and UAM placed computers in places 126 (2006) and 225 (2008), respectively. Other outstanding projects in Mexico are the National Laboratory for High Performance Computing in Mexico City (UNAM-UAM-CINVESTAV), the National Supercomputing Center of San Luis Potosi within the Instituto Potosino de Investigación Científica y Tecnológica (IPICYT), the Grids National Laboratory, the National Supercomputing Laboratory of the Southeast (LNS) from the Bemérita Universidad Autónoma de Puebla, and ABACUS CINVESTAV, which placed its supercomputer in the 255 place of the top 500 list of June 2015. In addition to these laboratories, a recent new supercomputer center was inaugurated at the University of Guadalajara, Centro de Análisis de Datos y Supercómputo (CADS), and the University Autonomous of the State of Mexico (UAEMEX) will be opening a center in the next year. Although we have a platform and experience in supercomputing, these supercomputing resources are not enough to conduct research and development for a country like Mexico. The joint efforts by institutions, organizations, and government continue to examine the direction and need in academia, government, society, and industry of computer power to advance research and development.

With an effort to continue to evolve in the uses of supercomputing and of these powerful machines in research and development in Mexico and Latin America, the International Supercomputing Conference in Mexico (ISUM) was founded by a group of researchers, supercomputing directors, IT directors, and technologists representing the largest research institutions, along with the support of the largest technology vendors in Mexico. This conference was established to provide a space for researchers and technologists to present their research works related to HPC. Building on the experience of the previous 9 editions, this 10th edition of ISUM was held in the progressive and industrial city of Monterrey, Nuevo Leon, Mexico, where more than 1,205 attendees had the opportunity to hear 5 international keynote speakers, 16 national and international speakers, 10 thematic tracks, and more than 60 research presentations. The conference covered themes in HPC architecture, networks, system software, algorithmic techniques, modeling and system tools, clouds, distributed computing, big data, data analytics, visualization and storage, applications for science and engineering, and emerging technologies. The thematic tracks included, Smart-Cities, Artificial Intelligence, Cybersecurity, Energy, Supercomputer Infrastructure, Women in STEM, Supercomputer Projects in Mexico, Supercomputing in Latin America, Biotechnology, and Supercomputing in Nuevo Leon, Monterrey. There were five workshops offered in various areas of supercomputing conducted by an international group of instructors. In addition, the conference had 2 plenary round tables and 10 round tables in the thematic tracks where important issues related to supercomputing were discussed; themes like strengthening graduate programs in supercomputing in Mexico, creating national and international project opportunities in supercomputing, and fostering the uses of supercomputing in industry for the development of Mexico and Latin America in areas such as artificial intelligence, biotechnology, smartcities, etc. These round tables gathered experts in the respective areas representing Mexico, Europe, and Latin America and included academia, industry, and government.

The central part of ISUM is the presentation of the latest research work conducted primarily but not limited to Mexico and Latin America. This book presents the selected works from more than 70 works presented at ISUM 2019. Each work was reviewed by three expert reviewers from an international group of experts in the respective area. These works are divided into five parts that include, Part I: Applications; Part II: Algorithm Techniques; Part III: HPC Architecture; Part IV: Parallel Computing; and Part V: HPC Modelling. Each section presents a series of works that you will find instrumental and enhancing to your repertoire of knowledge in the respective areas of study.

The book is aimed towards senior undergraduate and graduate students, as well as scientists in the fields of HPC, computer sciences, physics, biology, mathematics, engineering, and chemistry, who have an interest in the solution of a large variety of problems that make use of supercomputers. The material included in this book is adequate for both teaching and research.

The editors are grateful to the institutions and people who made possible ISUM 2019 through their support: Cesar Díaz Torrejón, Universidad Abierta y a Distancia de México (UnADM); Luis Díaz Sánchez, Universidad Autónoma del Estado de México (UAEMEX); Luis Gutiérrez Díaz de León, Universidad de Guadalajara; Felipe Bracho Carpizo y Fabián Romo, Universidad Autónoma de México (UNAM); Raúl Rivera, Centro de Investigación Científica y de Educación Superior de Ensenada (CISESE); Carlos Casasús López Hermosa, Corporación Universitaria para el Desarrollo de internet (CUDI); Salma Leticia Jalife Villalón, Secretaria de Comunicaciones y Transporte (SCT); and Moisés Torres Martínez, Sociedad Mexicana de Supercómputo (SOMEXSU A.C.) Universidad Abierta y a Distancia de México, and Red Mexicana de Supercómputo (REDMEXSU) Consejo Técnico Académico (CTA). We give special recognition to our corporate sponsors, without whom this event would not have been possible. Special recognition to ATOS, IBM/Sinergia Sys, DELL, Intel, Totalplay Empresarial, Fujitsu, IPICYT-CNS, Global Hitss, SparkCognition, Mellanox, Lenovo, and ITEXICO.

The following individuals were instrumental in leading the evaluation of these works: Juan Manuel Ramírez Alcaraz, Alfredo Cristóbal Salas, Andrei Tchernykh, Cesar Díaz Torrejón, Erwin Martin, Enrique Varela, Jaime Klapp, Liliana Barbosa Santillán, Luis Díaz Sánchez, Luis Gutiérrez Díaz de León, Moises Torres Martínez, Manuel Aguilar Cornejo, Rene Luna, Salvador Castañeda, and Sergio Nemeschnow. We thank them for the time spent in coordinating the evaluation process of these research works.

We give special thanks to the ISUM national and local committees, and Universidad Autónoma de Nuevo León for all their support in making this event possible. We give special thanks to Veronica Lizette Robles Dueñas, Marlene Ilse Martinez Rodriguez, Claudia Karina Casillas Godinez, Angie Fernández Olimón, Adriana Margarita Jimenez Cortez, and Araceli Gutierrez Campuzano for all their support in organizing all the logistics of this successful edition of ISUM.

The thematic track on "HPC Energy Applications and the ENERXICO Project" as well as the production of this book received funding from the ENERXICO project under the European Union's Horizon 2020 Programme, grant agreement n° 828947, and from the Mexican Department of Energy, CONACYT-SENER Hidrocarburos grant agreement n° B-S-69926, and from the Ibero-American Programme for the Development of Science and Technology (CYTED) under Project 516RT0512, CONICYT (Chile).

In conclusion we thank all the institutions who have supported this event throughout these 10 editions, especially this 10th anniversary of ISUM: BUAP LNS-SURESTE, UdeG, UCol, UNISON, ININ, CUDI, IPN, UAM, UNAM, CICESE, CIMAT-Merida, UAEMEX, CNS-IPICYT, ABACUS-CINVESTAV, CONACYT, SOMEXSU A.C., and REDMEXSU.

October 2019

Moisés Torres
Jaime Klapp

Organization

Sociedad Mexicana de Supercómputo A.C. (SOMEXSU A.C.) and Red Mexicana de Supercómputo (REDMEXSU).

Organizing Committee

Moisés Torres Martínez	SOMEXSU A.C. and Universidad de Guadalajara (UDG), Mexico
Jaime Klapp	Instituto Nacional de Investigaciones Nucleares (ININ), Mexico
César Carlos Díaz Torrejón	SOMEXSU A.C. and Universidad Abierta y a Distancia de Mexico (UnADM), Mexico
Salvador Castañeda Ávila	Centro de Investigación Científica y de Educación Superior de Ensenada, Baja California (CICESE), Mexico
Luis Enrique Díaz Sánchez	SOMEXSU A.C. and Universidad Autónoma del Estado de México (UAEMEX), Mexico
Luis Alberto Gutiérrez Díaz de León	Universidad de Guadalajara (UDG), Mexico
Raúl Rivera Rodríguez	Centro de Investigación Científica y de Educación Superior de Ensenada, Baja California (CICESE), Mexico
Andrei Tchernykh	Centro de Investigación Científica y de Educación Superior de Ensenada, Baja California (CICESE), Mexico
Isidoro Gitler	Laboratorio de Matemática Aplicada y Cómputo de Alto Rendimiento (CINVESTAV-ABACUS), Mexico
René Luna García	Instituto Politécnico Nacional (IPN), Mexico
Manuel Aguilar Cornejo	Universidad Autónoma Metropolitana (UAM), Mexico
Juan Manuel Ramírez Alcaraz	Universidad de Colima (UCOL), Mexico
Jesús Cruz Gúzman	Universidad Nacional Autónoma de México (UNAM), Mexico
Alfredo Santillán González	Universidad Nacional Autónoma de México (UNAM), Mexico
Raúl Hazas Izquierdo	Universidad de Sonora (UNISON), Mexico
Erwin Martín Panameño	Benemérita Universidad Autónoma de Puebla (BUAP), Mexico
Fabián Romo	Universidad Nacional Autónoma de México (UNAM), Mexico

Juan Manuel Ramírez Alcaraz	Universidad de Colima (UCOL), Mexico
Alfredo Cristóbal	Universidad Veracruzana (UV), Mexico
Liliana Barbosa	Universidad de Guadalajara (UdeG), Mexico
Carlos Franco Rebodera	Universidad de Guadalajara (UdeG), Mexico
Eduardo de la Fuente	Universidad de Guadalajara (UdeG), Mexico
Isabel Pedraza	Benemérita Universidad de Puebla (BUAP), Mexico

Program Committee

Members

Andrés Ávila, Chile
Alejandro Avilés, Mexico
Javier R. Balderrama, France
Carlos J. Barrios, Colombia
Lola Bautista, Colombia
Carlos Bederían, Argentina
Cristiana Bentes, Brazil
Cristina Boeres, Brazil
Rossana Bonasia, Mexico
Francisco Brasileiro, Brazil
Carlos Buil Aranda, Chile
Victor Calo, Saudi Arabia
Néstor Calvo, Argentina
Luis Fernando Castillo, Colombia
Marcio Castro, Brazil
Harold Castro, Colombia
Gerson Cavalheiro, Brazil
Marcia Cera, Brazil
Andrea Charao, Brazil
Esteban Clua, Brazil
Daniel Cordeiro, Brazil
Álvaro Coutinho, Brazil
Fernando Crespo, Chile
Marcela Cruchaga, Chile
Jesús Cruz, Mexico
Gregoire Danoy, Luxembourg
Alvaro de la Ossa, Costa Rica
Claudio Delrieux, Argentina
César Díaz, Colombia
César Díaz, Mexico
Gilberto Díaz, Venezuela
Bernabé Dorronsoro, France
Nicolás Erdody, New Zealand
Pablo Ezzatti, Uruguay

Ricardo Farias, Brazil
Alejandro Flores-Méndez, Mexico
Ruslan Gabbasov, Mexico
Verónica Gil Costa, Argentina
Isidoro Gitler, Mexico
Brice Goglin, France
Antonio Gomes, Brazil
José L. Gordillo, Mexico
Benjamín Hernández, USA
Gonzalo Hernández, Chile
Tiberio Hernández, Colombia
Salma Jalife, Mexico
Jaime Klapp, Mexico
Alejandro Kolton, Argentina
Roberto León, Chile
Francisco Luna, Spain
Rafael Mayo, Spain
Ricardo Medel, Argentina
Wagner Meira Jr., Brazil
Alba Melo, Brazil
Esteban Menezes, Costa Rica
Renato Miceli, Brazil
Pablo Mininni, Argentina
David Monge, Argentina
Sergio Nesmachnow, Uruguay
Luis Nuñez, Colombia
Julio Paciello, Paraguay
Elina Pacini, Argentina
Jairo Panetta, Brazil
Johnatan Pecero, Mexico
Gabriel Pedraza, Colombia
Guilherme Peretti Pezzi, Italy
Jorge Pérez, Belgique
Carlos Piedrahita, Colombia

Laercio Pilla, Brazil
Carlos Hernán, France
Javier Príncipe, Spain
Marcela Printista, Argentina
Juan Manuel Ramírez Alcaraz, Mexico
Raúl Ramos Pollan, Mexico
Vinod Rebello, Brazil
Olivier Richard, France
Genghis Ríos, Peru
Robinson Rivas, Venezuela
Ascanio Rojas, Venezuela
Isaac Rudomin, Spain
Alfredo Cristóbal Salas, Mexico
Alfonso Sales, Brazil
Liria Sato, Brazil
Lucas Schnorr, France
Hermes Senger, Brazil

Alejandro Soba, Argentina
Luiz Angelo Steffenel, France
Mario Storti, Argentina
Andrei Tchernykh, Mexico
Fernando Tinetti, Argentina
Patricia Tissera, Argentina
Claudio Torres, Chile
Moisés Torres, Mexico
Tram Truong Huu, Singapore
Manuel Ujaldón, Spain
Grabiel Usera, Uruguay
Carlos A. Varela, USA
Mariano Vasquez, Spain
José Luis Vazquez-Poletti, Spain
Pedro Velho, Brazil
Jesús Verduzco, Mexico
Nicolás Wolovick, Argentina

Editorial Committee

Chairs

Moisés Torres Martínez   SOMEXSU A.C. and Universidad de Guadalajara
                          (UDG), Mexico
Jaime Klapp   Instituto Nacional de Ciencias Nucleares (ININ),
                          Mexico

Sponsoring Institutions

- Sociedad Mexicana de Supercómputo (SOMEXSU A.C.)
- Red Mexicana de Supercómputo (REDMEXSU)
- Consejo Nacional de Ciencia y Tecnología (Conacyt)
- Instituto Nacional de Investigaciones Nucleares (ININ)
- Universidad de Guadalajara
- Universidad Autónoma de Nuevo León
- Nuevo Léon 4.0
- Laboratorio de Matemática Aplicada y Computo de Alto Rendimiento (Abacus) of the Centro de Investigación y de Estudios Avanzados of the Instituto Politécnico Nacional
- ENERXICO Project: European Union Horizon 2020 Programme, Grant Agreement No. 828947, and the Mexican CONACYT-SENER-Hidrocarburos, Grant Agreement No. B-S-69926
- Ibero-American Programme for the Development of Science and Technology (CYTED) under Project 516RT0512, CONICYT

Acknowledgments

The production of this book has been sponsored by the Sociedad Mexicana de Supercomputo (SOMEXSU A.C.), Red Mexicana de Supercomputo (REDMEXSU), Consejo Nacional de Ciencia y Tecnología (Conacyt), Instituto Nacional de Investigaciones Nucleares, Universidad de Guadalajara, Universidad Abierta y a Distancia de México (UnADM), Universidad Autónoma de Nuevo León, Nuevo León 4.0, Centro de Investigación y de Estudios Avanzados of the Instituto Politécnico Nacional (Cinvestav-Abacus), Universidad Nacional Autónoma de México, CYTED Project No. 516RT0512 (CONICYT, Chile), and the ENERXICO project (through the European Union Horizon 2020 Programme, Grant Agreement No. 828947, and the Mexican CONACYT-SENER-Hidrocarburos Grant Agreement No. B-S-69926).

Contents

Algorithm Techniques

HPC Architecture

Parallel Computing

HPC Modelling

Applications

Generation and Classification of Energy Load Curves Using a Distributed MapReduce Approach

Santiago Garabedian[1], Rodrigo Porteiro[1(✉)],
and Sergio Nesmachnow[2]

[1] UTE, Montevideo, Uruguay
{sgarabedian, rporteiro}@ute.com.uy
[2] Universidad de la República, Montevideo, Uruguay
sergion@fing.edu.uy

Abstract. In nowadays energy markets, suppliers are encouraged to model the electricity consumption behavior of their customers in order to improve the quality of service and provide better products with lower investment and operating costs. New load models to support power system are required to mitigate scalability issues, especially considering the increasing penetration of distributed energy resources, varying load demands, and large volumes of data from smart meters. Smart metering allows obtaining detailed measures of the power consumption in the form of large time series that encode load curves. Clustering methods are applied to group costumers according to their similarity, by extracting characteristics of their behavior. Traditional computing approaches are not efficient to deal with the aforementioned problem, particularly when it must be solved in real time. This article proposes applying distributed computing and statistical learning methods to the problem of load curves classification of electricity consumers, applying the Map-Reduce model over the Hadoop framework. A case study, using real representative smart meter data from Uruguay is presented. The obtained results validate the stability and robustness of the approach. The main findings suggest that distributed computing can help electricity companies to deal with large volumes of data in order to improve energy management, provide services to consumers, and support modern smart grid technologies.

1 Introduction

In the last decades, electrical grids have gone through a process of change, mainly due to three factors: the desregulation of electricity markets, the emergency of new renewable energy sources, and the incorporation of information and communication technologies to provide a better use of energy and improve the quality of service. The concept of *smart grid* emerged to define electrical grids that incorporate the proper utilization of smart meters, smart appliances, different (renewable) energy resources, and energy efficiency procedures for operation [5, 10]. In this new paradigm, consumers can adopt an active role in the network, changing the traditional model of passive consumers. The electric system can stimulate consumers to adapt their

M. Torres and J. Klapp (Eds.): ISUM 2019, CCIS 1151, pp. 3–17, 2019.
https://doi.org/10.1007/978-3-030-38043-4_1

consumption patterns according to different proposals oriented to fulfill different goals, by implementing demand response techniques [13, 14].

Energy consumption characterization is a key tool for smart grids to gain useful information and improve the quality of service. Load profiles or *load curves* allow characterizing the variation of the electrical load consumed by a customer versus time. Load curves vary according to customer type and several other factors (i.e., working day or not, temperature, holiday season, etc.). Typical examples of load curves include residential, industrial, and commercial, and within these categories different patterns can also be identified. Load curves provide useful information to producers to plan the electricity needed for a proper operation of the system at any time. In turn, consumers can also benefit from suggestions of customized energy utilization plans, and also ad-hoc billing plans [17].

Load curves are determined by direct measurements using smart meters. On large cities, this procedure generates large volumes of data that must be properly processed to extract valuable information. There are important challenges for handling the resulting data efficiently, reliably, and in reasonable time. Distributed computing [6] and computational intelligence [11] help researchers to process large volumes of data in reasonable execution time. Information from individual costumer can be compressed in a canonical form that reduces the amount of data to be managed and allows extracting consumption patterns, e.g. by applying clustering techniques to group costumers according to their similarity. These algorithms can be further enhanced by applying parallel/distributed approaches [1].

This article presents a specific proposal applying distributed computing for characterization and classification of load curves using real data from the smart grid system in Uruguay [9]. Statistical learning methods are applied for clustering customers regarding their use of energy, as measured by smart meters. A distributed MapReduce approach is applied for the analysis, in order to obtain a load curve representative of each costumer and also to apply clustering techniques to the obtained curves.

The main contributions of the research reported in this article include a MapReduce approach to characterize each costumer through a load curve that captures the dynamics of power consumption behavior over time. In addition, a classification is performed by applying the *k*-means statistical learning method to the load curves, to obtain customer groups with similar behavior. The experimental evaluation of the proposed approach was performed over the high performance computing platform of the National Supercomputing Center (Cluster- UY), Uruguay [12]. The main results of the analysis indicate that the combination of high-performance distributed computing and computational intelligence provides an excellent solution to handle the complexity of characterizing hundreds of thousands costumers in a real business environment.

The article is organized as follows. Next section introduces the procedure for obtaining load curves and describes the available data. Section 3 introduces the proposed MapReduce approach and the implementation of the proposed algorithm for customer clustering. The experimental evaluation of the proposed approach are reported in Sect. 4. Finally, Sect. 5 presents the conclusions and summarizes the main lines for current and future work.

2 Load Curves Analysis for the Smart Grid in Uruguay

This section introduces the procedure for obtaining load curves and describes the data considered for the processing.

2.1 Load Curve Analysis

Load curve analysis is a valuable tool for understanding energy consumption patterns and anticipate the power demand of customers [7]. Load analysis are useful for both distribution and end-user customers to identify specific situations than can impact on the electric network operation. Specific devices such as smart grid meters and load profilers allow recording periodical energy consumption measurements. Furthermore, load profiles can be inferred from customer billing and can be enhanced by crossing with information extracted from other data sources. Several load analysis methods have been proposed in the literature, applying different methods [2, 8, 15, 16, 19]. Load curves analysis are applicable to many problems. In particular, any device that measures electrical load and generates large data can be analyzed through the proposed solution.

When analyzing load curves, it is desirable to generate abstract solutions that allow adapting the analysis to the specific problem that is being solved. Following this approach, this article proposes a solution that represents a starting point for the development of smart tools for energy management, based on the classification of load curves.

2.2 Data Description and Load Curves Model

The analysis reported in this article considers data gathered using smart meters installed in the residential area of Montevideo, Uruguay. Smart meters have been widely deployed around the world in recent years. The availability of smart meter data enables both utilities and consumers to have a better understanding of how energy is used. In Uruguay, smart meters began to be installed in 2016 in the residential area of Montevideo and other main cities on the country [9]. Nowadays, about 10000 smart meters are installed. However, there is still much work to be done to generate knowledge and make decisions based on this data.

The dataset studied in the research is formed by measurements. Measurements were obtained with Kaifa Smart Meters, models MA110P, MA309P, and MA309D. Each measurement is composed of:

- *Device identifier* (integer), representing a unique code for the smart meter.
- *Date* (yyyy-mm-dd), indicating the date on which the measure was taken.
- *Time* (hh:mm:ss), indicating the hour on which the measure was taken.
- *Power* (float), indicating the real power measured.

Data from smart meters are not public, due to privacy issues. Therefore, for the purpose of studying and validating the distributed method for load curve analysis, a synthetic data set was generated. The synthetic data set is based on real power consumption data from houses in Montevideo.

A systematic procedure was applied for data generation:

1. A set of original data consisting in 7000 load curves is used.
2. Average load curves are calculated from original data to keep privacy, by filtering 6 weeks of measurements so experimental analysis can be done using several weeks in the past. The frequency of measurements is 15 min, because smart meters collects electricity consumption with this frequency.
3. Four canonical curves were generated using the baseline average load curve:

   - *Curve 1:* each point of the curve is obtained from the corresponding power value on average curve adding a noise. Noise is generated in each instant of time, taking the corresponding point in canonical curve x_i, generating the interval $\left[\frac{3}{4}x_i, \frac{5}{4}x_i\right]$, and sampling a new point from it using a uniform distribution. A sample curve (one week) is shown in Fig. 1.

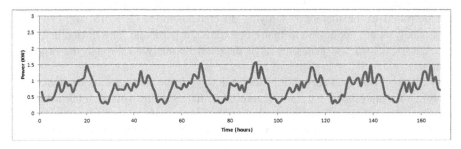

Fig. 1. Curve 1: Standard daily behavior replicated throughout the week. On weekends, power consumption is more homogeneously distributed during the day.

   - *Curve 2:* each point of the curve is obtained dividing the power value of the average curve by 3 and adding a constant $r = 0.3$ to flatten the curve and get a steady behaviour keeping a decent amount of energy. A sample curve (one week) is shown in Fig. 2.

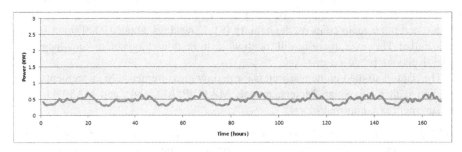

Fig. 2. Curve 2: Steady power consumption through the whole week.

   - *Curve 3:* Weekdays (Monday to Friday) are generated following the procedure for Curve 1 and weekends are generated following the procedure for Curve 2. Curve 3 captures the behavior of customers that have standard consumption on weekdays and low consumption on weekends. A sample curve (one week) is shown in Fig. 3.

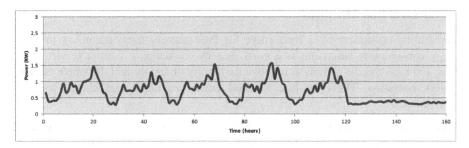

Fig. 3. Curve 3: Standard power consumption on weekdays, low power consumption on weekends.

- *Curve 4:* Weekdays (Monday to Friday) are generated following the procedure for Curve 2 and weekends are generated following the procedure for Curve 1. Curve 4 captures the behavior of customers that have low consumption on weekdays and standard consumption on weekends. A sample curve (one week) is shown in Fig. 4.

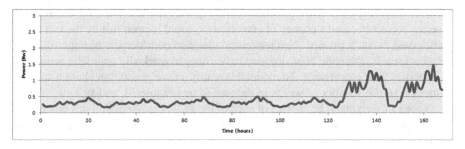

Fig. 4. Curve 4: Low power consumption on weekdays, standard power consumption on weekends.

4. In five years, it is estimated that the number of smart meters installed in Montevideo, Uruguay will be more than 100000. To model this scenario, data for 100000 costumers is generated, by taking one of the four canonical curves and adding noise according to the procedure described for Curve 1 to the canonical values. Thus, 250000 synthetic costumers are obtained from each canonical curve.

In all realistic time series there are usually missing or invalid values. However, the analysis reported in this article assumes that all data is received correctly, e.g., they were previously corrected by a cleansing procedure.

3 Generation and Classification of Load Curves

This section describes the design and implementation of the proposed method for generation of representative load curves and load curves classification.

3.1   General Considerations

Representing costumers by a load curve for later classify them according to their energy consumption behaviour is a good strategy for defining custom services and plans, and take specific actions to improve the quality of service and the whole electric network operation. The procedure for load curve generation and classification is described next.

Load Curve Generation. Relevant considerations are taken into account for load curve generation. On the one hand, it is important to consider the periodicity of energy utilization and possible variations in consumption behavior. Combining these two factors, a weekly representative load curve is used in the proposed analysis, because it captures clearly the periodicity. For example, it could happen that classifying costumers based on a daily curve result in a very similar energy utilization on weekdays and a very different one on weekends. Considering the whole week in the curve allows to ensure the similarity of behavior between two costumers.

On the other hand, the energy utilization of a costumer can vary by different dynamic circumstances. For example, no (or low) consumption due to a trip, the arrival of a new member of the family, the acquisition of a new household appliance, etc. In that sense, it is desirable to have a load curve representation that considers dynamic behaviour. Regarding historical information, Using only the last week for the analysis not seems correct because a change of classification could happen just by the fact that a unanticipated event happened. Neither seems adequate consider the average of many weeks backwards, since the behavior may have changed markedly and older weeks are less important than recent ones. To model this reality, curve generation phase takes two parameters: M, the number of weeks in the past to be considered, and $\boldsymbol{w} = (w_1, w_2, \ldots w_M)$ a vector of weights to be applied of each of the M weeks. Applying this procedure, a curve represented by a vector of 168 components, one for each hour of the week, is obtained: $representativeCurve = w_1 \times Week_1 + w_2 \times Week_2 + \ldots + w_m \times Week_M$ where $Week_i$ is the load curve of the i-th week (backwards in time). An hourly discretization was chosen, taking into account a compromise between keeping a small amount of data to avoid negative performance issues and capturing the necessary information to characterize the consumption behavior.

As an example, considering data for $M = 4$ weeks in the past and weights defined by $\boldsymbol{w} = (0.6, 0.2, 0.15, 0.05)$, then $representativeCurve = 0.6 \times Week_1 + 0.2 \times Week_2 + 0.15 \times Week_3 + 0.05 \times Week_4$. Figure 5 shows the application of the applied model. From the graphic, it is clear that the costumer behavior has changed the last week, therefore the representative load curve takes an intermediate shape between the ones for the previous three weeks and the one for last week. It can be observed that although the power consumption pattern changed only in the last week, the resulting curve adapts to the new behavior, because the corresponding weight for last week is greater than weights for the previous weeks.

Load Curve Classification. The second stage is load curves classification, which is performed using the k-means clustering algorithm. The main idea is to group load curves in k classes, to determine if they are characterized by a small number of representative patterns without losing significant information. Selecting the metric that

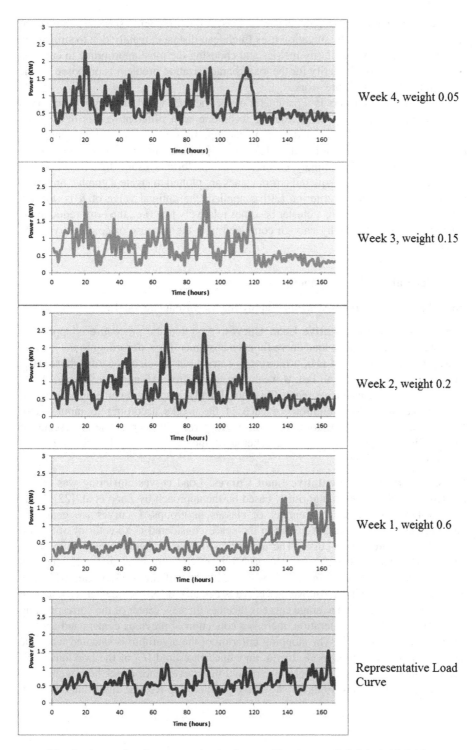

Fig. 5. A sample of representative load curve $M = 4$, $\boldsymbol{w} = (0.6, 0.2, 0.15, 0.05)$

better captures similarity is very related to the specific problem to solve. The proposed method for load curve classification uses Euclidean distance, mainly due to simplicity, but studying different similarity metrics and choosing the most appropriate to captures the desired notion of similarity for the load characterization problem is proposed as one of the main lines for future work.

The number of clusters is a parameter of the method, which usually is determined empirically, by executing the clustering technique with different values of k. More complex methods are able to determine the optimal value of k automatically, by applying multiobjective optimization [3]. In the proposed method, a single objective approach is applied. Preliminary executions are performed using different values of k and the obtained sum of squared errors values are plotted to create a graphic on which the well known "elbow" criterion [20] is applied: the optimal value of K is selected where the gain from adding a cluster becomes relatively low (i.e., the error reduction is considered to be not worthy enough compared with the increase of complexity in the clustering).

3.2   General Design Approach

Both phases of the proposed method apply the Map-Reduce model [4].

Generation of Representative Load Curves. A systematic procedure is applied to generate the representative load curve for each costumer. First, according to the number of weeks to be considered (M), a filtering is carried out to select records whose dates are within those weeks. The last M weeks are taken (from Monday to Sunday). Once filtered, measurements are aggregated by hour. Finally, after having an hourly curve for each of the M weeks, weighting of each of the weeks according to input vector $\boldsymbol{W} = (w_1, w_2, ..., w_m)$ is performed to get a single resulting curve (the representative curve). Figure 6 presents a generic schema of the parallel Map-Reduce algorithm designed for this stage.

Classification of Representative Load Curves. Load curves clustering was implemented using the k-means algorithm, based on the approach by Zhao et al. [22]. From the k value that defines the number of classes or groups, k curves are generated randomly as initial centers. A center in the space considered is a vector of 168 components that represents a curve. The algorithm follows an iterative procedure, computing the distance of each curve to each one of the k centers, and each curve is associated to the nearest center. In this way, a collection of curves associated with each of the centers is obtained. An average curve is calculated for each center, considering its associated curves. The average curve is taken as the new center of the corresponding class. At the end of each iteration, there is a collection of previous centers and another collection of new centers. The stopping criterion of the algorithm is satisfied when the new centers do not differ more than a predefined threshold (E) of the previous ones. Centers must be identified in order to carry out the convergence check homogeneously throughout the iterations. Figure 7 shows the parallel Map-Reduce algorithm designed.

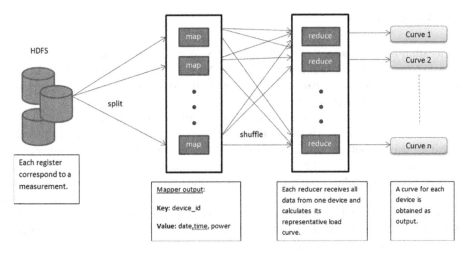

Fig. 6. Map Reduce parallel algorithm for computing representative load curves

In both Map-Reduce algorithms, implementing a combiner class would help to optimize communication costs between nodes, thus improving performance. Including a combiner when dealing with large volumes of data is proposed as one of the main lines of future work.

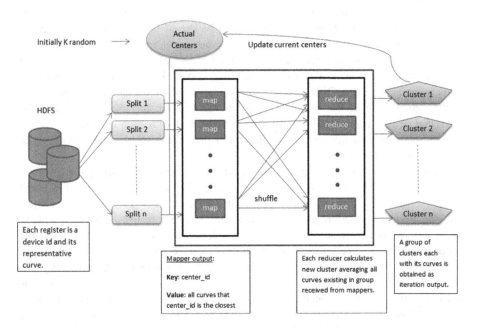

Fig. 7. Map Reduce parallel algorithm for load curves classification

3.3   Implementation

Generation of Representative Load Curves. A specific Map-Reduce algorithm was devised for generation of load curves, using the Apache Hadoop framework [21]. Input data is stored in Hadoop Distributed File System (HDFS) [18]. The main implementation details are provided below.

Mapper. A new class `LecturasMapper` was implemented, extending the `Mapper` class of Hadoop. The *map* function of `LecturasMapper` receives a record in text format and outputs a (*key, value*) pair, where the key is the device identifier and in the value are the rest of the fields: date, time, and power.

Reducer. A new class `CreatorCurvasReducer` was implemented, extending the `Reducer` class of Hadoop. The *reduce* function receives all values corresponding to the same key (i.e., all values associated to the same device). *Reduce* is responsible of filtering the *M* weeks and the aggregating per hour. It also calculates the weighted average to obtain the representative load curve.

Driver. The `main` function of the `CurvaRepresentativa` class fulfills the role of *driver*. In this case, the main function just configures the work, instantiate the *Mapper* and *Reducer* classes and establishes the input and output formats. The output of this step is a group of pairs containing the device id and its representative load curve.

Classification of Load Curves. For load curves classification, each collection of new centers found in a given iteration must be known in the next iteration by all nodes that collaborate in the solution. Thus, a mechanism for sharing information is needed. The proposed implementation makes use of the *Distributed Cache* of Hadoop, where the collection of centers is placed in a file that can be shared between Mappers. Furthermore, iterations are linked by using the *JobChaining* pattern (i.e., each iteration is a new *Job*). The Job of iteration *j* takes the output of the job of iteration *j*-1, i.e., a file with the centers and the collection of associated curves. Each Mapper reads the previous centers from the Distributed Cache. Finally, when the stopping criterion is reached, the output of the complete algorithm is obtained: the resulting centers (the curve that defines each class) and the curves associated with each center.

The main implementation details of each of the classes involved in the proposed solution are described next.

Mapper. A new class `MapperKMeans` was implemented, extending the `Mapper` class of Hadoop. The *map* function of this class receives a curve represented as a text string, interprets its content, and compares it with each one of the previous centers obtained from the Distributed Cache. Then, the Mapper creates a pair (*key, value*), where the key is the nearest center and the value is the curve itself. This way, the Reducer will receive the corresponding set of curves for each center.

Reducer. A new class `kMeansReducer` was implemented, extending the `Reducer` class of Hadoop. The *reduce* function receives a center as key and the collection of curves associated to it as value. Then, reduce averages all the center curves and gets a new center. The propose method uses Euclidean distance, but any otherdistance can be used depending on the notion of proximity that the decisionmaker wants to capture [19]. Finally, the new center calculated from the average is returned as a key and the collection of associated curves as value.

Driver. The `main` function of the `KMeansCurvas` class fulfills the driver role. It receives as parameters the paths of the file that defines the centers, the file with all the curves to be sorted, and the output directory. The JobChaining pattern is implemented, iterating until convergence is reached. For each iteration, a new Job is created, which takes the entry of the output directory of the Job corresponding to the previous iteration. The centers in each new iteration are obtained from the previous output and placed in the DistributedCache so that they are accessible to all Mappers of the new Job. To check convergence, the centers of the previous iteration and the current iteration are compared (one by one). In case that all the centers are closer than the E parameter to the previous ones, the algorithm is finished and the output of the last Mapper is the final output.

The output of the Map-Reduce algorithm for load curves classification is a collection containing for each resulting center its associated curves.

4 Experimental Analysis

This section presents the results of the experimental analysis of the proposed parallel distributed algorithm.

4.1 Methodology

The main goal of the analysis is to properly evaluate the accuracy of both algorithms (generation of representative load curves and load curves classification) and their execution time. The methodology consists in taking as input the measurements data described in Sect. 2.2 and applying the algorithm for generation of representative curves to obtain a curve for each of the 100000 customers. After that, the algorithm for load curves classification is applied to obtain a set of K classes of curves.

Execution Platform. Experiments were performed in an HP ProLiant DL380 G9 server with two Intel Xeon Gold 6138 processors (20 cores each) and 128 GB RAM, from the high performance computing infrastructure of National Supercomputing Center Cluster-UY [13].

4.2 Validation

The main details of the validation of the proposed algorithm are presented next.

Representative Load Curve. Preliminary experiments were performed to determine the appropriate value of parameter M (number of past weeks to consider). Results showed that using few weeks (1–2) in the past does not allow capturing the temporal dynamics of energy consumption behavior. The most appropriate value in preliminary experiments was $M = 4$. The weight in parameter $\boldsymbol{w}$ were set to capture the relative importance of each week, starting from $w1 = 0.6$ and the rest according to an exponential decay and taking into account that $\sum_{i=1}^{4} w_1 = 1$. Preliminary results allowed concluding that this selection of $\boldsymbol{w}$ allows appropriately weighting historical information. Furthermore, values of $\boldsymbol{w}$ do not affect the execution time.

Load Curve Classification. The representative load curves obtained in the first stage are used for clustering and the deviation/error is computed. A particular representative curve is composed of 168 values and it must be similar to the weekly pattern that generate the initial base curve, since initial baseline curves are homogeneous. Figure 8 depicts all representative curves in one plot, showing no detectable pattern.

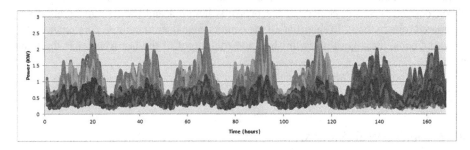

Fig. 8. All representative curves to be classified

4.3   Results

Representative Curve Results. A sample of representative curves was used to check the accuracy of the proposed algorithm (100000 customers, 49 GB). The expected result was obtained and the execution time was 379 s.

Load Curve Classification Results. An upper bound of the error incurred was computed. Curves were generated from its baseline, uniformly sampling between $\frac{3}{4}c_i^{(k)} \leq x_i \frac{5}{4}c_i^{(k)}$ for each component. Then $\left| x_i - c_i^{(k)} \right| \leq \frac{1}{2}c_i^{(k)}$. Considering that none of the canonical curves has values higher than 3 ($c_i^{(k)} \leq 3, \forall i, k$) the following inequality is verified: $\left| x_i - c_i^{(k)} \right|^2 \leq \frac{9}{4}c_i^{(k)}, \forall i, k$.

The error function in k-means algorithm is given by Eq. 1, where Δ is the set of curves, K is the number of clusters, $\mu^{(k)}$ is the center corresponding to cluster k and C_k are the collection of curves associated to $\mu^{(k)}$.

$$L(\Delta) = \sum_{k=1}^{K} \sum_{j \in C_k} \left\| x^{(j)} - \mu^{(k)} \right\|^2 \tag{1}$$

In the proposed analysis $K = 4$, $dim(x) = 168$ and $\#(\Delta) = 100000$ so,

$$L(\Delta) = \sum_{k=1}^{4} \sum_{j \in C_k} \left\| x^{(j)} - \mu^{(k)} \right\|^2 = \sum_{k=1}^{4} \sum_{j \in C_k} \sum_{i=1}^{168} \left| x_i^{(j)} - \mu_i^{(k)} \right|^2 \tag{2}$$

Thus, $\sum_{k=1}^{4} \sum_{j \in C_k} \sum_{i=1}^{168} \left| x_i^{(j)} - \mu_i^{(k)} \right|^2 \leq 4.100000.168\frac{9}{4} = 2.012 \times 10^8$ is obtained for the proposed analysis. If the algorithm groups curves as expected (each load curve is in the cluster corresponding to the center that generated the curve), then the error must verify the previous inequality. Experimental results showed that $L(\Delta) = 1.12 \times |10^7 \leq 2.012 \times 10^8$. Figures 9, 10, 11 and 12 show each group of curves separately. They clearly shows that curves were properly classied, as curves in each class are very similar among them.

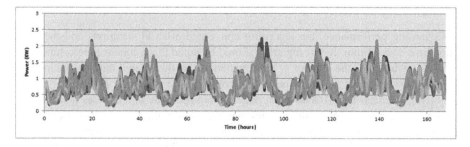

Fig. 9. Curves of class 1

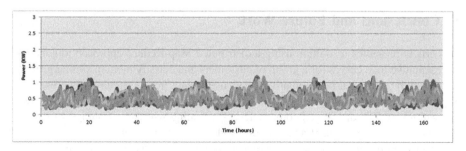

Fig. 10. Curves of class 2

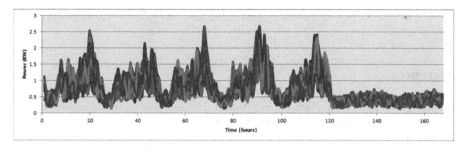

Fig. 11. Curves of class 3

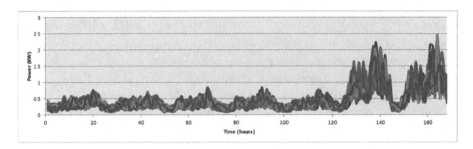

Fig. 12. Curves of class 4

Regarding performance, the algorithm converged after 11 iterations and the execution time was 19 min. In this regard, it should be noted that k-means time complexity is $O(TKn)$, where n is the number of input patterns, K is the desired number of clusters, and T is the number of iterations needed to complete the clustering process. The case study uses 4 clusters and 100000 input patterns, but probably in real cases no less than 20 clusters are needed. Also, in Uruguay there are one million costumers. Both facts determine that the execution time will be 50 times larger in a real scenario, which can be handled properly. These results demonstrate the viability of the proposed distributed approach for generating and classifying representative load curves.

5   Conclusions and Future Work

This article presented a solution using a distributed Map-Reduce approach to generate representative load curves for a group of customers and classify them in similar groups. A case study using real representative smart meter data from Uruguay was presented. Experimental results validated the scalability and robustness of the proposed approach, suggesting that The distributed computing helps dealing with large volumes of data to improve energy management and support modern smart grid technologies.

The main lines for future work are related to improve the Map-Reduce approach by implementing a Combiner class that reduces the information shared for generation of representative load curves. Different similarity metrics should be studied to captures different features that are relevant for the analysis. Furthermore, the solution can be extended to include new customers in a dynamic way, or implement demand response techniques.

References

1. Alba, E., Luque, G., Nesmachnow, S.: Parallel metaheuristics: recent advances and new trends. Int. Trans. Oper. Res. **20**(1), 1–48 (2013)
2. Amri, Y., Lailatul, A., Fatmawati, F., Setiani, N., Rani, S.: Analysis clustering of electricity usage profile using k-means algorithm. IOP Conf. Ser.: Mater. Sci. Eng. **105**, 12–20 (2016)

3. Curi, M.E., et al.: Single and multiobjective evolutionary algorithms for clustering biomedical information with unknown number of clusters. In: Korošec, P., Melab, N., Talbi, E.-G. (eds.) BIOMA 2018. LNCS, vol. 10835, pp. 100–112. Springer, Cham (2018). https://doi.org/10.1007/978-3-319-91641-5_9
4. Dean, J., Ghemawat, S.: MapReduce: simplified data processing on large clusters. Commun. ACM **51**(1), 107–113 (2008)
5. Ekanayake, J., Jenkins, N., Liyanage, K., Wu, J., Yokoyama, A.: Smart Grid: Technology and Applications. Wiley, New York (2012)
6. Foster, I.: Designing and Building Parallel Programs: Concepts and Tools for Parallel Software Engineering. Addison-Wesley Longman, Boston (1995)
7. Grandjean, A., Adnot, J., Binet, G.: A review and an analysis of the residential electric load curve models. Renew. Sustain. Energy Rev. **16**(9), 6539–6565 (2012)
8. Laurinec, P., Lucká, M.: Clustering-based forecasting method for individual consumers electricity load using time series representations. Open Comput. Sci. **8**(1), 38–50 (2018)
9. Malcon, J., Sardi, G., Carnelli, E., Franco, R.: Smart management of transmission network in UTE. In: Innovative Smart Grid Technologies Latin America (2015)
10. Momoh, J.: Smart Grid: Fundamentals of Design and Analysis. Wiley-IEEE (2012)
11. Nesmachnow, S.: An overview of metaheuristics: accurate and efficient methods for optimisation. Int. J. Metaheuristics **3**(4), 320–347 (2014)
12. Nesmachnow, S., Iturriaga, S.: Cluster-UY: scientific HPC in Uruguay. In: International Supercomputing in Mexico (2019)
13. Nesmachnow, S., et al.: Demand response and ancillary services for super-computing and datacenters. In: International Supercomputing in México, pp. 1–15 (2019)
14. Paterakisa, N., Erdinc, O., Catalão, J.: An overview of demand response: key-elements and international experience. Renew. Sustain. Energy Rev. **69**, 871–891 (2017)
15. Räsanen, T., Voukantsis, D., Niska, H., Karatzas, K., Kolehmainen, M.: Data-based method for creating electricity use load profiles using large amount of customer-specific hourly measured electricity use data. Appl. Energy **87**(11), 3538–3545 (2010)
16. Rhodes, J., Cole, W., Upshaw, C., Edgar, T., Webber, M.: Clustering analysis of residential electricity demand profiles. Appl. Energy **135**, 461–471 (2014)
17. Shaukat, N., et al.: A survey on consumers empowerment, communication technologies, and renewable generation penetration within smart grid. Renew. Sustain. Energy Rev. **81**, 1453–1475 (2018)
18. Shvachko, K., Kuang, H., Radia, S., Chansler, R.: The Hadoop distributed file system. In: IEEE 26th Symposium on Mass Storage Systems and Technologies, pp. 1–10 (2010)
19. Sun, M., Konstantelos, I., Strbac, G.: C-vine copula mixture model for clustering of residential electrical load pattern data. IEEE Trans. Power Syst. **32**(3), 2382–2393 (2017)
20. Thorndike, R.: Who belong in the family. Psychometrika **18**(4), 267–276 (1953)
21. White, T.: Hadoop: The Definitive Guide. O'Reilly Media, Inc., Sebastopol (2009)
22. Zhao, W., Ma, H., He, Q.: Parallel k-means clustering based on MapReduce. In: IEEE International Conference on Cloud Computing, pp. 674–679 (2009)

Spectrum Sample Calculation of Discrete, Aperiodic and Finite Signals Using the Discrete Time Fourier Transform (DTFT)

Julio Cesar Taboada-Echave[(✉)], Modesto Medina-Melendrez, and Leopoldo Noel Gaxiola-Sánchez

Division of Research and Postgraduate Studies, Tecnológico Nacional de México, Instituto Tecnológico de Culiacán, Culiacán, SIN, Mexico
{m17170010, modestogmm}@itculiacan.edu.mx,
drgaxiolasanchez@gmail.com

Abstract. A method for the calculation of spectrum samples of discrete, aperiodic and finite signals based on the DTFT is proposed. This method is based on a flexible discretization of the frequency variable that could produce equidistant, sparse or unique spectrum samples. It is implemented in a GPU platform as a Matrix-Vector product, being able to be applied on modern HPC systems. As a result, a general use tool is developed for the frequency analysis that achieves execution times in a linear relation with the length of the vector to be processed and the number of samples required. Finally, it is shown that the required execution time for the computation of equally spaced spectrum samples is competitive to the achievements of other tools for frequency analysis based on sequential execution.

Keywords: High performance computing · DTFT · Fourier analysis · GPU

1 Introduction

In digital signal processing, the transformation and analysis of information is fundamental. An alternative to this is the harmonic analysis also called Fourier analysis, which can be performed with a set of tools that enable a different interpretation of information by transforming it from time or space domain to frequency domain. Frequency domain analysis is based on the premise that all signals can be represented by the sum of different harmonic components, made up of sinuses and cosines. Tools for Fourier analysis include the Fourier Series (CTFS) for analyzing continuous and periodic signals; the Fourier Transform (CTFT) for continuous and aperiodic signals; the Discrete Time Fourier Series (DTFS) for discrete and periodic signals; and the Discrete Time Fourier Transform (DTFT) for discrete and aperiodic signals [1]. The inconvenience of DTFT for the analysis of discrete and aperiodic signals is that the resulting spectrum is a continuous function. The Fourier Discrete Transform (DFT), whose definition is derived from the DTFS or the DTFT according to several authors [2, 3], represents the first choice tool for the analysis of discrete, aperiodic and finite signals. The Fast Fourier Transform (FFT) [4], besides the direct version of the DFT, is

M. Torres and J. Klapp (Eds.): ISUM 2019, CCIS 1151, pp. 18–26, 2019.
https://doi.org/10.1007/978-3-030-38043-4_2

currently the most widely used algorithm for spectral analysis. The use of the DFT has as a restriction that the spectrum samples that are obtained correspond to equidistant elements forming a vector of equal length as the input sequence. To avoid such restriction in the use of DFT, some authors propose pruning operations, who allows removing samples not required [5–8], or filling with zeros (zero-padding), that allows to increase the number of samples in the frequency domain. These operations allow the application of techniques for the recovery of windows in the frequency or zoom operations. For applications where the detection of single sample or sparse samples is required, Goertzel's algorithm represents a valid option [9]. Even though the previous alternatives may overcome different requirements for frequency analysis, none of these represents a versatile alternative for general use because all are based or are variants of the FFT algorithm. This publication proposes a versatile method for frequency analysis of discrete, aperiodic and finite signals, this is based on the computation of specific DTFT samples and is implemented on a parallel processing unit. The direct implementation of the proposed method has an order of $O(N^2)$ to process a single dimension signal or an order of $O(N^3)$ to process a two dimension signal. This order of complexity makes the implementation prohibitive, unless a high performance platform is chosen for parallel processing. At current time, Graphic Processing Units (GPU) had been used successfully as parallel processing units, thus implementations of the direct version of the DFT has been done based on GPU [6, 10] with good results, especially when the sequence to be analyzed has a prime length size [11]. The proposed method is implemented in a parallel structure based on GPU, where each of the processing elements individually calculates a sample of the spectrum required by the user.

2 Calculation of the DTFT for Discrete, Aperiodic and Finite Signals

This section shows the basis for the reinterpretation of the DTFT as the right tool for the analysis of discrete, aperiodic and finite signals instead of the DFT.

A. Adaptation of DTFT.

The DTFT is positioned as the most suitable tool when Fourier analysis of discrete, aperiodic and finite signals is required, and its definitions is given by

$$X(e^{j\omega}) = \sum_{n=-\infty}^{\infty} x[n]e^{-j\omega n} \tag{1}$$

The disadvantage of the DTFT is that, despite processing a discrete and aperiodic input, the frequency variable ω is in the periodic continuous domain with a period of 2π. To adapt its implementation in modern computing systems, it is possible to discretize the continuous variable. In the case that the selected samples of the continuous variable are equidistant and of an equal number than the length of the input sequence, their implementation results equivalent to the DFT. It is important to note that each discrete element of the continuous variable corresponds to a unique sample of the spectrum. With these conditions in mind, a not necessarily invertible implementation can be obtained to compute versatile DTFT samples.

For the definition of the DTFT sampling is necessary to introduce a selection vector $\omega[k]$ in substitution of the continuous variable ω, thus, the synthesis equation can be rewritten as

$$X[k] = \sum_{n=0}^{N-1} x[n] e^{-j\omega[k]n} \quad 0 \leq k \leq K - 1 \tag{2}$$

where $\omega[k]$ represents the vector with the K required discretized frequencies and k represents its index. The vector $x[n]$ of length N represents the input sequence of a discrete and aperiodic signal, turning the equation into a finite summation.

B. Calculation of the DTFT as a matrix-vector product.

For the implementation of Eq. (2), it is convenient to arrange it in the form of a Matrix-Vector product, as observed in Eq. (3). In this way, a direct implementation in a parallel system is possible. The matrix consists of evaluations of the kernel transform, where each k row is formed by evaluations of the kernel for the frequency defined by $\omega[k]$.

$$X[k] = \begin{bmatrix} X[0] \\ X[1] \\ \vdots \\ X[K-1] \end{bmatrix} = \begin{bmatrix} 1 & e^{-j\omega[0]} & \cdots & e^{-j\omega[0](N-1)} \\ 1 & e^{-j\omega[1]} & \cdots & e^{-j\omega[1](N-1)} \\ \vdots & \vdots & \cdots & \vdots \\ 1 & e^{-j\omega[k-1]} & \cdots & e^{-j\omega[k-1](N-1)} \end{bmatrix} \begin{bmatrix} X[0] \\ X[1] \\ \vdots \\ X[N-1] \end{bmatrix} \tag{3}$$

The implementation in a parallel system of Eq. (3) can divide the task of computing a sample of the spectrum by each processing unit, individually. The computation of the sample within the thread is done by an iterative process of adding multiplication between the kernel transformed and the input sequence. The execution time of each execution thread is directly related to the length N of the input sequence. As result, $2N$ complex operations are performed on each thread.

A convenient way for its implementation in high performance computing equipment (HPC) is using GPU architectures, especially considering the multi-core characteristics of modern GPUs. A valid approach is to calculate in each core of the GPU one of the output samples, where each thread makes an iterative pass over all the input elements multiplying them with the kernels and carrying out their addition. For the calculation of the transform is necessary to determine the kernel values, which are calculated individually within each thread using the mathematical functions library of the GPU.

3 GPU Implementation

In order to perform the implementation in a parallel system, the Nvidia GPU platform was chosen. Currently, multiple HPC systems rely their computing power in GPU units [12], for instance, supercomputers based on Tesla units [13]. One of the advantages to choose a GPU as a hardware accelerator platform is that GPUs are available even in consumer grade computers, especially in high-performance computers. The GPU devices that dominate the consumer market are Nvidia with its GeForce series and ATI/AMD with its Radeon series [14]. The implementation of this proposal is made in a GPU of the Nvidia GeForce series with the set of CUDA libraries. It is important to consider that the final implementation can be developed indistinctly in CUDA C, or with the set of open-source libraries OpenCL for its operation in GPU of the families that support it like AMD/ATI or Intel. Based on the studies reported con the papers of Fang [15] and Karimi [16] where they compare the performance of CUDA C against OpenCL, CUDA C has been chosen.

A. Equipment description

A personal computer based on a Windows 10 Operating System, with a 1st generation Intel I7 950 processor, 24 GB RAM DDR3 was used for the test. Further, a Nvidia GTX 780-DC2-3GD5 GPU board was included as the parallel processing unit.

B. Control Algorithm

The system execution control is ruled by a sequential routine in the CPU that determines the number of processing units to be called in the GPU, as well as the GPU preprocessing routine itself. The main control routine described in Fig. 1 is intended to prepare the data for execution in the GPU system. In the case that complex data are processed, the x[n] input array could be separated in its real and imaginary part, xr[n] and xi[n] sequences respectively. In addition, the vector containing the required frequency samples, stored in the vector ω[k], must be passed as a parameter. The number

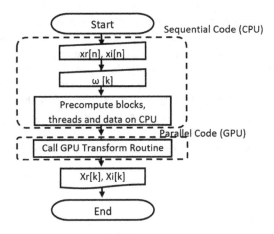

Fig. 1. Flowchart of the system.

of processing elements to be invoked in the GPU is calculated from the number of elements in ω[k].

In the GPU transformation routine, both the required elements of the kernel transform and the DTFT calculation are achieved.

For performance optimization, the closest memory resources in the GPU are used. The input sequence is first passed from the global memory to the shared memory. Data that is kept constant or unique in each thread is sent to the local memory of each thread. Once the data is processed and the results are obtained, they are stored on GPU's global memory and later copied to the CPU memory for their use.

C. Parallel Algorithm

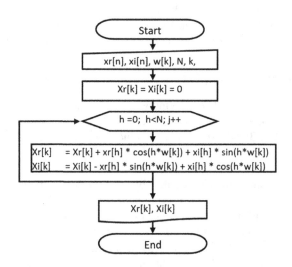

Fig. 2. Flowchart of the GPU thread.

For the calculation of the DTFT in the parallel processing unit based on GPU, K processing threads are invoked where k represents the unique identificator (ID) of each CUDA thread. These thread IDs are directly related to the index of the samples to be calculated. The processing function receives as inputs the real and imaginary part of the input sequence (xr[n], xi[n]), the vector ω[k], the number of elements N in the input sequence and the number of elements K in the discretized frequency vector. These elements are illustrated in Fig. 2. It is important to mention that, for performance reasons, the DTFT kernels are calculated in the GPU. In addition, both the input sequence and the discretized frequency vector are previously stored in the shared memory and in the local memory of the thread for the case of being required more than once.

4   Validation and Performance Analysis

In order to validate the tool, a set of tests was done. The main goal is to validate the proposed characteristic of versatility. To determine the accuracy of the tool, a comparison between the obtained samples and those of the FFT has been done.

A. Validation of versatility

For the validation of the developed proposal's versatility, tests were carryout processing a synthetic signal composed of N = 64 input elements. For this signal were calculated equally spaced samples of the whole period with K = N (Fig. 3), with K = 2 N (Fig. 4) and with K = 2/N (Fig. 5). Equally samples on a spectrum's window from $3/4\pi$ to $5/4\pi$ with K = 32 were calculated and showed on Fig. 6. Non equally spaced samples from 0 to π were calculated and showed on Fig. 7. And finally, specific arbitrary samples were calculated and showed on Fig. 8. All the scenarios were compared against the continuous DTFT witch was estimated with 12,000 samples of the spectrum.

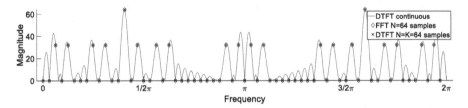

Fig. 3. Equidistant samples of the DTFT with $K = N$ (equivalent to a DFT).

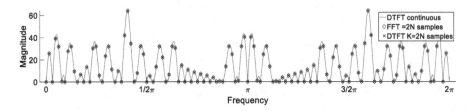

Fig. 4. Equidistant samples of the DTFT with $K = 2\ N$ (equivalent to a oversampled DFT).

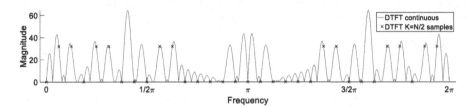

Fig. 5. Equidistant samples of the DTFT with $K = N/2$ (equivalent to a subsampled DFT).

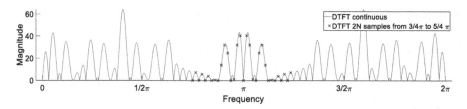

Fig. 6. Samples of the DTFT from *3/4π* to *5/4π* with *K = 32* (equivalent to a pruned oversampled DFT)

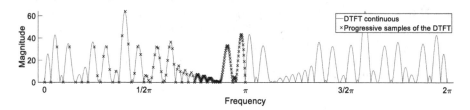

Fig. 7. Non-equally spaced samples of the DTFT from *0* to *π*

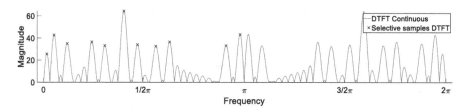

Fig. 8. Specific samples of the DTFT

The results of Fig. 3 could be compared against a DFT where the number of coefficients is equal to the length of the signal. Results in Fig. 4 could be compared against an oversampled DFT who has to be filled with zeros to be calculated. Results in Fig. 5 could be compared against a DFT where half of the coefficients were dropped after the calculations. Results in Fig. 6 could be compared against a pruned over-sampled DFT, which performs unnecessary operations with zeros. Results in Fig. 7 and Fig. 8 couldn't be compared against the DFT, because such tool cannot obtain non-equally spaced spectrum samples. Thus, the disadvantage of the DFT is its lack of versatility and in some cases the additional needed operations.

B. Execution Time

To determine the average time, 1000 executions of each instruction were carried out in an iterative cycle within Matlab, registering the total time. For each execution of different length, the register of the first execution was omitted to exclude the overhead made by the Matlab. The additional overhead for the control of the Matlab iterative cycle is not taken into account.

In order to compare the performance of the proposal method between the sequential version on CPU an parallel version on GPU, run-time tests are carried out by processing vectors of different lengths. The comparison is initially done with the implementation of the same method implemented on CPU. It is important to point out that the host to device transport overhead is omitted in both GPU implementations analysis as the signal is transferred directly in the device's global memory using the tools built into Matlab. The results obtained are shown in the graphs of Fig. 9, the experiments consist of processing sequences of lengths from 1 to 2048 on the DTFT. The results show that for vector longer than 394 elements the parallel version shows a better performance.

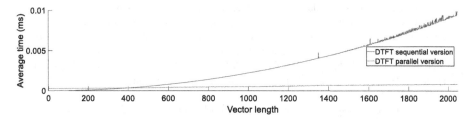

Fig. 9. Run time for sequential and parallel version.

The run times are carried out in order to analyze the viability of the proposed method. Even when the implementation is superior to the direct version on CPU in terms of speed, this could be improved with a more efficient methods matrix multiplication algorithm as cuBLAS.

5 Conclusions

The objective of this paper is to introduce and validate the basis of a versatile method for the Fourier analysis based on the DTFT of discrete, aperiodic and finite signals. This method allows to obtain a tool in which all possible scenarios can be achieved. The implementation takes great advantage from hardware accelerator available for HPC. In this implementation, it can be seen that the tool presents enough performance as to be used in the scenarios where the requirement of versatility is needed. Due to the simplicity of the algorithm, it is possible to implement it in other parallel platforms, including FPGA devices and other GPU devices like AMD and Intel.

Acknowledgment. The authors of this paper are grateful to the Tecnológico Nacional de México, Campus Culiacán, especially to the Division of Postgraduate Studies and Research for the facilities provided. I would also like to express my gratitude to the Consejo Nacional de Ciencia y Tecnología (Conacyt) for the support given during the course of the master's degree studies.

References

1. Oppenheim, A.V., Willsky, A.S.: Señales y Sistemas 2da. ed. Prentice Hall Hispanoamericana, México (1997)
2. Opepnheim, A.V., Shafer, R.W.: Tratamiento de señales en tiempo discreto. Pearson Educacion, Madrid (2011)
3. Proakis, J.G., Manolakis, D.G.: Digital Signal Processing. Principles, Algorithms, and Applications. Prentice Hall, Upper Saddle River (1996)
4. Cooley, J.W., Tukey, J.W.: An algorithm for the machine calculation of complex fourier series. Am. Math. Soc. **301**, 297 (1965)
5. Alves, R.G., Osorio, P.L., Swamy, M.N.S.: General FFT pruning algorithm. In: Proceedings of 43rd IEEE MidWest Symposium on Circuits and Systems, Lansing (2000)
6. Angulo Rios, J., Castro Palazuelos, D., Medina Melendrez, M., Santiesteban Cos, R.: A GPU based implementation of input and output prunning of composite length FFT using DIF DIT transform decomposition. In: Congreso Internacional de Ingenieria Electromecanica y de Sistemas CIEES, Ciudad de Mexico (2016)
7. Melendrez, M.M., Estrada, M.A., Castro, A.: Input and/or output pruning of composite length FFTs using a DIF-DIT transform decomposition. IEEE Trans. Sig. Process. **57**(10), 4124–4128 (2009)
8. Markel, J.D.: FFT prunning. IEEE Trans. Audio Electroacust. **4**, 305–311 (1971)
9. Goertzel, G.: An algorithm for the evaluation of finite trigonometric series. Am. Math. Monthly **65**(1), 34–35 (1958)
10. Stokfiszewski, K., Yatsymirskyy, M., Puchala, D.: Effectiveness of fast fourier transform implementations on GPU and CPU. In: International Conference on Computational Problems of Electric Engineerings (CPEE), pp. 162–164 (2015)
11. Shu, L.: Parallel implementation of arbitrary-sized discrete fourier transform on FPGA. In: 2016 3rd International Conference on Advanced Computing and Communication Systems (ICACCS), Coimbatore, India (2016)
12. Nvidia (2018). https://www.nvidia.com/en-us/high-performance-computing/. Accessed 17 Nov 2018
13. Oak Ridge National Laboratory (2018). https://www.ornl.gov/news/ornl-launches-summit-supercomputer. Accessed 17 Nov 2018
14. Evangelho, J.: AMD Claims Radeon Is #1 Gaming Platform – Here's Their Proof, Forbes, 23 April 2018. https://www.forbes.com/sites/jasonevangelho/2018/04/23/radeon-vs-geforce-which-brand-is-truly-the-1-gaming-platform/#4cfb19276a95. Accessed 17 Dec 2018
15. Fang, J., Varbanescu, A.L., Sips, H.: A comprehensive performance comparison of CUDA and OpenCL. In: 2011 International Conference on Parallel Processing, Taipei (2011)
16. Karimi, K., Dickson, N.G., Hamze, F.: A performance comparison of CUDA and OpenCL, arXiv (2010)

Software Defined Data Center for High Performance Computing Applications

J. E. Lozano-Rizk[1](✉), J. I. Nieto-Hipolito[1], R. Rivera-Rodriguez[2],
M. A. Cosio-Leon[3], M. Vazquez-Briseno[1], J. C. Chimal-Eguia[4],
V. Rico-Rodriguez[1], and E. Martinez-Martinez[1]

[1] Universidad Autonoma de Baja California, Ensenada, B.C., Mexico
{lozanoj,jnieto,mabel.vazquez,
vrico,evelio}@uabc.edu.mx
[2] Centro de Investigacion Cientifica y de Educacion Superior de Ensenada,
Ensenada, B.C., Mexico
rrivera@cicese.edu.mx
[3] Universidad Politecnica de Pachuca, Hidalgo, Mexico
ma.cosio.leon@upp.edu.mx
[4] Instituto Politecnico Nacional, Mexico City, Mexico
jchimale@ipn.mx

Abstract. In recent years, traditional data centers have been used to host high-performance computing infrastructure, such as HPC clusters, addressing specific requirements for different research and scientific projects. Computes, storage, network, and security infrastructure is usually from heterogenous manufacturers and has multiple management interfaces.

This process implies a higher demand on data center administrators to manually attend the problems or particular configurations that require each of the HPC applications, which can affect its performance, together with the fact that it can present a poor resource allocation on Data Center. Software-Defined Data Centers (SDDC) have emerged as a solution for automating the management and self-provisioning of computing, storage, network, and security resources dynamically according to the software-defined policies for each of the applications running in the SDDC. With these paradigms in mind, this work aims to answer whether HPC applications can benefit in their performance using the advantages that SDDC offers to other applications such as *business* or *enterprise*. The results of this article are (i) we identify SDDC main components. (ii) we present an experimental approach to use SDDC network component for High-Performance MPI-based applications.

Keywords: SDDC · SDN · Data center · HPC · MPI

1 Introduction

Traditional data centers have been used to host high-performance computing (HPC) infrastructure, such as HPC clusters. The computational components used in clusters are usually from different manufacturers. This scheme requires administrators to perform several configuration rules or policies on every device to meet compute,

© Springer Nature Switzerland AG 2019
M. Torres and J. Klapp (Eds.): ISUM 2019, CCIS 1151, pp. 27–41, 2019.
https://doi.org/10.1007/978-3-030-38043-4_3

storage, network, and security requirements for HPC applications. This process can affect applications performance and also an unbalanced computational resources allocation on the data center. Also, HPC clusters often run a standard operative system (OS) and software stack across all compute nodes limiting the flexibility of their computational resources [1], especially when need to execute parallel applications from multi-disciplinary scientific projects with specific requirements.

Software-Defined Data Centers (SDDC) have emerged as a solution for automating the management and self-provisioning of computing, storage, network, and security resources dynamically according to particular configurations or policies for each of the applications running in the SDDC.

In this paper, we identify and study the SDDC main components and how can HPC applications get benefits when using them. Also, we present an experimental approach to test HPC application performance and its interaction with the SDDC network component.

The rest of the article is organized as follows: Sect. 2 describes the Software- defined data center main components. In Sect. 3, presents a brief review of research works and its interaction with SDDC network component. Section 4 describes an experimental approach using SDN functionalities with an HPC MPI-based application, the simulation model, and the results of the tests. Conclusion and future work are presented in Sect. 5.

2 Software Defined Data Center

The software-defined data center (SDDC) is an architecture that allows IT infrastructure as compute, storage, networking, and security to be abstracted and defined in software to function as enterprise-wide resources [2]. SDDC is based on resource virtualization, and its main components are software-defined: network, compute, storage, and security, as shown in Fig. 1. In software-defined systems, simple management and automation are one of the main objectives.

SDDC depends on the abstracted resources extensibility from virtualized elements, and it is possible to manage them through the Application Programming Interface (API) provided by each of the elements.

The Distributed Management Task Force [3] describes the functionalities that SDDC should achieve, and they are:

1. Access to logical computing, network, storage, and other resources.
2. Resource discovery.
3. Automated provisioning of logical resources based on workload requirements.
4. Measurement and management of resource consumption.
5. Orchestration based on policies to allocate resources according to workloads.
6. Security (authorization, authentication, auditing), intrusion detection, and prevention systems (IDS and IPS), firewalls.

In [4] authors defined the following characteristics for SDDC:

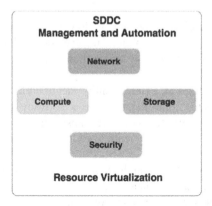

Fig. 1. SDDC main components

1. Standardized: By logically resource utilization, the infrastructure becomes homogeneous, even if it is provided through a set of standard x86 hardware, eliminating unnecessary complexity and the commitment to use vendor- specific or proprietary elements.
2. Homogeneous: An unified platform, optimized for the entire data center, to be able to support any workload.
3. Adaptive: With the automated resource provisioning, the infrastructure is self-programmable according to the application's requirements, even if it changes at runtime, allowing the highest level of agility, and efficiency.
4. Automated: A management orchestrator with intelligence to eliminate complex management scripts, and be able to perform operations with minor manual effort, obtaining significant cost savings.
5. Resilient: As the SDDC model is based on intelligent software that allows hardware abstraction, it is possible to compensate for the hardware failures that may arise, delivering high availability at the minimum cost.

With a software layer, known as the data center abstraction layer, the standardized compute, storage, network, and security resources are presented as software-defined elements. These elements are identified as Software-Defined Network (SDN), Software-Defined Storage (SDS), Software-Defined Security (SD-Sec), Software-Defined Compute (SDC), which we will detail in the following subsections.

2.1 Software Defined Network

Software-Defined Networks (SDN) provide a mechanism to allow applications dynamically request network services or parameters as available bandwidth, QoS policies, security, among others [5]. According to [6], there are four fundamental aspects of SDN design:

1. The control and data planes are decoupled, removing the control functionalities from the network devices, which will become them as a simple data packet forwarding elements.
2. Forwarding decisions are given by the data flow, instead of considering data packet destination. All packets in a data flow receive identical service policies in the forwarding devices. The data flow abstractions unify the behavior of different devices in the network.
3. The control logic becomes an external entity identified as the SDN or NOS (Network Operating System) controller. NOS is a software platform that runs on a server, provides the essential resources and abstractions to enable the forwarding devices' programming based on a centralized logic, as a traditional operating system works.
4. The network is programmable through the software applications that run in the SDN controller and interact with the data plane devices. The programmability functions are considered the most valuable elements in the SDN.

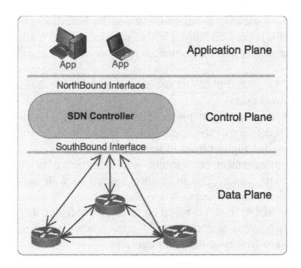

Fig. 2. SDN general architecture

Figure 2 shows the SDN general architecture. In data centers whose scenarios change rapidly, the technological value represented by the SDN is essential for solving scalability, security, and mobility problems. Traditional data centers will be able to gradually adopt hybrid networks, combining SDN and traditional networks taking advantage of any existing devices in the network to improve their management.

2.2 Software Defined Storage

SDS facilitate and simplify the storage components abstraction to maintain a quality of service (QoS) according to the application's needs. With this in mind, SDS separates the data plane and the control plane. The data plane (also known as infrastructure layer) refers to the use of storage devices from many manufacturers, both physical and virtual. While in the control plane, policies are defined to provide automated provisioning to respond to a variety of end-user requests through the elements APIs. Figure 3 shows SDS general architecture.

Traditional storage devices are managed through an individually installed driver. The SDS creates a single central control unit known as the SDS controller, to manage the different system elements regardless of their provider, instead of installing a driver on each device.

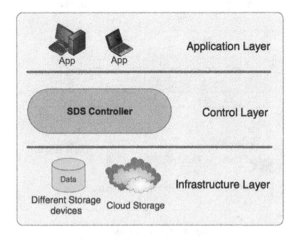

Fig. 3. SDS general architecture

In [7] authors described the SDS main functionalities, and they are:

1. Automated: Enable the implicit management to reduces the maintenance cost of the storage infrastructure, in response to the users request at runtime.
2. Programmability: Defining a standard API for management, provisioning, and maintenance of storage devices and services. Providing resource control for several system components to allow automatization.
3. Virtualized data path: Block, file, and object interfaces that support applications written to these interfaces.
4. Scalability: The ability to scale storage infrastructure without disrupting service availability or application's performance (for example, QoS and SLA configuration).
5. Transparency: The ability of storage users to monitor and manage their storage consumption based on available resources and costs.

One of the essential SDS features is the ability to control and manage all policies in the system [8]. With these policies, it is possible to maintain a high level of QoS handled by the storage control layer, such as failover, resource migration, among others.

2.3 Software Defined Security

SDSec provides a flexible and centralized security solution by abstracting the security mechanisms from the hardware layer to a software layer [9]. SDSec separates the forwarding and processing plane from the security control plane, virtualizing the security functions. One of the main objectives is to secure virtual storage, virtual network, and virtual servers.

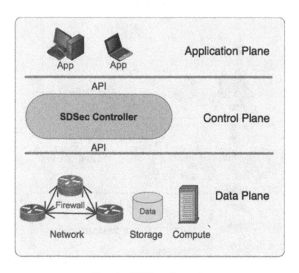

Fig. 4. SDSec elements

SDSec facilitates the deployment of security policies to cover several elements in IT infrastructure. These elements are: a secure archive of data-sensitive applications, host-to-hosts transfers data flows using secure network nodes, virtual machine or container failover and recovery, among others. Securing IT storage, connectivity, and computing infrastructure with SDSec provides a single control to manage these elements in the SDDC, as it is illustrated in Fig. 4.

2.4 Software Defined Compute

Software-defined computing (SDC) is based on server virtualization. Server virtualization is defined as a software-based technology that allows the execution of different operating systems at the same time (virtual machines), within a physical server [10]. Virtualization allows multiple applications (hosted as virtual machines or containers) to be run on the same server while providing computing resource isolation.

In *full virtualization* or *hardware-level virtualization*, a system has an operating system that runs a process called the hypervisor. The hypervisor is capable of communicating directly with the kernel host. Above the hypervisor resides the virtual hardware layer, and the operating system installed on the virtual machine communicates to the virtual hardware layer [11].

Lightweight virtualization technology has emerged as an alternative to traditional hypervisor-based virtualization [12]. Container-based virtualization was developed to improve the sharing of computing resources, allowing multiple iso- lated namespaces, and facilitating the creation and maintenance of customized environments according to specific user and applications requirements. These containers, create abstractions of the guest processes directly without the need of an OS guest, reducing the overhead of creating a new virtual machine with an operating system guest for each application [13].

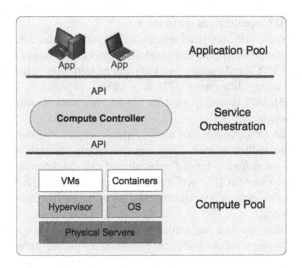

Fig. 5 SDC main components

Both virtualization technologies are managed by SDC controller enabling the service orchestration according to applications requirements, as is represented in Fig. 5.

One of the most significant transformations that virtualization has led to is infrastructure-as-a-service (IaaS) is cloud computing. Users can access virtually unlimited computing power whenever they need it, paying for only what they use [14]. In SDC is not only the virtualization of the computer server and operative system resources, but is also the abstraction layer through the APIs enabling the entire infrastructure into a programmable instrument that can be used for HPC applications.

3   SDDC and HPC

High-performance computing is used to solve large problems in science and engineering, providing computing capabilities to improve applications performance. This scheme requires the management of very high scale workloads to minimize HPC application job completion time. SDDC policy-driven automation supports the provisioning and management of computing, storage, and network services, allowing HPC applications to meet their computational resources requirements. There are research works that have used some of the SDDC components to meet specific applications requirements. Regarding the compute component, in [11], a review of containers technology was performed to identify their use in HPC applications requirements. Also, in [12] performed a multi-objective approach to distribute the workload to multiple OS containers running on several servers.

The network technology used to interconnect HPC compute nodes in the data center became a critical factor to be able to transfer large amounts of data flows in the less possible time to achieve applications time-constraint requirements. The network traffic is usually an east-to-west traffic pattern and contained within a single data center. Software-defined networks (SDN) is one of the SDDC's main components that can be used to optimize HPC applications performance.

We identified some HPC applications research works that have used one or more SDN parameters to improve applications performance. For the aim of our research, we studied MPI-based HPC applications and their interaction with software-defined networks. Message Passing Interface (MPI) is a library of routines for inter-process communication [15]. MPI is widely used for parallel applications running in a cluster computing environment.

In [16] designed an algorithm that aims to minimize the number of jumps in the longest path in the reduction tree. This algorithm only focuses on obtaining the available routes in the software-defined network and calculates the shortest path to be used in the reduction tree. In [17] performed a data packet forwarding scheme in the SDN according to the application requirements, focusing on two network parameters: bandwidth and latency.

In the next section, we will perform an experimental approach executing an MPI-based application among compute nodes connected by a software-defined network. Our experiment objective is to analyze the HPC-MPI application performance when transferring data flows from source to destination hosts selecting different end-to-end networks paths according to application requirements and data center's network path conditions. The data flow forwarding process in the SDN will be implemented using the network programmability functions in the simulated data center.

4 SDN and HPC Experimental Approach

The experiment consists in the measurement of the MPI application completion time when transferring data flows among two hosts (source to destination) within the data center. When the source node transfers its data flow to the destination node, there are two options for network path selection:

1. The SDN controller decides the network path to be used in the data flow transfer process. In this case, the SDN controller computes and configures the path that will be used for the data flow transfer process. By default, the SDN controller uses the SPF (Shortest Path First) algorithm for path selection.

2. Use the SDN programmability functions to dynamically configure the path to be used in the data flow transfer process. In this particular case, we can use the end-to-end available bandwidth and delay parameters for path selection. With these parameters, we can compute and dynamically configure the optimal network path according to the MPI application requirements.

In an SPF scenario, we identified the path with minimal hops (cost metric) between source to destination hosts. In a bandwidth-aware, we select the path with the minimum available bandwidth. In a delay-aware, we use the minimal end-to-end delay between source to the destination node. These forwarding methods are represented in Eqs. (1), (2) and (3):

(a) SPF using several hops as Cost metric:

$$p = min(Cost(P^{s,d})) \tag{1}$$

(b) Bandwidth-aware:

$$B(p) = min(B(P^{s,d})) \tag{2}$$

(c) Delay-aware:

$$D(p) = min(D(P^{s,d})) \tag{3}$$

Where:

$P^{s,d} = $ Available paths from source to destination hosts
$D(p) = $ Minimal path delay
$B(p) = $ Minimal path available bandwidth

For the simulation environment, we used a workstation with Intel processor, 16 GB of RAM, 512 GB hard drive, macOS High Sierra operating system, and installed VirtualBox version 5.1 virtualization software. Within VirtualBox, we created one virtual machine with Linux Ubuntu 14 operating system for Mininet simulator.

Figure 6 shows the topology used for this experiment. We use a 3-tier data center topology, and it was implemented in Mininet simulator [18].

In the virtual machine with the Mininet simulator, the topology was implemented by developing a Python program that refers to components of the Mininet CLI (Command Line Interface). Inside Mininet, we used OpenFlow enable switches for network simulation. OpenFlow [19] is a protocol used to enable communication between the SDN controller and the network switches, in other terms, it is the SouthBound Interface, as is described in Sect. 2.1.

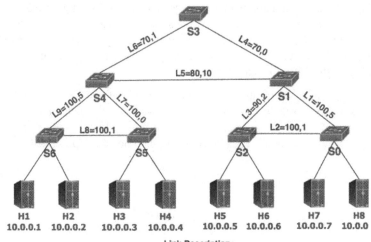

Fig. 6. Experimental topology

The switches links and hosts were configured with their respective values in bandwidth and delay parameters as are shown in Fig. 6. The compute hosts are from H1 to H8. We configured an MPICH cluster [20] in Mininet simulator for running MPI jobs among compute hosts.

Next, we describe the methodology used to get optimal path considering applications requirements and their configuration in the Mininet simulator:

1. According to experimental topology, convert each link to a vector system with delay, available bandwidth, and the number of hops values.
2. Define the paths of host H1 to host H8.
3. Make the sum of the corresponding values for each path (delay and hops), in the case of bandwidth, get the minimum available in each of the paths. Store the information in a list arrangement (paths).
4. Search within the list of paths that comply with the forwarding methods represented in Eqs. (1), (2) and (3) to get their optimal path.
5. Configure data flow rules in each OpenFlow switches to use the optimal path.

When running the simulation, Mininet creates networks links connecting physical ports for each OpenFlow switches.

Listing 1.1 shows a fragment of the Python code developed in Mininet for the experimental topology.

Listing 1.1. Python code using Mininet CLI for the experimental topology

```
#!/usr/bin/python
from mininet.net import Mininet
from mininet.link import TCLink
from mininet.node import OVSSwitch, Controller, Remote Controller
. . . . .
from mininet.cli import CLI
. . . . .
# Add compute hosts
h1 = self.addHost('h1')
h2 = self.addHost('h2')
. . .
h7 = self.addHost('h7')
h8 = self.addHost('h8')
# Add switches to network domain
s0 = self.addSwitch('s0', dpid="0000000000000001")
s1 = self.addSwitch('s1', dpid="0000000000000002")
. . . .
s5 = self.addSwitch('s5', dpid="0000000000000006")
s6 = self.addSwitch('s6', dpid="0000000000000007")
# Host and Switch connection
self.addLink(h1, s6, bw=100)
self.addLink(h2, s6, bw=100)
. . .
self.addLink(h7, s0, bw=100)s
elf.addLink(h8, s0, bw=100)

# Add network links for all switches in network domain
self.addLink(s0, s1, bw=100, delay='5ms', loss=0, jitter='0ms')
self.addLink(s0, s2, bw=100, delay='1ms', loss=0, jitter='0ms')
. . . .
self.addLink(s5, s6, bw=100, delay='1ms', loss=0, jitter='0ms')
def run():
        c = Remote Controller('c0','127.0.0.1',6653)
        net = Mininet(topo=DataCenterA(), link=TCLink, controller=None)
        net.addController(c)
        net.start()
```

We used an MPI parallel application for completion time test. This application was designed to send and receive messages among hosts. In our case, the application sends and receives messages of 1000000 bytes between H1 and H8 hosts for 40 times and then finish the data transfer process. Algorithm 1 describes the MPI application general process.

Algorithm 1 MPI Application general process

INPUT: *NP* {get the number of MPI processes}
OUTPUT: *CompTime* {return the completion time in seconds}
numtests ← 40 {number of tests to execute}
messb ← 1000000 {message size}
i ← 0 {test number, first test starts at 0}
inittime ← *MPIWtime*() {initial time}
while ($i <$ *numtests*) **do**
    MPIRecv(&*messb, MPIChar, sourcen, tag, MPICommWorld*) {receive messages}
    MPISend(&*messb, MPIChar, destn, tag, MPICommWorld*) {send messages}
    i ← *i* + 1
end while
endtime ← *MPIWtime*() {end time}
CompTime ← (*endtime* − *inittime*) {return completion time in seconds}

The MPI application was executed 25 times for each of the SPF, bandwidth-aware, and delay-aware data forwarding method. We measured the application completion time in seconds.

Table 1 shows available networks paths and metrics (number of hops, available bandwidth rate, and delay) from H1 to H8 hosts. Using the data forwarding schemes, SPF selected PathID 3, because it is the one with fewer hops. For bandwidth-aware, we have two choices: PathID 7 and 8; both have a maximum bandwidth rate but different hop numbers and delay metrics. For this experiment, we selected the PathID 7 with maximum bandwidth rate and fewer hops compared to PathID 8. For delay-aware, PathID 6 has minimal delay among all paths.

Table 1. Network paths and metrics from Host 1 to Host 8 in experimental topology

Path ID	Network path	Hops	Bandwidth (Mbps)	Delay (ms)
1	S6, S4, S3, S1, S0	5	70	11
2	S6, S4, S3, S1, S2, S0	6	70	9
3	S6, S4, S1, S0	4	80	20
4	S6, S4, S1, S2, S0	5	80	18
5	S6, S5, S4, S3, S1, S0	6	70	7
6	S6, S5, S4, S3, S1, S2, S0	7	70	5
7	S6, S5, S4, S1, S0	5	80	16
8	S6, S5, S4, S1, S2, S0	6	80	15

Listing 1.2. Example commands to configure data flow rules in OpenFlow Switches

```
# Add flow in OF Switch S1 using source and destination MAC Address
# Forwad data flow using port 2
mininet> sh ovs-ofctl add-flow s1 dl src=00:00:00:00:00:01,
dl_dst=00:00:00:00:00:02,actions=output:3

# Display all configured rules in OF Switch S0
mininet > sh ovs-o fctl dump-flows s0
NXST FLOW reply ( xid=0x4 ):

cookie=0x67, duration=1533.636s, table=0, n_packets=0, n_bytes=0,
idle_timeout=1800, hard timeout=1800, idle age=1533, priority=20,
ip, nw_src=10.0.0.1/32 _nw dst=10.0.0.8/_32, nw proto=6 actions=output:2


cookie=0x2b00000000000039, duration=76160.88s, table=0, n packets=395210,
n_bytes=422185120, idle age=963, hard age=65534, priority=2,
in_port=1 actions=output:2,CONTROLLER:65535


cookie=0x2b00000000000027, duration=76168.703s, table=0, n_packets=4, n_bytes=168,
idle_age=65534, hard age=65534, priority=0 actions=drop

# Remove all existing data flow rules on Switch S1
mininet> sh ovs-ofctl del-flows s1
```

Using Mininet simulator, we created data flow rules in OpenFlow switches to configure the corresponding PathID referred in the same table. We have two options to configure data flow rules in OF switches:

1. Using OpenFlow commands in Mininet interface.

2. Using the NorthBound Interface provided by the SDN Controller (REST-CONF API).

In our experiment, we created the data flow rules in each of the OpenFlow switches using the Mininet command-line interface. An example of these commands is described in Listing 1.2.

4.1 Experiment Results

As mentioned in the previous section, the MPI application sends messages between H1 and H8 hosts. We executed this MPI applications 25 times for each data forwarding process.

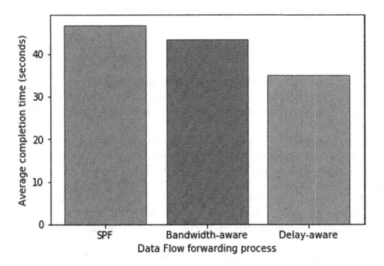

Fig. 7. Data flow forwarding process comparison

Figure 7 shows application completion time results using three different data forwarding schemes. SPF took an average of 46.8 s, Bandwidth-aware 43.4 s and Delay-aware 34.9 s to finish the message transfer process between H1 and H8 hosts. As a result, we can observe that MPI application gets better performance when using Delay-aware path selection rather than SPF or Bandwidth-aware.

In this case, we dynamically set data flow rules in OpenFlow switches according to the path selection method we needed to use. This automation process is one of the main SDN advantages allowing applications to configure data flow rules for path selection at runtime to meet their network requirements.

5   Conclusions

In this work, we described the SDDC main components identifying their advantages. Also, we reviewed some research works that get the benefits of using Software Defined Networks, one of the main SDDC components. Related to SDN, we performed an experimental approach running an MPI-based HPC application in an SDN-based data center. Experiments results showed that the HPC application improved its completion time when using SDN functionalities, as configuring data flow rules at runtime in OpenFlow switches for network path selection according to their requirements.

As future work, we propose a strategy design to provide Quality of Service for HPC applications considering a distributed data center topology based in SDDC components. This strategy implies a multi-objective approach to improve HPC applications performance.

References

1. Kirkley, J.: Virtualization, the Cloud and HPC. InsideHPC (2014)
2. Avramov, L., Portolani, M.: The Policy Driven Data Center with ACI. Cisco Press (2015)
3. DMTF. https://www.dmtf.org/sites/default/files/standards/documents/DSP-IS05011.0.0.pdf. Accessed 10 Feb 2019
4. Darabseh, A., Al-Ayyoub, M., Jararweh, Y., Benkhelifa, E., Vouk, M., Rindos, A.: SDDC: a software defined datacenter experimental framework. In: 3rd International Conference on Future Internet of Things and Cloud, pp. 189–194. IEEE Computer Society (2015)
5. Stallins, W.: Software-defined networks and openflow. Internet Protocol J. **16**, 1 (2013)
6. Kreutz, D., Ramos, F., Verissimo, P., Rothenberg, E., Azodolmolky, S., Uhlig, S.: Software-defined networking: a comprehensive survey. Proc. IEEE **103**(1), 1476 (2015)
7. Carlson, M., et al.: Software Defined Storage. Storage Networking Industry Association (2015)
8. Darabseh, A., Al-Ayyoub, M., Jararweh, Y., Benkhelifa, E., Vouk, M., Rindos, A.: SDStorage: a software defined storage experimental framework. In: 2015 IEEE International Conference on Cloud Engineering, pp. 341–346. IEEE Computer Society (2015)
9. Darabseh, A., Al-Ayyoub, M., Jararweh, Y., Benkhelifa, E., Vouk, M., Rindos, A.: SDSecurity: a software defined security experimental framework. In: 2015 IEEE International Conference on Communication Workshop, pp. 1871–1876. IEEE (2015)
10. Portnoy, M.: Virtualization Essentials, 2nd edn. Wiley, New York (2016)
11. Medrano-Jaimes, F., Lozano-Rizk, J.E., Castañeda-Avila, S., Rivera-Rodriguez, R.: Use of containers for high-performance computing. In: Torres, M., Klapp, J., Gitler, I., Tchernykh, A. (eds.) ISUM 2018. CCIS, vol. 948, pp. 24–32. Springer, Cham (2019). https://doi.org/10.1007/978-3-030-10448-1_3
12. Rewer, C., Tchernykh, A., Cortes-Mendoza, J., Rivera-Rodriguez, R., et al.: Energy consumption and quality of service optimization in containerized cloud computing. In: 2018 Ivannikov Ispras Open Conference (ISPRAS), pp. 47–55. IEEE (2019)
13. Adufu, T., Choi, J., Kim, Y.: Is container-based technology a winner for high performance scientific applications? In: 17th Asia-Pacific Network Operations and Management Symposium (APNOMS), pp. 507–510. IEEE (2015)
14. Douglis, F., Krieger, O.: Virtualization. IEEE Internet Comput. **17**, 6–9 (2013). IEEE Computer Society

15. Sloan, J.: High Performance Linux Clusters, 1st edn. O'Reilly (2004)
16. Makpaisit, P., Ichikawa, K., Uthayopas, P.: MPI Reduce algorithm for OpenFlow- enabled network. In: Proceedings of the 15th International Symposium on Communi- cations and Information Technologies (ISCIT), pp. 261–264 (2015)
17. U-chupala, P., Ichikawa, K., et al.: Application-oriented bandwidth and latency aware routing with OpenFlow network. In: Proceedings of the IEEE 6th International Conference on Cloud Computing Technology and Science, pp. 775–780 (2014)
18. Mininet SDN simulator. Accessed 20 Mar 2019
19. OpenFlow. Open Networking Foundation. https://www.opennetworking.org. Accessed 20 Mar 2019
20. MPICH. http://www.mpich.org. Accessed 10 Feb 2019

ETL Processing in Business Intelligence Projects for Public Transportation Systems

Alfredo Cristobal-Salas[1]([⊠]), Andrei Tchernykh[2],
Sergio Nesmachnow[3], Ceila-Yasmin García-Morales[1],
Bardo Santiago-Vicente[1], José-Eduardo Herrera-Vargas[1],
Carolina Solís-Maldonado[4], and Raúl-Alejandro Luna-Sánchez[4]

[1] Facultad de Ingeniería en Electrónica y Comunicaciones,
Universidad Veracruzana, Poza Rica, Mexico
acristobal@uv.mx, zeila.yazzmin@gmail.com,
bardosantiago.v@gmail.com
[2] Centro de Investigación Científica y de Educación Superior de Ensenada,
Ensenada, Mexico
chernykh@cicese.mx
[3] Facultad de Ingeniería, Universidad de la República, Montevideo, Uruguay
sergion@fing.edu.uy
[4] Facultad de Ciencias Químicas, Universidad Veracruzana, Poza Rica, Mexico
{casolis, raluna}@uv.mx

Abstract. Defining a business intelligence project for a transportation system with more than 10 k-users per day could become a challenging problem. A transportation system like this would generate more than 400 million of registers per month when monitoring users each minute. That is why, some strategies need to be applied to the ETL process to correctly handle the data generated by big transportation systems. This paper explores different operational database (OD) architectures and analyze their impact on processing time of the ETL stage in a business intelligence. The database architectures reviewed are: one centralized OD, one logical-centralized OD and distributed OD. This model is being tested with the transportation system defined in the city of Poza Rica, Mexico. This system contains more than three million simulated registers per day and the entire ETL process is done under 136 s. This model runs on a Quad-core Intel Xeon processor 8 GB RAM OSX Yosemite 10.10.5 computer.

Keywords: ETL · Business intelligence · Multithread · Transport system · Decision making

1 Introduction

In recent years, mobility has become a challenge in most of the cities all other the globe. There are common problems in large cities such as: overpopulation, the increase of vehicular traffic, the overcoming of the capacity of roads and highways. All this is linked to the accelerated growth of populations that exceed the capacity of cities to adapt to the new demands of the population. Public transport is not exempt from the impact of these problems; there are still unanswered questions related to the adaptation

© Springer Nature Switzerland AG 2019
M. Torres and J. Klapp (Eds.): ISUM 2019, CCIS 1151, pp. 42–50, 2019.
https://doi.org/10.1007/978-3-030-38043-4_4

of transport routes to changes in the population, the efficient use of transport units, and the increase in mobility capacity of the population within cities. Making the transport system fault tolerant or adaptable to sudden changes is also a desirable feature.

However, these new characteristics of a transportation system require the use of complex techniques for monitoring, analysis, prediction and simulation of usage trends. This problem is obvious in large cities such as: Mexico City, Shanghai, New York, etc. [1–3]. These cities need to be more efficient to facilitate population mobility. One solution to this problem is to analyze people mobility and, in order to complete this task, massive volume of data need to be loaded, interpreted and contextualized. For instance, in public transportation systems, it is necessary to analyze where users board a bus, how much time they spend traveling along a route, how fast is the entire transportation system growing over the time, etc.

When a city provides hardware, software, data and personnel to population in order to help them in their daily activities, such as the examples before, then this city can be called 'smart' [4–6]. Smart cities has grown on the coverage of the concept 'society 4.0' where population demands information in order to fulfill expectations as can be seen in references [7–9]. This expectations could involve important decision making processes like in [10, 11].

That is why, this paper focuses on the objective of reviewing different strategies to load large amounts of data coming from different sources into a Data Warehouse. Even though, this problem is quite common on data analytics and, several papers have reported different kind of solutions to this problem [12–15], this paper reviews parallel alternatives for performing the ETL process.

There is some other work already done in this area. For instance, there are optimizations of the process using a MAS-based and fault-tolerant distributed ETL workflow engine [16]. There is some other work that presents a parallel processing solution that splitting big and complex SQL query into small pieces in distributed computing [17]. In paper [18], an improvement of the ETL processing in data warehouses using high-performance joins for changed data capture is presented.

Paper [19] presents a distributed ETL engine based on MAS and data partition technology. There are also work on massive data load on distributed database systems [20]; also, there are work on using agent-based parallel ETL system for massive data [21]. Even, there is work on defining an architecture for big data processing on intelligent transportation systems [22].

The rest of the paper is organized as follows: in section two, the system modelling is presented. Section three presents the system design, section four presents details for system implementation and some of the preliminary results are discussed. Finally, some conclusions are presented in section five.

2 System Modeling

In this section, a system modelling for a public transportation system (PTS) is presented. Let's first define $S = \{s_i | s_i = <s_{id}, s_{lat}, s_{lng} > \}$ as a station where:

s_{id} It is the station ID.

s_{lat} It is the station latitude.

s_{lng} It is the station longitude.

n = |S| is the number of station in the PTS

Let's also define an user as follows: $U = \left\{ u_j / u_j = <u_{id}^j, u_{lat}^j, u_{lng}^j, u_d^j > \right\}$ where:

u_{id}^j It refers to the user ID.

u_{lat}^j It is the user latitude.

u_{lng}^j It is the user longitude.

u_d^j It is the date when data was captured

Finally, the total number of users in the PTS is defined by $m = |U|$.

On the other hand, let's define a range of dates to analyze the existing information in the operational database (OD). Let's define that business intelligence process is oriented to know how many users are present in a station in a range of dates. Then, some definitions are needed; they are listed next.

D_a It is the beginning of the data range.

D_b It is the end of the data range

$$f(s_i, u_j, D_a, D_b) = \begin{cases} 1; (s_{lat1} < u_{lat} < s_{lat2})^\wedge (s_{lng1} < u_{lng} < s_{lng2})^\wedge (D_a \leq u_d \leq D_b) \\ 0; \; Otherwise \end{cases} \quad (1)$$

$f(s_i, u_j, D_a, D_b)$ Defines the presence of a user in a station s_i if:

$$(s_{lat1} < u_{lat} < s_{lat2})^\wedge (s_{lng1} < u_{lng} < s_{lng2})^\wedge (D_a \leq u_d \leq D_b) = 1$$

Then, let's define the number of users in a station (δ) as follows:

$$\delta = \sum_{i=1}^{n} \sum_{j=1}^{m} f(s_i, u_j, D_a, D_b) \quad (2)$$

The Eq. (2), counts all users in all stations in the transportation system in a fix period of time, where $s_i \in S \forall u_j \in U$. Now, let's define α as the number of users present in the station s_i. The definition is as follows:

$$\alpha = \sum_{j=1}^{m} f(s_i, u_j, D_a, D_b) \quad (3)$$

The Eq. (3), counts all users in i-th station, where $\forall u_j \in U$. In a similar way, let's define β as the number of users in a sub-set of stations. The definition is as follows:

$$\beta = \sum_{i=1}^{p} \alpha_i \quad (4)$$

Equation (4) represents the count of the users in a set of stations, where $p < n$. Finally, let's define all users in a route, which is a sub-set of stations. The definitions is as follows:

$$\gamma = \sum_{i=1}^{p} \sum_{j=1}^{m} f\left(s_i, u_j, D_a, D_b\right) \tag{5}$$

Equation (5) represents the number of users in the route R, where $s_i \in R^{\wedge} u_j \in U$. Now, it is necessary to implement this model in order to analyze the processing time.

3   System Design

In this section, three software architectures are presented to analyze large volumes of data in a business intelligence process. In this section, the work to be done is divided into three stages: the description of the ETL process, the ETL project design and the visualization of data.

3.1   ETL Process Description

During the description process of the ETL process, we have an operational database (OD) with a table containing the following fields:

< userID, user latitude, user longitude, TimeStamp >

This table grows significantly due to the fact that users' data are captured with high frequency. For example, for a PTS with 100k users whose geolocation it is being captured once per minute, in one hour (60 min), of software use there would be 6 million queries.

Due to the magnitude of the number of records, several strategies are proposed to accelerate the ETL process: (1) the use of distributed computing to concurrently read registers in one big database that contains all information coming from all users (see Fig. 1a). (2) A centralized operational database with one table and multiple data read threads to implement parallel access to database elements (see Fig. 1b). (3) An operational database with multiple tables where each table contains information organized by PTS users, regions of the transportation system, routes, schedules, dates of data acquisition, or some other organization (see Fig. 1c). (4) Finally, in Fig. 1d, it is shown a multiple operational databases containing the same information than in previous cases but data is organized in different databases which are accessed by different threads and different software worker.

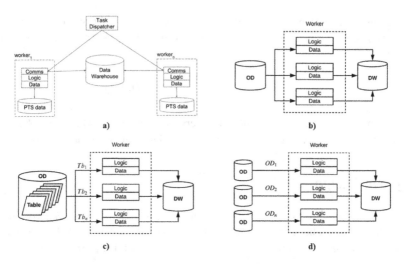

Fig. 1. Different software and database architectures to improve access to data. (a) Distributed architecture, (b) One centralized database architecture. (c) Multiple table but one database, (d) Multiple databases architecture; all of them for a multi-threaded multiple workers software.

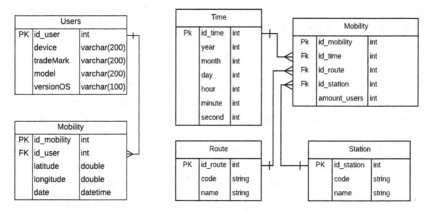

Fig. 2. Operational databases design for a PTS.

Fig. 3. Data warehouse to analyze data from a PTS.

Figure 2 shows details about the operational database which contains user geo-positions. This operational database contains two tables 'users' and 'mobility'. Table 'users' contains information about the user <id, device, tradeMark, model, versionOS> and the table 'mobility' contains information about each user geo-position <id_user, latitude, longitude, date>. On the other hand, Fig. 3 shows the Data Warehouse design which has four tables: data, route, station, userPerStation.

This database is organized as a data cube with the following dimensions *route x station x date* and the data stored is the number of users $< \alpha >$ (see Fig. 4 for a graphical representation and implementation using Pentaho Schema Workbench).

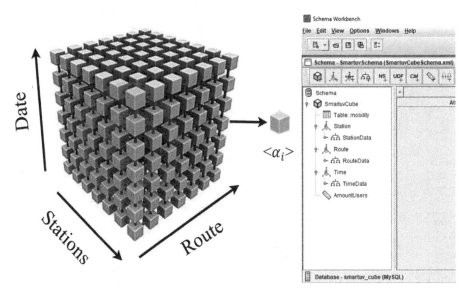

Fig. 4. Data cube representation for the data warehouse design and its implementation using Pentaho schema workbench.

4 Implementation and Preliminary Results

Master-node and slave-nodes are implemented in Java 8. Databases are implemented using MySQL 5.7.24 running on MAMP server 4.1. Communication between master- and slaves-nodes are implemented by using Java-Sockets and Pentaho Data Integration. All test are done in a Quad-core Intel Xeon processor 8 GB RAM OSX Yosemite 10.10.5 computer.

To test this software, data is obtained from the transportation system defined for the city of Poza Rica, Mexico. This PTS has 45 routes and 1024 stations, and it stores the 3,456,000 register of users' geo-positions (latitude, longitude). The ETL process is graphically represented in Fig. 5 using Pentaho Data Integration.

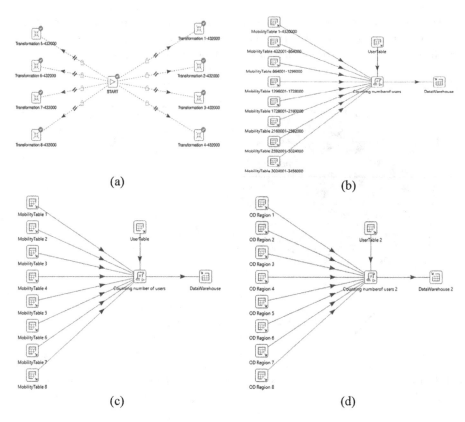

(a)

(b)

(c)

(d)

Fig. 5. ETL process design implemented in Pentaho data integration with eight concurrent requests for information from the operational database.

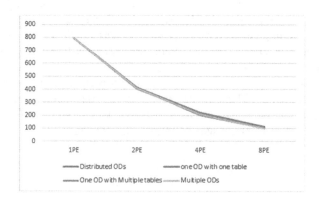

Fig. 6. System performance as increasing the number of threads and processing elements.

In Fig. 6, the results of executing the algorithm with different concurrent requests for information are presented. From this figure, it is possible to see that execution time is reduced as augmenting the number of concurrent requests.

5 Conclusions

In a public transportation system, data acquisition can become a problem when databases grow rapidly. The only sense of having a data acquisition process is to analyze the information in order to make some decisions based on the data acquired. There are several ideas about how to keep track of a system user: cards, image recognition, face recognition, GPS, etc. However, the amount of data could become a problem.

This paper presents the algorithm to improve the performance of ETL process when analyzing data coming from large databases containing public transportation user's mobility. This paper presents different architectures that can process big databases that holds information about public transportation users. Preliminary results show that data analysis can become fully parallel and this feature allow the improvement of execution time.

Acknowledgements. This research is sponsored in part by the Mexican Agency for International Development Cooperation (AMEXCID) and the Uruguayan Agency for International Cooperation (AUCI) through the Joint Uruguay-Mexico Cooperation Fund. This research work reflects only the points of view of the authors and not those of the AMEXCID or the AUCI.

References

1. Sharif, A., Li, j., Khalil, M., Kumar. R., Irfan, M., Sharif, A.: Internet of things—smart traffic management system for smart cities using big data analytics. In: 2017 14th International Computer Conference on Wavelet Active Media Technology and Information Processing (ICCWAMTIP), pp. 281–284. Chengdu (2017)
2. Liu, Y.: Big data technology and its analysis of application in urban intelligent transportation system. In: 2018 International Conference on Intelligent Transportation, Big Data & Smart City (ICITBS), pp. 17–19. Xiamen (2018)
3. Yang, Q., Gao, Z., Kong, X., Rahim, A., Wang, J., Xia, F.: Taxi operation optimization based on big traffic data. In: 2015 IEEE 12th International Conference on Ubiquitous Intelligence and Computing and 2015 IEEE 12th International Conference on Autonomic and Trusted Computing and 2015 IEEE 15th International Conference on Scalable Computing and Communications and Its Associated Workshops (UIC-ATC-ScalCom), pp. 127–134. Beijing (2015)
4. de Moreno, I.F.: La sociedad del conocimiento. General José María Córdova 5(7), 40–44 (2009)
5. García, F.: Engineering contributions to a multicultural perspective of the knowledge society. IEEE Revista Iberoamericana de Tecnologias del Aprendizaje 10(1), 17–18 (2015)
6. Kumar, N., Goel, S., Mallick, P.: Smart cities in India: features, policies, current status, and challenges. In: 2018 Technologies for Smart-City Energy Security and Power (ICSESP), pp. 1–4. Bhubaneswar (2018)

7. Ynzunza., C., Landeta, I., Bocarando, J., Aguilar, F., Larios, M.: El entorno de la industria 4.0: Implicaciones y Perspectivas Futuras. In: Conciencia Tecnológica, ISSN: 1405–5597
8. Lom, M., Pribyl, O., Svitek, M.: Industry 4.0 as a part of smart cities. In: 2016 Smart Cities Symposium Prague (SCSP), pp. 1–6. Prague (2016)
9. Gokalp, M., Kayabay, K., Akyol, M., Eren, P., Koçyiğit, A.: Big data for industry 4.0: a conceptual framework. In: 2016 International Conference on Computational Science and Computational Intelligence (CSCI), pp. 431–434. Las Vegas, NV (2016)
10. Ferreira, N., et al.: Urbane: A 3D framework to support data driven decision making in urban development. In: 2015 IEEE Conference on Visual Analytics Science and Technology (VAST), pp. 97–104. Chicago, IL (2015)
11. Zhao, M.: Urban traffic flow guidance system based on data driven. In: 2009 International Conference on Measuring Technology and Mechatronics Automation, pp. 653–657. Zhangjiajie, Hunan (2009)
12. Zhang, S., Jia, S., Ma, C., Wang, Y.: Impacts of public transportation fare reduction policy on urban public transport sharing rate based on big data analysis. In: 2018 IEEE 3rd International Conference on Cloud Computing and Big Data Analysis (ICCCBDA), pp. 280–284. Chengdu (2018)
13. Guido, G., Rogano, D., Vitale, A., Astarita, V., Festa, D.: Big data for public transportation: a DSS framework. In: 2017 5th IEEE International Conference on Models and Technologies for Intelligent Transportation Systems (MT-ITS), pp. 872–877. Naples (2017)
14. Yuan, W., Deng, P., Taleb, T., Wan, J., Bi, C.: An unlicensed taxi identification model based on big data analysis. IEEE Trans. Intell. Transp. Syst. 17(6), 1703–1713 (2016)
15. Wu, P., Chen, Y.: Big data analytics for transport systems to achieve environmental sustainability. In: 2017 International Conference on Applied System Innovation (ICASI), pp. 264–267. Sapporo (2017)
16. Huang, J., Guo, C.: An MAS-based and fault-tolerant distributed ETL workflow engine. In: Proceedings of the 2012 IEEE 16th International Conference on Computer Supported Cooperative Work in Design (CSCWD), pp. 54–58. Wuhan (2012)
17. Yang, P., Liu, Z., Ni, J.: Performance tuning in distributed processing of ETL. In: 2013 Seventh International Conference on Internet Computing for Engineering and Science, pp. 85–88. Shanghai, (2013)
18. Tank, D., Ganatra, A., Kosta, Y., Bhensdadia, C.: Speeding ETL processing in data warehouses using high-performance joins for changed data capture (CDC). In: 2010 International Conference on Advances in Recent Technologies in Communication and Computing, pp. 365–368. Kottayam (2010)
19. Wang, G., Guo, C.: Research of distributed ETL engine based on MAS and data partition. In: Proceedings of the 2011 15th International Conference on Computer Supported Cooperative Work in Design (CSCWD), pp. 342–347. Lausanne, (2011)
20. Azqueta, A., Patiño, M., Brondino, I., Jimenez, R.: Massive data load on distributed database systems over HBase. In: 2017 17th IEEE/ACM International Symposium on Cluster, Cloud and Grid Computing (CCGRID), pp. 776–779. Madrid (2017)
21. Chen, G., An, B., Liu, Y.: A novel agent-based parallel ETL system for massive data. In: 2016 Chinese Control and Decision Conference, pp. 3942–3948. Yinchuan (2016)
22. Guerreiro, G., Figueiras, P., Silva, R., Costa, R., Jardim, R.: An architecture for big data processing on intelligent transportation systems: an application scenario on highway traffic flows. In: 2016 IEEE 8th International Conference on Intelligent Systems (IS), pp. 65–72. Sofia (2016)

Molecular Rotors in Viscous Fluids: A Numerical Analysis Aid by GPU Computing

Daniel Gutiérrez-Garibay[✉] and Humberto Híjar[✉]

Engineering School, La Salle University Mexico,
Benjamin Franklin 45, 06140 Mexico City, Mexico
{dgg,humberto.hijar}@lasallistas.org.mx

Abstract. Molecular rotors are microscopic structures composed of two coupled parts that can rotate mutually. They have promising applications in viscosity measurement and flow detection in micro-sized and complex geometries. We propose a model for studying molecular rotors as classical systems moving in viscous environments, subjected to internal interactions and stochastic forces. Our model is expressed as a set of non-linear stochastic Langevin equations that are solved numerically using a Brownian Dynamics procedure. Attention is focused on the calculation of the two-time correlation function of the internal angular variable. For small internal forces, this correlation turns out to have a very slow time decay and its correct estimation requires long numerical experiments. We propose a CUDA implementation for a computer cluster with TESLA GPUs that calculates angular correlation functions in parallel. The implementation reduces the used computational time considerably in comparison with the one consumed by a usual serial scheme. It allows for the simulation of massive molecular rotors ensembles from which reliable results can be obtained. It is discussed how the GPU implementation can be improved in modern GPUs architectures.

1 Introduction

Molecular rotors (MRs) are customarily described as microscopic structures composed of two coupled parts that can rotate one with respect to the other in a continuous manner [1]. In recent years, the analysis and synthesis of MRs have attracted significant attention in physics, chemistry and nanosciences [2].

Constituent parts of MRs are usually classified by their moments of inertia. The part having the largest moment of inertia is called the stator (S) and the one corresponding to the smallest moment of inertia is referred to as the rotor (R). A rather large variety of MRs have been synthesized that differ significantly on their physical and chemical properties, thus serving for a correspondingly large amount of purposes. For relevant situations in nanotechnology, MRs mounted on a solid or on a surface have been studied experimentally [3]. These MRs must be distinguished from those that can float freely in a liquid or vapor phase [4]. In terms of their internal structure, MRs can be classified as those in which S and R are covalently linked from those in which they are not [5]. Examples of the latter include molecules containing two interlocked rings (catenanes) [6], and molecules with a ring mounted on a rod (rotaxanes) [7].

© Springer Nature Switzerland AG 2019
M. Torres and J. Klapp (Eds.): ISUM 2019, CCIS 1151, pp. 51–62, 2019.
https://doi.org/10.1007/978-3-030-38043-4_5

Fluorescent MRs are special systems possessing excited energy states that can relax following two alternate mechanisms, namely: rotation and light emission [8]. When the rotation mechanism is inhibited by the environment MRs emit more light. On the contrary, when rotation is favored, light emission is reduced. An external property that can modify these relaxation mechanisms is the viscosity of the thermal bath. In a fluid with high viscosity relaxation by light emission is stimulated. Using this effect MRs could be used as microscopic viscometers [9]. External flow is an additional mechanism that alters rotational dynamics [10]. By this mean, MRs can be used to explore flow in complex geometries [11]. Furthermore, chemical interactions between MRs and dissolved substances perturb the internal energetic states and also inhibit internal rotations [12]. Therefore, this type of fluorescent MRs can be used as microscopic chemical sensors [13].

Analytical models have been proposed that describe the action of external electric fields applied on MRs [14]. In these models the time evolution of the internal angular degree of freedom is considered to be the solution of stochastic differential equations with additive thermal noise (Langevin equations). Molecular rotors are subjected to internal potentials and electric fields have the effect of tilting such potentials, thus promoting the rotation in a preferred direction [15].

Here, a general model is proposed for analyzing MRs floating in equilibrium viscous fluid. At first order in a series expansion, the internal interaction energy is shown to be a periodic cosine potential. In addition, stochastic thermal forces are considered to produce Brownian fluctuations that are modeled through equations of the Langevin type. Due to the nonlinear character of the proposed equations, a Brownian Dynamics (BD) numerical scheme is implemented to obtain the relevant dynamical information. In particular, orientational correlation functions related to spectral characteristics are calculated that exhibit a very slow decaying. In addition, because of the stochastic nature of the system, it is necessary to realize a sufficiently large number of simulations to obtain proper statistical results.

In order to obtain results in a feasible time, it is proposed to calculate the structural correlation functions under a parallel scheme running on GPUs. It is shown that the proposed scheme improves significantly the performance of the numerical implementation when compared with the corresponding traditional serial scheme. Then it is demonstrated that GPU computing is very useful in allowing the simulation of sufficiently large MRs ensembles from which more reliable physical information can be inferred. Specifically, it is found that angular correlations contain two contributions, one arising from libration around states of internal mechanical equilibrium and the other one from hops between such states. For large viscosity, these mechanisms evolve over widely separated time-scales. In this limit, a simplified method for superposing these effects is proposed and used to fit the numerical results.

This paper is organized as follows. In Sect. 2, the stochastic model for describing the time evolution of a MR is constructed that includes a first order approximation for the torque between its internal components. Also, the statistical properties of the stochastic forces acting on the MR are presented. In Sect. 3, the specific BD algorithm implemented to solve the resulting non-linear stochastic equations is described. Furthermore, the definition of the structural correlation function is introduced and an approximated analytical form for this quantity is given. Subsequently, in Sect. 4 it is explained the method used to parallelize the BD algorithm on GPUs. In Sect. 5, the results obtained from the numerical implementation are presented and the advantage of using parallel computing is shown. Finally, in Sect. 6 the main results of the present analysis are summarized.

2   Dynamic Model of Molecular Rotors

Consider the structure shown in Fig. 1. It consists of two parts, S and R, that can rotate mutually. The stator (S) is composed of two semi-spheres with radii R_S and mass $M_S/2$. These hemispheres are joined by an axis that supports the rotor (R). This latter is modeled as a dumbbell with two spheres of mass M_R and radii R_R, separated by a mass-less bar with length $2R_D$. An internal structural energy is introduced by assuming that S and R have points, $\vec{r_S}$ and $\vec{r_R}$, respectively, that attract each other through the function $\Phi(|\vec{r_S} - \vec{r_R}|)$. The structure in Fig. 1 is assumed to be microscopic and to be immersed in a fluid with temperature T and viscosity η. Moreover, the motion of the system is assumed to be confined to the plane containing the dumbbell ($x - z$ plane).

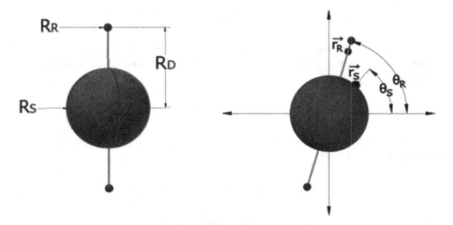

Fig. 1. Mechanical model for a MR with a spherical stator and a rotating dumbbell.

Let θ_S and θ_R represent, respectively, the angles that S and R form with the z axis. The dynamic equations for these variables can be obtained by considering the balance of angular momentum, namely

$$I_S\ddot{\theta}_S = -\gamma_S\dot{\theta}_S - \Gamma + \tau_S(t), \tag{1}$$

$$I_R\ddot{\theta}_R = -\gamma_R\dot{\theta}_R + \Gamma + \tau_R(t), \tag{2}$$

where time derivatives are indicated by overdots.

In Eqs. (1) and (2), I_S and I_R are moments of inertia, whereas γ_S and γ_R represent angular drag coefficients. These quantities have the explicit form:

$$I_S = 2M_S R_S^2/3, I_R = 2M_R R_D^2, \gamma_S = 8\pi\eta R_S^3, \text{ and } \gamma_R = 12\pi\eta R_R R_D^2.$$

Terms $\tau_S(t)$ and $\tau_R(t)$ in Eqs. (1) and (2) are stochastic torques induced by the medium surrounding the MR. As it is usual, it will be assumed that $\tau_S(t)$ and $\tau_R(t)$ are Gaussian-Markov processes with zero mean, that obey the fluctuation-dissipation theorems (FDT)

$$\langle \tau_S(t)\tau_S(t')\rangle = 2\gamma_S k_B T \delta(t-t'), \tag{3}$$

$$\langle \tau_R(t)\tau_R(t')\rangle = 2\gamma_R k_B T \delta(t-t'), \tag{4}$$

respectively, where $\langle \ldots \rangle$ indicate an equilibrium average and k_B is the Boltzmann constant.

Also in Eqs. (1) and (2), $\Gamma(\theta_S, \theta_R)$ is the internal torque exerted on R by S. $\Gamma(\theta_S, \theta_R)$ can be written in the general form

$$\Gamma = f\left(r_R^2 + r_S^2 - 2r_R r_S \cos(\theta_R - \theta_S)\right)r_S r_R \sin(\theta_R - \theta_S), \tag{5}$$

where f is a function of the square distance $|\vec{r}_S - \vec{r}_R|^2$ with units of force over distance. By expanding f in terms of the ratio $r_S/r_R < 1$, and maintaining only the leading term one obtains

$$\Gamma = -\Lambda \sin(2(\theta_R - \theta_S)), \tag{6}$$

where $\Lambda = r_S^2 r_R^2 [df(z)/dz]_{z=r^2}$. Under this approximation Eqs. (1) and (2) can be rewritten in the form

$$\ddot{\theta}_1 = -\beta_{11}\dot{\theta}_1 - \beta_{12}\dot{\theta}_2 - \omega^2 \sin(2\theta_1) + q_1(t), \tag{7}$$

$$\ddot{\theta}_2 = -\beta_{21}\dot{\theta}_1 - \beta_{22}\dot{\theta}_2 + q_2(t), \tag{8}$$

where new state variables have been introduced through the definitions $\theta_1 = \theta_R - \theta_S$ and $\theta_2 = (I_R\theta_R + I_S\theta_S)/(I_R + I_S)$. Furthermore, coefficients in Eqs. (7) and (8) are abbreviations for

$$\omega^2 = \left(\frac{1}{I_R} + \frac{1}{I_S}\right)\Lambda, \beta_{11} = \frac{\gamma_R I_S}{I_R} + \frac{\gamma_S I_R}{I_S}, \beta_{12} = \frac{\gamma_S}{I_S} + \frac{\gamma_R}{I_R},$$

$$\beta_{21} = \frac{\gamma_R I_S}{(I_R + I_S)^2} + \frac{\gamma_S I_R}{(I_R + I_S)^2}, \text{ and } \beta_{22} = \frac{\gamma_R}{I_R + I_S} + \frac{\gamma_S}{I_R + I_S}.$$

Finally, $q_1(t)$ and $q_2(t)$ stand for the combinations of the stochastic torques:

$$q_1(t) = \frac{1}{I_R} \tau_R(t) - \frac{1}{I_S} \tau_S(t) \tag{9}$$

and

$$q_2(t) = \frac{1}{I_R + I_S} (\tau_R(t) + \tau_S(t)), \tag{10}$$

respectively.

3 Numerical Solution

The system of stochastic differential equations Eqs. (7) and (8) can be solved numerically. With this aim, it is transformed into a system of four differential equations of first order for the variables θ_1, θ_2, $\dot{\theta}_1$, and $\dot{\theta}_2$. Then, a Runge-Kutta method is implemented to solve the resulting expressions using a time-step with size Δt. Brownian Dynamics is incorporated by sampling stochastic forces τ_S and τ_R at every simulation step from Gaussian distributions with zero mean and standard deviations

$$\sigma_S = \sqrt{\frac{2\gamma_S k_B T}{I_S^2 \Delta t}}, \tag{11}$$

and

$$\sigma_R = \sqrt{\frac{2\gamma_R k_B T}{I_R^2 \Delta t}}, \tag{12}$$

respectively. A similar implementation has been recently used for the simulation of Brownian motors that operate by morphological changes [16, 17].

Solutions given by the algorithm are time series $\theta_1(t_i)$ and $\theta_2(t_i)$, where the discretized time is $t_i = i\Delta t$, for $i = 0, 1, 2, \ldots, N$. Here, N is the number of simulation steps. These series were used to calculate numerically the dynamic correlation

$$X(t) = \frac{\langle cos(\theta_1(t))cos(\theta_1(0))\rangle - \langle cos(\theta_1)\rangle^2}{\langle cos^2(\theta_1)\rangle - \langle cos(\theta_1)\rangle^2}, \tag{13}$$

which is the relevant function occurring in scattering phenomena in suspensions of MRs [18]. In practice, the main contribution to $X(t)$, $\langle cos(\theta_1(t))cos(\theta_1(0))\rangle$, can be estimated using the usual moving time-origin scheme, namely

$$\langle cos(\theta_1(t_{i+n}))cos(\theta_1(t_i))\rangle \simeq \frac{1}{N-n+1} \sum_{j=0}^{N-n} cos(\theta_1(t_{j+n}))cos(\theta_1(t_j)). \tag{14}$$

From the analytical point of view, for large values of Λ, only small fluctuations around the minimum of the structural potential, $\theta_1 = 0$, could be expected. In this case, $X(t)$ contains contributions from this libration mechanism only. These contributions can be calculated by approximating the interaction potential as a harmonic potential. Then, the nonlinear character of Eq. (7) is neglected and the equilibrium probability distribution for θ_1 can be found. Using this distribution it can be shown that [19]

$$X_1(t) = \frac{\cosh\left(\frac{k_B T}{2\Lambda}e^{-\alpha t}\right) - 1}{\cosh\left(\frac{k_B T}{2\Lambda}\right) - 1},$$ (15)

where $\alpha = 2\Lambda/\beta_{11}$. Thus, in this limit, $X(t)$ decays exponentially to zero at characteristic time of the order of $1/\alpha$.

For small internal forces, thermal noise can activate jumps between the minimum energy states of the cosine potential [20]. It has been shown that $X(t)$ has a decay of the form

$$X_2(t) = \frac{e^{-2\kappa_2 t}}{\cosh\left(\frac{2k_B T}{\Lambda}\right)},$$ (16)

where κ_2 is the rate of escape from the harmonic potential well. Further approximations yield $\kappa_2 = 8\eta_1$, where

$$\eta_1 = \frac{\Lambda}{8\pi\beta_{11}}e^{-\frac{\Lambda}{k_B T}},$$ (17)

is the Kramers activation rate for a jump over a single potential barrier of high Λ with maximum and minimum approximated at the quadratic order.

These theoretical predictions show that two separated time-scales can be identified in MRs dynamics corresponding to libration around the minima of the cosine potential and activated jumps over the potential barrier. By introducing a bridging parameter defined as the ratio of the characteristic times, $\varepsilon = e^{-\frac{\Lambda}{k_B T}}$, a simple superposition of Eqs. (15) and (16) gives

$$X(t) = \frac{1}{1+\varepsilon}X_1(t) + \frac{\varepsilon}{1+\varepsilon}X_2(t),$$ (18)

which recovers both results in the proper limit.

Moreover, in the limit $\Lambda \ll k_B T$, $X(t)$ is expected to decay very slowly. Consequently, the numerical estimation of this function requires long experiments that could reduce the statistical error arising from small sampling at large values of t. Reducing the computation time employed in the calculation of $X(t)$ is fundamental, because obtaining the time series solution for $\theta_1(t)$ is a problem $O(N)$, while obtaining $X(t)$ requires $O(N^2)$ operations. Therefore, estimating correlation functions is more time consuming than solving the system of dynamic equations itself, and represent a bottleneck that should be reduced to improve efficiency and permit the simulation of larger samples.

4   GPU Parallel Computation Scheme

In order to speed up the computation of the correlation function contribution $X'(t_i)$, we propose an hybrid procedure in which BD solutions of Eqs. (7) and (8) are computed in a serial manner on the CPU, while correlation functions are calculated in parallel using the GPUs provided by the Tesla K20m in the computer cluster. In order to achieve sufficient statistics we use ensembles of 5000 MRs and let its dynamic evolve along four million steps in time.

The inherent character of the correlation function is that the result of each pair of elements in the multiplication depends exclusively on that pair, then it's possible to run $N_{threads}$ operations at the same time without affecting the final result. Because of this property, we considered that a program that can run the operations in parallel will reduce the total time of the calculation without altering the result, and the multiple processors of a GPU are ideal for this.

To solve the correlations we use the approximation of divide the data in several parts and run each multiplication of a pair of elements in one CUDA thread, and due to the architecture available in the server, Tesla K20m with a compute capability 3.5 [21], launch a kernel of $N_{threads}$ threads M_{block} times, then sum each resulting block with the previous and finally sum $N_{threads}$ elements in the host side to obtain the ith term of the correlation function, as shown in the Fig. 2.

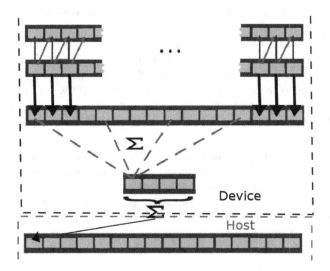

Fig. 2. Diagram of the process followed to calculate the correlation function.

Also as a side advantage of the use of GPUs we can obtain the random torques for τ_R and τ_S with *curandSetPseudoRandomGeneratorSeed* using a Mersenne Twister MTGP32 pseudo-random generator. in parallel instead of calculating each random number in each simulation step.

5 Results

5.1 Comparison Against Serial Calculations

Correlation functions where calculated according to the parallel scheme described in Sect. 4, as well as following a purely serial scheme executed in a **Intel Xeon E5-2670** processor. This was done with the purpose of assessing the efficiency of the proposed GPU parallel method. In addition, this series of numerical experiments allowed us to have a first insight on the behavior of correlation functions and on the physical consistency of the proposed algorithm. With this in mind ensembles of 600 independent MRs where studied that evolved over 4×10^6 time-steps of size $\Delta t = 10^{-4} u_t$, where u_t are units of time. Notice that hereafter, simulation units (s.u.) rather than physical units will be considered. Specifically, simulations were conducted using $k_B T = 1$, $R_S = 1$, and $M_S = 1$, as units of energy, distance, and mass, respectively. Time units are defined from $u_t = \sqrt{M_S R_S^2 / (k_B T)}$.

Then different ensembles of MRs were studied changing the value of the interaction strength Λ from $\Lambda = 1 s.u.$ to $\Lambda = 10 s.u.$ in regular increments. All other simulation variables remained fixed at the values $M_R = 1 M_S$, $R_D = 2 R_S$, $R_R = 0.1 R_S$, $\eta = 20 s.u..$ Using these parameters it could be anticipated that $1/\beta_{11} \in (4.71, 47.13) u_t$. On the other hand, relation time $1/\kappa_2$, is expected to go from $1/\kappa_2 = 2187 u_t$ for $\Lambda = 1$, to $1/\kappa2 = 1.4 \times 10^{10} u_t$ for $\Lambda = 10$. Thus, the selected parameters permit us to explore the two separated scales associated libration and jumping mechanisms discussed in Sect. 4.

Numerical results in both parallel and serial implementations exhibited the expected behavior through a fast decay for $\Lambda \le 3$, a slower decay for $3 < \Lambda \le 7$ and a very slow decay for $\Lambda \ge 8$. In the previous cases, statistical noise in measurements of $X(t_i)$ was present and seemed to be the dominant contribution for $t > 100 u_t = t_f$, $t > 200 u_t = t_m$, and $t > 300 u_t = t_s$, respectively. Consequently, we decided to use the complete time-series to calculate correlation functions, but cut the calculation at t_f, t_m, and t_s, respectively.

The execution times t_{ex} for obtaining correlation functions were measured in hours, h, for the previously established conditions. Results are summarized in Fig. 3 were execution times for parallel and serial implementations are presented. It can be readily observed that in all cases parallel computations had a better performance. The maximum percentage difference was found to be 50%, obtained for simulations with $\Lambda = 1$. Therefore, parallel GPU computing could reduced significantly the computation time employed in the analysis of stochastic systems described by differential equations of the Langevin type.

5.2 Correlation Functions

Results of the previous description were obtained using the following simulation parameters $\Delta t = 1 \times 10^{-4} u_t$, $R_D = 2$, $R_R = 0.1$ and $M_R = 1$, the viscosity $\mu = 2$ and interaction variable corresponding $\Lambda = 1, 2, \ldots, 10$.

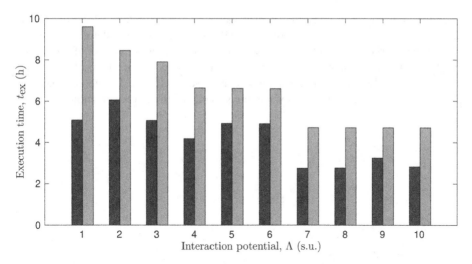

Fig. 3. Execution time comparison (CUDA in blue and Serial in yellow) of the program through 10 sets of experiments for 600 MRs Λ (1–3) calculated with 30000 samples, Λ (4–6) calculated with 20000 samples, Λ (7–10) calculated with 10000 samples. (Color figure online)

Each MR evolved for 4×10^7 simulation steps, after a thermalization period of 2×10^7 steps. To obtain trustworthy results for the correlations, ensembles of 5000 MRs with each set of parameters were executed and individual correlations were averaged. Results of this procedure are shown in Fig. 4.

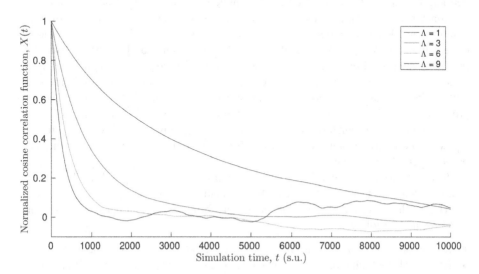

Fig. 4. Cosine correlation function $X(t)$ obtained by the parallel method for $\Lambda = 1$, 3 and 9.

In Fig. 4, it can be observed that at large values of Λ the correlation decreases faster. Accordingly, at larger interaction potentials MRs spend less time in deformed states.

With the purpose of validating our method, we compared the results of the cosine correlation function obtained by the numerical simulations versus the results obtained of evaluation of Eq. (18), this comparison can be see in Fig. 5. The good agreement that can be noticed exhibits the physical consistency of the implementation.

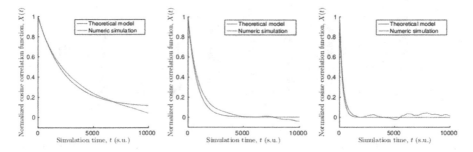

Fig. 5. Comparison of the cosine correlation obtained from the analytical model, Eq. (18), and simulations with values of $\Lambda = 1$, 3 and 9. Red: numeric simulations. Blue: theoretical model. (Color figure online)

6 Conclusions

The stochastic motion of MRs was analyzed using BD simulations. The non linear and periodic features of the considered model implied a slow decay of the structural correlation functions at large internal energies. As a consequence, the computation time required for calculating correlation functions using standard serial procedures could be extremely large. With the purpose of improving the efficiency of the method, a parallel procedure supported by GPUs was developed. The basic idea was to assign the multiplication pairs involved in two-times correlation function calculations to de minimal GPU units, so these operations can run in parallel. afterwards, a running average procedure was applied to obtain statistical result ensembles of independent MRs.

The reliability of our procedure was confirmed by showing that numerical results reproduce correctly theoretical predictions for correlation functions of Brownian particles in periodic potentials.

It was demonstrated that, in terms of execution time, our proposal has better performance than the usual serial scheme for correlation calculations.

The implementation of a parallel algorithm brings various improves versus the serial method as follows:

- Reduction of the total execution time in around 47% vs the serial method.
- In spite of the limitations of the available computer cluster, an improvement in the time is shown in the parallel method. This, in conjoint with the advances in the performance of GPUs and CPUs reported by Nvidia [22, 23], lead us to conclude that with an update in the hardware available the improvement could be greater.

The same limitations in hardware reduced the GPU's performance when many programs ran in a single card. However, these limitations could be solved in newer architectures.

Results in the present manuscript could be of interest in some other fields where calculation of correlation functions is relevant. For instance, two-point correlation functions are important in the analysis of large scale structures in the Universe and the advantages and drawbacks of using GPUs for calculating them have been explored in detail in Refs. [24–26]. Correlation coefficients are also relevant in the real time analysis of neural activity and their computation on the massive parallel architecture provided by GPUs has been conducted in Ref. [27].

Acknowledgments. H.H. thanks La Salle University Mexico for financial support under grant NEC-08/18. D.G-G. thanks La Salle University Mexico for financial support.

References

1. Kottas, G.S., Clarke, L.I., Horinek, D., Mich, J.: Artificial molecular rotors. Chem. Rev. **105**, 1281–1376 (2005)
2. Cao, J., Lu, H.-Y., Chen, C.-F.: Synthesis, structures, and properties of peripheral o-dimethoxy-substituted pentiptycene quinones and their o-quinone derivatives. Tetrahedron **65**, 8104–8112 (2009)
3. Khuong, T.V., Dang, H., Jarowski, P.D., Maverick, E.F., Garcia-Garibay, M.A.: Rotational dynamics in a crystalline molecular gyroscope by variable-temperature ^{13}C NMR, ^{2}H NMR, X-ray diffraction, and force field calculations. J. Am. Chem. Soc. **129**(4), 839–845 (2007). PMID: 17243820
4. Akers, W., Haidekker, M.A.: A molecular rotor as viscosity sensor in aqueous colloid solutions. J. Biomech. Eng. **126**(3), 340–345 (2004)
5. Comotti, A., Bracco, S., Ben, T., Qiu, S., Sozzani, P.: Molecular rotors in porous organic frameworks. Angew. Chem. Int. Ed. **53**, 1043–1047 (2014)
6. Armspach, D., et al.: Catenated cyclodextrins. Chem. A Eur. J. **1**(1), 33–55 (1995)
7. Kim, K., Lee, J.W.: Rotaxane dendrimers. Top. Curr. Chem. **228**, 111–140 (2003)
8. Haidekker, M.A., Theodorakis, E.A.: Environment-sensitive behavior of fluorescent molecular rotors. J. Biol. Eng. **4**, 11 (2010)
9. López-Duarte, I., Vu, T.T., Izquierdo, M.A., Bull, J.A., Kuimova, M.K.: A molecular rotor for measuring viscosity in plasma membranes of live cells. Chem. Commun. **50**, 5282–5284 (2014)
10. Haidekker, M.A., Akers, W., Lichlyter, D., Brady, T.P., Theodorakis, E.A.: Sensing of flow and shear stress using fluorescent molecular rotors. Sens. Lett. **3**, 42–48 (2005)
11. Mustafic, A., Huang, H.-M., Theodorakis, E.A., Haidekker, M.A.: Imaging of flow patterns with fluorescent molecular rotors. J. Fluorescence **20**, 1087–1098 (2010)
12. Dong, J., et al.: Ultrathin two-dimensional porous organic nanosheets with molecular rotors for chemical sensing. Nat. Commun. **8**, 1142 (2017)
13. Valeur, B.: Molecular fluorescence. In: Digital Encyclopedia of Applied Physics, pp. 477–531 (2009)
14. Horinek, D., Michl, J.: Molecular dynamics simulation of an electric field driven dipolar molecular rotor attached to a quartz glass surface. J. Am. Chem. Soc. **125**(39), 11900–11910 (2003)

15. Kudernac, T., et al.: Electrically driven directional motion of a four-wheeled molecule on a metal surface. Nature **479**, 208–211 (2011)
16. Ambía, F., Híjar, H.: Stochastic dynamics of a brownian motor based on morphological changes. Rev. Mex. Fis. **63**, 314–327 (2017)
17. Híjar, H.: Operation of theoretical brownian motors based on morphological adaptations. Physica A **513**, 781–797 (2019)
18. Marchesoni, F., Vij, J.K., Coffey, W.T.: Nonlinear budó model for dielectric relaxation: comparison with new experimental data. Z. Phys. B – Condens. Matter **61**, 357–366 (1985)
19. Gutiérrez-Garibay, D.: Análisis teórico y numérico de la dinámica estocástica de giroscopios moleculares. Master's thesis, La Salle University Mexico, Mexico City, Mexico (2019, in progress)
20. Marchesoni, F., Vij, J.K.: Brownian motion in a periodic potential: application to dielectric relaxation. Z. Phys. B – Condens. Matter **58**, 187–198 (1985)
21. NVIDIA Corporation. Programming guide v10.0.130. https://docs.nvidia.com/cuda/cuda-c-programming-guide/index.html#cuda-general-purpose-parallel-computing-architecture. Accessed 18 Feb 2019
22. NVIDIA Corporation. Programming guide v10.0.130. https://docs.nvidia.com/cuda/cuda-c-programming-guide/index.html#from-graphics-processing-to-general-purpose-parallel-computing__memory-bandwidth-for-cpu-and-gpu. Accessed 18 Feb 2019
23. NVIDIA Corporation. Tesla v100 performance guide. https://images.nvidia.com/content/pdf/v100-application-performance-guide.pdf. Accessed 18 Feb 2019
24. Barda, D., Bellisbc, M., Allend, M.T., Yepremyane, H., Kratochvilf, J.M.: Cosmological calculations on the GPU. Astron. and Comput. **1**, 17–22 (2013)
25. Alonso, D.: CUTE solutions for two-point correlation functions from large cosmological datasets. arXiv:1210.1833 [astro-ph.IM] (2013)
26. Ponce, R., Cardenas-Montes, M., Rodriguez-Vazquez, J.J., Sanchez, E., Sevilla, I.: Application of GPUs for the calculation of two point correlation functions in cosmology. arXiv:1204.6630 [astro-ph.IM] (2012)
27. Gembris, D., Neeb, M., Gipp, M., et al.: Correlation analysis on GPU systems using NVIDIA's CUDA. J. Real-Time Image Proc. **6**, 275–280 (2011). https://doi.org/10.1007/s11554-010-0162-9

SPH Numerical Simulations of the Deformation of a Liquid Surface in Two Dimensions

Cristian Cáliz-Reyes[1], Laura A. Ibarra-Bracamontes[1],
Rosanna Bonasia[2(✉)], and Gonzalo Viramontes-Gamboa[1]

[1] Universidad Michoacana de San Nicolás de Hidalgo, Av. Francisco. J. Múgica
S/N, C.U., 58030 Morelia Mich, Mexico
laibarrab@gmail.com
[2] CONACYT-Instituto Politécnico Nacional, ESIA, UZ, Miguel Bernard,
S/N, Edificio de Posgrado, 07738 Mexico City, Mexico
rbonasia@conacyt.mx

Abstract. The Smoothed Particles Hydrodynamics (SPH) numerical method, DualSPHysics, was applied to simulate numerically the deformations generated when a solid object hits a liquid surface. In order to simplify the study, the simulations were carried out in 2D, with the hitting solid having a circular geometry. With the aim of comparing numerical and experimental results, a real quasi-2D cell was made using two acrylic walls with a 5 mm separation filled with water, using a slightly thinner Teflon disc as the hitting object. The simulation was able to reproduce qualitatively all the experimental phenomenology of the system, particularly the three main structures observed in the real quasi-2D (and also reported in 3D) situation: a crown splash, an air cavity, and a liquid jet. The maximum values reached by the depth of the cavity and the height of the jet were determined for two different impact velocities both numerically and experimentally. The numerical simulation better reproduced the experimental cavity depth than the jet height, with a percentage of average accuracy of 94% and 64% respectively. Accuracy was improved up to 85% for the maximum jet height when the effect of gravitational forces was increased and the maximum resolution was used in the numerical simulations. The differences found between experimental and simulation results can be attributed to the absence of a suitable model for surface tension in the single-phase system used to represent the free surface in the simulations, as well as to the confinement effects present in the experiments.

Keywords: SPH model · Splash deformation

1 Introduction

The deformation generated in a liquid surface either by the impact of a solid object or by a liquid is known as splash. Associated with the splash, a series of movements on the liquid surface can be identified. For example, if a solid object striking perpendicular to the liquid surface generates the deformation, the impact causes a release of liquid on the

© Springer Nature Switzerland AG 2019
M. Torres and J. Klapp (Eds.): ISUM 2019, CCIS 1151, pp. 63–75, 2019.
https://doi.org/10.1007/978-3-030-38043-4_6

surface forming what is known as a splash crown. Subsequently, the solid object descends displacing the liquid in its path and forming a hole called the air cavity. Finally, when the air cavity is closed due to the hydrostatic pressure exerted by the liquid, a jet is generated and expelled from the surface, which is defined as the liquid jet.

The splash is a phenomenon associated with fluid mechanics and shows the response of a liquid surface due to the energy transferred by the impact of an object. It is a common phenomenon in nature and can occur in industrial phenomena that handle liquids. For example, its study is of a great interest in industries dealing with ink injection printers. Some studies have been developed for the applications of the splash phenomenon in naval architecture, in the design of seaplanes, as well as in the military area for the development of missiles [23]. Some other works have focused on the analysis of the most appropriate way to enter the water during diving to avoid damage to the body; moreover, few related works try to understand how some basilisk lizards and shorebirds can walk on the surface of the sea [9].

Various experimental, theoretical and numerical studies, have been carried out in relation to the splash phenomenon. Among the numerical works is the one made by Alam et al. [1] that used the Semi-Implicit Particle Movement technique to determine the deformation of the splash crown by the vertical impact of a wedge in 2D. Wang et al. [24] used the numerical Border Integral Equation method to study the behavior of the air cavity formed by the impact of a wedge on the water surface. Other numerical studies, included within the Computational Fluid Mechanics, have been developed and applied to the splash phenomenon, based on Eulerian and Lagrangian methods [6, 10, 14].

The Smoothed Particles Hydrodynamics (SPH) is a meshless Lagrangian method that was developed to model continuous medium physics, avoiding the limitations of finite difference methods. It was applied for the first time forty years ago to solve astrophysical problems [8, 15]. The numerical method has proven to be robust and applicable to a wide variety of fields. For example, in the case of Fluid Dynamics, it has been applied in: multiphase flows [5, 18], gravity currents [17], free surface flow [19], sediment transport [26], among others. According to this method, the relevant physical quantities are calculated for each particle as an interpolation of the values of the nearest neighbor particles. The Lagrangian nature of the SPH method endows it with some advantages compared to the usual limitations of the Eulerian models. For example, there are no restrictions imposed either on the geometry of the system or the initial conditions, so that the latter can be easily programmed without the need for complicated grid algorithms such as those used in finite element methods. In addition, the number of particles increases in the regions where the fluid is present, in such a way that the computational effort is concentrated mainly in those regions and no time is wasted calculating the neighboring areas. The SPH model continues to evolve with new improvements in the approximations, stability and reliability of the model.

The code used in the present work, DualSPHysics [4], is an open source developed by a network of Universities. Thanks to the power of GPUs (graphics cards with parallel computing power), DualSPHysics can simulate real engineering problems using high resolution in a reasonable computing time. The code has already been used to model the interaction of waves with floating bodies [2, 12], to analyze the upward movement of floating solids of different densities, and it has been validated with analytical models, experimental measurements and other numerical methods [7].

In this work, DualSPHysics is used to simulate the 2D deformations generated on a water surface as a result of the impact of a solid disc. First, physical experiments carried out to quantify splash magnitudes in a quasi-2D cell are described in general terms. Subsequently, the theoretical bases of the SPH method are presented. Finally, numerical simulations of physical experiments are described and results are compared with the experimental values. Limitations of the presented application of the numerical method and proposals for its improvement are discussed.

2 The Studied System

The goal of this research is to reproduce the deformations observed experimentally on a liquid surface hit by a solid object of circular cross section, using the DualSPHysics code.

The authors obtained experimental results in a simplified 2D system in a previous work [3]. The experimental values of the splash were obtained using a vertical rectangular quasi-two-dimensional cell. The volume available within the cell had the following dimensions: height $H = 62$ cm, width $W = 40.5$ cm and thickness $E = 0.5$ cm. Distilled water was used as test liquid. To generate the deformations on the water surface, a Teflon disc of $D = 2.54$ cm in diameter and a thickness $e = 0.32$ cm was used. The solid disc was released in free fall from the top of the cell at a height Z above the water surface. The disc impact velocity on the liquid surface was controlled by varying the liquid level L within the quasi-2D cell. Figure 1 shows a diagram of the experimental cell with the mentioned variables to control the impact velocity. It is worth noting that the experiments described in Cáliz-Reyes et al. [3] were carried out within a cell of reduced thickness ($E << H, W$), which produces confinement effects in the studied system. This implies that experimental results are affected by the presence of adjacent walls during the displacement of the disc when falling. This conditions imposes restrictions on the behavior of the disc, when it descends in a limited free fall, and in the response of the liquid during the induced deformations on its surface. Using image analysis, the maximum depth of the air cavity (Hc) and the maximum height of the liquid jet (H_j) were quantified. Figure 2 shows two of the characteristic fluid structures formed in the liquid surface during the splash [3]. To measure their magnitudes, the liquid level was taken as a reference before being deformed. Table 1 shows the experimental values that were taken into account in the numerical simulations, such as the water level and the impact velocity of the solid disc. Moreover, the maximum cavity depth and the maximum jet height, are also shown, for two impact velocity values.

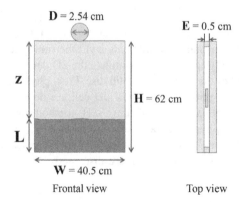

Fig. 1. Scheme of the physical model to generate the splash deformations on the liquid surface when impacting with a solid disc.

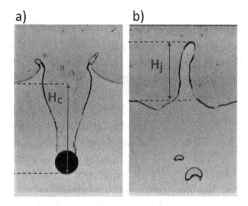

Fig. 2. Two of the fluid splash formations observed in the quasi-2D cell: (a) the air cavity; (b) the liquid jet. Both deformations are measured with respect to the free liquid surface level before the impact of the solid disc [3].

Table 1. Experimental values considered for the validation of the 2D simulation results. Values correspond to a quasi-2D splash generated using a solid disc of diameter $D = 2.54$ cm [3].

Water level L (cm)	Impact velocity V_i (cm/s)	Maximum cavity depth H_c (cm)	Maximum jet height H_j (cm)
35	200	10.77	5.48
50	128	7.83	1.61

3 Methodology

3.1 The DualSPHysics Model

The DualSPHysics code was designated for the numerical simulations of the experiments described in the previous section. The code has a pre-processing software that can use a wide range of input files for the creation of geometries. Advanced post-processing tools allow users to measure the physical magnitudes of any flow property at arbitrary locations within the domain.

The SPH method is based on integral interpolants so that the Navier-Stokes equations (governing equations of the model) are discretized using the kernel interpolation function. The governing functions are approximated as:

$$A(\vec{r}) = \int A(\vec{r}')W(\vec{r} - \vec{r}', h)d\vec{r}' \qquad (1)$$

where h is the smoothing length and $W(\vec{r} - \vec{r}', h)$ is the kernel (i.e. the weighting function). The integral interpolant can be expressed in discrete notation as:

$$A(\vec{r}) = \sum_b m_b \frac{A_b}{\rho_b} W_{ab} \qquad (2)$$

where the summation applies to all particles (b) within the region defined by the kernel function $(W_{ab} = W(\vec{r_a} - \vec{r_b}, h))$. The smoothing kernel function approximates a Dirac delta as the smoothing length tends to zero. It depends on the smoothing length and the non-dimensional distance between particles. m_b and ρ_b are mass and density respectively.

In DualSPHysics it is possible to choose between two types of kernel: Cubic Spline [16] and Quintic Wendland [25]. For the present work, the 5 degree smoothing kernel function was used.

For the solution of the momentum equation, DualSPHysics provides different options for the inclusion of the dissipation effect. In our experiments, the particle Reynolds number is of the order of 10^4, being a value greater than the Reynolds number established for a laminar flow. This indicates that turbulent flows can be generated. For this reason, the laminar viscosity + Sub-Particle Scale (SPS) Turbulence model was used for the simulations proposed here. The concept of SPS [11] describes the effect of turbulence in the Moving Particle Semi-Implicit (MPS) model. The conservation equation is defined as:

$$\frac{dv}{dt} = -\frac{1}{\rho}\nabla P + g + v_0\nabla^2 v + \frac{1}{\rho} \cdot \vec{\tau} \qquad (3)$$

where $\vec{\tau}$ represents the SPS stress tensor. It is modeled using Favre-averaging (for a compressible fluid):

$$\frac{\tau_{ij}}{\rho} = -2v_t S_{ij} - \frac{2}{3}k\delta_{ij} - \frac{2}{3}C_I \Delta^2 \delta_{ij} |S_{ij}|^2 \tag{4}$$

where τ_{ij} is the sub-particle stress tensor, v_t is the turbulence eddy viscosity, k the SPS turbulence kinetic energy, $C_I = 0.0066$, $|S| = (2S_{ij}S_{ij})^{1/2}$, S_{ij} the element of SPS strain tensor. The laminar viscous term is treated as:

$$\left(v_0 \nabla^2 v\right)_a = \sum_b m_b \frac{4v_0 r_{ab} \cdot \nabla_a W_{ab}}{(\rho_a + \rho_b)(r_{ab}^2 + \eta^2)} v_{ab} \tag{5}$$

where v_0 is the kinematic viscosity (typically 10^{-6} m²/s for water).

3.2 Numerical Simulations of the Physical Model

The numerical model seeks to represent the physical phenomenon that is observed on the surface of a liquid when it is impacted by a solid object of circular geometry. In order to simplify the system to a 2D model, a quasi-two-dimensional cell was used in the experimental system and a disc was used to generate the surface deformations in the water.

First, the computational domain was defined using two points in the space that allowed us to dimension the volume of the liquid to be studied in 3D. When the system is simplified to the 2D case, the numerical value assigned to one of the spatial coordinates, that is not taken into account, is repeated, generating a plane in space. For convenience, the XZ plane was chosen, where the X axis was located along the fluid interface, and the Z axis in the direction of the disc free fall.

In order to validate the numerical results, the conditions used in the experiments were implemented. For example, to define the volume of the liquid, the water level in the cell was considered along with the rest of the dimensions of the cell. A cylinder with a diameter of 2.54 cm and a thickness of 0.32 cm, was defined to represent the experimental disc, with the weight corresponding to the density of the material used (Teflon in this case). Once the disc geometry was generated, the property of the solid object was defined such that it could behave according to the rigid body dynamics. The magnitude and direction of the gravity force were indicated. The initial conditions of the liquid were defined such that the position and velocity of fluid particles represent an initial state of rest. The initial position of the disc and a zero initial velocity were also defined, so that once released, the disc would be subjected to the force of gravity and, on impact with the liquid surface, it would take a velocity of magnitude similar to the one obtained in the experiments.

As boundary conditions, a solid wall condition was established, both for the sidewalls and for the base of the computational domain. The shifting algorithm was included to take into account anisotropic particle spacing in regions close to the free surface or in violent flows. For the displacement of the solid disc, a dynamic boundary condition was used. According to this boundary condition, solid particles satisfy the same equations as fluid particles but do not move according to the forces exerted on them. Finally, for the fluid-solid interaction the fluid-driven object condition was

Table 2. Defined constants and parameters used in the numerical simulations.

Constants	
Particle assignment in the mesh	1 particle per node
Gravity	-9.81 m/s^2 in the Z direction
Density	1000 kg/m^3
Viscosity	0.000001 m^2/s
Smoothing length coefficient (coefh)	1.2
Resolution (dp)	0.002 m
Parameters	
Precision	double
Time step algorithm	Symplectic
Smoothing Kernel	Wendland
Viscosity model	Laminar + SPS
Minimum time step (DtMin)	0.00001 s
Simulation time (TimeMax)	3 s

applied. This condition allows to derive the object movement by its interaction with fluid particles: the forces acting on each particle of the rigid body are computed according to the sum of the contribution of all surrounding fluid particles.

Table 2 shows some constants and parameters used for the numerical simulations. Parameters of interest, maximum depth of the cavity H_c and maximum height of the jet H_j, were measured with the Paraview software.

3.3   Simulations in 2D

For the 2D simulations, a computational domain was defined delimiting an XZ plane of dimensions $W = 40$ cm wide and $H = 62$ cm high, the same measures used in the experiments for the quasi-2D cell. The solid disc was defined in 2D as a solid circle of radius $R = 1.27$ cm.

In the simulations the velocity at which the solid object impacts on the liquid surface was generated in a similar way as in the experiments: the disc was released from a certain height and fell by gravitational effects. Unlike in the experiments, the speed of the disc is affected by confinement and friction effects due to its proximity to the walls of the quasi-2D cell.

A convergence analysis was carried out for the resolution of the simulations in order to determine the adequate minimum distance between fluid particles (dp). By increasing the resolution, better numerical results should be obtained, but this in turn implies increasing the number of particles and consequently the computation time. The simulation resolution, dp, and the smoothing length are the variables that characterize the smoothing kernel, on which the performance of the SPH model strongly depends. Few studies have shown inconsistencies in the mathematical formalism of the kernel functions used in models like DualSPHysics, mainly due to errors inherent to the discretization of the equations or to truncation problems [20, 22]. Those effects are particularly evident when an interface between two phases is assumed. Moreover,

Korzani et al. [13] demonstrated that the ratio of the cylinder diameter to the initial distance between particles affects the simulations results. Taking all these considerations into account, we observed how certain fluid particles belonging to the free surface easily detached showing high velocities. This can be considered as a reflection of the instabilities that generate in the free surface, which can reduce the accuracy in the numerical results.

The experimental case used as reference is the one that corresponds to the impact velocity of the disc on the water surface $V_i = 200$ cm/s, which generated a maximum jet height of $H_j = 5.48$ cm, and a maximum cavity depth of $H_c = 10.77$ cm (see Table 1).

The experimental impact velocity is the average value obtained from several experiments conducted under the same conditions [3]. In addition, the numerical value of the impact velocity is not an initial condition imposed in the simulation, it depends on the value of the height at which the disc was released. The numerical values of the impact velocity obtained in the simulations are within the range of variation of the corresponding experimental values.

Convergence in the numerical results depends on different factors, such as: resolution in simulation (related to the particle size), boundary conditions according to the phenomenon of interest, the main forces that describe the system behavior. For the latter case, the model proposed to deform the liquid surface shows some limitations. For example, the particles detected close to the free surface are only restricted in their diffusive movement towards low concentration regions, due to the high particle concentration gradient present at the interface.

Table 3 shows the results obtained in the 2D simulations by varying the resolution for a fixed impact velocity of the disc, $V_i = 200$ cm/s. From the table, the numerical result for the maximum cavity depth shows a relative error percentage lower than 10% for all resolutions applied. But for a high simulation resolution ($dp = 0.0008$ m), the height of the jet reaches a value of $H_j = 9.9$ cm, which is sufficiently far from the value obtained experimentally. At lower resolution (e.g. $dp = 0.002$ m), the jet height reaches the value of $H_j = 6.1$ cm, which corresponds to a relative error percentage of 11%.

As particle size decreases, the gravitational force less affects the jet height, and a lower numerical convergence is obtained. Besides, due to the lack of a suitable model for the surface tension force, the growth of the liquid jet is overestimated. To overcome this situation, the gravitational forces were increased to compensate this effect. Table 3

Table 3. Numerical results for the maximum cavity depth and jet height obtained by varying the resolution in simulation and using an impact velocity of $V_i = 200$ cm/s, some results consider increased gravitational forces ($igf = 2$ g).

Simulation resolution, dp (m)	Number of particles, N_p	Maximum cavity depth, H_c (cm)	Maximum jet height, H_j (cm)	Maximum cavity depth igf, H_{cg} (cm)	Maximum jet height igf, H_{jg} (cm)
0.0008	220,933	11.1	9.9	9.3	7.1
0.001	141,828	11.4	7.5	10	6.3
0.002	35,763	10.5	6.1	9.9	5.5
0.003	16,047	9.8	5.6	8.7	4.3

also shows numerical results for the case in which the gravitational forces are increased. Better results are obtained including a factor of 2 in the acceleration due to gravity (2 g) and a higher resolution. For example, with a resolution $dp = 0.001$ m, the maximum jet height reaches a value of $H_{jg} = 5.5$ cm, and the maximum cavity depth reaches a value of $H_{cg} = 9.9$ cm. Both numerical results show a percentage of relative error lower than 10% with respect to the experimental results.

4   Results

2D Numerical Simulations of Liquid Surface Deformations Using Solid Walls as Boundary Conditions

The characteristic surface deformations of the splash that could be generated when a solid object hits a liquid are shown in Fig. 3. Numerical results show qualitatively the stages observed in the quasi-2D experiments. Three of the typical splash fluid structures are formed: a crown splash, an air cavity and a liquid jet. Both in the experiment and in the numerical simulation, the deformation in the surface of the liquid was induced upon impacting a solid disc with a velocity of approximately 250 cm/s.

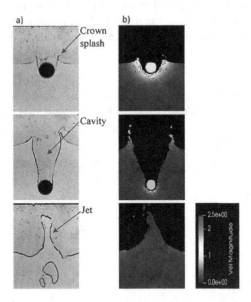

Fig. 3. Stages of the splash obtained from: (a) experiments in a quasi-2D cell; (b) 2D numerical simulations using DualSPHysics. The images correspond to the formation of the crown splash and the cavity during the entrance of the disc, and the ejection of the liquid jet. The color scale for the velocities in the numerical simulations is shown in m/s.

Table 4 shows a comparison between experimental and numerical values of the nondimensional maximum cavity depths and maximum jet heights.

Three cases are considered for comparison: Case 1 corresponds to an impact velocity V_i = 128 cm/s with a simulation resolution of dp = 0.002 m; Case 2 corresponds to an impact velocity V_i = 200 cm/s with a simulation resolution of dp = 0.002 m; Case 3 corresponds to an impact velocity V_i = 200 cm/s with a simulation resolution of dp = 0.001 m and increased gravitational forces. Furthermore, the respective Froude numbers, which relates the inertial forces to the gravitational forces, is also shown. The Froude number is generally expressed as:

$$Fr = \frac{V}{\sqrt{gl}} \tag{6}$$

In this system, its characteristic velocity (V) was assumed as the impact velocity of the solid object (V_i), and as the characteristic length (l) the disc diameter (D) was considered.

From Table 4, it can be seen that for a fixed value of the disc size, a decrease in the value of the Froude number corresponds to a lower impact velocity, while the maximum cavity depth and the jet height show a tendency to decrease.

Comparing experimental and numerical results for a fixed value of the impact velocity, a small difference in the maximum cavity depth, showing an error lower than 10% is observed. Therefore, the model reliably reproduces the formation of the cavity that provokes a deformation towards the interior of the liquid during the impact of the solid disc, transferring part of its kinetic energy to the fluid while the disc descends forming the cavity.

Table 4. Comparison between experimental and numerical nondimensional results for the maximum cavity depth and the maximum jet height, for two impact velocities, with $D = 2.54$ cm.

	Experimental results	Numerical results	Experimental results	Numerical results	Numerical results
	V_i = 128 cm/s	Case 1	V_i = 200 cm/s	Case 2	Case 3
Nondimensional maximum cavity depth (H_c/D)	3.08	3.37	4.24	4.15	3.90
Nondimensional maximum jet height (H_j/D)	0.63	1.01	2.20	2.40	2.17
Froude number (Fr)	2.56	2.56	4.0	4.0	2.83

However, when comparing the results for the jet heights, the relative errors between numerical and experimental results increase. For example, in Case 1, for a lower impact velocity and a low resolution, the absolute differences are of the order of 1 cm. But jet height in Case 1 is of the order of a few centimeters, giving as result a relative error greater than 50%. In Case 2, the impact velocity is twice than the one applied in Case 1. Lower differences between experimental and numerical results for the jet height are obtained at low resolution with a relative error of 10%. As the resolution increases (see Table 3), the maximum jet height differs more from the experimental result. Inertial forces are more dominant over gravitational and surface tension forces. Finally, in Case 3 the same impact velocity of the Case 2 is considered, and a greater gravitational force is imposed. This was done to compensate the lack of an explicit surface tension model and the low effect of gravitational forces when particle size is reduced as resolution increases. Better numerical results are obtained at a higher resolution than in Case 2, with a relative error of less than 5%. Even though the absolute differences between experimental and numerical results are of the order of 1 cm, the relative error is 15% for the highest resolution considered here.

Moreover, when the induced deformation causes an increase in the surface area in the opposite direction to gravity, surface instabilities occur and cause the fluid particles to detach at high velocity overcoming the surface tension forces. This low effect of surface tension forces could be one of the reasons why the jet grows to a greater extent than in the experiments. A similar phenomenon has already been observed when a sphere hits the surface of a granular medium generating a very high jet due to the absence of surface tension forces [21].

5 Conclusions

The SPH numerical model DualSPHysics was used to reproduce the deformations induced in a liquid surface by the impact of a solid object in two dimensions. The maximum cavity depth and the maximum jet height for fixed values of the impact velocity of the disc were calculated. Numerical results showed a good approximation to the experimental results, especially for the cavity depths. This allowed the validation of the DualSPHysics code for low impact speeds.

2D simulations were carried out applying solid walls as boundary conditions. Simulations qualitatively reproduced the deformations observed in the liquid free surface hit by a solid disc. In the range of values of Froude numbers considered here, between 2 and 5, inertial forces dominate over gravitational forces. This causes a great transfer of energy from the disc to the liquid at the impact moment, producing displacement of liquid and the opening of a cavity in the free surface. Due to the absence of a suitable model for surface tension in a single fluid phase system, and to the confinement conditions for 2D simulations, the numerically calculated jet height showed greater differences with respect to the experimental results at low impact velocities and high resolutions. In the experiments, the presence of nearby side walls contributes to fluid returning and to energy absorption that could affect the height of the emerging jet.

Numerical results should be improved incorporating a model that considers the effects of surface tension so to obtain a better representation of the interfacial deformations in a two-phase liquid-gas system.

Acknowledgments. Cáliz-Reye thanks CONACyT, UMSNH, and Santander scholarship by funding his research stay. Ibarra-Bracamontes would like to thank Andrew Belmonte for the collaborative work on the experimental results.

References

1. Alam, A., Kai, H., Susuki, K.: Two-dimensional numerical simulation of water splash phenomena with and without surface tension. J. Mar. Sci. Tech. **12**, 59–71 (2007)
2. Bouscasse, B., Colagrossi, A., Marrone, S., Antuono, M.: Nonlinear water wave interaction with floating bodies in SPH. J. Fluids Struct. **42**, 112–129 (2013)
3. Cáliz-Reyes, C.: Analisis de la deformacíon en 2D de la superficie del agua al variar su tension superficial durante la caída de un disco sólido (Unpublished master's thesis). Universidad Michoacana de San Nicolás de Hidalgo, Morelia, Mich. México (2019)
4. Crespo, A.J.S., et al.: DualSPHysics: open-source parallel CFD solver on Smoothed Particle Hydrodynamics (SPH). Comput. Phys. Commun. **187**, 204–216 (2015). https://doi.org/10.1016/j.cpc.2014.10.004
5. Cuomo, G., Panizzo, A., Dalrymple, R.A.: SPHH-LES two phase simulation of wave breaking and wave-structure interaction. In: Proceedings: 30th International Conference on Coastal Engineering, pp. 274–286 (2006)
6. Dou, P., Wang, Z., Ling, H.: Research method of the splash character of prismatic planing craft. J. Har. Eng. Univ. **39**(3), 422–427 (2018)
7. Fekken, G.: Numerical simulation of free surface flow with moving rigid bodies. Ph.D. thesis, University of Manchester, United Kingdom (2004)
8. Gingold, R.A., Monaghan, J.J.: Smoothed Particle Hydrodynamics: theory and application to non-spherical stars. Mon. Not. R. Astr. Soc. **181**, 375–389 (1977)
9. Glasheen, J., Macmahon, T.: Vertical water entry of disks at low Froude numbers. Phys. Fluids **8**(8), 2078–2083 (1996)
10. Gorla, C., Concli, F., Stahl, K., et al.: Simulations of Splash Losses of a Gearbox. Adv. Tribol. (2012) https://doi.org/10.1155/2012/616923
11. Gotoh, H., Shao, S., Memita, T.: SPH-LES model for numerical investigation of wave interaction with partially immersed breakwater. Coast. Eng. J. **46**(1), 39–63 (2001)
12. Hadžić, I., Henning, J., Peric, M., Xing-Kaeding, Y.: Computation of fluid-induced motion of floating bodies. Appl. Math. Model. **29**, 1196–1210 (2005)
13. Korzani, M.G., Galindo-Torres, S.A., Scheuermann, A., Williams, D.J.: Parametric study on smoothed particle hydrodynamics for accurate determination of drag coefficient for a circular cylinder. Water Sci. Eng. **10**(2), 143–153 (2017)
14. Li, M., Li, Q., Kuang, S., Zou, Z.S.: Computational investigation of the splashing phenomenon induced by the impingement of multiple supersonic jets onto a molten slag-metal bath. Ind. Eng. Chem. Res. **55**(12), 3630–3640 (2016)
15. Lucy, L.: A numerical approach to testing the fission hypothesis. J. Astron. **82**, 1013–1924 (1977)
16. Monaghan, J.J., Lattanzio, J.C.: A refined method for astrophysical problems. Astron. Astrophys. Edp Sci. **149**(1), 135–143 (1987)
17. Monaghan, J.J., Cas, R.F., Kos, A., Hallworth, M.: Gravity currents descending a ramp in a stratified tank. J. Fluid Mech. **379**, 39–70 (1999)
18. Monaghan, J.J., Kocharyan, A.: SPH simulation of multi-phase flow. Comput. Phys. Commun. **87**, 225–235 (1995)
19. Monaghan, J.J., Kos, A.: Solitary waves on a cretan beach. J. Waterw. Port Coast. Ocean Eng. **125**, 145–154 (1999)
20. Sigalotti, L., et al.: A new insight into the consistency of Smoothed Particle Hydrodynamics. Appl. Math. Comput. **356**, 50–73 (2019)
21. Thoroddsen, S.T., Shen, A.: Granular jets. Phys. Fluids **13**, 4–6 (2001)

22. Vaughan, G.L., Healy, T.R., Bryan, K.R., Sneyd, A.D., Gorman, R.M.: Completeness, conservation and error in SPH for fluids. Int. J. Numer. Meth. Fluid. **56**, 37–62 (2008)
23. Vincent, L., Xiao, T., Yohann, D., Jung, S., Kanso, E.: Dynamics of water entry. J. Fluid Mech. **846**, 508–535 (2018)
24. Wang, J., Lugni, C., Faltinsen, O.M.: Experimental and numerical investigation of a freefall wedge vertically entering the water surface. Appl. Ocean Res. **51**, 181–203 (2015)
25. Wendland, H.: Piecewise polynomial, positive definite and compactly supported radial functions of minimal degree. Advances in Computational Mathematics, vol. 4, pp. 389–396. Baltzer Science Publishers, Baarn/Kluwer Academic Publishers (1995). https://doi.org/10. 1007/BF02123482
26. Zou, S., Dalrymple, R.A.: Sediment suspension simulation under flow with SPH-SPS method. In: Proceedings: 30th International Conference on Coastal Engineering (2006)

SiO$_2$ Electronic Structure in Gas Giants' Planetary Cores: A Density Functional Theory Approach

J. M. Ramírez-Velásquez[✉] and Joshua M. Salazar

School of Physical Sciences and Nanotechnology, Yachay Tech University,
100119 Urcuqui, Ecuador
{jmramirez,joshua.salazar}@yachaytech.edu.ec

Abstract. Modern physical models and computational tools allow us to probe into the deepest and extremest conditions of high-pressure and high-temperature systems such as planetary cores. Gas giants planets, despite of being mainly composed of light elements as Hydrogen, Helium and Ammonia ices, inside the thick gas layers under their atmospheres all of them they should be composed of heavy elements laying in the center of the planet. Those heavy elements, by the suggestion of the density calculations based on the observed volume and measured mass by gravitational effects, must be mainly metallic oxides, iron compounds, silicate allotropes, and other similar heavy elements forming a rocky core, with an structure resembling the mantles of the rocky planets in our System. With the aid of the Quinde I Supercomputer, a *Density Functional Theory* simulation is performed under SiO$_2$ quartz structures found on Earth to approach the Seifertite crystal phase of the same composition, by applying extreme pressure conditions. The obtained electronic configuration of the obtained structure lies inside the range of expected values for the band gap energies at different pressures.

Keywords: Super computing · HPC · Quantum Mechanics · Quinde I

1 Introduction

Probing into planetary cores, even in our planet Earth, is an extremely hard task. The deepest hole ever dug on Earth is the *Kola Superdeep Borehole*, led by a Soviet Union research team; its true vertical depth is roughly 12, 289 m and took almost 20 years to complete [1]. Thus, due to the complexity of this kind of observational operation, we must rely on indirect methods to probe into the planet's internal structure by analyzing several factors, such as gravitational effects, oblateness, and seismic data. These methods, however, are still inaccurate for determining the structures of the materials inside because the high temperatures and pressures exerted on the planet's inner shells might alter the expected compositions in exotic ways. For example, it is expected that we would find *metallic hydrogen* phases inside some gas giants, such as Jupiter [10].

Computational simulations and high-pressure experiments are fundamental for understanding those exotic compositions, but our experiments are limited to the pressures generated in Diamond Anvil Cells [11] and we cannot simultaneously study

© Springer Nature Switzerland AG 2019
M. Torres and J. Klapp (Eds.): ISUM 2019, CCIS 1151, pp. 76–85, 2019.
https://doi.org/10.1007/978-3-030-38043-4_7

high pressures and high temperatures; for example, in Jupiter's mantle we have pressures surpassing 10 Mbar and temperatures over $10k$ kelvin. Therefore, simulations become a relatively easy and cheap way to study materials as opposed to conducting high-pressure experiments. Density Functional Theory (dft), based on Quantum Mechanics, allows us to analyze the internal behavior of crystalline solid structures and predict many of the properties of the desired compounds [8].

1.1 Neptune: A Blue and Icy Giant

Neptune is the farthest planet on our solar system and is mainly composed of gases and a rocky core, stratified by densities in three main layers (Fig. 1): a cloudy atmospheric surface, mainly composed of hydrogen and helium [21]; an "icy" (not cold, but semi-solid) mantle made up of methane, carbon and hydrogen, with precipitation of diamonds produced by the extreme pressures (up to 300 Mbar) [19]; and finally, a rocky sphere made of iron, nickel, and silicates similar to Earth (see for example [18], Table 1).

Table 1. Neptune layers composition

Outer atmosphere		Icy mantle		Rocky core	
H_2O	81.5%	H_2O	56.5%	SiO_2	38.0%
CH_4	15.5%	CH_4	32.5%	MgO	25.0%
Other	<4.0%	NH_3	11.0%	FeS	25.0%
–		Other	10.0%	FeO	12.0%
–		–		Other	13.0%

From protoplanetary formation theories [5], we know that the composition of the rocky core of Neptune should be similar to that of Earth because it may have been formed in an accretion disk of the early solar nebula that gave birth to the now-visible planets in our system. Hence, $CaIrO_3$ (typically, the structure is baptized with the name of the first compound that showed that geometry [20]) structures of $MgSiO_3$ and SiO_2 allotropes are expected to be found in Jupiter, Uranus, and Neptune [22].

Then, by applying extreme pressures to SiO_2 structures, we may approach the present materials of Neptune's rocky core.

Because of the high silicate composition of the core, we expect to find SiO_2 in the Seifertite phase [17]. Seifertite has been found at pressures above 35 GPa [6], and the samples available on Earth come from Martian meteorite samples, which provides strong evidence of the existence of common silicates among the rest of the planets of our solar system [4].

Neptune

Fig. 1. Neptune layers and compositions. We have remade the picture taken from [10].

2 Theoretical Methods

Our computations are based on the dft. All the physical properties of solids, such as thermal conductivity, heat capacity, and band structure, are given by their electronic structures [12]:

$$\hat{H}\Psi = \left(\hat{T} + \hat{V}_{e-e} + \hat{V}_{ext}\right)\Psi = E\Psi. \tag{1}$$

This is the Schrödinger equation for a multi-electronic system, where $\hat{H}$ is its Hamiltonian, $\hat{T}$ is the kinetic term, $\hat{V}_{e-e}$ is the inter-electronic term, and $\hat{V}_{ext}$ is the external potential. It is well known that the resulting nonlinear differential equation requires the use of approximate and numerical methods to find physical solutions (for instance see [7]).

The full Hamiltonian used for describing the motion of the electrons in an atomic lattice is given by:

$$\hat{H} = -\frac{\hbar^2}{2m_e}\sum_{i=1}^{N}\nabla_i^2 + \sum_{i=1}^{N}V_{e-n}(\boldsymbol{r}) + \sum_{i=1}^{N}\sum_{j<i}^{N}U_{e-e}\left(\boldsymbol{r}_i, \boldsymbol{r}_j\right). \tag{2}$$

where the terms are: kinetic energies, electron-nuclei interactions, and electron-electron interactions.

Using many-body theory [15], we can turn the problem into a single-body problem. Imagine an electron gas, uniformly distributed over space; then, let us introduce a proton from outside the system and let it move in a straight line until it goes out again (Fig. 2).

As it passes through, it attracts, radially, the nearby electrons, screening the positive charge. This event creates a locally 'more negative' region that acts as a new particle

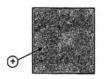

Fig. 2. Uniform electron gas with a positive charge passing by (figure from Mattuck, A Guide to Feynman Diagrams in the Many-Body Problem)

inside the gas: a *quasiparticle*. So, instead of considering each electron in the problem, we set everything in terms of a charge density function and then we may analyze how the electron gas is disturbed by the possible interactions:

$$\rho(r) = \langle \psi(r)|\psi(r)\rangle. \tag{3}$$

From the Eq. (2) and after applying Coulombic potentials, we get:

$$\hat{H} = -\frac{\hbar^2}{2m_e}\sum_{i=1}^{N}\nabla_i^2 + \frac{1}{2}\sum_{i\neq j}^{N}\frac{e^2}{|r_i - r_j|} - \sum_{j=1}^{N}\sum_{\alpha=1}^{N}\frac{Z_\alpha e^2}{|r_j - R_\alpha|}. \tag{4}$$

In this Hamiltonian, we neglect the ion-ion interactions and use the following notation: the $R\alpha$ vectors represent the position of the nuclei, r_i the position of the electrons, and the factor of $\frac{1}{2}$ is to avoid double-counting electrons. Now, assuming that the expected value of the *total energy* obtained from the Hamiltonian is only dependent on the electron density, we may write:

$$\begin{aligned}
E_{\text{Total}[\rho]} &= \langle \psi|T + V_{e-e} + V_{\text{ext}}|\psi\rangle \\
&= F[\rho] + \langle \psi|V_{\text{ext}}|\psi\rangle \\
&= F[\rho] + \int \rho V_{\text{ext}}d^3r,
\end{aligned} \tag{5}$$

where we define a universal functional $F[\rho]$ that contains all the electron interaction and energies: kinetic, Coulombic, and *exchange – correlation* energies (containing all the *quasiparticle* behavior), and can be written as:

$$\begin{aligned}
F[\rho] &= T[\rho] + V_{e-e}[\rho] \\
&= T[\rho] + V_C[\rho] + E_{\text{xc}}[\rho] \\
&= -\frac{\hbar^2}{2m_e}\langle \psi|\nabla^2|\psi\rangle + \frac{1}{2}\int\int\frac{\rho(r)\rho(r')}{|r-r'|} + E_{\text{xc}}[\rho].
\end{aligned} \tag{6}$$

The *quasiparticle* formalism requires that the "interaction cloud" be considered in the total energy calculation; therefore, the exchange-correlation term contains all the interactions within the *quasiparticle*.

This shows that the nature of the new energies depends on the applied universal functional. The *Hohenberg – Kohn* theorem [9] ensures the existence of a universal functional, but does not tell us anything about how to construct it. Also, it states that the external potential (lattice of the solid) is unique for a given ground-state electron density.

The full Hamiltonian of the interaction (Eqs. 2 and 4) strictly depends on the charge density alone; thus, Eq. (1) now becomes:

$$
\sum_{i=1}^{N} \left[-\frac{\hbar^2}{2m_e} \nabla_i^2 + \frac{e^2 \rho(r_i)}{|r_i - r_j|} \bigg|_{j \neq i} \\
- \sum_{\alpha=1}^{N} \frac{Z_\alpha \rho(r_i)}{|r_i - R_\alpha|} + V_{xc}(r_i) \right] = \epsilon_i \psi(r_i).
\tag{7}
$$

Now, the most important property of an electronic ground state density is its energy, which may be calculated by variational calculus [14]:

$$
E_{gs} = \min_{\psi} \langle \psi | \hat{H} | \psi \rangle.
\tag{8}
$$

Also, we can minimize the universal functional in Eq. (6) such that the obtained wave function is consistent with a charge density ρ, as follows:

$$
\begin{aligned}
F[\rho] &= \min_{\psi \to \rho} \langle \psi | T + V_{e-e} | \psi \rangle \\
&= \langle \psi_{min}^{\rho} | T + V_{e-e} | \psi_{min}^{\rho} \rangle.
\end{aligned}
\tag{9}
$$

Since the ground state of the system will be the configuration with minimal energy, considering the Eq. (5), we have the following relation:

$$
\begin{aligned}
E_{\text{Total}}[\rho] &\geq E_{gs}[\rho] \\
\langle \psi | V_{ext} | \psi \rangle + F[\rho] &\geq E_{gs}.
\end{aligned}
\tag{10}
$$

In general, the expectation value of V_{ext} will not change by choosing either basis ψ or ψ_{gs}. Therefore:

$$
\langle \psi_{min}^{\rho} | T + V_{e-e} | \psi_{min}^{\rho} \rangle \geq \langle \psi_{gs} | T + V_{e-e} | \psi_{-gs} \rangle,
\tag{11}
$$

but after the minimization, the obtained energy of the system will correspond to the ground state. Then, the latter expression is only true for:

$$
\langle \psi_{min}^{\rho} | T + V_{e-e} | \psi_{min}^{\rho} \rangle = \langle \psi_{gs} | T + V_{e-e} | \psi_{-gs} \rangle.
\tag{12}
$$

Therefore, this ensures us that, after iterations, we converge to the ground-state energy:

$$E_{gs} = \int \rho_{gs}(r)V_{ext}(r)d^3r + \langle \psi_{gs}|T + V_{e-e}|\psi\_gs \rangle$$
$$= \langle \psi_{gs}|V_{ext}|\psi\_gs \rangle + F[\rho_{gs}].$$

(13)

To obtain the correct energies, we have to use calculus of variations to minimize the charge density. We will denote a small Functional Variation with δ. Therefore, we will look for extreme values of the charge density:

$$\int \delta\rho(r)d^3r = 0.$$

(14)

Hence, considering the total energy expression in Eq. 5, we want to minimize it to approach the ground-state energies:

$$E_{Total} = V_{n-e}[\rho] + V_{e-e}[\rho]$$
$$+ T[\rho] + E_{xc}[\rho] \geq E_{gs}[\rho]$$
$$= \int \rho_{gs}(r)V_{n-e}(r)d^3r$$
$$+ \iint \frac{\rho(r)\rho(r')}{|r-r'|}d^3rd^3r'$$
$$+ T[\rho] + E_{xc}[\rho].$$

(15)

Applying variations to the energy functional:

$$\delta E_{Total} = \int \delta\rho \left[V_{n-e} + \int \frac{\rho(r')}{|r-r'|}d^3r' \right.$$
$$\left. + \frac{T[\rho]}{\delta\rho}\bigg|_{\rho=\rho_{gs}} + \frac{E_{xc}[\rho]}{\delta\rho}\bigg|_{\rho=\rho_{gs}} \right] d^3r = 0.$$

(16)

In order to wrap up some terms, we can define an external potential and an extra effective potential associated with the exchange-correlation energy:

$$V_{xc}(r) = \frac{E_{xc}[\rho]}{\delta\rho}\bigg|_{\rho=\rho_{gs}}$$

(17)

$$V_{eff}(r) = V_{n-e} + \frac{E_{xc}[\rho]}{\delta\rho}\bigg|_{\rho=\rho_{gs}} + \int \frac{\rho_{gs}(r')}{|r-r'|}d^3r' + V_{xc}(r).$$

(18)

Thus, Eq. (16) becomes:

$$\delta E_{\text{Total}} = \int \delta\rho \left[\frac{T[\rho]}{\delta\rho} \bigg|_{\rho=\rho_{gs}} + V_{\text{eff}}(\mathbf{r}) - \varepsilon \right] d^3\mathbf{r} = 0, \qquad (19)$$

where ε represents a Lagrange multiplier that contains the constraint of particle conservation for the minimization process [2]. Finally, the whole problem can be reduced to solve the following one-particle equation that contains all the manybody interactions wrapped up into an effective potential, as previously defined. This is the *Kohn – Sham equation*:

$$\left(-\frac{\hbar^2}{2m} \nabla^2 + V_{\text{eff}} - E_j \right) \phi_j(\mathbf{r}) = 0, \qquad (20)$$

$$\rho_{gs}(r) = \sum_{j=1}^{N} |\phi_j(\mathbf{r})|^2. \qquad (21)$$

This set of equations is self-consistent [13] and can be iterated over and over again starting from a homogeneous electron gas or an inhomogeneous one [9], depending on the *ansatz* applied over the system. After the first set of solutions and eigenenergies are obtained, a new electron density is calculated from the previously calculated wave functions until energy convergence is achieved.

To accelerate the calculations, the wave functions are expanded under a Fourier series, depending on the boundary conditions of the problem (a periodic lattice would allow us to consider Bloch waves [3]) and are cut off up to an arbitrary energy value so that convergence is unaffected [20].) Also, extra symmetry points are obtained within the first Brillouin Zone to reduce the wave function calculation complexity [16].

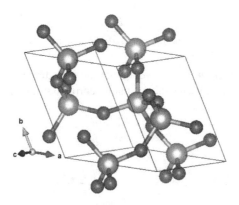

Fig. 3. Typical SiO_2 quartz structure at STP conditions. Has as lattice parameters: (a, b, c) = (5.022, 5.022, 5.511) Å, a P 3121 space group in Hermann Mauguin convention, showing a trigonal cell with (α, β, γ) = (90, 90, 120)°, and density of 2.49 [g/cm^3]

3 Discussion and Results

From the typically-found-on-Earth silica SiO_2 structures (Fig. 3), a dft simulation for calculating the optimal spatial distribution of the electronic density and the involved ions can be calculated by applying the adequate conditions to the main stress tensor of the unit cell of the crystal. So, using an energy cutoff of 500 eV for the plane wave expansion, an appropriately generated k – point sampling mesh with the Monkhorost-Pack method [16], and the LDA approximation for the electron density energy functional on VASP 5.3 software, the following energy gap dependence with pressure was found (Fig. 4):

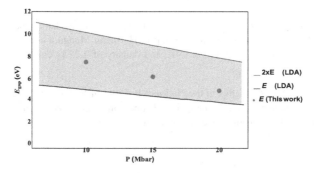

Fig. 4. Typical SiO_2 quartz structure at STP conditions. Has as lattice parameters: (a, b, c) = (4.114, 4.527, 5.081) Å, a Pbcn space group in Hermann Mauguin convention, showing a orthorombic cell with (α, β, γ) = (90, 90, 90)°, and density of 4.22 [g/cm³]

The shaded area represents the energy range of possible gaps in the Seifertite crystal structure. The LDA approximation usually underestimates the band gap for high pressures, so the energies obtained by U06 are doubled to get an upper bound for this energy [22]. The calculated points are inside the proposed range and there is also an energy decrease that depends on the increase in pressure. The optimal spatial configuration of the system results in a Seifertite structure with a higher density as a result of the high pressure (Fig. 5).

dft calculations allows us to get a great insight and a powerful theoretical tool for analyzing physical systems that would otherwise be impossible to study using current technologies.

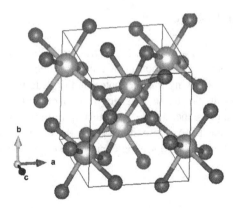

Fig. 5. Typical SiO$_2$ quartz structure at STP conditions. Has as lattice parameters: (a, b, c) = (4.114, 4.527, 5.081) Å, a Pbcn space group in Hermann Mauguin convention, showing a orthorombic cell with (α, β, γ) = (90, 90, 90)°, and density of 4.22 [g/cm^3]

Acknowledgement. Special thanks to the National Institute of Supercomputing of Ecuador for allow us to perform the simulations in the Quinde I supercomputer, located at Innópolis, Urcuquí, Ecuador. We would like to thank Professor H. Pinto for his valuable review and commentaries over the initial manuscript.

References

1. Ault, A.: Ask smithsonian: whats the deepest hole ever dug (2015)
2. Bartolotti, L.J.: Time-dependent Kohn-Sham density-functional theory. Phys. Rev. A **26**(4), 2243 (1982)
3. Bloch, F.: Z. Phys. **52**, 555 (1928). https://link.springer.com/article/10.1007/BF01339455
4. Bouvier, A., Blichert-Toft, J., Albarede, F.: Martian meteorite chronology and the evolution of the interior of Mars. Earth Planet. Sci. Lett. **280**(1–4), 285–295 (2009)
5. Bryden, G., Lin, D., Ida, S.: Protoplanetary formation. I. neptune. Astrophys. J. **544**(1), 481 (2000)
6. El Goresy, A., et al.: Seifertite, a dense orthorhombic polymorph of silica from the Martian meteorites Shergotty and Zagami. Eur. J. Mineral. **20**(4), 523–528 (2008)
7. Griffiths, D., Schroeter, D.: Introduction to Quantum Mechanics. (2018). ISBN 9781107189638
8. Hafner, J., Wolverton, C., Ceder, G.: Toward computational materials design: the impact of density functional theory on materials research. MRS Bull. **31**(9), 659–668 (2006)
9. Hohenberg, P., Kohn, W.: Inhomogeneous electron gas. Phys. Rev. **136**(3B), B864 (1964)
10. Hubbard, W.B., MacFarlane, J.J.: Structure and evolution of Uranus and Neptune. J. Geophys. Res. Solid Earth **85**(B1), 225–234 (1980)
11. Jayaraman, A.: Diamond anvil cell and high-pressure physical investigations. Rev. Mod. Phys. **55**(1), 65 (1983)
12. Kittel, C., McEuen, P.: Introduction to Solid State Physics (2018). ISBN 9781119454168
13. Kohn, W., Sham, L.J.: Self-consistent equations including exchange and correlation effects. Phys. Rev. **140**(4A), A1133 (1965)

14. Levy, M., Nagy, Á.: Variational density-functional theory for an individual excited state. Phys. Rev. Lett. **83**(21), 4361 (1999)
15. Mattuck, R.: A Guide to Feynman Diagrams in the Many-Body Problem, 2nd edn (2012). ISBN 9780486131641
16. Monkhorst, H.J., Pack, J.D.: Special points for brillouin-zone integrations. Phys. Rev. B **13** (12), 5188 (1976)
17. Oganov, A.R., Lyakhov, A.O.: Towards the theory of hardness of materials. J. Superhard Mater. **32**(3), 147 (2010)
18. Podolak, M., Weizman, A., Marley, M.: Planet. Space Sci. **43**, 1517 (1995)
19. Ross, M.: The ice layer in Uranus and Neptune—diamonds in the sky? Nature **292**(5822), 435 (1981)
20. Sholl, D., Steckel, J.: Density Functional Theory: A Practical Introduction (2011). ISBN 9781118211045
21. Tyler, G., et al.: Voyager radio science observations of Neptune and Triton. Science **246** (4936), 1466–1473 (1989)
22. Umemoto, K., Wentzcovitch, R.M., Allen, P.B.: Dissociation of MgSio$_3$ in the cores of gas giants and terrestrial exoplanets. Science **311**(5763), 983–986 (2006)

Three Body Problem Applied to the Helium Atom System: The Independent Electron Approximation (IEA)

J. M. Ramírez-Velásquez[(✉)] and Jennifer A. Sanchez

School of Physical Sciences and Nanotechnology, Yachay Tech University, 100119 Urcuqui, Ecuador
{jmramirez,jennifer.sanchez}@yachaytech.edu.ec

Abstract. In this study the most simple approximation to the numerical solution for a Helium atom system is computed, dividing the problem in two independent Hydrogen systems and neglecting the inter-electronic term. The radial and spherical harmonic functions yield certain tendencies, relating the evolution of the quantum numbers and the shape of the probability density functions (PDF), that correspond to each combinations of n, l and m. The radial and angular PDF components return the already known result: there exist more probability to find the electron in its more stable level of energy, close to the nucleus. Also, it was computed the numerical/analytic solution for a Hamiltonian in which the inter-electronic term was replaced with a constant C in order to find a condition relating the energies and the inter-electronic distance.

Keywords: Super computing · HPC · Quantum Mechanics · Quinde I

1 Introduction

In 17th century Newton achieved the goal of describing the dynamics of the solar system, a discovery that would change the paradigm of how the humanity sees the universe and the role we all play in it forever. This breaking innovation was possible through the gravitational potential, that describes the interactions of two bodies, and how their presences affects the dynamics and trajectory of the other.

Since the two body problem was successfully described by the gravitational potential, this model was extrapolated to the quantum world in order to describe the dynamics of the atomic components. At atomic scale the potential that guides the atomic interactions is the Coulomb potential, in which the electrons and nucleus play the role of the bodies that interact [1]. The two body problem is represented by the simplest and more abundant element in the Universe: the Hydrogen atom. The hydrogen atom was mathematically fully described by the Coulomb potential, being one of the very few realistic systems that can be solved at all, in exact closed form [2].

In the three-body problem, three bodies move in space under their mutual gravitational interactions as described by Newton's theory of gravitation. The solutions to this problem require that future and past motions of the bodies be uniquely determined based solely on their present positions and velocities. In general, the motions of the

© Springer Nature Switzerland AG 2019
M. Torres and J. Klapp (Eds.): ISUM 2019, CCIS 1151, pp. 86–95, 2019.
https://doi.org/10.1007/978-3-030-38043-4_8

bodies take place in three dimensions (3D), and there are no restrictions on their masses nor on the initial conditions [4].

After the success at modeling the hydrogen atom, this model was tested to explain a system apparently simple, just a bit more complex that the two body problem, adding up one more body. This variation is now known as the three body problem, and nowadays it supposes one of the major challenges to physicists [3]. Introducing one more body suppose a qualitative increase in the complexity of the calculation to describe the dynamics of the three bodies, making it too complicated to obtain similar types of solutions [1]. The difficulty to achieve an analytic solution to this problem comes from the addition of one more term in the Hamiltonian of the system: the inter-electronic term. This term describes the repulsion that the electrons exert in each other, affecting the dynamics of the system (Eq. 1).

$$ H = \frac{e^2}{4\pi\epsilon_0 |r_1 - r_2|} - \frac{e^2}{2\pi r_1 \epsilon_0} - \frac{e^2}{2\pi r_2 \epsilon_0} - \frac{\tilde{n}^2 \nabla_1^2}{2m} - \frac{\tilde{n}^2 \nabla_2^2}{2m}. \tag{1} $$

Where r_1 and r_2 represent the radial position of the electron 1 and 2 respectively; E_0 is the permitivity of free space; e is the charge; m is the electron mass and ñ is the Planck constant.

The Coulomb three body problem has been one of the most important examples in the non-integrable Hamiltonian systems [4]. In the past, many physicists, astronomers and mathematicians attempted unsuccessfully to find closed form solutions to the problem, but such solutions do not exist because motions of the three bodies are in general unpredictable [1]. In the atomic world this system is represented by one of the most extensively studied systems, due to its unique properties: the Helium atom (He).

In early 20th century the failure to find a stable solution for the classical helium atom heralded the demise of Niels Bohr's program of semiclassical atomic physics [4]. This event give raise to a serie of numerical approaches and approximations conditioned to certain characteristics, in order to solve the problem. As we can see in Eq. 1 the Hamiltonian for the helium atom is the sum of the Hamiltonian for the hydrogen atom for each electron plus the inter-electronic term, which is inversely proportional to the distance between the electrons.

In principle, the first intuitive approximation is to neglect the inter-electronic term that causes all the trouble in the analytic calculations for a solution, in order to have a separable Hamiltonian that is two times the Hydrogen Hamiltonian. Each equation will have an independent solution with the form of the Hydrogen atom wave function, just with a variation in the charge, putting $2e^2$ instead of e^2 (due to the atomic number of the Helium atom is 2). This research will be focused on the computation of a solution for the helium atom using the Independent Electron Approximation (IEA) that consist in neglecting the inter-electronic term and solving with the separated Hamiltonian as two independent Hydrogen systems.

2 Mathematical Methods

In order to study the independent hydrogen systems we must obtain two equation to describe each electron. Taking the Eq. 1 and neglecting the inter electronic term, we can obtain a separable Hamiltonian that is expressed in Eqs. 2 and 3:

$$H_1 = -\frac{e^2}{2\pi r_1 \epsilon_0} - \frac{\tilde{n}^2 \nabla_1^2}{2m}, \tag{2}$$

$$H_1 = -\frac{e^2}{2\pi r_2 \epsilon_0} - \frac{\tilde{n}^2 \nabla_2^2}{2m}. \tag{3}$$

Then, we solve the Schrödinger equation using H_2 and H_1 separately[1]:

$$H_1 \psi_1 = E \psi_1 \tag{4}$$

$$H_2 \psi_2 = E \psi_2. \tag{5}$$

In order to find independent numerical solutions we use separation of variables, to decompose the wave function in its radial and angular dependence.

$$\psi(r, \theta, \phi) = R(r) Y_l^m(\theta, \phi) = R(r) \Theta(\theta) \Phi(\phi). \tag{6}$$

First, we solve for the radial wave equation. The Schrödinger equation for radial dependence reduces to:

$$\frac{\partial^2 R}{k^2 \partial r^2} = R \left(-\frac{2e^2 m}{(kr)(2\pi k \epsilon_0 \tilde{n}^2)} + \frac{(l+1)l}{(kr)^2} + 1 \right), \tag{7}$$

then, making the following changes of variables:

$$\rho = Kr \tag{8}$$

$$\rho_0 = \frac{2e^2 m}{2\pi k \epsilon_0 \tilde{n}^2}. \tag{9}$$

The Eq. 7 reduces to:

$$\frac{\partial^2 R}{\partial \rho^2} = R \left(\frac{(l+1)l}{\rho^2} - \frac{\rho_0}{\rho} + 1 \right). \tag{10}$$

---

[1] We verify all these results with the use of the NDSolve routine from Mathematica with all its default values. For a future larger version of the code we expect to run our Mathematica script into a supercomputer.

Then, after solving the differential equation and an approximation through a Taylor serie, we finally can find the Radial solution:

$$U(\rho) = C_0 e^{\rho} \rho^{l+1}, \tag{11}$$

where:

$$\rho = \frac{r}{an}; \tag{12}$$

Being a the Bohr radius and n the principal quantum number.

To solve for the angular dependence we use again separation of variables, leaving each function depending on a different angle, as we can see in Eq. 6. The solutions for each function are:

$$\Theta(\theta) = A P_l^m(\cos(\theta)), \tag{13}$$

$$\Phi(\phi) = e^{im\phi}. \tag{14}$$

After combining both functions and normalizing them, we can finally obtain the angular function:

$$Y_l^m(\theta, \phi) = \epsilon e^{im\phi} P_l^m(\cos(\theta)) \sqrt{\frac{(2l+1)(l-|m|)!}{4\pi(|m|+l)!}}. \tag{15}$$

Where m is the magnetic quantum number, the l is the azimuthal quantum number and the $P_l^m(\cos(\theta))$ are the associated Legendre functions.

Since the Helium atom need contributions of Hamiltonians H_1 and H_2 the general wave function for the Helium will be the product of the independent solutions;

$$\psi(r_1, r_2) = \psi_{nml}(r_1)\psi_{l'm'n'}(r_2). \tag{16}$$

Finally, the energies for a generic atomic number Z are dependent only on the principal quantum number, a particularity of the Coulombian potential systems. For the Helium atom $Z = 2$;

$$E_n = -\frac{m\left(\frac{Ze^2}{4\pi\epsilon_0}\right)^2}{n^2\left(2\tilde{n}^2\right)} \tag{17}$$

2.1 Helium Hamiltonian Variation: Constant Addition

We introduce a variation in the helium Hamiltonian adding up a constant C (strictly positive defined) to the classical Coulomb potential, representing the neglected inter-electronic term. Due to this, C will be inversely proportional to the distance between the electrons:

$$V_{ee} = \frac{2e^2}{(4\pi\epsilon_0)|r_1 - r_2|}. \tag{18}$$

Since the radial differential equation is the one that depend on the potential, just that part of the solution will be treated. The new radial equation will have an extra term:

$$\frac{\partial^2 R}{\partial \rho^2} = R\left(\frac{(l+1)l}{\rho^2} - \frac{\rho_0}{\rho} + 1 + \rho'\right), \tag{19}$$

where:

$$\rho' = \frac{2\pi C}{e^2 k\epsilon_0}. \tag{20}$$

Performing a similar process than with the hydrogen radial equation we found:

$$R'_{nl}(r) = \frac{C_o \rho^{l+1} e^{\rho(2-\omega)}}{r}, \tag{21}$$

where:

$$\omega = \rho' + 1. \tag{22}$$

Then to complete the radial equation we need to multiply by the contribution of the independent radial equation of the other electron. Then we arrive to the Radial equation:

$$R_{nl}(r) = \frac{C_o^2 \rho^{2l+2} e^{\rho(3-\omega)}}{r^2}. \tag{23}$$

In order to make $R_{nl}(r)$ normalizable, it is necessary that:

$$3 - \omega \leq 0, \tag{24}$$

then, in terms of the energy, it has to be fulfilled that:

$$E \leq \frac{C}{8}, \tag{25}$$

this condition always holds for bound states in which the energies are negative.

3   Argues and Results

In Figs. 1, 2 and 3 are shown the radial functions behavior for different combinations of n and l going from 0 to 4.

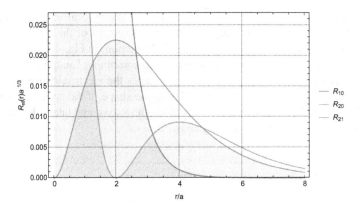

Fig. 1. Radial wave functions R_{nl} of the helium atom with $n = 1, 2$ and $l = 0, 1$.

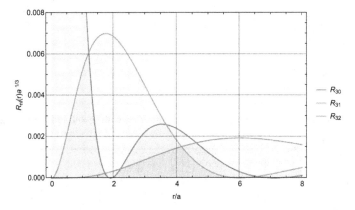

Fig. 2. Radial wave functions R_{nl} of the helium atom with $n = 3$ and $l = 0, 1, 2$.

In Fig. 1 it can be observed the behavior of the radial functions, that corresponds to R_{10}, R_{20} and R_{21}. It can be seen that each of them have an oscillatory behavior in a certain domain, excepting the R_{10} that tends to plus infinity in the y axis and to zero in the x axis. For R_{20}, there exist a local maximum before going to the infinity just like R_{10} and, finally, R_{21} shows also a local maximum before going to zero at plus infinity. The local maximum that can be observed are the regions that used to be negative in the radial wave function of the hydrogen atom. Then, this solutions have a similar behavior in general but with a totally positive output. In Fig. 2 there are presented the radial functions corresponding to the R_{30}, R_{31} and R_{32}. In this case, we can observe that the R_{30} certainly have a local maximum but, as it happened with $n = 1, 2$, the l equal zero tend to the plus infinity in the y axis. In contrast, R_{31} and R_{32} also present local maxima (R_{32} less prominent), that correspond to the negative regions for the hydrogen radial functions, before tending to infinity in the x axis. In Fig. 3 are presented the radial functions for the R_{40}, R_{41}, R_{42} and R_{43}. Here can be seen again the behavior to the infinity at l equal zero, as in the previous plots, with fewer local maxima than in the past cases. It can be seen a tendency relating the increment of the l number and the decrease of the local maxima that have each radial function. In Fig. 4 it is presented the case for the spherical harmonics of the Helium atom combining l and m going form 0 to 3. It can be seen the evolution of the different shapes the electronic orbitals, as l and m take different values. As l changes from 1 to 2 the shape of the spherical harmonics changes, from a single circumference to two along the x axis, and later it becomes more like an helix, that replicates along the y axis.

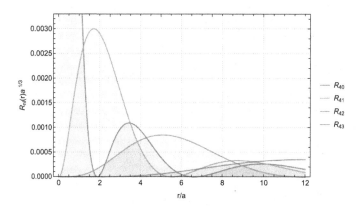

Fig. 3. Radial wave functions R_{nl} of the helium atom with $n = 4$ and $l = 0, 1, 2, 3$.

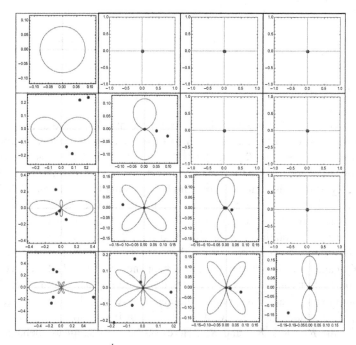

Fig. 4. Spherical Harmonics Y^{lm} of the helium atom with $l = 0, 1, 2, 3$ and $m = 0, 1, 2, 3$.

3.1 Probability Density Functions

Taking the same order, as the previous section, it is presented the shape of the probability density functions for each radial contribution, with n going from 1 to 4 and l from 0 to 3.

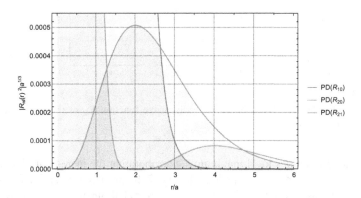

Fig. 5. Probability Density Function of the radial wave function R_{nl} of the helium atom with $n = 1, 2$ and $l = 0, 1$.

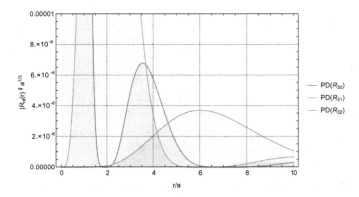

Fig. 6. Probability Density Function of the radial wave function R_{nl} of the helium atom with $n = 3$ and $l = 0, 1, 2$.

In Fig. 5 the probability density functions of R_{10} and R_{20} go to the plus infinite just as its correspondent radial wave functions. In contrast, the local maximum of the PDF that correspond to R_{21} is considerably less that the previous maximum. This indicates a larger probability of the electron to be nearer to the nucleus than farther away, a conclusion that agrees with the stability of the electron being nearer to its ground level of energy. In Fig. 6 the probability density functions of R_{30} go to infinity in the way y axis, as seen before for the l equal zero radial functions. The R_{31} and R_{32} show their respective local maximums, that according to the scale, are much less that the

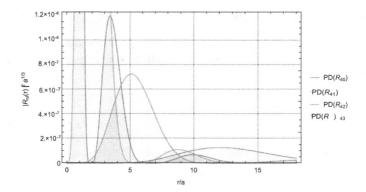

Fig. 7. Probability Density Function of the radial wave function R_{nl} of the helium atom with $n = 4$ and $l = 0, 1, 2, 3$.

respective radial functions local maximums, corroborating the increment of stability of the electron as it is nearer to the nucleus. In Fig. 7 the probability density functions of R_{40} go to infinity, as it is common for l equal to zero radial functions, having more local maximums as the n increases. For the other radial functions, it can be seen a tendency of increasing the prominence of the maximums as l decreases. Each of the maximums are much less that the maximums correspondent to the radial equations. Finally, Fig. 8

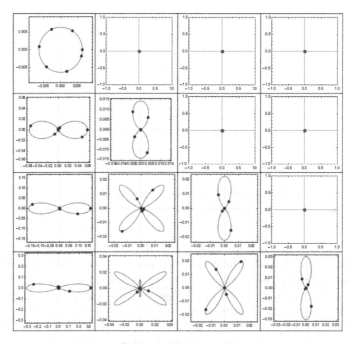

Fig. 8. Probability Density Function of the spherical harmonics Y^{lm} of the Helium atom with $l = 0, 1, 2, 3$ and $m = 0, 1, 2, 3$.

presents the spherical harmonics probability density function for l and m going from 0 to 3. We can observe a similar behavior to the spherical harmonic corresponding function, in the evolution of the shape of the orbitals, as the quantum numbers change. What is different is the width of the branches, which became slimmer in comparison with the previous case. This can be explained by the tendency of the particle to keep closer to the central parts of the total orbital space, since it is more stable in the middle of each branch. Then this explains why it is more likely to find the particle in a slimmer region.

4   Conclusions

This study does show the simplest approximation to the helium atom system which is considering the helium as two hydrogen independent systems, neglecting the inter-electronic term. Even thought this approximation does not give enough accuracy to considerate extrapolating it to more complex system, it does give initial values from where to begin to construct more sophisticated and accurate methods. In the radial wave function it could be observed the tendency of the one with l equal zero to go to infinity in the y axis, and the increment in local maxima as the n evolved. For the rest of the radial function the tendency was the increment prominence of the local maxima as the l was decreasing. In the spherical harmonics function we could observe the evolution of the shape of the orbitals as the quantum numbers evolved, replicating in the x and y axis, evolving from a circle to two circles and then a helix that reproduced in the other axis. Finally, the probability density function plots of the radial and spherical parts of the wave function yield the same conclusion: there exist more probability to find the electron in its more stable level of energy, close to the nucleus and that is why the local maxima become much less in the radial case and the branches were slimmer in the spherical harmonics case.

Acknowledgement. Special thanks to the National Institute of Supercomputing of Ecuador for allow us to perform the simulations in the Quinde I supercomputer, located at Innópolis, Urcuquí, Ecuador.

References

1. Kondyukov, G.: The Three Body Coulomb Problem: An Examination of Bound States and Stability as a Function of Individual Masses. Ph.D. thesis, Florida State University (2015)
2. David, G.: Introduction to Quantum Mechanics: Pearson New International Edition. PE (2008)
3. Kornilov, O.: The quantum halo state of the helium trimer. Science **348**(6234), 498–499 (2015). https://doi.org/10.1126/science.aaa9102
4. Kunitski, M., et al.: Observation of the Efimov state of the helium trimer. Science **348**(6234), 551–555 (2015). https://doi.org/10.1126/science.aaa5601

Solution of Schrödinger Equation Not Implementing Conventional Separation of Variables: Using the Trial and Error Brute Force Permutation Method

J. M. Ramírez-Velásquez$^{(\boxtimes)}$ and Ismael Villegas

School of Physical Sciences and Nanotechnology, Yachay Tech University,
100119 Urcuqui, Ecuador
{jmramirez, jhonny.villegas}@yachaytech.edu.ec

Abstract. The Schrödinger equation is practically the base of quantum mechanics and the most use technique to solved this differential equation has been the separation of variable technique. From separation of variable process is possible obtain the time independent Schrödinger equation [TISE]; a useful equation for independent time potential. However, there are another situations in quantum mechanics that involves other mathematical ways to solve this equation. The methods implemented in this document are given by different potentials and avoiding the conventional separation of variables. The goal of this work is search wave functions that satisfy the Schrödinger equation with other unusual conditions. That makes easier reach more specific solution than in comparison are complicated to reach using the common separation of variables.

Keywords: Super computing · HPC · Quantum mechanics · Quinde I

1 Introduction

At the beginning of the XX century, the concept of wave-particle duality was introduced in physics, mainly due to the contribution of Planck and Einstein. The Max Planck's work about black body radiation and his conclusion of quantization of light was crucial for the posterior Einstein's interpretation. Albert Einstein inferred that Planck's quanta should be photons; small energy packages. Additionally, due to the photoelectric effect, he concluded that photons behave as particles exchanging momentum (1);

$$p = \frac{h}{\lambda} = \hbar k. \tag{1}$$

In 1923, Louis-Victor de Broglie proposed to generalize this duality to all known particles, even particles with mass such as electrons. That assumption leads to understand that only certain discrete rotational frequencies about the nucleus of an atom are allowed. Following up on de Broglie's ideas, Erwin Schrödinger in 1925

M. Torres and J. Klapp (Eds.): ISUM 2019, CCIS 1151, pp. 96–107, 2019.
https://doi.org/10.1007/978-3-030-38043-4_9

decided to find a proper wave equation for the electron (2) [1]; inspired in the principle of least action of Hamilton applied in optics:

$$ i\hbar \frac{\partial}{\partial t} \Psi(r,t) = -\frac{\hbar^2}{2m} \nabla^2 \Psi(r,t) + V(r)\Psi(r,t). \tag{2}$$

The left term of (2) represents the total energy of the studied system and the two terms of the right side are similar to kinetic and potential energy. In the Copenhagen interpretation of quantum mechanics, the wave function is the most complete description that can be given of a physical system. Separation of variables is the physicist's first line of attack on any partial differential equation, but it has some limitations. For instance, it assumes that the Ψ (r, t) is only the product of a time dependent and a space dependent part (9); it limits for other more eccentric possible solutions for Quantum mechanics. Furthermore, it supposes in the process of that potentials are time independent and it cannot be always necessarily true.

$$ \Psi(r,t) = \psi(r)\varphi(t). \tag{3}$$

2 Theoretical Mathematical Methods

First, it is necessary to know the conventional process of separation of variable. The next part will emphasize in the objection of the Time Independent Schrödinger Equation [*TISE*] by the change (9). Then, the relation (9) will be changed by other that not implies separation of variable itself (18); it will be applied for harmonic oscillator potential (10). Then as well, a time dependent potential will be studied; considering a moving potential with constant velocity (21).

It is possible to consider that it is other step obligatory to study Quantum mechanics, because nature is enough complex to have more types of systems and wave functions related to them. Again, by the Copenhagen interpretation, a wave function is the most complete description that can be given of a physical system. Since the beginning of physics, its goal has been describe nature with mathematics and Quantum mechanics is our most powerful tool for this objective.

2.1 Schrödinger Equation [TISE]

The time-independent Schrödinger equation describes discrete stationary states. For example, if the potential is equal to zero, it is possible obtain n satisfactory solutions with $n \in Z$ and n allowed energies; discretization of energy. Those specific functions describe a state of the studied system; a vector independent of time, more precise an eigenvector of the Hamiltonian. It predicts that wave functions can form standing waves to respect time with a related allowed energy. Those wave functions and their energies are fundamental to understand the nature of atoms, its orbitals, and matter itself. So, it is essential to understand our daily reality in the smallest scale. These stationary states are particularly important as their individual study later simplifies the task of solving the time-dependent Schrödinger equation for any state. Now, to solve the partial differential Eq. (2) is possible to use (9) to obtain the following expressions:

$$\frac{\partial}{\partial t}\Psi(r,t) = \frac{\partial}{\partial t}\psi(r)\varphi(t) = \psi(r)\frac{d\varphi(t)}{dt}, \tag{4}$$

$$\frac{\partial^2}{\partial x^2}\Psi(r,t) = \frac{\partial^2}{\partial x^2}\psi(r)\varphi(t) = \varphi(t)\frac{d^2\psi(x)}{dx^2}. \tag{5}$$

The anterior changes seems easier and simple, but behind this step is feasible to omit some mathematical restrictions of partial derivatives. This chance makes possible replace the partial derivatives for common derivatives, and it makes easier the solution process. The next step consists in replace (4) and (5) in the time dependent Schrödinger Eq. (2) and divided this new expression by $\psi(x)\phi(t)$ (9);

$$i\hbar\frac{1}{\varphi}\frac{d\varphi}{dt} = -\frac{\hbar^2}{2m}\frac{1}{\psi}\frac{d^2\psi}{dx^2} + V(r). \tag{6}$$

This new expression has each side depending only of one single variable. The left side depends only of time and the other side only depends of the position, for this case positions is only one dimensional (x). From the left side of this expression comes the respective eigenvalue, E in (7) of a solution of this new differential equation and from the right side comes the Hamiltonian operator for one dimension;

$$i\hbar\frac{d\varphi}{dt} = E\varphi, \tag{7}$$

$$\hat{H}\psi = E\psi = -\frac{\hbar^2}{2m}\frac{d^2\psi}{dx^2} + V(x)\psi. \tag{8}$$

Now, the partial differential equation has came in a two normal differential equations. Furthermore, the first differential equation is easy to solve because it is a differential equation of first order, as shown in Sect. 2.2. Plugging $\phi(t)$ in (6) gives us a general solution to respect time (9) and the mathematical expression for stationary states for discrete values of E; its eigenvalues:

$$\varphi(t) = e^{iEt/\hbar}$$

$$\Psi(x,t) = \psi(x)e^{iEt/\hbar}, \tag{9}$$

by using novel transformations and separations of variables, the exact analytical solution of energy eigenvalues as well as the wave functions is obtained (8). This can be applied for systems non-relativistic region that evolve in time and with a correction it can be applied with the relativistic corrections (11).

2.2 Harmonic Oscillator Potential

In synthesis, a harmonic oscillator is composed by something moving around an equilibrium position by action of a restoring force in relation with the position. Harmonic Oscillator is an important case studied a lot in classical mechanics; specially because it is equivalent in many areas of science. Similar mathematical models can be applied for example for RLC circuits, rotational mechanics, between others which obey the principle of least action. The areas in which harmonic oscillator also included also quantum mechanics. Schrödinger Equation is enough versatile to apply many different kind of potential energies and in consequence it can study many kind of exotic systems. One of the most common studied potential is the case for a "spring" and its associated potential (10) [1]:

$$V(x) = \frac{1}{2}m\omega^2 x^2 + C(x). \tag{10}$$

That potential is used in Fig. 1 for the case of stationary states with its related eigenvalues. This case has a strong relevance because its is a good approximation for the vibrations of a diatomic molecule. Diatomic molecules are a good analogy of a two-body version of the quantum harmonic oscillator. The classical way to visualize molecules was imagine diatomic gases as two small pieces of matter joined by a spring with a related constant as in the Hooke's law. The vibrations of molecules as heat is a consequence of the repelling and attractive forces of the "spring". For a mono atomic gas the measuring of the heat capacity was satisfactory with classical methods, but for a diatomic was a failure compared with experimental data. To solve that problem was necessary omit the Energy Equipartition theorem of statistical mechanics and introduce the discretization of energy by the work of Max Planck. This way of think about energy as discrete number is one of the most important contributions of quantum mechanics, the eigenvalues of a wave function, of a quantum state itself. Other similar cases of quantum harmonic oscillators are modelling photons, and a charge with mass in a uniform magnetic field: the Landau quantization.

Harmonic oscillator can be solved plugging (10) into TISE (8); it gives us n possible solutions independent of time. In three spatial dimensions, the generalized uncertainty principle is considered under an isotropic harmonic oscillator interaction in both non-relativistic and relativistic regions [2]:

$$\hat{H} = \frac{\hat{p}^2}{2m} + \frac{\beta}{m}\hat{p}^4 + O(\beta^2) + \frac{1}{2}m\omega_0^2\hat{x}^2. \tag{11}$$

For a case of non-relativistic conditions and an harmonic oscillator as the potential the Ehrenfest's theorem is not valid in the case of Generalized Uncertainty Principle [3], so we should take the classical limit by replacing commutators by brackets. For this case the operator p is modified by a factor β (12). The change over the commutators follow the expressions (13) and (14). The operators $\hat{X}$ and $\hat{P}$ are the addition of the contribution of each part of the system; the harmonic part and the correction for non-relativistic motion:

$$\hat{P} = \hat{P}\left(1 + \beta\hat{p}^2\right), \tag{12}$$

$$\frac{1}{i\hbar}\left[\hat{X}, \hat{P}\right] = 1 + \beta\hat{p}^2 \rightarrow \{\hat{X}, \hat{P}\} = 1 + \beta\hat{p}^2, \tag{13}$$

$$\frac{1}{i\hbar}[\hat{x}, \hat{p}] = 1 \rightarrow \{x, p\} = 1. \tag{14}$$

For the case of this work, $\beta \rightarrow 0$ for simplicity; giving us the classical Harmonic oscillator. All of this is evidence of the versatility of the harmonic oscillator. The harmonic oscillator is frequently used in physics, because a mass at equilibrium under the influence of any conservative force, in the limit of small motions, behaves as a simple harmonic oscillator.

Now, the most direct computational way by brute force to solve [TISE] (8) with a harmonic potential (10) is a function that satisfies the *Weber differential Eq.* (15). It implies that the result and the function are entire function of z with no branch cut discontinuities:

$$y'' + y\left[v - \frac{z^2}{4} + \frac{1}{2}\right] = 0. \tag{15}$$

The solution wave functions for a potential as (10) by [TISE] can be expressed in terms of the function parabolic cylinder $D_v(z)$ (16); as shown in Sect. 2.1:

$$\psi_n(x) = D_{[n]}\left[\sqrt{\frac{2m\omega}{\hbar}}x\right] + D_{[-n-1]}\left[i\sqrt{\frac{2m\omega}{\hbar}}x\right]. \tag{16}$$

The importance of this step is transform an unknown problem in other mathematically proved and this is good jump to avoid the tedious algebraic method to get the solution for harmonic oscillator. The solutions are the same that the methods by operators and it ensures us that this solution is mathematically correct by the corrections of *Weber Eq.* (15). One of the most interesting properties of wave function is its strong relation with *complex numbers*. it necessary for our understanding of nature that this be as accurate as possible and prove that the result are complete complex function with no branch cut discontinuities. Additionally, it is an additionally way to satisfy some properties of the Hilbert space as an euclidean space [4]. Again, the energy is discrete and follow (17):

$$E_n = \hbar\omega\left[n + \frac{1}{2}\right]. \tag{17}$$

Omitting the contribution the second term of (16) and contrasting it with the harmonic potential it is possible to get again The information of Fig. 1.

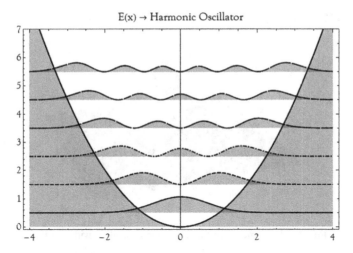

Fig. 1. Probability densities representations for the first six bound eigenstates, n = 0 to 5. Stationary states to respect position.

This is only the time independent part, but it is possible to find the whole contribution of the harmonic oscillator in time; assuming the time is orthonormal with respect the position and the omitting the contribution of the second term of (16) that depend of *i*. According with conventional separation of variables (9) is feasible to make a representation of the wave function to respect time depending all by the energy, which in turn depends on *n*; for example with *n* = 0; Fig. 2; this can be analysed with other *n* ∈ N for example Fig. 3. However the previous assumption limits the function only as a pick not changing in time represented Fig. 2 any of the other *n* possible solutions that satisfy this restrictions as for example *n* = 4; Fig. 3;

$$\Psi(r,t) = \psi(r)\rho(t)\beta(r,t). \tag{18}$$

If we want to consider the omitted assumptions; it possible think in this as other system. However, statistical mixtures of states are different from a linear combination. A statistical mixture of states is a statistical ensemble of independent systems [4]. According with Kempf et al. [4], statistical mixtures represent the degree of knowledge whilst the uncertainty within quantum mechanics is fundamental. We can consider the omitted assumptions as other quantum state orthonormal with respect the taken function. Previously, we assume that the second parameter of (16) will not contribute because this is to respect a complex value; now we take that contribution but orthonormal with respect to the previous. Other way of study more complete systems is the product of two different system (18). In this case beta are the previous omitted contributions.

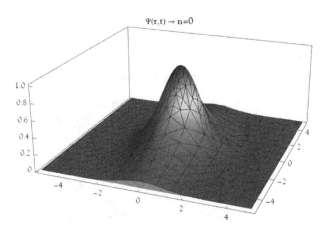

Fig. 2. Harmonic wave function time dependent with $n = 0$.

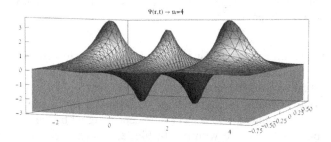

Fig. 3. Harmonic wave function time dependent with $n = 4$.

2.3   Moving Delta Potential

According to Griffiths, the Dirac delta function is an infinitely high, infinitesimally narrow spike at the origin, whose area is 1 (20). Qualitatively, it corresponds to a potential which is zero everywhere, except at a single point, where it takes an infinite value (19) [1]. This situation can be used to reproduce situations where a particle is free to move in two regions of space with a barrier of infinite potential between the two regions. Technically, the is divided in two regions and this is in some aspects similar with an infinite squared well, but inverted and with an infinitesimal length of the well. An practical example applied is an electron can move almost freely in a conducting material, but if two conducting surfaces are put close together, the interface between them acts as a barrier for the electron that can be approximated by a delta potential [5], Bastard:

$$\delta(x) \equiv \begin{cases} 0, & \text{if } x \neq 0 \\ \infty, & \text{if } x = 0 \end{cases}, \tag{19}$$

$$\int_{-\infty}^{\infty} \delta(x)dx = 1. \tag{20}$$

For situation as the electrons case (mentioned before), a potential dependent of delta can be applied (21); where obviously $\delta(x)$ is the Dirac delta function. For this potential, its behavior is as attractive delta function potential and look for the bound states. The delta has been defined to occur at the origin for simplicity; a shift in the delta function's argument does not change any of the proceeding results, and this fact is very important for the proposed mathematical problem:

$$V(x) = -\alpha\delta(x). \tag{21}$$

Additionally, for the proposed problem of this is necessary to apply the energies of this system (22) to make a construction of other more complex system and find its wave functions:

$$E_{n\delta} = -\frac{\alpha^2 m}{2\hbar^2}, \tag{22}$$

$$\psi(x) = \sqrt{\frac{\alpha m}{\hbar}}e^{-\alpha m|x|/\hbar^2}. \tag{23}$$

At the beginning of this work was mentioned that the conventional separation of variable has some limitation with respect potential that depends of time, for that case the potential (21) will be modify to change the potential to someone that moves in time; as a pick moving in the x axis. A moving potential is possible by a change in the position and a position changing at an non-relativistic velocity can be expressed by the classical simple equation of motion:

$$x_f = x_0 + vt$$

by a modification in the sign, for the $-\alpha$ in the potential definition (21).

$$V(x,t) = -\alpha\delta(x - vt). \tag{24}$$

For this document and for simplicity, i only consider a one-dimensional potential well, but analysis could be expanded to more dimensions.

3 Applied Cases

For this part we will analyse two cases and at the final point decompose the contribution of the system that affect all the wave function. These cases do not use the conventional Schrödinger Equation, instead it is as a checking to satisfy the constraints of the Schrödinger Eqs. (4) and (5) by brute force; and compare the systems by the known energies of other studied systems.

$$\hat{H}\psi = E\psi = [E_1 + E_2 + \ldots]\psi. \tag{25}$$

The energies of a collection of systems can create a high factor of degeneration but if it is analogized in their ground states is possible reduce the noise produced by the whole sum of contributions. But this can implies that after this process is possible express the function in term of n and find the remaining functions for higher level. For this reason in this document will study the cases at $n = 0$.

3.1   Case 1

For this case, i use a function and i try to prove (25) by not common separation of variable. In other words, i will operate with the objective to find the eigenvalues and the express the function in terms of those eigenvalues/energies for the following expression, as a test function.

$$\Psi(x,t) = \sqrt[4]{\frac{m\omega}{\hbar\pi}} \exp\left[-\frac{m\omega\left(\frac{1}{2}a^2(1+e^{-2it\omega}) - 2axe^{-it\omega} + \frac{it\hbar}{m} + x^2\right)}{2\hbar}\right]$$

Now it is necessary to clear algebraically the expression to make a new expression in term of the energies

$$\Psi(x,t) = \left(\frac{m\omega}{\hbar\pi}\right)^{1/4} \exp\left[-\frac{1}{2}it\omega\right] \exp\left[-\frac{m\omega x^2}{2\hbar}\right]$$
$$\exp\left[-\frac{a^2 m\omega}{4\hbar}\right] \exp\left[-\frac{a^2 m\omega e^{-2it\omega}}{4\hbar}\right] \exp\left[\frac{amx\omega e^{-it\omega}}{\hbar}\right]$$

Now, it is obvious that the first term and the third are the time independent wave function of harmonic oscillator of the Sect. 2.3 with $n = 0$ and the second term is the $\phi(t)$ of the Sect. 2.2, also with $n = 0$. So, i will regroup those terms in a single function, the time dependent harmonic oscillator function $\Psi_{HO}(x,t)$.

$$\Psi(x,t) = \Psi_{HO}(x,t) \exp\left[-\frac{a^2 m\omega}{4\hbar}\right] \exp\left[-\frac{a^2 m\omega e^{-2it\omega}}{4\hbar}\right]$$
$$\exp\left[\frac{amx\omega e^{-it\omega}}{\hbar}\right].$$

Giving that this expression is now in terms of the harmonic oscillator with $n = 0$ is a good step to put the energies in term of the energy of the harmonic oscillator, also with $n = 0$.

$$E_n = \hbar\omega \left[\frac{1}{2}\right]$$

Changing by E_n

$$\Psi(x,t) = \Psi_{HO}(x,t)\exp\left[-\frac{a^2m}{2\hbar^2}E_n\right]\exp\left[-\frac{a^2me^{-2it\omega}}{2\hbar^2}E_n\right]$$
$$\exp\left[\frac{2amxe^{-it\omega}}{\hbar^2}E_n\right]$$

Now, By this algebraic clearance is possible to see some contestants that can be grouped in terms of other known energy, for this case the energy of a delta function potential (22) at $n = 0$, by the condition that $\alpha = a$ of this function.

$$E_{n\delta} = -\frac{\alpha^2 m}{2\hbar^2}$$

The new expression is

$$\Psi(x,t) = \Psi_{HO}(x,t)\exp\left[E_{n\delta}E_n\left(-\frac{4xe^{-it\omega}}{a}+e^{-2it\omega}+1\right)\right]$$

By definition, the values of energies are constants and it is not different for harmonic oscillator or a delta well potential.

$$\chi = \exp[E_{n\delta}E_n] = e^{-m\omega a^2/4\hbar}$$

With this new change that after i generalize for all addition of states as a normalization value.

$$\Psi(x,t) = \Psi_{HO}(x,t)\cdot\chi\cdot\chi^{-4xe^{-it\omega}/a}\cdot\chi^{e^{-2it\omega}}$$

In addition χ is not only a constant it can be expressed as:

$$\chi = \left(e^{-\frac{am}{\hbar^2}}\right)^{\frac{a\omega\hbar}{4}} = \left(e^{-\frac{am}{\hbar^2}}\right)^{\frac{q}{2}E_n}$$

It implies that the third term that depends of x by a change can be transform in the wave function for a delta well potential (23) with out the normalization factor. Now the third therm can be expressed in terms of the wave function of delta well potential with $n = 0$ (23).

$$\sqrt{\frac{\hbar}{\alpha m}}\psi_\delta(x) = e^{-\alpha m|x|/\hbar^2} = \chi^{aE_n|x|/2}.$$

Taking and arbitrary $|x| = \sqrt{x^2}$ over χ and applying in the previous whole expression.

$$\Psi(x,t) = \chi\cdot\Psi_{HO}(x,t)\cdot\left(\sqrt{\frac{\hbar}{\alpha m}}\psi_\delta(x)\right)^{-4E_ne^{-it\omega}/2}\cdot\chi^{e^{-2it\omega}}.$$

Now, the new expression is in terms of the $\psi\delta(x)$ and we can apply the (25) and with this we can take the other parameter which is missing. So, for the left member of the Schrödinger equation.

$$i\hbar\frac{\partial\Psi}{\partial t} = \Psi\left[-\frac{1}{2}ma^2\omega^2 e^{-2it\omega} + amx\omega^2 e^{-it\omega} + \frac{1}{2}\omega\hbar\right], \tag{26}$$

and for the right member of the equation.

$$-\frac{\hbar^2}{2m}\left[-\frac{m\omega}{\hbar} + \frac{m^2\omega^2}{\hbar^2}(x - ae^{-it\omega})^2\right]\Psi + \left[\frac{1}{2}m\omega^2 x^2\right]\Psi$$

Clearing this expression.

$$\Psi\left[\frac{1}{2}\omega\hbar + amx\omega^2 e^{-it\omega} - \frac{1}{2}ma^2\omega^2 e^{-2it\omega}\right]. \tag{27}$$

Now it is obvious that both expressions (26), (27) are equal and as a consequence it satisfy the Schrödinger equation and the Eq. (25). It means that the values inside the parenthesis are the eigenvalues of the studied system.

$$\Psi\left[E_n - \frac{8}{a}E_n E_\delta x e^{-it\omega} + 4E_n E_\delta e^{-2it\omega}\right]$$

The enclosed factors are the energies for this expression is the those energies depend of time similar as a Taylor series. First, we have the E_n that we can drop as a common factor.

$$\Psi \cdot E_n\left[1 + 4E_\delta e^{-2it\omega} - \frac{8}{a}E_\delta x e^{-it\omega}\right]$$

As a series, every single factor has a contribution for the whole state. The main contribution is the energy of the harmonic oscillator and it decreased as the time and position take a role in the contribution given a potential that depends of time (24).

4   Conclusions

In conclusion, the "separation of variables is the physicist's first line of attack on any partial differential equation" [1] but it has some limitation with respect some complex potentials and its necessary use our knowledge of eigenfunctions and its related eigenvalues to clarify easily what system we have in our hands. In nature, isolated systems are strange and as a physicist our work is synthesize our world with the most loyal mathematical representation. The best argue is the simplicity of an equation.

Acknowledgement. Special thanks to the National Institute of Supercomputing of Ecuador for allow us to perform the simulations in the Quinde I supercomputer, located at Innópolis, Urcuquí, Ecuador.

References

1. Griffiths, D.J.: Introduction to Quantum Mechanics. Pearson Prentice Hall, Upper Saddle River (2005)
2. Hassanabadi, H., Hooshmand, P., Zarrinkamar, S.: The generalized uncertainty principle and harmonic interaction in three spatial dimensions. Few-Body Syst. **56**(1), 19–27 (2014). https://doi.org/10.1007/s00601-014-0910-7
3. Nozari, K., Azizi, T.: Gravitational induced uncertainty and dynamics of harmonic oscillator. Gen. Relativ. Gravit. **38**(2), 325–331 (2006)
4. Kempf, A., Mangano, G., Mann, R.B.: Hilbert space representation of the minimal length uncertainty relation. Phys. Rev. D **52**, 1108 (1995)
5. Bastard, G.: Wave Mechanics Applied to Semiconductor Heterostructures. Editions de Physique, Les Ulis (1988)

Lagrangian Approach for the Study of Heat Transfer in a Nuclear Reactor Core Using the SPH Methodology

F. Pahuamba-Valdez[2], E. Mayoral-Villa[1], C. E. Alvarado-Rodríguez[3], J. Klapp[1(✉)], A. M. Gómez-Torres[1], and E. Del Valle-Gallegos[2]

[1] Instituto Nacional de Investigaciones Nucleares, Carretera México – Toluca s/n, La Marquesa, 52750 Ocoyoacac, Estado de México, Mexico
jaime.klapp@inin.gob.mx
[2] Instituto Politécnico Nacional, Escuela Superior de Física y Matemáticas, Instituto Politécnico Nacional, Ciudad de México, Mexico
[3] Departamento de Ingeniería Química, División de Ciencias Naturales y Exactas, Universidad de Guanajuato, Noria Alta s/n, 36050 Guanajuato, Guanajuato, Mexico

Abstract. Numerical modeling simulations and the use of high-performance computing are fundamental for detailed safety analysis, control and operation of a nuclear reactor, allowing the study and analysis of problems related with thermal-hydraulics, neutronic and the dynamic of fluids which are involved in these systems. In this work we introduce the bases for the implementation of the smoothed particle hydrodynamics (SPH) approach to analyze heat transfer in a nuclear reactor core. Heat transfer by means of convection is of great importance in many engineering applications and especially in the analysis of heat transfer in nuclear reactors. As a first approach, the natural convection in the gap (space that exists between the fuel rod and the cladding) can be analyzed helping to reduce uncertainty in such calculations that usually relies on empirical correlations while using other numerical tools. The numerical method developed in this work was validated while comparing the results obtained in previous numerical simulations and experimental data reported in the literature showing that our implementation is suitable for the study of heat transfer in nuclear reactors. Numerical simulations were done with the DualSPHysics open source code that allows to perform parallel calculations using different number of cores. The current implementation is a version written in CUDA (Compute Unified Device Architecture) that allows also the use of GPU processors (Graphics Processor Unit) to accelerate the calculations in parallel using a large number of cores contained in the GPU. This makes possible to analyze large systems using a reasonable computer time. The obtained results verified and validated our method and allowed us to have a strong solver for future applications of heat transfer in nuclear reactors fuel inside the reactor cores.

© Springer Nature Switzerland AG 2019
M. Torres and J. Klapp (Eds.): ISUM 2019, CCIS 1151, pp. 108–124, 2019.
https://doi.org/10.1007/978-3-030-38043-4_10

1   Introduction

Safety analysis in a nuclear reactor is a subject of big interest for the evaluation of operational transients and prevention of severe accidents. Due to the multi physical nature of the phenomena taking part in a nuclear reactor core, the use of numerical modeling and high-performance computing has become a must in the development of numerical tools for analysis of nuclear reactors. In a boiling water reactor (BWR) the nuclear fuel, the moderator, the control elements and part of the heat removal system are found in the same structure within the vessel of the reactor. This array presents the complexity that water is used both, as moderator (fundamental in the neutronic behavior of the reactor and totally related to power generation) while it serves as vehicle of heat removal as a coolant. When water and fuel come into contact, the latter transfers heat to the water triggering the vapor generation. The vapor generated goes through the turbines of the turbo generators transforming the enthalpy of vapor into electrical power. When the transition occurs (onset of nucleate boiling) the properties of heat transfer are affected by the nucleation and the process of boiling alters the dynamics of the fluid. In BWR reactors, the transition of the liquid phase into gas plays and important role in the design and control of the reactor. The most important thermal limits for design and operation of the boiling reactor are related with the capability of the water to continue the coolant process even though the change of phase from liquid to gas.

An important phenomenon that must be considered in the BWR, is the reaching of a critical heat flux in the cladding of the fuel in which a film of vapor can be formed in the cladding acting as a thermal isolator, damaging the heat transfer and thus, increasing dramatically the temperature in the fuel. Consequently, the fuel overheats and can melt. This phenomenon is known as '*dry-out*' and, as already stated, it is of great interest to study in detail. One of the first steps in the analysis of this phenomenon is to analyze the heat transfer in the space between the fuel rod and the inner cladding wall. This space, known as gap, is full of helium and is usually coarse approximated by heat conduction phenomenon in current numerical tools. Since heat transfer in such gap plays an important role in the heat transfer from fuel to coolant outside of the cladding wall, it is imperative to improve the numerical models in the gap. For that, the natural convection model developed, verified and validated in this paper becomes very important.

Furthermore, to analyze the flow pattern of the coolant on the other side of the cladding wall is also a key aspect in nuclear reactor analysis. The turbulent behavior of the fluid, mostly in the region of heat transfer favors the transfer of heat in the system and its control is important to optimize its proper functioning. For this reason, special designs can be made to induce turbulence that can favor, along with the boiling processes, the extraction of heat generated by the fission processes. This phenomenon will be studied in detail in a future development to extend the current one.

In general, to study these systems, traditionally, Eulerian methods have been used such as finite elements, finite volumes and finite differences. These type of methods and Computational Fluid Dynamics (CFD) programs running in a supercomputer have demonstrated to be an important tool in the design, control and operation of PWR reactors which operates at high pressure and thus without boiling. Nevertheless, for

BWR's, due to the transition phase, its application presents some noteworthy restrictions and limits, especially while dealing with mobile and diffused interphases, phase transitions, complex geometry and dynamic systems or turbulent fluids, which are cases that represent many of the fundamental phenomena that take place in a BWR reactor. The main limitation of Eulerian solutions is that the systems are solved by the discretization of coupled differential equations that solve the system in a mesh which is not dynamic or adaptive to the structural changes that are present, so the use of approximations must be applied. At the same time the incorporation of other physical and chemical effects results in an increase of the complexity of the numeric solution that can carry strong numeric instabilities. The traditional techniques for one-dimensional models are based on simplified models where empirical correlations and approximations are incorporated introducing uncertainties hard to quantify. Therefore, it is necessary to incorporate physical models of first principles to represent the main phenomena that occur in the boiling water reactors such as boiling and condensation, mass and energy exchange between phases, transport of particles, etc. in substitution of the empirical correlations that additionally have intervals of limited validity.

To overcome these difficulties, the use of a free mesh simulation like the SPH method has been considered as a promissory option. SPH is a Lagrangian methodology and is based on interpolation theory that uses points, generally called particles, to discretize the continuous medium. The SPH is a computational method used to simulate the dynamics of continuous mediums such as the mechanics of solids and the flux of fluids. Initially, it was developed by Gingold and Monaghan [1] for problems related to astrophysics. Its use expands over several fields of investigation including astrophysics, ballistics, volcanology and oceanography. The equations in the medium or continuous fluid which are the conservation of mass, moment and energy of the fluid, are present in Lagrangian form and later discretized using the SPH methodology.

The numerical simulations were performed with the DualSPHysics free code (for details please refer to [5] and www.dual.sphysics.org). One of the main advantages of the DualSPHysics code is its parallel structure. The code is written in the C++ language using the Open Multi-processing application that allows to perform calculations in parallel using different number of cores according to the computer equipment used. In addition, there is a version written in CUDA (Compute Unified Device Architecture) that allows to use the GPU processors (Graphics Processor Unit) to accelerate the calculations in parallel using many cores contained in the GPU. The ability of GPUs to perform numerical simulations using the SPH method is demonstrated by Harada [7] where a speedup of 28 was achieved by simulating 60,000 particles. The DualSPHysics code is organized mainly in three stages: (1) the creation of the list of neighbors, (2) the computation of the interaction between neighbors, (3) the integration in time, referring to the update of the system. Crespo et al. [5] verified that the interaction stage is the one that consumes the most computation time in a numerical simulation. Based on the above, to improve the calculation performance it is necessary to perform the interaction stage in parallel, in this way the sequential calculation is avoided, and the interaction of several particles is calculated at the same time using different cores.

In the second part of this work the general characteristics of the SPH approach are presented together with the considerations needed to introduce the bases for the implementation to analyze heat transfer in the fuel of nuclear reactors. In the third section the results obtained for the study of heat convection, which is of great importance in many applications of engineering and especially in the analysis of heat transfer in nuclear reactors, are presented. The 2D models developed here will be extended to 3D models to study the natural convection in the gap (space that exists between the fuel rod and the cladding) and the comparison with previous numerical simulations. Section 4 contains the conclusions of this work.

2   SPH Methodology

The generalities of the SPH approach are described in this section. The equations that govern the dynamics of the continuous media (fluids and deformable solids) are transformed into integral equations through the use of an interpolation function. Thus, in SPH the medium is represented numerically by a finite set of observation points, or particles, by means of a smoothing procedure in which the estimated value of a function $f(x)$ at a point x is given by the expression

$$\tilde{f}(x) = \int_{\Omega} f(x')W(x - x', h)dx', \tag{1}$$

where $W(x - x', h)$ is the smoothing function usually called kernel, which is a function of the position x and a smoothing length h that determines the domain of influence Ω.

If a fluid of density $\rho(x)$ is considered, the interpolation integral shown in Eq. (1) can be written as

$$\int_{\Omega} \left[\frac{f(x')}{\rho(x')} \right] W(x - x', h)\rho(x')dx'. \tag{2}$$

To evaluate this integral the domain Ω is subdivided into N elements of volume (particles) each of mass m_b and density ρ_b, in such a way that the sum of the masses of all the particles is the total mass of the fluid. Thus, the mass of each particle (m_b) can be identified as

$$m_b = \rho(x')dx', \tag{3}$$

where dx' is the volume differential and $\rho(x')$ is the density.

Equation 2 can be discretized in a set of particles by replacing the interpolation integral with the summation over the mass of the particle m_b

$$\tilde{f}(x) = \sum_{b=1}^{N} m_b \frac{f_b}{\rho_b} W(|x - x_b|, h), \tag{4}$$

where the subscript b refers to the quantity evaluated in position b.

An advantage of the SPH method is that its formulation allows the first derivative to be estimated in a simple way considering the kernel as a differentiable function obtaining:

$$\frac{\partial \tilde{f}(x)}{\partial x} = \sum_{b=1}^{N} m_b \frac{f_b}{\rho_b} \frac{\partial W(|x - x_b|, h)}{\partial x}. \tag{5}$$

In this way, in SPH each derivative is calculated from the exact derivative of the kernel function. This feature allows to calculate the gradient of any function $f(r)$ in a simple manner through the kernel gradient in such a way that

$$\tilde{\nabla} f(r) = \sum_{b=1}^{N} m_b \frac{f_b}{\rho_b} \nabla W(|r_a - r_b|, h) = \sum_{b=1}^{N} m_b \frac{f_b}{\rho_b} \nabla_a W_{ab}, \tag{6}$$

where r is the position vector.

A graphic description of the kernel function is shown in Fig. 1. The smoothing length is usually constant, however there are works that report algorithms to use a variable h value in each particle [2, 3].

The kernel function can be written as follows on the position r and the smoothing length h

$$W(r, h) = \frac{\sigma}{h^\nu} f(q), \tag{7}$$

where $q = r/h$ and v is the number of spatial dimensions.

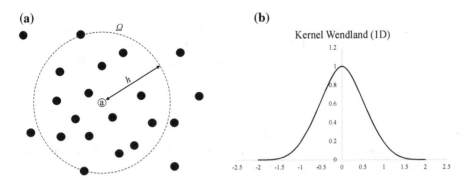

Fig. 1. (a) Representation of the particle of interest "a", neighboring particles (black points), smoothing length (h) and domain of interest (Ω) in the kernel function, (b) example of a kernel function (Wendland) in 1D.

The normalization condition is expressed as:

$$\sigma \int f(q)\, dV = 1,$$

where $dV = dq$, $2\pi q dq$ and $4\pi q2 dq$ in 1D, 2D and 3D, respectively.

2.1 SPH Formalism Used for the Equations of Fluid Dynamics

In this section are described the equations that govern the fluid dynamics in SPH formalism which are obtained from the continuous form of each equation using the methodology shown in the interpolation section.

The equation of continuity described in Lagrangian form is presented in Eq. (8) as

$$\frac{d\rho}{dt} = -\rho \nabla \cdot v. \tag{8}$$

For particle a we have:

$$\frac{d\rho_a}{dt} = -\rho_a (\nabla \cdot v)_a. \tag{9}$$

Using Eq. (6) to evaluate the gradient, it is obtained:

$$\frac{d\rho}{dt} = -\rho_a \sum_{b=1}^{N} m_b \frac{v_b}{\rho_b} \cdot \nabla_a W_{ab}. \tag{10}$$

The momentum conservation equation is defined as

$$\frac{dv}{dt} = \frac{-1}{\rho} \nabla P + g + v_0 \nabla^2 v + \frac{1}{\rho} \nabla \cdot \tau, \tag{11}$$

where the laminar term $(v_0 \nabla^2 v)$ is treated as in Eq. (12) and τ represents the stress tensor. The wall shear stress tensor is calculated from the SPH model according to the Eq. (12) that is completely described in [5].

$$\begin{aligned}
\frac{dv_a}{dt} = &-\sum_b m_b \left(\frac{P_b}{\rho_b^2} + \frac{P_a}{\rho_a^2} \right) \nabla_a W_{ab} + g \\
&\sum_b m_b \left(\frac{4 v_0 r_{ab} \cdot \nabla_a W_{ab}}{(\rho_a + \rho_b)(r_{ab}^2 + \eta^2)} \right) v_{ab} + \\
&\sum_b m_b \left(\frac{\tau_{ij}^b}{\rho_b^2} + \frac{\tau_{ij}^a}{\rho_a^2} \right) \nabla_a W_{ab}
\end{aligned} \tag{12}$$

2.2 SPH Model for Natural Convection

For the numerical simulation the conservation equations of momentum, mass and energy in Lagrangian formalism are considered:

$$\frac{d\rho}{dt} = -\rho \nabla \cdot v, \tag{13}$$

$$\frac{dv}{dt} = \frac{-1}{\rho}\nabla P + \frac{\mu}{\rho}\nabla^2 v + F^B, \tag{14}$$

$$\frac{dT}{dt} = \frac{1}{\rho C_p}\nabla \cdot (k\nabla T), \tag{15}$$

where ρ is the density, t is the time, v is the velocity vector, P is the pressure, μ is the viscosity, F^B is the buoyant force, T is the temperature, C_p is the heat capacity and k is the thermal conductivity coefficient.

The motion of the fluid due to the change in temperature is provided by Boussinesq approximation:

$$F^B = -g\beta(T - T_r), \tag{16}$$

where g is the gravitational acceleration vector, β is the thermal coefficient of volumetric expansion, T is the temperature of the fluid and T_r is the reference temperature of the fluid.

The momentum, continuity and energy equations can be discretized using the SPH formalism and gives:

$$\frac{d\rho}{dt} = -\rho_a \sum_{b=1}^{N} m_b \frac{v_b}{\rho_b} \cdot \nabla_a W_{ab}, \tag{17}$$

$$\frac{dv_a}{dt} = -\sum_{b=1}^{N} m_b \left(\frac{P_b}{\rho_b^2} + \frac{P_a}{\rho_a^2} + \Gamma\right)\nabla_a W_{ab} + g, \tag{18}$$

$$\frac{dT_a}{dt} = \frac{1}{Cp}\sum_{b=1}^{N} \frac{m_b(k_a + k_b)(r_a - r_b)\cdot\nabla_a W_{ab}}{\rho_a\rho_b(r_{ab}^2 + \eta)}(T_a - T_b). \tag{19}$$

Equations (17)–(18) are coupled by the Tait state equation

$$P = B\left[\left(\frac{\rho}{\rho_r}\right)^\gamma - 1\right], \tag{20}$$

where P is the pressure, ρ is the density of the fluid, ρ_r is the reference density, $B = c_0^2\rho_r/\gamma$, $\gamma = 7$ for liquids and $\gamma = 1.4$ for gases.

To consider a change in the reference density ρ_r in Eq. (20) due to the temperature change, the following model is used by the coefficient of volumetric expansion.

$$V_f = V_0\left[1 + \beta(T_f - T_0)\right], \tag{21}$$

where V_f and V_0 are the final and initial volumes respectively and T_f and T_0 are the final and initial temperature, respectively. Relating density, mass and volume

$$\rho = \frac{m}{V}, \tag{22}$$

and substituting the volume from (22) in Eq. (21):

$$\rho_f = \rho\left(\frac{1}{1 + \beta(T_f - T_0)}\right), \tag{23}$$

in this way the reference density $\rho_r = \rho_f$ is evolved in Eq. (23) at each time step, thus the fluid tends to the value of a new density when the fluid temperature changes. This calculation is performed per particle at each time step.

Finally, in Eq. (24) the value of the coefficient of thermal conductivity per particle is calculated by the following expression

$$k_a = \alpha\rho_f Cp. \tag{24}$$

where α is the thermal diffusivity coefficient. With the previous model the change of temperature and density of the fluid affects the coefficient of thermal conductivity considering a more robust model in comparison with the models that consider constant k.

2.3   The Integration Algorithm, (Verlet)

The values of position, density and speed are updated every time step using the Verlet algorithm [6], which does not require multiple calculations for each time step and has a lower computational load compared to other integration techniques. The Verlet algorithm consists of two parts: in the first part, the integration of position, density and velocity is carried out using Eqs. (25)–(28). The second option of Eqs. (25)–(27) is applied every certain number of steps ($t_s \approx 50$). The second option of the algorithm prevents the results from diverging from the correct solution over time.

$$v_a^{t+1} = v_a^{t-1} + 2\Delta t\left(\frac{dv_a}{dt}\right)^t \quad \text{each } t_s \approx 50 \quad v_a^{t+1} = v_a^t + \Delta t\left(\frac{dv_a}{dt}\right)^t, \tag{25}$$

$$\rho_a^{t+1} = \rho_a^{t-1} + 2\Delta t\left(\frac{d\rho_a}{dt}\right)^t \quad \text{each } t_s \approx 50 \quad \rho_a^{t+1} = \rho_a^t + \Delta t\left(\frac{d\rho_a}{dt}\right)^t \tag{26}$$

$$T_a^{t+1} = T_a^{t-1} + 2\Delta t\left(\frac{dT_a}{dt}\right)^t \quad \text{each } t_s \approx 50 \quad T_a^{t+1} = T_a^{t-1} + 2\Delta t\left(\frac{dT_a}{dt}\right)^t \tag{27}$$

$$r_a^{t+1} = r_a^t + \Delta t v_a^t + 0.5\Delta t^2 \left(\frac{dv_a}{dt}\right)^t, \tag{28}$$

Each time step (Δt) reported in Eqs. (25)–(28) is calculated using Eq. (31) to establish a time step that ensures stability in the simulation. Equation (31) is calculated from Eqs. (29) and (30). Equation (29) is calculated based on the maximum acceleration in the fluid, that is, the value of the particle with the greatest acceleration is considered. Equation (30) considers the speed of sound ($c_s = c_0 \rho^3$) as well as the value of the viscosity v. In addition, the passage of time is controlled using the Courant-Friedrich-Levy (CFL) condition [4],

$$\Delta t_f = min_a \left(\sqrt{h/\left|\frac{dv_a}{dt}\right|}\right), \tag{29}$$

$$\Delta t_{cv} = min_a \frac{h}{c_s + max\left|hv_{ij}r_{ij}/\left(r_{ij}^2 + \eta^2\right)\right|}, \tag{30}$$

$$\Delta t = CFL \cdot min\left(\Delta t_f, \Delta t_{cv}\right), \tag{31}$$

where h is the smoothing length, $v_{ij} = v_i - v_j$ and $\eta^2 = 0.01\ h^2$.

3   Results

For the verification and validation of the mathematical modelling, two concentric tubes were simulated according to the results shown by Yang and Kong [8], in which the same ratio of $L/D_i = 0.8$ is considered according to Fig. 2, where in (b) we present the initial conditions for the validation study cases. In all cases the temperature of the contours is maintained constant and the only change is the relationship that exists in the dimensionless numbers of Rayleigh (Ra) and Prandtl (Pr), specifically the value of the thermal diffusivity of the fluid (α).

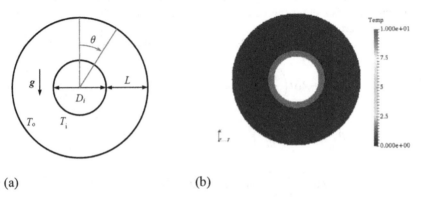

(a)   (b)

Fig. 2. (a) Dimensions of the concentric tube system and (b) Initial conditions for SPH simulations.

$$Ra = \frac{g\beta L^3 \Delta T}{v\alpha} ; Pr = \frac{v}{\alpha}.$$

Numerical simulations for different cases were performed, for Ra = 10^2 and Pr = 10, Ra = 10^4 and Pr = 10, Ra = 10^6 and Pr = 10. In all cases the steady state was reached and then the isothermal profiles between the concentric tubes were obtained. Figure 3 shows these results.

These results correspond well with the data reported in [8]. Validation was done also comparing with experimental data presented in [9]. For this case, Fig. 4 shows the experimental system studied, which consists of a system of concentric cylinders aligned horizontally, where the two cylinders are at constant temperature of different magnitude, the inner cylinder being the highest temperature, as well as the components used to maintain the experimental conditions. The external diameter of the inner cylinder is 3.56 cm, with a thickness of 0.51 cm and the inner diameter of the outer cylinder is 9.25 cm, with a thickness of 0.45 cm, which maintains a relation L/D_i = 0.8.

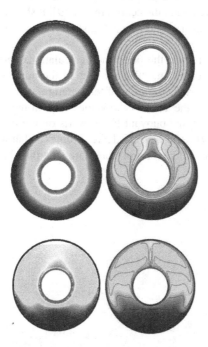

Fig. 3. Comparison of the isothermal profile results with DualSPHysics and those reported by Yang and Kong [8]. From top to bottom we present the cases for Ra = 10^2 and Pr = 10, Ra = 10^4 and Pr = 10, and Ra = 10^6 and Pr = 10, respectively.

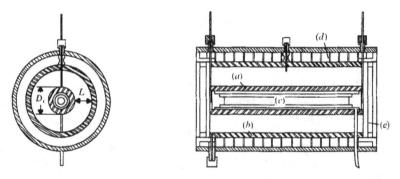

Fig. 4. Diagram of the experimental facility. (a) Internal cylinder. (b) External cylinder. (c) Heater. (d) Cooling water channels. (e) Window. (Taken from reference [9]).

Figure 5 shows the temperature profiles for one of the water tests above, Ra = 10^5 taken from reference [9]. The thermic limit layers near both cylinders are well defined, as is the temperature inversion in the central region [9]. It should be noted that for these results, the experiment was allowed to reach a steady state, it took at least 8 h for the circulation of the water.

As it can be seen in Fig. 5, the performed calculations agree in a comprehensive manner with the experimental data. The analysis of the numerical results is shown in the Figs. 6, 7, 8 and 9 where distribution of temperature, density, thermal conductivity and velocity are shown. In the Table 1 the values used in the simulation are reported.

In Fig. 6, the effect that the buoyant force exerts on the fluid is appreciated, when forming what colloquially it is denominated like "plume". What shows a steady state with a 1 plume, since four different convection states are identified in numerical simulations,

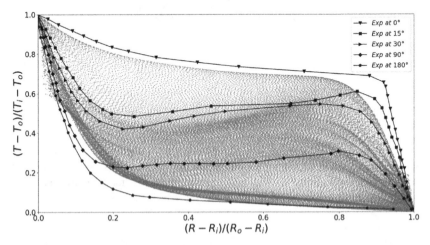

Fig. 5. Dimensionless distribution of radial temperature in water for $Ra = 2.09 \times 10^5$, $Pr = 5.45$, $L/Di = 0.8$. The profiles for $\theta = 0°$, 15°, 30°, 90° and 180° were taken from [9] and compare with the SPH numerical results (red area). (Color figure online)

state stable with 1 plume (SP1), unstable state with 1 plume (UP1), stable state with n (n > 1) plumes (SPN) and unstable state with n (n > 1) plumes (UPN). In Fig. 5 a comparison is made between the results of the simulation carried out in the DualSPHysics code and the results obtained were published in the reference experiment [9].

Finally, another model was studied. In this case, a two-dimensional case with analytical solution, which consists on a plate with dimensions $L = H = 10$ cm and boundary conditions of constant temperature, $T_1 = 0$ °C. The fluid is at an initial temperature, $T_0 = 100$ °C [10]. Figure 10 shows the problem to be solved, with the spatial domain established together with the boundary conditions and the initial conditions.

Table 1. Parameters used in the simulation of concentric tubes.

Parameter	Value
Initial distance between particles	0.02 cm
Viscosity (laminar viscosity treatment + SPS)	1×10^{-6} m^2/s
Initial temperature of the fluid	278.15 K
Step algorithm	Verlet
Kernel	Wendland
Simulation time	3.15 s
Temperature of the cold boundary	278.15 K
Temperature of the hot boundary	348.15 K
Specific heat capacity at constant pressure (Cp)	4.1813 kJ/kgK
Thermal diffusivity coefficient (α)	1.84×10^{-7} m^2/s
Volumetric expansion coefficient (β)	5.82×10^{-4} °C^{-1}
Boundary particles	17644
Fluid particles	143192

In reference [10] the problem was simulated with a number of particles SPH, $N = 1600$, as shown in Fig. 11. The numerical results obtained for different instants of time are presented in Fig. 12.

Table 2 shows the parameters used in the second simulation and the Fig. 12 shows different time instants of the simulation, which show the temperature distribution in the established domain.

The final test show that the mathematical modelling and its solution using the SPH method presents good accuracy for simple cases with analytical solution. Moreover, when the variable thermal conductivity is applied in the mathematical modelling, the accuracy increases for values at the center of the solution comparing whit the numerical results shown by the reference [10].

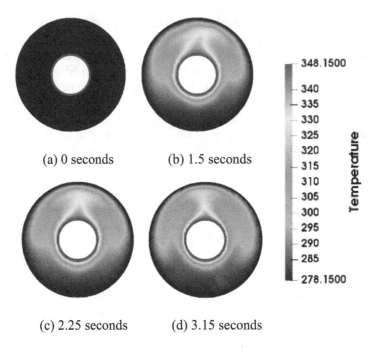

(a) 0 seconds   (b) 1.5 seconds

(c) 2.25 seconds   (d) 3.15 seconds

Fig. 6. Distribution of the temperature at different simulation times.

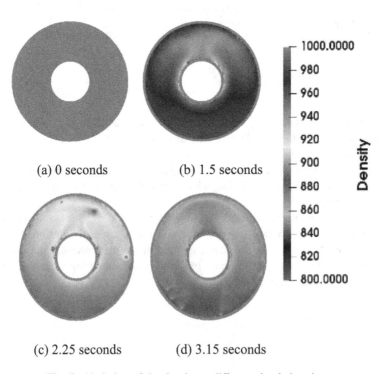

(a) 0 seconds   (b) 1.5 seconds

(c) 2.25 seconds   (d) 3.15 seconds

Fig. 7. Variation of the density at different simulation times.

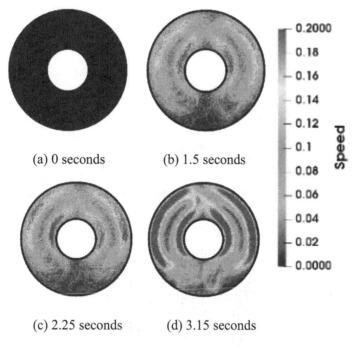

(a) 0 seconds   (b) 1.5 seconds

(c) 2.25 seconds   (d) 3.15 seconds

Fig. 8. Speed profiles at different simulation times.

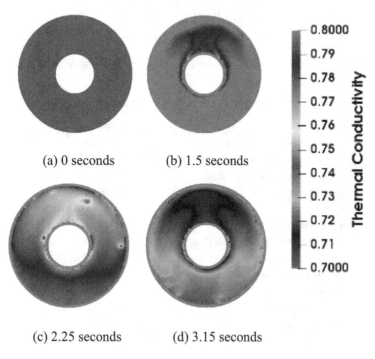

(a) 0 seconds   (b) 1.5 seconds

(c) 2.25 seconds   (d) 3.15 seconds

Fig. 9. Change of thermal conductivity at different simulation times.

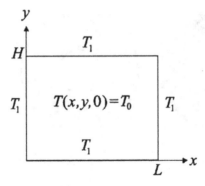

Fig. 10. 2D spatial domain with boundary conditions of constant temperature and initial conditions (Taken from [10]).

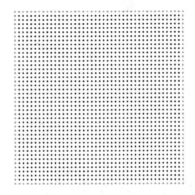

Fig. 11. Spatial discretization of the 2D spatial domain using SPH particles.

Table 2. Simulation parameters used in the second simulation.

Parameter	Value
Initial distance between particles	0.25 cm
Viscosity (laminar viscosity treatment + SPS)	1×10^{-6} m^2/s
Initial temperature of the fluid	373.15 K
Step algorithm	Verlet
Kernel	Wendland
Simulation time	8 s
Temperature of the boundary	273.15 K
Specific heat capacity at constant pressure	4.1813 kJ/kgK
Thermal diffusivity coefficient	1.0×10^{-4} m^2/s
Volumetric expansion coefficient	6.95×10^{-4} °C^{-1}
Boundary particles	81
Fluid particles	1600

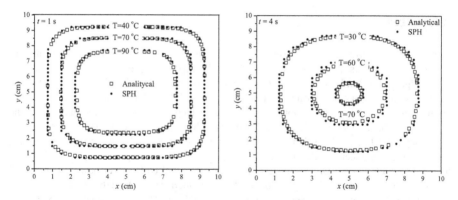

Fig. 12. Comparison of isothermal contours for the SPH numerical results and the analytical solution for $t = 1.0$ and $t = 4.0$ s [10].

4 Conclusions

Despite being a relatively new method for the solution of fluid dynamics problems, the SPH method is more flexible and versatile than mesh-based methods. It has been shown that with the developed tool it is possible to model the heat transfer under natural convection between two concentric rings like the phenomenon of heat transfer between fuel rod and inner cladding wall (heat transfer in fuel gap), which is a fundamental step in safety analysis of nuclear reactors related to thermal limits. Once the verification and validation of the model is finished, next step is to expand to a 3D version of the code in order to be able to perform practical analysis and comparisons with other numerical models that solve in traditional way the heat transfer in the fuel elements of a nuclear reactor.

Acknowledgements. The authors are grateful for the financial support received from the strategic project No. 212602 (AZTLAN Platform) of the Energy Sustainability Sector Fund CONACyT-SENER for the elaboration of this work. Likewise, the author Felipe de Jesus Pahuamba Valdez thanks the National Polytechnic Institute and CONACyT for the scholarship received for their master's studies and Dr. Carlos Enrique Alvarado Rodriguez, for the technical assistance provided for the realization of this project. We acknowledge funding from the European Union's Horizon 2020 Programme under the ENERXICO Project, grant agreement No. 828947 and under the Mexican CONACYT- SENER-Hidrocarburos grant agreement No. B-S-69926. The authors thank ABACUS: Laboratory of Applied Mathematics and High-Performance Computing of the Mathematics Department of CINVESTAV-IPN for providing the computer facilities to accomplish this work.

References

1. Gingold, R.A., Monaghan, J.J.: Smoothed particle hydrodynamics: theory and application to non-spherical stars. Mon. Not. R. Astron. Soc. **181**, 375–389 (1977)
2. Rodríguez-Paz, M., Bonet, J.: A corrected smooth particle hydrodynamics formulation of the shallow-water equations. Comput. Struct. **83**(17–18), 1396–1410 (2005)
3. Sigalotti, L.D.G., López, H., Donoso, A., Sira, E., Klapp, J.: A shock-capturing SPH scheme based on adaptive kernel estimation. J. Comput. Phys. **212**, 124–149 (2006)
4. Monaghan, J.J., Kos, A.: Solitary waves on a cretan beach, journal of waterway port, coastal, and ocean. Engineering **125**, 145–154 (1999)
5. Crespo, A.J.C., et al.: DualSPHysics: open-source parallel CFD solver based on smoothed particle hydrodynamics (SPH). Comput. Phys. Commun. **187**, 204–216 (2015)
6. Verlet, L.: Computer experiments on classical fluids. I. Thermodynamical properties of Lennard-Jones molecules. Phys. Rev. **159**, 98–103 (1967)
7. Harada, T., Koshizuka, S., Kawaguchi, Y.: Smoothed particle hydrodynamics on GPUs. In: Proceedings of the Computer Graphics International, pp. 63–70 (2007)
8. Yang, X., Kong, S.C.: Smoothed particle hydrodynamics method for evaporating multiphase flows. Phys. Rev. E **96**, 033309 (2017). https://doi.org/10.1103/PhysRevE.96.033309
9. Kuehn, T.H., Goldstein, R.J.: An experimental and theoretical study of natural convection in the annulus between horizontal concentric cylinders. J. Fluid Mech. **74**(4), 695–719 (1976). https://doi.org/10.1017/S0022112076002012
10. Rook, R., Yildiz, M., Dost, S.: Modeling transient heat transfer using SPH and implicit time integration. Numer. Heat Transfer Part B: Fundam. **51**(1), 1–23 (2007). https://doi.org/10.1080/10407790600762763

Algorithm Techniques

Public Transportation System Real-Time Re-organization Due to Civil Protection Events

Alfredo Cristóbal-Salas[1]([⊠]), Andrei Tchernykh[2],
Sergio Nesmachnow[3], Bardo Santiago-Vicente[1],
Raúl-Alejandro Luna-Sánchez[4], and Carolina Solis-Maldonado[4]

[1] Facultad de Ingeniería en Electrónica y Comunicaciones,
Universidad Veracruzana, Poza Rica, Mexico
acristobal@uv.mx, bardosantiago.v@gmail.com
[2] Centro de Investigación y de Educación Superior de Ensenada,
Ensenada, Mexico
chernykh@cicese.edu.mx
[3] Facultad de Ingeniería, Universidad de la República, Montevideo, Uruguay
sergion@fing.edu.uy
[4] Facultad de Ciencias Químicas, Universidad Veracruzana, Poza Rica, Mexico
{raluna, casolis}@uv.mx

Abstract. The Civil Protection Department provides assistance to the population when minor or major disasters occur. These events happen without expecting and some of them could affect people using transportation system. Examples of these types of events are: car crashes, explosions, or some kind of accident on the road, among many others. That is why, transportation systems need to consider these types of events to guarantee physical integrity of users. In these cases, authorities should provide real-time solutions that may reduce affectations and keep population's mobility inside a city. That is why, this paper presents a model for a transportation system that help users to reach their final destination when a civil protection events occur. In this model, civil protection authorities can disable a set of stations, users receive a notification and they are solicited to request for a new path recommendation. This new path will not contain any of the stations disabled. The model finds a new path recommendation using a non-dominant function trying to balance between two objectives: Minimize the total riding time and Maximize the distance of the new path stations from the civil protection event. This model was tested for the city of Poza Rica, Mexico which has 45 routes and 1024 stations. In this city, an explosion was simulated and the time to solve all users' paths is measured. Software, that implements this model, runs on a Quad-core Intel Xeon processor 8 GB RAM OSX 10.5 computer.

Keywords: Multi-thread · Public transportation · Civil protection · Decision making · Critical events

© Springer Nature Switzerland AG 2019
M. Torres and J. Klapp (Eds.): ISUM 2019, CCIS 1151, pp. 127–136, 2019.
https://doi.org/10.1007/978-3-030-38043-4_11

1 Introduction

Most of the cities in the globe have a civil protection department which is in charge of planning and management of crisis and incidents taking place within the city. Also, it is responsible for protecting population against threats of aggression, disasters of all kinds and catastrophes, environmental threats, monitoring of operations and reporting accidents and preparation of rescue measures and coordination of emergency resources. Civil protection departments have participated in very well-known events like terrorist attacks in New York [1], Madrid [2], Paris [3], Jerusalem [4], among others. Also, they have participated in earthquakes [5, 6], hurricanes [7, 8] and some other critical events.

In Mexico, there are a Civil Protection Authorities (CPA) at federal, state and municipal levels. They all coordinate the fire departments and they have close contact with civil organizations for specific cases such as the wild animal life or organizations specialized in events like floods, earthquakes, among others.

Public transportation might be affected by any civil protection related event from an obstacle on the road to a major catastrophe. However, the occurrence of these events should not interrupt the transportation system. In other words, the entire transportation system should auto-organize as soon as possible to keep serving users even though any incident occurs in the city.

There is recent research work to help population in case of weather events [9–12] or seismic events [13], vulcanological events [14], or general emergencies like in reference [15]. There are also research works related to dynamic reorganization or adaptation of the public transportation system to unexpected events, such as [16–23].

Unlike previous research works, this paper presents a model that allows the interaction of civil protection authorities with public transportation system when an event occur in the city without the interruption of the entire system. This software has two main objectives: (1) Avoid user's exposure to dangerous events and (2) Keep the users mobility going even if there are these type of events. Details about how these two objectives are fulfilled are presented next.

The rest of this paper is organized as follows. Section 2 proposes the transportation system modeling. Section 3 presents the measuring path alternatives; Sect. 4 presents the system design, implementation and optimization. Section 5 presents the experimental results and, finally in the Sect. 6 some conclusions are presented.

2 System Modeling

This section presents a model to define a public transportation system as a graph with a set of stations and a set of paths, $PTS = G(S, P)$. In this model, some stations might be disabled due to civil protection incidents and the entire PTS should be redesigned in real-time. The model is explained next.

2.1 Defining a Station (S)

A station is a place where users can get on or get off from transportation units. A station could have a physical space or construction; however, it could also be just a space in

the road where transportation units can just stop by. Then, the *i-th* station is defined as:
$s_i = <lat, lng, \psi, \rho, \delta, \phi>$ where:

lat	It is the latitude of a specific station.
lng	It is the longitude of a specific station.
ψ	It is a sequence of time-schedule for that station.
ρ	This variable is a set of stations that are nearby, i.e., stations which are within a maximum walking distance.
δ	It is the distance between the station and the nearest civil protection event.
ϕ	It is the availability of a station. A station is not available when it is overcrowded, it is under maintenance or some other reason.

To clarify the previous description, the definition of the station s_{36F} is presented next.

$$s_{36F} = <20.03458, -96.23454, (07:15, 08:12, 09:34, 10:19, 11:27, 12:16), \{20Q, 36R, 2M\}, 0, 1>$$

2.2 Defining a Path (P)

A path is a sequence of stations where users can go from an initial station to a final one. In other words, a path is considered as valid if it can take a user from an initial to a final station. However, this model considers that a path could start from the initial station or any other one which is nearby the initial. Similarly, a path ends in the final station or any other one which is nearby the final.

This model is non-deterministic, then, any station could have multiple options where users can go from a specific station. Thus, a sequence is considered as valid when the sequence arrives to a final station or some other one which is nearby the final. Under this perspective, a path can be defined as follows:

$$P = (S, V, f, I, F) \tag{1}$$

S	It is a set which contains all stations in the PTS. Example $S = \{s_1, \ldots, s_n\}$.
V	It is a set of input sequences that helps to select the next station when there are several options to choose.
f	It is a function that decides which is the next station to go. $f : S \times V \times \{0, 1\} \to ST$, where T is a time stamp.
$I \subseteq S$	It is a sub-set of stations considered as initial, i.e., where user starts the journey.
$F \subseteq S$	It is a sub-set of stations considered as final, i.e., where user ends the journey.

2.3 Example of the Model Execution

In this section, let's review an example of a PTS that implements the model defined above. Figure 1 shows a PTS which contains ten stations. User wants to travel from station s_1 to station s_{10}; let's also define four input sequences: A = (1,0), B = (0,1), C = (1,0,0), D = (0,1,0), E = (0,0,1), F = (1,0,0,0), G = (0,1,0,0), H = (0,0,1,0), I = (0,0,0,1). The results of the model for each input string is presented next.

$$PTS = (\{s_1, s_2, s_3, s_4, s_5, s_6, s_7, s_8, s_9, s_{10}\}, P)$$

Input sequence: V = (A, H)
The execution of the model shows the following evaluation of the function f:

1. $f(s_1, A, 1) = \{s_2, 10:30\}$
2. $f(s_2, H, 1) = non\,defined$
3. $output : error$

Evaluation shows an error due to the function $f(s_2, H, 1)$ is not defined then the model rejects the path as a valid path to go from station s_1 to s_8.

Input sequence: V = (B, G)
Running the model using the input sequence produces the following output.

1. $f(s_1, B, 1) = \{s_3, 05.32\}$
2. $f(s_3, G, 1) = \{s_8, 08:37\}$
3. $s_8 \in F$
4. $output : acepted.Path = (s_1, s_3, s_8)$

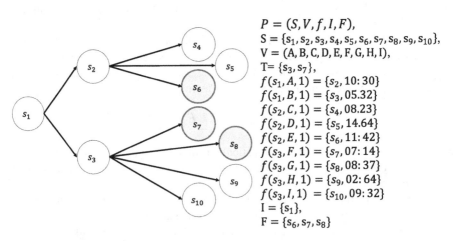

$$P = (S, V, f, I, F),$$
$$S = \{s_1, s_2, s_3, s_4, s_5, s_6, s_7, s_8, s_9, s_{10}\},$$
$$V = (A, B, C, D, E, F, G, H, I),$$
$$T= \{s_3, s_7\},$$
$$f(s_1, A, 1) = \{s_2, 10:30\}$$
$$f(s_1, B, 1) = \{s_3, 05.32\}$$
$$f(s_2, C, 1) = \{s_4, 08.23\}$$
$$f(s_2, D, 1) = \{s_5, 14.64\}$$
$$f(s_2, E, 1) = \{s_6, 11:42\}$$
$$f(s_3, F, 1) = \{s_7, 07:14\}$$
$$f(s_3, G, 1) = \{s_8, 08:37\}$$
$$f(s_3, H, 1) = \{s_9, 02:64\}$$
$$f(s_3, I, 1) = \{s_{10}, 09:32\}$$
$$I = \{s_1\},$$
$$F = \{s_6, s_7, s_8\}$$

Fig. 1. Portion of a public transportation system with ten stations where it is possible to travel from station $\{s_1\}$ to stations $\{s_6, s_7, s_8\}$.

3   Measuring Paths

This section presents how each path is evaluated in order to select the path more suitable for the user where two objectives are balanced: total traveling time and distance between station and the civil protection event. The definition of these two measures is presented next.

3.1   Total Traveling Time in Paths (T_{total})

This variable measures the time spent by a user when riding the transportation system. This variable considers two values: time on-board (T_{travel}) and waiting time (T_{wait}).

$$T_{total} = T_{travel} + T_{wait} \qquad (2)$$

Time on-board (T_{travel}). This value is the time that user spends using the transportation system. This time is the summation of all times defined in the function f for each trajectory from one station to the next one. For example, $T_{travel}(s_1, s_2, s_4) = 10{:}30 + 08{:}23 = 18{:}53$.

Waiting time (T_{wait}). It is the difference between the current time and the next scheduled time (ψ) for a transportation unit to arrive to a station.

3.2   Distance Between Station and Events (T)

When there is an event that affects the transportation system, the stations which are nearby the event have to be disabled. All stations which are disabled are contained in the set $D = \{s_a, \ldots, s_z\}$; where $D \subseteq S$. For example, let's assume that a civil protection event has occurred for the transportation system defined in Fig. 1. Then $D = \{s_3, s_8\}$ is the set which contains all stations affected. In this case, all evaluations of function f that consider the disabled stations have to be temporary disabled. In this case, the resultant transportation system is described in Fig. 2.

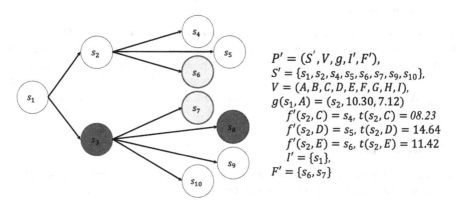

$$P' = (S', V, g, I', F'),$$
$$S' = \{s_1, s_2, s_4, s_5, s_6, s_7, s_9, s_{10}\},$$
$$V = (A, B, C, D, E, F, G, H, I),$$
$$g(s_1, A) = (s_2, 10.30, 7.12)$$
$$f'(s_2, C) = s_4, \; t(s_2, C) = 08.23$$
$$f'(s_2, D) = s_5, \; t(s_2, D) = 14.64$$
$$f'(s_2, E) = s_6, \; t(s_2, E) = 11.42$$
$$I' = \{s_1\},$$
$$F' = \{s_6, s_7\}$$

Fig. 2. Modified transportation system when there has occurred a civil protection event that affected the stations $D = \{s_3, s_8\}$.

Also, $\forall s_i \in S$ in P' has to compute the distance between each station and the civil protection event (δ_i). Then, the distance between the path and the event is the $Min(\delta_i)$. When the event has finished, $D = \emptyset$ meaning that all stations are now available again and all $\delta_i = 0$ (See Fig. 3).

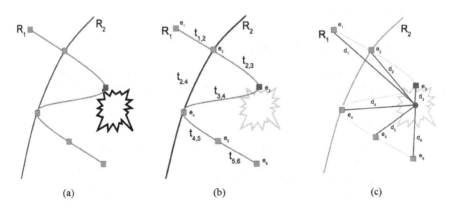

(a)   (b)   (c)

Fig. 3. Graphical description of (a) occurrence of an unexpected event, (b) total time to complete the journey (T_{total}). (c) The path distance from the event (Γ).

4 System Design

This section presents the design details of a distributed computer system to allow civil protection authorities to issue an alert to all users of the transportation user. Once the alert has occurred, users are forced to redirect their trajectory to avoid areas where unexpected incidents have occurred in the city. This model is implemented in under client-server software architecture (see Fig. 4). Details of this implementation are described next.

4.1 Client Modules

This software has two client modules: (1) 'User oriented' software client. This module is used to keep interact users when incidents occur. Also, the module allows users to solve their path-planning requests. (2) 'Civil protection authority' (CPA) software client. In this module, civil protection authorities can disable or enable stations in the transportation system. This module does not allow direct communication with users or with transportation units.

4.2 Server Module

Software architecture considers two server modules as can be seen in Fig. 4 called: User and CPA servers. The functionality for each server is described next.

(1) User server. This server computes the total traveling time (T_{total}) for each path-planning and the distance between stations and events (Γ).

(2) Civil protection authority (CPA) Server. This server takes care of all operations related to activating or deactivating stations. These operations are done when a request is received from client-side software. This server receives a JSON containing the geo-positions of the affected area and it computes the distance between the geo-position of the affected area and all the stations in the transportation system.

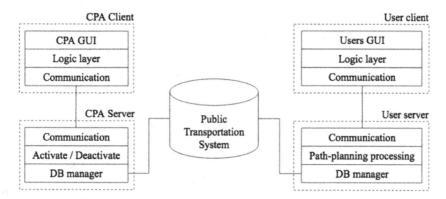

Fig. 4. Client-server software architecture.

5   Implementation and Preliminary Results

This section presents results of the model implementation presented in this paper. The client-user module is implemented as a mobile application for Android 4.4 or higher while the server-user module is implemented in Java 8. The CPA-user module is implemented as a Web + JavaScript application while the CPA-server version is implemented in Java 8. The database is implemented with the MySQL administrator 5.7.24.

This software is being tested in the city of Poza Rica, Mexico where there is high probability of an explosion due to the presence of oil, gas and energy companies. This transportation system contains 45 taxi and bus routes with 1,024 stations in total. The entire transportation system contains a total of 1,048,576 trajectories available to go. This algorithm first solves the problem of finding a path to travel from the initial to final station using the R-Library called **NSGA2R** and the function **nsga2** which implements a genetic algorithm. This algorithm need to minimize the two objectives: Min (ψ) and Min (δ). Figure 5 shows how the execution time reduces when increasing the number of processes in R using the **mclapply** function.

The paths recommended by the genetic algorithms are stored in the vector called **value**. This vector is filled after the execution of the function **nsga2** R-function. For instance, this vector contains the sequence of stations to complete the path and the values of the functions γ and δ. Once the path is defined then a review process eliminates all paths containing the stations disabled, then, finally the remaining paths are presented as a result.

Figure 5 shows the execution time for the algorithm varying the number of cores in the `mclapply` R-function. As expected, the execution time is reduced significatively when augmenting the number of available cores. This algorithm runs on a Quad-core Intel Xeon processor 8 GB RAM OSX 10.5 computer.

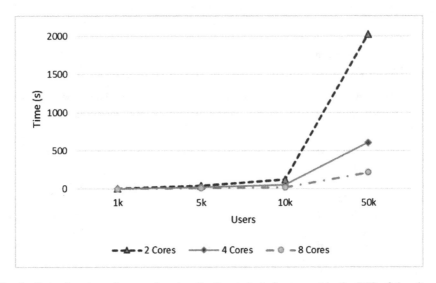

Fig. 5. Execution time of processing deactivating trajectories request in the PTS of the city of Poza Rica, Mexico.

6 Conclusions

This paper presents the definition and implementation of an algorithm to disable paths of a transportation system when unexpected events occur in a city. When one of these events occurs, the city authorities must take care of the population by keeping users away from the affected area but at the same time the city must continue with their mobility in the most regular way. This paper considers events such as explosions, accidents, floods, tree falls due to strong winds, etc. In all cases, the authorities must react in a matter of minutes to avoid affecting the civilian population.

The results presented shows that it is possible to run this algorithm in a regular computer with desired results. Even more, this algorithm allows civil protection authorities re-adjust the PTS under five minutes with more than 50,000 users. These results, of course, will change varying the geoposition of the incident and the amount of users in the PTS. However, these results bring hope to authorities to provide a more reliable and secure transportation system.

Acknowledgements. This research is sponsored in part by the Mexican Agency for International Development Cooperation (AMEXCID) and the Uruguayan Agency for International Cooperation (AUCI) through the Joint Uruguay-Mexico Cooperation Fund.

This research work reflects only the points of view of the authors and not those of the AMEXCID or the AUCI.

The authors are grateful for the support and facilities of the authorities of the Municipality of the city of Poza Rica de Hidalgo to carry out this investigation, especially to the Directorate of Civil Protection for providing relevant information to conclude this research work.

References

1. El País Newspaper Homepage. https://bit.ly/2IPnGGj. Accessed 20 Feb 2019
2. El País Newspaper Homepage. https://bit.ly/2GR0SDP. Accessed 20 Feb 2019
3. TIME Newspaper Home Page. https://bit.ly/2LjRTiy. Accessed 20 Feb 2019
4. The New York Times Newspaper Homepage. https://nyti.ms/2GQf53W. Accessed 20 Feb 2019
5. Forbes México Home Page. https://bit.ly/2PzhwdS. Accessed 20 Feb 2019
6. The New York Times Newspaper Homepage. https://nyti.ms/2xV0KQm. Accessed 20 Feb 2019
7. The New York Times Newspaper Homepage. https://nyti.ms/2xifCGw. Accessed 20 Feb 19
8. Forbes México Newspaper Home Page. https://bit.ly/2GHy9A8. Accessed 20 Feb 2019
9. Bumbary, T.M.: Utilizing a network of wireless weather stations to forecast weather in developing countries. In: Integrated STEM Education Conference, pp. 109–111 (2017)
10. Wibisono, M.N., Ahmad A.S.: Weather forecasting using knowledge growing system (KGS). In: 2nd International Conferences on Information Technology, Information Systems and Electrical Engineering (ICITISEE), pp. 35–38 (2017)
11. Majumdar, I., Banerjee, B., Preeth, M.T., Hota, D.M.K.: Design of weather monitoring system and smart home automation. In: IEEE International Conference on System, Computation, Automation and Networking (ICSCA), pp. 1–5 (2018)
12. Naik, N.: Flooded streets—a crowdsourced sensing system for disaster response: a case study. In IEEE International Symposium on Systems Engineering (ISSE), pp. 1–3 (2016)
13. Gula, T., Grosu, C., Nanuti, D., Mocanu, M., Ciolofan, S.N.: ArcGIS based visualization tool for assessment of earthquakes impact. In: Ninth International Conference on Complex, Intelligent, and Software Intensive Systems, pp. 308–313 (2015)
14. Criollo, C.L., Gómez, A.B., Guerrero, N.O., Granados, H.D.: Strategic planning of information from research and volcano monitoring institutions in latin America. In: Workshop on Engineering Applications - International Congress on Engineering, pp. 1–5 (2015)
15. Rego, A., Garcia, L., Sendra, S., Lloret, J.: Software defined networks for traffic management in emergency situations. In: Fifth International Conference on Software Defined Systems (SDS), pp. 45–51 (2018)
16. Boni, G., et al: User oriented multidisciplinary approach to flood mapping: the experience of the Italian civil protection system. In: IEEE International Geoscience and Remote Sensing Symposium (IGARSS), pp. 834–837 (2015)
17. Meiying, J., Hainana, L., Led, N.: The evaluation studies of regional transportation accessibility based on intelligent transportation system: take the example in Yunnan Province of China. In: International Conference on Intelligent Transportation, Big Data and Smart City, pp. 862–865 (2015)
18. Zhang, Z., Zhu, M., Zhou, H.: Dynamical complexity analysis of beijing transportation network based on district structural information. In: Chinese Control and Decision Conference (CCDC), pp. 755–760 (2018)

19. Zhang, Z., Ma, W., Zhang, Z., Xiong, C.: A transportation network stability analysis method based on betweenness centrality entropy maximization. In: Chinese Control and Decision Conference (CCDC), pp. 2741–2745 (2018)
20. Wang, F., Zhang, J.J.: Transportation 5.0 in CPSS: towards ACP-based society-centered intelligent transportation. In: IEEE 20th International Conference on Intelligent Transportation Systems (ITSC), pp. 762–767 (2017)
21. Aulya, R., Hindersah, H., Prhiatmanto, A.S., Rhee, K.H.: An authenticated passengers based on dynamic QR code for bandung smart transportation systems. In: 6th International Annual Engineering Seminar (InAES), pp. 23–27 (2016)
22. Rajput, P., Chaturvedi, M., Patel, P.: Advanced urban public transportation system for Indian scenarios. In: ICDCN 2019 Proceedings of the 20th International Conference on Distributed Computing and Networking, pp. 327–336 (2019)
23. Lin, F., Hsieh, H.: SRC: an intelligent and interactive route planning maker for deploying new transportation services. In: SIGSPATIAL Special, pp. 6–7 (2019)

Multi-objective Evolutive Multi-thread Path-Planning Algorithm Considering Real-Time Extreme Weather Events

Alfredo Cristóbal-Salas[1(✉)], Andrei Tchernykh[2],
Sergio Nesmachnow[3], Bardo Santiago-Vicente[1],
Raúl Alejandro Luna-Sánchez[4], and Carolina Solis-Maldonado[4]

[1] Facultad de Ingeniería en Electrónica y Comunicaciones,
Universidad Veracruzana, Poza Rica, Mexico
acristobal@uv.mx, bardosantiago.v@gmail.com
[2] Centro de Investigación y de Educación Superior de Ensenada,
Ensenada, Mexico
chernykh@cicese.edu.mx
[3] Facultad de Ingeniería, Universidad de la República, Montevideo, Uruguay
sergion@fing.edu.uy
[4] Facultad de Ciencias Químicas, Universidad Veracruzana, Poza Rica, Mexico
{raluna, casolis}@uv.mx

Abstract. Public transportation systems (PTS) should not only guarantee the mobility of users in the city but also, it should guarantee users health during trips. For example, users with health problems such as: high blood pressure, migraine, fever, asthma, back pain, dizziness, among others could be affected in their health when using the system in extreme weather conditions. This paper proposes an algorithm that makes path recommendations maximizing protection to weather conditions and minimizing the total traveling time until reaching the final destination. This paper presents the execution of this algorithm for thousands of user requests running on a Quad-core Intel Xeon processor 8 GB RAM OSX 10.5.

Keywords: Smart-cities · Transportation · Path-planning · Health · Extreme weather

1 Introduction

In recent years, most cities have intense weather patterns; this trend seems to continue the next coming years. Some of these patterns are: torrential rains, heat waves, intense cold, strong winds, among others. These patterns are beginning to be a common phenomenon on several cities around the world. This tendency is so evident that international organizations such as the United Nations [1], UNESCO [2] and the European Union [3] contemplate this issue directly in their work plans.

In particular, the Mexican Federal Government analyzes climate change, and its effects, on Mexican inhabitants through the National Institute of Ecology and Climate Change [4]. This institute has several studies on the effects of climate change in

© Springer Nature Switzerland AG 2019
M. Torres and J. Klapp (Eds.): ISUM 2019, CCIS 1151, pp. 137–146, 2019.
https://doi.org/10.1007/978-3-030-38043-4_12

different sectors in Mexico [5]. Government policies on this issue has been strengthened over time. These policies have been included in several free trade agreements between Mexico and other countries to prevent environment deterioration. Such is the case of the USMCA trade agreement with the United States of America and Canada [6]. All these international policies let us see that climate change and its impact on the population should be considered as a priority. That is why, the population in urban areas must adjust their daily lives to these extreme weather conditions.

Consider the case of people with health problems such as high blood pressure, fever, migraine, allergies, asthma, back problems, diabetes, etc. This sector of the population could be affected when they are exposed to extreme weather conditions. For example, people with respiratory problems should not be exposed to sudden changes in temperature; the same goes for people with diabetes, who should not spend a lot of time without checking their glucose levels. Even elderly people how could be affected when seated for long periods of time.

Public transportation users are vulnerable to weather when they are on board at buses, taxis, subway, etc., or when they walk between transfer stations. This is why, public transportation authorities should consider reducing the exposure of users to climatic events that put their health at risk.

This paper proposes a strategy to recommend the use of public transportation that reduces traveling time; but this strategy also reduces health risks when vulnerable people are using the public transportation units.

There are several studies about people mobility in public transportation. There are studies about static travel planning considering different construction techniques [7–13]. There are also studies about tracking routes in multimodal units [14]. Similarly, there are studies on dynamic planning [15–17] and analysis of multiple objectives [18–20]. Moreover, there are studies on user's mobility who use private transportation as the one presented in [21]. In addition, there are some studies that present software architectures based on ontologies that use multiple criteria for decision-making techniques to design a customized route planning system [22–24].

However, this paper presents a different approach because it is oriented to reduce health problems not provoked by transportation system but provoked by climatic events. Paper orientation gives another meaning to traveling time minimization, but it also introduces a proposal on how it is possible to prevent affectations to user's health by checking transfer stations.

This paper is organized as follows: in section two, the modeling of the system is presented. The third section presents how the user protection measurements are defined.

Section four present the design of the algorithm while section five presents a parallelization of the Algorithm. Finally, in section six, some conclusions of the utility of the algorithm as a tool for the protection of public transport users are presented.

2   System Modeling

In this section, we present a mathematical model of a public transportation system *(PTS)* that considers weather conditions in order to make path-recommendations. *PTS = G(S, P)* where S is a set of stations and P is a set of paths between stations. Some definitions are presented next:

2.1   Defining Stations

A station is where users can get on and get off from transportation units. A station is also a space where users wait until the transportation unit arrives to that location. Stations could be physical which means that there is a physical construction, or they could be virtual which means that there is a space used as a station but there is no construction or special designated space for that station. For this paper, there are two types of stations: simple stations and transfer stations.

2.1.1   Simple Stations

A simple station, the i-th station in the transportation system at time t, is represented as $s_i^t = \langle \alpha_i^t, \beta_i^t, e_i^t, \delta_i \rangle$. Variables are described next:

α_i^t This function retrieves the next scheduled arrival of a transportation unit to the *i-th* station at time t. For instance, $\alpha_{17E}^{09:15}$ retrieves the next scheduled-time when a transportation unit would arrive to the station 17E. When current time is 09:15 h then the value of α would be $\alpha = 09:23$ h; while $\alpha_{17E}^{15:35} = 15:57$. These values are statically assigned to each station.

β_i^t This function retrieves the number of users in the *i-th* station at time *t*. For instance, $\beta_{17E}^{16:24}$ retrieves the number of users already present at station 17E at 16:24 h; then, an answer would be $\beta = 28$ while $\beta_{17E}^{20:18} = 52$. These values come from statistical analysis done at each station in the *PTS*.

e_i^t This function retrieves all stations nearby the station s_i^t under some criteria of proximity. For example:

$$e_i^{08:46} = \{\langle s_{20F}^{08:46}, 65 \rangle, \langle s_{11H}^{08:46}, 70 \rangle, < s_{8C}^{08:46}, 120 > \}$$

These values are statically assigned to each station in the PTS.

δ_i This variable is the adaptation of the *i-th* station to extreme weather conditions. This value comes from a checklist applied to that particular station which contributes to rate how well adapted is that station to extreme weather. For instance, if the station has roof, walls, sits, or it is adapted to avoid floods, it is near to a safe place, etc. All features previously described make a station has a better protection rate $0 \leq \delta_i \leq 1$.

With these previous definitions, it is possible to define a set of stations in the entire transportation system. This set is defined as $S = \left\{ s_1^t, s_2^t, \ldots, s_\eta^t \right\}$ where $\eta = |S|$ is the number of stations in the PTS.

2.1.2   Transfer Stations

A transfer station is a tuple defined as: $\varphi^t_{xy} = <s^t_x, s^t_y, w_{xy}, \sigma_{xy}, \tau>$ and it is required when users need to change transportation units to continue their journey. The description of its elements is presented next.

$s^t_x \epsilon S$ This is a station where users get off from a transportation unit.

$s^t_y \epsilon S$ This is a station where users wait until they get on a transportation unit in order to continue their journey.

w_{xy} It is the time users spend when walking from station s^t_x to station s^t_y.

σ_{xy} It represents the level of protection of a transfer station to extreme weather conditions $0 \leq \sigma_{xy} \leq 1$. When considering a transfer station with station s^t_x and station s^t_y, then, $\sigma_{xy} = (\delta_x + \delta_y)/2$.

τ The status of a transfer station is represented as $\tau = \{0, 1\}$ where

$$\tau = \begin{cases} 0, & \textit{the transfer station is not} - \textit{available} \\ 1, & \textit{the transfer station is available} \end{cases}$$

After these definitions, the set of all transfer stations in the transportation system is defined as: $\Theta = \left\{\varphi^t_{ab}, \ldots, \varphi^t_{yz}\right\}$ where $\psi = |\Theta|$ is the total number of transfer stations.

2.2   Defining Path Recommendations

Public transportation system has two types of paths: simple paths and complex paths recommendations. The details of their definition are presented next.

2.2.1   Simple-Path Recommendation

A simple path in the transportation system is a sequence of stations needed to travel from one station to another. They are represented as: $p^t_{az} = \left(s^t_a, \ldots, s^t_z\right)$ where s^t_a is the beginning of the path and s^t_z is the final destination. The number of stations in the path is defined as: $\mu = |p^t_{az}|; \ 0 < \mu \leq \eta$. If the station s^t_z is the next station from s^t_a then $\mu = 1$. If user requires two stations to travel from s^t_a to s^t_z then $\mu = 2$ and so on.

The set containing all paths in the transportation system is defined as: $P = \{p^t_{12}, \ldots, p^t_{wz}\}$. The number of paths in P is defined as $= |P|$.

2.2.2   Complex-Path Recommendation

A complex path is a sequence of two or more simple paths joined by transfer stations. They are represented as follows: $\phi^t_{az} = \left(s^t_a, \ldots, \varphi^t_{mn}, \ldots, s^t_z\right)$. The entire complex path could be disabled if at least one transfer station is disabled ($\tau = 0$).

2.3   Flexible Path Recommendation

Under this public transportation model, it is possible that a transfer station could be disabled ($\tau = 0$) when the number of users exceeds its capacity, or a transportation authority decides to disable it. So, in other to make the transportation system more flexible, the model finds additional paths starting or finishing in alternative stations.

These additional paths are added to the original set of paths and the system now has to find an optimal recommendation considering all possible paths.

To clarify this concept, let's present an example. Be p'_{ij} the path needed to be more flexible. To make this happen, it is necessary to find all stations which are nearby the initial station (s^t_i). This set of stations could be $I = \{s^t_1, s^t_2, s^t_3\}$. Also, it is necessary to find all stations which are nearby the final station (s^t_j); this set of stations could be $F = \{s^t_a, s^t_b\}$. Thus, a set of alternative paths to the original path p'_{ij} could be defined as follows: $e^t_{ij} = \{p^t_{1a}, p^t_{1b}, p^t_{2a}, p^t_{2b}, p^t_{3a}, p^t_{3b}\}$. Therefore, $E = \{e^t_{ab}, \ldots, e^t_{yz}\}$ defines a set of alternative paths in the transportation system. From this perspective, if a path is disabled for some reason, then, the transportation system has some alternative paths still to consider.

3 Measuring User Protection

In this section, it is defined how the transportation system could protect users from extreme weather conditions. There are two variables to consider: total traveling time and user protection in transfer stations. The definition of them is presented next.

3.1 Total Traveling Time in Paths (T_{total})

The total traveling time is a variable that counts the amount of time that a user spends in the transportation system. This variable considers three values: time on-board (T_{board}), walking time (T_{walk}) and waiting time (T_{wait}).

$$T_{total} = T_{board} + T_{walk} + T_{wait} \tag{1}$$

- Time on-board (T_{board}). This value is the time that user spends on board of a transportation unit.
- The walking time (T_{walk}). This variable is the time needed to walk from the final station of the first path to the initial station of the next path.
- The waiting time (T_{wait}). It is the difference between the current time and the next scheduled time for a transportation unit to arrive to a transfer station.

The computation of T_{total} varies when a path is simple or complex, more information on these variations are shown next.

3.2 For Simple Paths

Let's define $t_{i(i+1)}$ as the time spent by users when traveling on transportation units from station s^t_i to the immediate next station s^{t+1}_{i+1}. Then, the time (β_{ij}) spent by users traveling in a path (p'_{az}) could be defined as follows:

$$\beta_{ij} = \sum_{i=1}^{n} t_{i(i+1)} \tag{2}$$

Then, for simple paths like $p_{az}^t = \left(s_a^t, \ldots, s_z^t\right)$, T_{board} is computed as the time spent in the path p_{ij}^t without leaving the transportation unit. Thus, $T_{board} = \beta_{ij}$, $T_{walk} = 0$ because the user does not need to walk during the travel. $T_{wait} = \alpha_a^t$; where α_a^t is the time spent by users waiting at the initial station s_a^t.

3.3 For Complex Paths

In case of a complex path, like the following: $\phi_{az}^t = \left(s_a^t, \ldots, \varphi_{mn}^t, \ldots, \varphi_{wy}^t, \ldots, s_z^t\right)$, the time on-board (T_{board}) is the summation of the time to ride the three paths: p_{am}^t, p_{nw}^t, p_{yz}^t. Then

$$T_{board} = \beta_{am} + \beta_{nw} + \beta_{yz} \tag{3}$$

The value of T_{walk} considers the walking time inside the transfer station φ_{mn}^t to go from station s_m^t to station s_n^t and inside the transfer station φ_{wy}^t from station s_w^t to station s_y^t. Then, this variable is computed as follows:

$$T_{walk} = w_{mn} + w_{wy} \tag{4}$$

Finally, the waiting time (T_{wait}) considering the transfer stations φ_{mn}^t, φ_{wy}^t is defined as $T_{wait} = \alpha_a + \alpha_n + \alpha_y$ where α_a is the waiting time at station s_a^t, α_n is the waiting time at station s_n^t and, α_y is the waiting time at station s_y^t.

3.4 Defining the Total User Protection (Υ)

The value of the total user protection variable is computed considering the protection to extreme weather that each transfer station.

3.4.1 For Simple Paths

Considering the path $p_{az}^t = \left(s_a^t, \ldots, s_z^t\right)$ then $\Upsilon = \delta_a$ where δ_a is the protection of the initial station s_a^t.

3.4.2 For Complex Paths

Let's again consider the complex path : $p_{az}^t = \left(s_a^t, \ldots, \varphi_{mn}^t, \ldots, \varphi_{wy}^t, \ldots, s_z^t\right)$, this path has two transfer stations and each station has a value for adaptation to extreme weather defined as: σ_{mn} and σ_{wy}. Also, δ_a is the protection of the initial station s_a^t. Then, total user protection is defined as follows:

$$\Upsilon = \delta_a + \sigma_{mn} + \sigma_{wy} \tag{5}$$

4 Path Selection Algorithm

This section shows the algorithm to recommend a path in the transportation system that considers $ax\{\Upsilon\}, Min\{T_{total}\}$ (See Table 1).

Table 1. Algorithm to select a path recommendation using evolutive computing.

1.	$P' = P \cup E$
2.	For all $p_{ij}^t \in P'$ with initial station s_a^t, and final station s_z^t.
3.	For all φ_{xy}^t *in the path*
4.	If $\tau = 0$ then
5.	status=0
6.	end if
7.	end for
8.	if status $\neq 0$
9.	*Compute* T_{total}
10.	Compute Υ
11.	Store path in vector χ
12.	Increment β_i^t in all transfer stations at time t.
13.	end if
14.	end for
15.	Select a path from χ that fulfills both objectives: $Max\{\Upsilon\}, Min\{T_{total}\}$.

Experimentation for this algorithm considers the city of Poza Rica's public transportation system (PR-PTS). This system has 45 routes, 1024 stations and a total of 1024×1024 paths where users can travel from a station to any other station in the PTS.

Using this PTS, the algorithm has to select a path that fulfils both objectives: $Max\{\Upsilon\}, Min\{T_{total}\}$. In order to explain how the algorithm works, a pair of stations from PR-PTS are selected.

Initial station: station [A-EB500] named "Civic Plaza" belonging to route [RB03-A] "Downtown – November 20th".

Final station: station [B-EB196] named "Gas station Lopez" belonging to the route [RTX05-B] "Technologic - Downtown".

This pair of stations have three paths in the PR-PTS to take users from initial station to final station. However, the initial station has thirteen nearby stations and the final station has four nearby stations. Thus, the algorithm considers 3 solutions for user-selected initial and final stations; but there are also (13 * 4) alternative solutions.

Each alternative path which consist of an alternative initial station and an alternative final station. In the case of the PR-PTS has 10 possible paths in average. Thus, the algorithm has to decide an optimal path that satisfies both objectives: $Max\{\Upsilon\}, Min\{T_{total}\}$ between 3 + [(13 * 4) * 10] = 523 possible solutions.

Figure 1 shows the evaluation of all 523 possible paths to travel from initial station to final station. X-axis considers the total time (T_{total}) spent by user in the PR-PTS and y-axis considers the protection value (Υ) of a path for user sensitive to extreme weather conditions.

Figure 2 shows the Pareto front of paths that fulfills both objectives: $Max\{\Upsilon\}$, $Min\{T_{total}\}$.

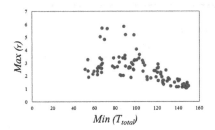
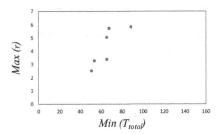

Fig. 1. Evaluation of all possible paths going from initial to destination stations.

Fig. 2. Paths that fulfills both objectives: $Max\{\Upsilon\}, Min\{T_{total}\}$.

5 Algorithm Parallelization

This section presents the parallelization of the requests for path recommendations made by public transportation users. For example, Fig. 3 shows the time spent the computation of selecting a path recommendation for 2, 4, 8, 16 thousands of users. As can be seen, the algorithm is time consuming. However, Fig. 4 shows how processing time can be reduced when using concurrent programming. Distributing tasks between the processing elements is a well-known technique for reducing computation time.

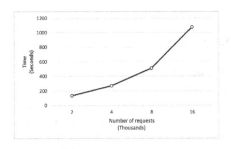
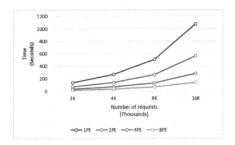
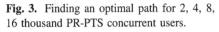

Fig. 3. Finding an optimal path for 2, 4, 8, 16 thousand PR-PTS concurrent users.

Fig. 4. Optimization of the algorithm using distributed computing.

6   Conclusions

This paper presents a research oriented to help people sensitive to extreme weather conditions such as: elders, pregnant women, children, etc. This research involves an algorithm that makes path recommendations considering the minimum time needed to travel from one station in the PTS to another one. At the same time, the algorithm considers maximizing the user protection against extreme climate conditions.

The algorithm considers all paths possible including alternative paths to departure from stations which are nearby the initial station or arrive to a station which is nearby the final station. Once all paths are defined, then, the algorithm uses a non-dominant function to decide which path better fulfills bi-objective criteria to maximize user protection and minimize the total time users spend in the transportation system.

This paper also shows how to improve the algorithm performance by distributing the requests for path recommendations between several processing units.

Acknowledgements. This research is sponsored in part by the Mexican Agency for International Development Cooperation (AMEXCID) and the Uruguayan Agency for International Cooperation (AUCI) through the Joint Uruguay-Mexico Cooperation Fund. This research work reflects only the points of view of the authors and not those of the AMEXCID or the AUCI.

The authors are grateful for the support and facilities of the authorities of the Municipality of the city of Poza Rica de Hidalgo to carry out this investigation, especially to the Directorate of Civil Protection for providing relevant information to conclude this research work.

References

1. United Nations Homepage. http://www.un.org/en/sections/issues-depth/climate-change/index.html. Accessed 06 Feb 2019
2. UNESCO Homepage. https://unesdoc.unesco.org/ark:/48223/pf0000190101. Accessed 06 Feb 2019
3. European Union Homepage. https://ec.europa.eu/clima/policies/eccp_en. Accessed 06 Feb 2019
4. NIECC Homepage. https://www.gob.mx/inecc. Accessed 06 Feb 2019
5. Mexican Government Homepage NIECC. https://www.gob.mx/inecc/acciones-y-programas/mexico-ante-el-cambio-climatico?De=IGOBMX. Accessed 06 Feb 2019
6. USTR Homepage, Agreement between the United States of America, the United Mexican States, and Canada Text (2018). https://ustr.gov/trade-agreements/free-trade-agreements/united-states-mexico-canada-agreement/agreement-between
7. Liu, C., Pai, T., Chang, C., Hsieh, C.: Path-planning algorithms for public transportation systems. In: ITSC 2001. 2001 IEEE Intelligent Transportation Systems. Proceedings (Cat. No.01TH8585), pp. 1061–1066 (2001)
8. Liu, C.: Best-path planning for public transportation systems. In: Proceedings of the Fifth International IEEE Conference on Intelligent Transportation Systems, pp. 834–839, Singapore (2002)
9. Wang, M., Shan, H., Lu, R., Zhang, R., Shen, X., Bai, F.: Real-time path planning based on hybrid-VANET-enhanced transportation system. IEEE Trans. Veh. Technol. **64**(5), 1664–1678 (2015). https://doi.org/10.1109/TVT.2014.2335201

10. Villagra, J., Milanés, V., Pérez, J., Godoy, J.: Smooth path and speed planning for an automated public transport vehicle. Rob. Auton. Syst. **60**(2), 252–265 (2012)
11. Guo, Z.: Transfers and path choice in urban public transport systems. In: Urban Studies and Planning, Massachusetts Institute of Technology (2008)
12. Souza, A., Yokoyama, R., Maia, G., Loureiro, A., Villas, L.: Real-time path planning to prevent traffic jam through an intelligent transportation system. In: 2016 IEEE Symposium on Computers and Communication (ISCC), Messina, Italy, pp. 726–731 (2016). https://doi.org/10.1109/iscc.2016.7543822
13. Wang, J., Sun, Y., Liu, Z., Yang P., Lin, T.: Route planning based on Floyd algorithm for intelligence transportation system. In: 2007 IEEE International Conference on Integration Technology, Shenzhen, China, pp. 544–546 (2007). https://doi.org/10.1109/icitechnology.2007.4290376
14. Zografos, K., Androutsopoulos, K.: Algorithms for itinerary planning in multimodal transportation networks. IEEE Trans. Intell. Transp. Syst. **9**(1), 175–184 (2008). https://doi.org/10.1109/TITS.2008.915650
15. Li, W., Wenquan, L.: Best-routing algorithm for public transportation systems. J. SE Univ. Nat. Sci. Ed. **34**(2), 265–267 (2004)
16. Chou, J.S., Cheng, M.Y., Hsieh, Y.M., Yang, I.T., Hsu, H.T.: Optimal path planning in real time for dynamic building fire rescue operations using wireless sensors and visual guidance. Autom. Constr. **99**, 1–17 (2019)
17. Sabar, N.R., Bhaskar, A., Chung, E., Turky, A., Song, A.: A self-adaptive evolutionary algorithm for dynamic vehicle routing problems with traffic congestion. Swarm Evol. Comput. **44**, 1018–1027 (2019)
18. Aifadopoulou, G., Zillaskopoulos, A., Chrisohoou, E.: Multiobjective optimum path algorithm for passenger pretrip planning in multimodal transportation networks. Transp. Res. Rec. **2032**(1), 26–34 (2007). https://doi.org/doi.org/10.3141/2032-04
19. Gutiérrez-Jarpa, G., Laporte, G., Marianov, V., Moccia, L.: Multi-objective rapid transit network design with modal competition: the case of concepción, Chile. Comput. Oper. Res. **78**, 27–43 (2017)
20. Peña, D., Tchernykh, A., Nesmachnow, S., Massobrio, R., Drozdov, A.Y., Garichev, S.N.: Multiobjective vehicle type and size scheduling problem in urban public transport using MOCell. In: 2016 International Conference on Engineering and Telecommunication (EnT), pp. 110–113 (2016). https://doi.org/10.1109/ent.2016.032
21. Sadeghi, A., Kim, K.: Ontology based personalized route planning system using a multi-criteria decision-making approach. Expert Syst. Appl. **36**(2), 2250–2259 (2009)
22. Chien, S.: Optimization of bus route planning in Urban commuter networks. J. Public Transp. **6**(1), 53–79 (2003). https://doi.org/10.5038/2375-0901.6.1.4
23. Dib, O., Moalic, L., Manier, M.A., Caminada, A.: An advanced GA–VNS combination for multicriteria route planning in public transit networks. Expert Syst. Appl. **72**, 67–87 (2017)
24. Tsai, C.Y., Chung, S.H.: A personalized route recommendation service for theme parks using RFID information and tourist behavior. Decis. Support Syst. **52**(2), 514–527 (2012)

Multi-objective Optimization of Vehicle Routing with Environmental Penalty

Luis Bernardo Pulido-Gaytan[1], Andrei Tchernykh[1(✉)],
Sergio Nesmachnow[2], Alfredo Cristóbal-Salas[3], Arutyun Avetisyan[4],
Harold Enrique Castro Barrera[5], and Carlos Jaime Barrios Hernandez[6]

[1] CICESE Research Center, 22860 Ensenada, BC, Mexico
{lpulido, chernykh}@cicese.edu.mx
[2] Universidad de la República, Montevideo, Uruguay
sergion@fing.edu.uy
[3] Universidad Veracruzana, Veracruz, Mexico
acristobal@uv.mx
[4] Ivannikov Institute for System Programming of the RAS, Moscow, Russia
arut@ispras.ru
[5] University of Los Andes, Bogotá, Colombia
hcastro@uniandes.edu.co
[6] Industrial University of Santander, Bucaramanga, Colombia
cbarrios@uis.edu.co

Abstract. Cities host more than half of the population in only 2% of the earth's surface and consume 75% of the resources extracted from the planet, this abrupt demographic growth in urban areas has worsened the level of pollution in the city, as well as the problems of road congestion. Therefore, smart cities propose the incorporation of technologies to optimize the use of existing infrastructure and thus, achieve a sustainable and inclusive city. In this context, we propose an optimization method based on a multi-objective cellular genetic algorithm to determine an adequate routing of vehicles that allows to diminish the environmental impact in highly concurred areas, while providing alternative routes that minimize the associated costs of moving from one place to another, this under the premise that not always the shortest path represents the best solution.

The presented algorithm simultaneously minimizes three important objectives: the time, the amount of pollutants emitted and an environmental penalty, where the latter represents the implicit cost of moving through a certain segment of the map. That is, an approximate set of Pareto is obtained, which contains alternative routes that avoid traveling through areas with a high degree of pollution and that, in turn, minimize the time and quantity of emissions when traveling through a certain network of routes. Our experimental analysis based on several quality indicators, like Hypervolume and Spread, shows a competitive performance of the proposed approach in terms of convergence and diversity, this with respect to NSGA II and SPEA2, well-known multi-objective algorithms in the literature.

Keywords: Vehicle routing · Multi-objective optimization · Evolutionary algorithms · Metaheuristics

© Springer Nature Switzerland AG 2019
M. Torres and J. Klapp (Eds.): ISUM 2019, CCIS 1151, pp. 147–162, 2019.
https://doi.org/10.1007/978-3-030-38043-4_13

1 Introduction

The cities are considered elementary pieces for the future, since they play a preponderant role in socio-economic aspects of the whole world, these urban areas host more than half of the population in only 2% of the earth's surface, but they consume 75% of the resources that are extracted from the planet [1]. This abrupt demographic growth in urban areas lead to a wide range of problems such as difficulties in waste management, lack of resources, environmental pollution, human health problems, road congestion, among many others [2], for this reason thinking of sustainable urban development is a discussion that has received constant attention from researchers for several years.

In this way, smart cities (SCs) propose the incorporation of technologies for the cohesion of all aspects that involve social, institutional and infrastructure problems in an urban ecosystem [3]; areas as diverse as civil administration, education, health services, public safety, housing, energy, transport, and logistics, can be improved, interconnected and made more efficient thanks to the incorporation of technology [4]. SCs allow reducing costs, making responsible use of resources and encouraging the active participation of citizens in decision-making processes, to achieve a sustainable and inclusive city.

The main challenges for cities on urban mobility are often related to the inability of public transport systems to satisfy needs of a growing number of users [5], as well as the inefficiency of infrastructure in urban areas. However, since modifying the existing commercial infrastructure represents a high monetary cost, it has been chosen to apply various computational intelligence techniques for the generation of management solutions, such as the introduction and application of variable speed limits, the imposition of differentiated prices for roads, or the optimization of the time in traffic signals, all this to improve in some way the performance of the existing road network.

Due to its potential to improve road safety, reduce traffic congestion and improve the mobility of people and goods, Intelligent Transport Systems (ITS) or "Smart Mobility" have generated considerable enthusiasm in the scientific community [6]. In addition to safety and mobility, ITS play an essential role in the reduction of pollutants, as well as to the decrease in energy consumption [7]. However, in many cases these objectives conflict, so a single solution that simultaneously optimizes all the objectives does not exist. The solution consists of a set of non-dominated solutions, called Pareto front or Pareto optimal set. In most cases, for NP-hard problems, its calculating is impractical. It can contain an infinite number of non-dominated solutions. Therefore, the goal is to obtain a good approximation of the real Pareto front in a computable time. Heuristics and metaheuristics are a popular class of algorithms to find a high-quality solution for Multi-objective Optimization Problems (MOPs) [8].

In this paper, we propose an optimization method based on a multi-objective cellular genetic algorithm to determine an adequate routing of vehicles that allows to diminish the environmental impact in highly concurred areas, while providing alternative routes that minimize the associated costs of moving from one place to another, this under the premise that not always the shortest path represents the best solution. The presented algorithm simultaneously minimizes three important objectives: the time, the amount of pollutants emitted and an environmental penalty, where the latter represents the implicit cost of moving through a certain segment of the map. That is, an approximate set of Pareto is obtained, which contains alternative routes that avoid traveling through areas with a high degree of pollution and that, in turn, minimize the time and quantity of emissions when traveling through a specific network of routes.

This paper is structured as follows. The next section briefly reviews related works, models, and algorithms for vehicle routing problems. Section 3 presents the formal description of the vehicle routing problem to be addressed. Section 4 introduces multi-objective evolutionary algorithms (MOEAs), and the proposed MOEA to solve the problem. Section 5 reports the experimental evaluation, including a comparison against multi-objective evolutionary algorithms commonly used in the literature. Finally, Sect. 6 formulates the conclusions of the paper and future work.

2 Related Work

This section presents a brief overview of models and algorithms for vehicle routing problems and their derivatives. Given the nature of the problem, most of these works are based on computational intelligence techniques to improve solution.

The Vehicle Routing Problem (VRP) was formulated as a mathematical programming model by Dantzig and Ramser [9]. Later, in 1964 Clarke and Wright proposed a seminal heuristic method [10]. In 1981, Lenstra and Kan [11] demonstrated that VRP is NP-hard. Since then different models and algorithms have been developed for related problems, most of these works are based on models proposed a few decades ago, where when applying computational intelligence techniques it has been possible to find approximate solutions in a computable time.

Real-time traffic information has been a key factor for the VRP [12], where ITS have been introduced to take advantage of the data in real time by providing reasonable routes [13]. Regulations on vehicles and access times have been enacted to reduce air or noise pollution, and control traffic flows in urban areas [12].

A common problem in these systems is finding an optimal route that minimizes the costs of going from one place to another. However, in most cases, the shortest path is not always the best solution, from user satisfaction point of view. Under this premise, mono-objective approaches present a notable disadvantage with respect to multi-objective approaches; this is their inability to optimize more than one aspect at a time when offering solutions to the problem. On the other hand, given the magnitude of the search space when dealing with realistic and highly non-deterministic instances such as road networks today, the exact algorithms do not seem to be viable, since the main objective is to find potential solutions in times computationally reduced. Therefore, techniques such as simulated annealing, taboo search or genetic algorithms are commonly implemented methods to solve this particular problem.

In this way, techniques for solving combinatorial problems can be classified into two main categories: exact and heuristic algorithms. The exact algorithms guarantee to find the global optimum solved. Heuristics and metaheuristics are more efficient and flexible, and allow approximate global optimum in computable time.

2.1 Exact Methods

The Dijkstra algorithm is one of the exact algorithms based on the tagging method, which is to find the route with the lowest cost (usually refers to the shortest route) from a node to all nodes in a network of routes. Its computation complexity is $O(n^2)$ where n is the number of nodes in the network [14]. Also, other algorithms such as Floyd-Warshall [15], Bellman-Ford-Moore, incremental graph, threshold, topological ordering, among others, also used to find the shortest path.

Pallotino and Scutellà [16] stated that transportation problems often offer compensation between two or more objectives, for example, minimizing the time of arrival at a final destination and the cost of the route. Müller-Hannemann and Weihe [17] reported on a railway routing problem that faces a compromise between the monetary cost and the travel time. In these cases, it is necessary to find a set of solutions that take into account more than one objective simultaneously. Although some of these exact algorithms have a multi-objective version, when examining a large part of the graph for the calculation of each of the routes, they present a poor performance in terms of the computational time required.

2.2 Metaheuristic Methods

Given the magnitude of the search space when dealing with realistic instances, it is necessary to use heuristics or metaheuristics that allow calculating solutions of acceptable quality in reasonable times.

Bell [18] applied the metaheuristic method of optimizing ant colonies (ACO) to minimize the total cost of travel in large instances. ACO approach [19] has been used extensively to search for the shortest routes, since it is capable of reacting to dynamic changes in traffic conditions. In the same way, Possel [20] implemented the simulated annealing algorithm to solve a bi-level optimization problem in which minimizing externalities are the objectives, and link types which are associated with certain link characteristics are the discrete decision variables.

Likewise, genetic algorithms (AG) have been widely used for VRP and in general to solve search problems and combinatorial optimization. They simulate the way species evolve and adapt to their environment, according to the Darwinian principle of natural selection. Through these techniques, multiple contributions have been made to the design of transport networks (topology and routes). In this way, under the premise that not always the shortest route represents the best solution Chakraborty [21] proposed a genetic algorithm where it is possible to choose routes with respect to different criteria, such as road congestion, environmental problems or comfort of handling, this despite an implicit increase in the resulting cost.

Fagúndez [22] proposed to minimize the total cost of travel in the problem of distributing a group of passengers traveling from the same origin to different destinations in several taxis.

Sharma [23] implemented a multi-objective evolutionary algorithm to solve a transportation network design problem when the planner is environmentally conscious and thereby tries to minimize health-damage cost due to vehicular emissions along with total system travel time while performing optimal capacity expansion.

3 The Multi-objective VRP

This section introduces the vehicle routing problem with an environmental penalty and its mathematical formulation as a multi-objective optimization problem.

3.1 Problem Description

VRP models a realistic scenario, where a set of vehicles, located in different points of origin decide to move to different destinations. The optimization problem consists of properly routing these vehicles under the premise that not always the shortest path represents the best solution, this from the point of view of user satisfaction. In this way, it is required to minimize three important objectives simultaneously: time, the amount of pollutants emitted and an environmental penalty, where the latter represents the implicit cost of moving through a particular segment of the map. That is, an approximate set of Pareto must be obtained, which contains alternative routes that avoid traveling through areas with a high degree of pollution and that, in turn, minimize the time and quantity of emissions when moving through a network of routes.

3.2 Mathematical Formulation

The mathematical formulation of the VRP considers the following elements:

- Let $G(V, E)$ be a connected graph representing the underlying topology of a route network, where $V = \{1, \ldots, m\}$ is the set of intersections (vertices) and $E = \{(i,j) | i,j \in V, i \neq j\}$ denotes the set of connections (edges) between vertices in G.
- Let $e_{ij} = \{d_{ij}, v_{ij}, cont_{ij}, p_{ij}, incl_{ij}\}$ the connection between the vertex i and the vertex j, which has five non-negative values associated with it, $d_{ij}, v_{ij}, cont_{ij}, p_{ij}$ and $incl_{ij}$, which denote the distance, maximum speed allowed, environmental pollution, environmental penalty and inclination of the route $(i, j) \in E$.
- A set of vehicles $B = \{b_1, .., b_n\}$, where $b_k = \{\beta_k, s_k, m_k, FT_k\}$, β_k the coefficient of fuel consumption, s_k the speed (constant), m_k the weight and FT_k the traction force of the vehicle b_k, for $k = \{1, \ldots, n\}$.
- A subset of start vertices $V_{in}^{b_k} \subseteq V$ and a subset of target vertices $V_{out}^{b_k} \subseteq V$.
- $t_{ij}^{b_k} = d_{ij}/s_k$ represents the time required to travel the edge e_{ij} for the vehicle b_k, where $s_k \leq v_{ij}$.
- A route $r_{ab}^{b_k}$ for each vehicle $b_k \in B$ composed of adjacent edges $r_{ab}^{b_k} = \langle e_{a1}, e_{12}, \ldots, e_{zb} \rangle$ where $e \in E$ and l_{ab} represent the length of the route $r_{ab}^{b_k}$.
- Let $T_{ab}^{b_k} = \sum_{(i,j) \in r_{ab}^{b_k}} t_{ij}^{b_k}$ the time to travel the route $r_{ab}^{b_k}$ for b_k.
- Let $P_{ab}^{b_k} = \sum_{(i,j) \in r_{ab}^{b_k}} p_{ij}^{b_k}$ the environmental penalty when traveling the route $r_{ab}^{b_k}$ for b_k.
- Let $c_{ij}^{b_k} = t_{ij}^{b_k} \cdot \beta_k \cdot VSP_{ij}^{b_k}$ the pollutants emitted of the vehicle b_k when going from the vertex i to the vertex j, where $VSP_{ij}^{b_k} = FT_k \cdot s_k/m_k$.

- Let $C_{ab}^{b_k} = \sum_{(i,j) \in r_{ab}^{b_k}} c_{ij}^{b_k}$ the pollutants emitted of the vehicle b_k when traveling the route $r_{ab}^{b_k}$.
- Let $T = \sum_{k=1}^{n} T_{ab}^{b_k}$ be the time for all vehicles when traveling the set of routes.
- Let $P = \sum_{k=1}^{n} P_{ab}^{b_k}$ be the penalty for all vehicles when traveling the set of routes
- Let $C = \sum_{k=1}^{n} C_{ab}^{b_k}$ be the emissions for all vehicles when traveling the set of routes.

It is then sought to identify that set of non-dominated solutions that minimize the time needed for each of the vehicles to go from the point of entry to the exit point, while minimizing the amount of emissions and the environmental penalty, where the latter represents the implicit cost of traveling through a certain area in G, thus contributing to the reduction of environmental impact or pollution in that region. Therefore, it is possible to express the problem to be treated as a scheduling problem, composed of processors, jobs and optimization criteria, that is:

$$G \,|B|\, min\{T, P, C\}$$

4 Multi-objective Evolutionary Algorithms

This section introduces MOEAs and describes the proposed multi-objective optimization algorithm with an environmental penalty for the vehicle routing problem.

4.1 Evolutionary Algorithms

Evolutionary algorithms (EAs) are nature-inspired search methods that emulate the evolution process of the species to solve optimization problems. The common underlying idea behind these techniques is the next: given a population of individuals within some environment that has limited resources, competition for those resources causes natural selection. This, in turn, causes a rise in the fitness of the population. Given a quality function to be maximized, it is possible to randomly create a set of candidate solutions, i.e., elements of the function's domain. Then a quality function is applied to these as an abstract fitness measure [24]. Likewise, most EAs use recombination, mixing information from two or more candidate solutions to create new individuals as well as a mutation operator to diversify the population.

However, commonly the objectives to be optimized are compromised among themselves, for example, a solution that reduces traffic congestion will be affected in the distance to travel to reach the destination position. For this reason, multiple works have focused on obtaining a set of solutions that balance two or more objectives in conflict, this through multi-objective optimization algorithms.

MOEAs are a posteriori method based on the principles of EA for optimization with a single objective. These are an attractive strategy to address multi-objective optimization problems (POMO) given their ability to work simultaneously with a set of possible solutions, which can belong to the optimal set of Pareto. Also, said solution set is possible to achieve in a single execution, unlike a traditional method where solutions are found in independent executions. Additionally, these are less susceptible to the shape and continuity of the Pareto front; that is, they can operate with concave or discontinuous fronts.

MOEAs are designed taking into account two main goals: (1) approximating the Pareto front, (2) maintaining diversity instead of converging to a reduced section of the Pareto front.

In this work, we focus on cGAs, particularly, in the Multi-objective Cellular Genetic Algorithm (MOCell) [25]. The main feature of this approach is that the population is distributed in a two-dimensional toroidal grid, to then assign a neighborhood to each individual. A toroidal mesh is used to ensure that all individuals have the same number of neighbors. MOCell performs this type of population distribution in order to restrict the number of individuals that can interact with each other, promoting the exploration of the search space so that genes are transmitted between neighborhoods without the need for focus only on the best individual of each subgroup, and maintaining a high diversity due to the "slow" diffusion of the genetic material. On the other hand, since individuals can only interact with a small group of neighbors, they seek to encourage exploitation in each neighborhood, using the ranking and distance stacking techniques proposed in NSGA-II [26] in each neighborhood and thus promote elitism when applying genetic operators.

4.2   Encoding and Solution Representation

One of the main challenges when designing an evolutionary algorithm is to represent the real world within the same algorithm, which means creating a data structure that represents the characteristics of the problem and its context, which must be designed in such a way that a computational system can manipulate it. In other words, all the information inherent to the problem and its context are phenotypes and their codification, creates a data structure in an environment of EA that contains the genotypes [24]. In this way, the generation of a coding that allows adequate mapping of the phenotype space to that of genotypes is of vital importance in the performance of an evolutionary algorithm, since it will depend on whether the search is executed in the entire space of possible solutions or in a subset of it.

When this type of metaheuristics is applied to the problem of vehicle routing or in general to the design of transport networks (topology and routes of the routes) the usual scheme of an EA changes, due to difficulties such as: (a) a route may contain a number of node variables, where its maximum dimension is $n - 1$ for a graph of n nodes, and (b) a random sequence of edges usually does not correspond to a valid path [27]. To address these problems, we adopted an indirect approach proposed by Gen et al. [27], which mainly consists of coding certain guide information to build a route, instead of the route itself. As is well known, a gene in a chromosome is composed of two factors: the locus, that is, the position of the gene located within the structure of the chromosome, and the allele, that is, the value that the gene takes. In this coding method, the position of a gene is used to represent the node ID, and its allele is used to represent the priority assigned to that node [28].

The illustration of the priority-based coding and its decoded path to go from vertex v_1 to vertex v_4 are shown in Fig. 1 (right), this in terms of the connected undirected graph presented in Fig. 1 (left). Initially, it is verified that v_2 and v_5 have adjacencies with the initial vertex, which have priorities of 1 and 4, respectively. Since the vertex v_5 has a higher priority, it is placed in the route. Subsequently, for v_5 there are adjacencies with v_3 and v_6, of which v_6 has the highest priority, which is included in the resulting route. Then the set of adjacent vertices is formed for v_6 and v_7 of them is selected. The process continues until the target vertex v_4 is reached.

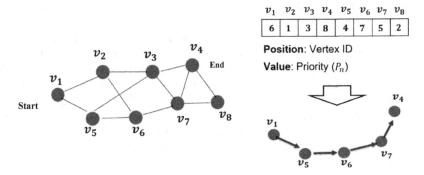

Fig. 1. A connected undirected graph with eight nodes and 12 edges (left) and an example of indirect encode (right).

The main advantages of the priority-based coding method are: (1) any permutation of the coding corresponds to a route (feasibility); (2) most of the existing genetic operators can easily be applied to coding; (3) any route has a corresponding coding (legality); (4) at most case, there exists one-to-one mapping from encodings to paths (non-redundancy); (5) any point in the solution space is accessible for genetic search (completeness) [29].

4.3   Objective Functions and Fitness Evaluation

The optimization problem is formulated with three different objective functions. f_1 includes the sum of the time of each vehicle when traveling a route, which is calculated through the quotient of the distance between the speed of the vehicle in course. f_2 represents the sum of the cost generated by each vehicle when traveling a route. This cost is given by two factors, the cost produced by traveling the distance of the route and the environmental penalty, that is, the implicit cost per kilometer of traveling through a certain area of the map. f_3 includes the sum of the pollutants emitted of each vehicle when traveling a route, given by the vehicle specific power.

4.4   Evolutionary Operators

Genetic operators mimic the process of inheriting genes to create new descendants in each generation. The use of different genetic operators has a significant influence on the performance of any evolutionary algorithm.

Population Initialization. Permutations of length m are randomly generated, where m is the number of nodes in G. Subsequently, the individuals are distributed in a toroidal grid of cells (see Fig. 5).

Selection. A tournament selection is chosen to select the parents (two individuals survive) in the neighborhood of the studied individual.

Recombination. By making use of an indirect coding, it is possible to apply any recombination operator for permutation chromosomes, this without affecting the validity of the resulting path. In this sense, an order crossover was used. In this genetic operator, are chosen two crossover points at random, and copy the segment between them from the first parent (P_1) into the first offspring. So, starting from the second crossover point in the second parent, the remaining unused numbers are copied into the first child in the order that they appear in the second parent (see Fig. 2).

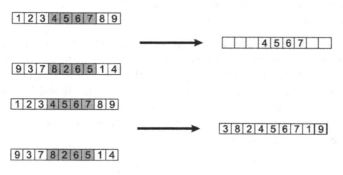

Fig. 2. Example of order crossover (CX) [24]

Mutation. Given the nature of the VRP, we look for a mutation operator that allows making specific changes in the chromosomes, so that the resulting route changes only the direction of one of its edges. For this reason, in this paper, we propose to make use of the swap mutation in the implementation of the MOEA, which basically consists of randomly selecting two positions (genes) in the chromosome and exchanging their values (see Fig. 3).

Fig. 3. Example of swap mutation [24]

Figure 5 illustrates the behavior of the performed implementation.

5 Experimental Results

5.1 Quality Indicators

In the literature, a large number of metrics have been proposed to evaluate the performance of MOEAs [30]. In this paper, we apply several of them with the purpose of evaluating the results obtained from proposed MOEA and in turn, compare their performance concerning other algorithms commonly used in the literature, this in terms of convergence and diversity of the set of non-dominated solutions found for the vehicle routing problem.

In this way, we have chosen the Hypervolume (I_{HV}) to assess these two criteria together and Spread (I_Δ) to evaluate the dispersion of a non-dominated solution set.

On the other hand, given the optimal Pareto front (PF) is not known for the problem instances studied, we use an artificial Pareto front (PF_a), which is built by merging all the Pareto front approximations computed by the tested algorithms in every independent run into one single front.

Hypervolume (I_{HV}) [25]. This quality indicator calculates the volume covered by members of a non-dominated set of solutions PF for problems where all objectives are to be minimized. Mathematically, for each solution $i \in PF$, a hypercube v_i is constructed with a reference point W and the solution i as the diagonal corners of the hypercube. The reference point can simply be found by constructing a vector of worst objective function values. Thereafter, a union of all hypercubes is found and its hypervolume (I_{HV}) is calculated:

$$I_{HV} = volume\left(\bigcup_{i=1}^{|PF|} v_i\right)$$

Spread (I_Δ) [25]. I_Δ is a diversity indicator that measures the extent of spread achieved among the obtained solutions. It is defined as:

$$I_\Delta = \frac{d_f + d_l + \sum_{i=1}^{|PF|-1}|d_i - \bar{d}|}{d_f + d_l + (|PF| - 1)\bar{d}},$$

where d_i is the Euclidean distance between consecutive solutions, $\bar{d}$ is the mean of these distances, and d_f and d_l are the Euclidean distances to the extreme solutions of the exact Pareto front in the objective space. This measure takes a zero value for an ideal distribution, pointing out a perfect spread out of the solutions in the Pareto front.

5.2 Experimental Setup

All the algorithms used in this paper (MOCell, NSGA-II, and SPEA2) were implemented in Java, using the JMetal framework [31], an open-source library aimed at the development, experimentation, and study of metaheuristics for solving multi-objective optimization problems.

As an instance of the problem, we use a related graph composed of 6104 nodes (see Fig. 4), which represents the underlying topology of the road network of the Oldenburg city [32]. Said graph was segmented into three different types of zones, which symbolize areas with different environmental penalties, that is, an associated environmental cost of moving through a certain area of the city or of the graph. An edge that is in a green zone has a penalty equal to 0 ($p = 0$), a yellow zone $p = 2$ and a red zone $p = 4$. On the other hand, for the considered problem instance, we run 30 independent executions and, the evaluated approximation sets are normalized by the maximum values for every objective function.

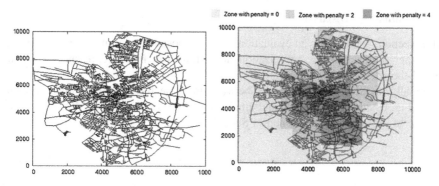

Fig. 4. City of Oldenburg (OL) road network [32] (left) and segmented OL road network based on environmental penalties (right)

A comparative analysis was performed between the proposed algorithm and three algorithms which are representative of the state-of-the-art: NSGA-II and SPEA2. For this, the same genetic operators were used for all cases, as well as the same parameters (see Table 1). The size of the initial population was defined as 100 individual, a binary tournament was used for parent selection, and defined 10,000 fitness evaluation as stopping criteria, assessing the performance by using Hypervolume (I_{HV}) and Spread (I_Δ).

Table 1. Parameterization of the algorithms.

Parameter	Value
Stopping condition	25000 function evaluation
Population size	100 individuals (10×10)
Neighborhood	8 surrounding neighbors
Selection parents	Binary tournament (9,2)
Recombination	CX
Probability of recombination	0.9
Mutation	Swap
Probability of mutation	0.2
Density estimator	Crowding distance

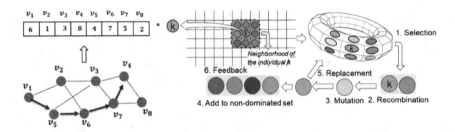

Fig. 5. Solution representation for the VRP and reproduction steps.

5.3   Results and Discussion

In this section, we describe an evaluation of the proposed algorithm and its comparison with other multi-objective optimization algorithms which are representative of the state-of-the-art.

Initially, to illustrate the conflict between the objectives to be optimized in this paper, Fig. 6 shows the initial and final population generated by MOCell for the instance of the problem mentioned in Sect. 5.2.

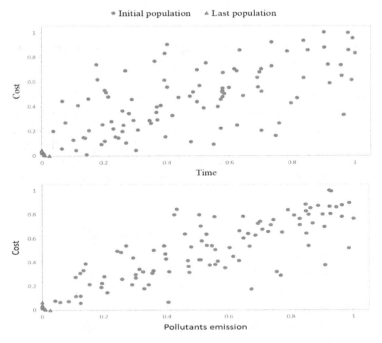

Fig. 6. Set of non-dominated solutions obtained by MOCell for conflicting objectives, compared to the initial population.

We can observe in broad strokes the magnitude of the space of possible solutions, that is, possible routes for a vehicle to move from one point to another. Likewise, we can show graphically how the algorithm evolves the population as the generations pass, making changes in individuals that represent an improvement in the quality of each of the feasible solutions for each objective function.

Figure 7 shows the approximate Pareto front generated by each of the implemented algorithms, whose specifications are mentioned in Sect. 5.2. Also, the Pareto artificial front is shown, which is built by merging all the Pareto front approximations computed by the tested algorithms in every independent run into one single front.

It is observed that for the conflicting objectives cost and quantity of emissions, MOCell was the only algorithm that found both optimal solutions and routes that contemplate the two conflicting objectives, which allows the decision makers to reduce the costs associated with the transfer from one place to another, without neglecting ecological aspects.

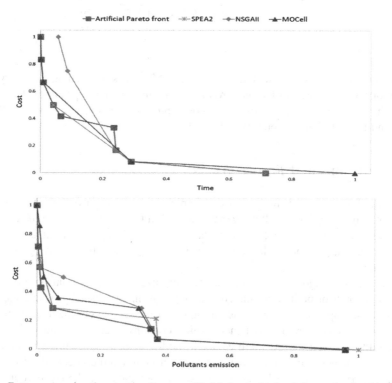

Fig. 7. Better approximation to the Pareto artificial front obtained for each algorithm with respect to the Spread quality indicator.

Table 2 shows the results obtained by each algorithm in the multi-objective metrics defined in Sect. 5.1. For each metric, the best value, the mean and standard deviation are reported.

It is easy to see that NSGA-II and SPEA2 have difficulties in diversity. The comparison shows that the MOCell algorithm outperformed the rest of the MOEAs in terms of diversity, achieving value in I_Δ 145% better than NSGA-II and 149% better than SPEA2. On the other hand, in hypervolume, the NSGA-II and MOCell algorithms presented similar results, this indicates that the solutions found by the cellular algorithm present a better dispersion along the approximate Pareto front, while in terms of convergence they may be similar.

Table 2. Quality metrics

Metric		MOCell	NSGA-II	SPEA2
Hypervolume (I_{HV})	Max	0.521	0.520	0.512
	Mean	**0.518**	0.515	0.420
	σ	0.0130	0.0145	0.0448
Spread (I_Δ)	Max	0.628	0.982	1.360
	Mean	**0.718**	1.760	1.790
	σ	0.0631	0.4490	0.2393

The previous results show that the proposed MOEA is an accurate and very efficient tool for the problem of vehicle routing with environmental penalties. In general terms, the proposed approach provides a good approximation to the approximate Pareto front, and the solution sets preserve diversity.

6   Conclusions and Future Work

This paper has presented the design and implementation of an optimization method based on a multi-objective cellular genetic algorithm to determine an adequate routing of vehicles diminishing the environmental impact in highly concurred areas, while providing alternative routes that minimize the associated costs of moving from one place to another.

The presented algorithm simultaneously minimizes three important objectives: the time, the amount of pollutants emitted and an environmental penalty, where the latter represents the implicit cost of moving through a certain segment of the map. That is, an approximate set of Pareto is obtained, which contains alternative routes that avoid traveling through areas with a high degree of pollution and that, in turn, minimize the time and quantity of emissions when traveling through a certain network of routes.

The experimental results based on several quality indicators, like Hypervolume and Spread, shows a competitive performance of the cellular type genetic algorithm for the conditions and characteristics of the proposed problem, this with respect to NSGA II and SPEA2 in terms of convergence and diversity, well-known multi-objective algorithms in the literature. Achieving value in I_Δ 145% better than NSGA-II and 149% better than SPEA2. This allows us to affirm that cellular-type genetic algorithms can be a useful tool for tactical planning in vehicle routing.

The main lines of future work include the use of graph segmentation algorithms to reduce the search for routes in areas that are not viable, that is, to execute the search only in those areas where the best routes are potentially found. And in this way, allow the execution of the proposed approach in larger instances. Another interesting line is the characterization of zones based on estimated data of concurrency by zones, in order to define the environmental penalty contemplating information in real time.

References

1. Bocquier, P.: World urbanization prospects: an alternative to the UN model of projection compatible with the mobility transition theory. Demogr. Res. **12**, 197–236 (2005)
2. Chourabi, H., et al.: Understanding smart cities: an integrative framework. In: Proceedings of Annual Hawaii International Conference on System Sciences, pp. 2289–2297 (2012)
3. Albino, V., Berardi, U., Dangelico, R.M.: Smart cities: definitions, dimensions, performance, and initiatives. J. Urban Technol. **22**, 3–21 (2014)
4. Washburn, D., Sindhu For Cios, U.: Making leaders successful every day helping CIOs understand smart city initiatives (2010)
5. Peña, D., Tchernykh, A., Radchenko, G., Nesmachnow, S., Ley-Flores, J., Nazariega, R.: Multiobjective optimization of greenhouse gas emissions enhancing the quality of service for urban public transport timetabling
6. Barth, M.J., Wu, G., Boriboonsomsin, K.: Intelligent transportation systems and greenhouse gas reductions. Curr. Sustain. Energy Rep. **2**, 90–97 (2015)
7. Massobrio, R., Fagúndez, G., Nesmachnow, S.: A parallel micro evolutionary algorithm for taxi sharing optimization
8. Nesmachnow, S.: An overview of metaheuristics: accurate and efficient methods for optimisation. Int. J. Metaheuristics **3**(4), 320 (2014)
9. Dantzig, G.B.: The truck dispatching problem. Source Manag. Sci. **6**, 80–91 (1959)
10. Clarke, G., Wright, J.W.: Scheduling of vehicles from a central depot to a number of delivery points. Oper. Res. **12**(4), 568–581 (1964)
11. Lenstra, J.K., Kan, A.H.G.R.: Complexity of vehicle routing and scheduling problems. Networks **11**(2), 221–227 (1981)
12. Kim, G., Ong, Y.S., Heng, C.K., Tan, P.S., Zhang, N.A.: City Vehicle Routing Problem (City VRP): a review. IEEE Trans. Intell. Transp. Syst. **16**, 1654–1666 (2015)
13. Lee, W.-H., Tseng, S.-S.: A knowledge based real-time travel time prediction system for urban network. Expert Syst. Appl. **36**, 4239–4247 (2009)
14. Fu, M.: A practical route planning algorithm for vehicle navigation system. In: Fifth World Congress on Intelligent Control and Automation, vol. 6, pp. 5326–5329 (2004)
15. Floyd, R.W.: Algorithm 97: shortest path. Commun. ACM **5**, 345 (1962)
16. Pallottino, S., Scutella', M.G., Scutellà, M.G.: Shortest Path Algorithms in Transportation models: classical and innovative aspects. In: Marcotte, P., Nguyen, S. (eds.) Equilibrium and Advanced Transportation Modelling. Centre for Research on Transportation, pp. 245–281. Springer, Boston (1997). https://doi.org/10.1007/978-1-4615-5757-9_11
17. Müller-Hannemann, M., Schnee, M.: Finding all attractive train connections by multi-criteria pareto search. In: Geraets, F., Kroon, L., Schoebel, A., Wagner, D., Zaroliagis, C.D. (eds.) Algorithmic Methods for Railway Optimization. LNCS, vol. 4359, pp. 246–263. Springer, Heidelberg (2007). https://doi.org/10.1007/978-3-540-74247-0_13
18. Bell, J.E., McMullen, P.R.: Ant colony optimization techniques for the vehicle routing problem. Adv. Eng. Inform. **18**, 41–48 (2004)

19. Tatomir, B.: Travel time prediction for dynamic routing using Ant Based Control. In: Proceedings of the 2009 Winter Simulation Conference (WSC), pp. 1069–1078 (2009)
20. Possel, B., Wismans, L.J.J., Van Berkum, E.C.: The multi-objective network design problem using minimizing externalities as objectives: comparison of a genetic algorithm and simulated annealing. Transportation (Amst) **45**, 545–572 (2018)
21. Chakraborty, B., Maeda, T., Chakraborty, G.: Multiobjective route selection for car navigation system using genetic algorithm (2005)
22. Fagúndez, G., Massobrio, R., Nesmachnow, S.: Online taxi sharing optimization using evolutionary algorithms. In: Proceedings of the 2014 Latin American Computing Conference, CLEI 2014 (2014)
23. Sharma, S.: Multiobjective network design for emission and travel-time trade-off for a sustainable large urban transportation network. Environ. Plan. B Plan. Des. **38**, 520–538 (2011)
24. Eiben, A.E., Smith, J.E.: Introduction to Evolutionary Computing, vol. 2. Springer, Heidelberg (2015). https://doi.org/10.1007/978-3-662-44874-8
25. Nebro, A.J., Durillo, J.J., Luna, F., Dorronsoro, B., Alba, E.: MOCell: a cellular genetic algorithm for multiobjective optimization. Int. J. Intell. Syst. **24**, 726–746 (2009)
26. Deb, K., Pratap, A., Agarwal, S.: A fast and elitist multiobjective genetic algorithm: NSGA-II. IEEE Trans. Evol. Comput. **6**(2), 182–197 (2002)
27. Gent, M., Cheng, R.: Genetic algorithms for solving shortest path problems
28. Lin, L., Gen, M.: Priority-based genetic algorithm for shortest path routing problem in OSPF. Stud. Comput. Intell. **187**, 91–103 (2009)
29. Gen, M., Altiparmak, F.: A genetic algorithm for two-stage transportation problem using priority-based encoding. OR Spectr. **28**(3), 337–354 (2006)
30. Coello, C.A.C.: Evolutionary Algorithms for Solving Multi-Objective Problems. Springer, New York (2007). https://doi.org/10.1007/978-0-387-36797-2
31. Durillo, J.J., Nebro, A.J.: jMetal: a Java framework for multi-objective optimization. Adv. Eng. Softw. **42**(10), 760–771 (2011)
32. Brinkhoff, T.: A framework for generating network-based moving objects. Geoinformatica **6**(2), 153–180 (2002)

Algorithm for Removing Secondary Lines Blended with Balmer Lines in Synthetic Spectra of Massive Stars

Celia R. Fierro-Santillán[1]([✉]), Jaime Klapp[1],
Leonardo Di G. Sigalotti[2], and Janos Zsargó[3]

[1] Departamento de Física, Instituto Nacional de Investigaciones
Nucleares (ININ), La Marquesa, Estado de México, Mexico
celia.fierro.estrellas@gmail.com,
jaime.klapp@inin.gob.mx
[2] Área de Física de Procesos Irreversibles, Departamento de Ciencias Básicas,
Universidad Autónoma Metropolitana-Azcapotzalco (UAM-A),
Mexico City, Mexico
leonardo.sigalotti@gmail.com
[3] Departamento de Física, Escuela Superior de Física y Matemáticas,
Instituto Politécnico Nacional, Mexico City, Mexico
jzsargo@esfm.ipn.mx

Abstract. In order to measure automatically the equivalent width of the Balmer lines in a database of 40,000 atmosphere models, we have developed a computer program that mimics the work of an astronomer in terms of identifying and eliminating secondary spectral lines mixed with the Balmer lines. The equivalent widths measured have average errors of 5%, which makes them very reliable. As part of the FIT*spec* code, this program improves the automatic adjustment of an atmosphere model to the observed spectrum of a massive star.

Keywords: Algorithm · Database · Artificial intelligence · Balmer lines · Stellar atmospheres

1 Introduction

The main restriction when studying astronomical objects is the impossibility of directly experiencing them. The massive stars have a period of evolution characteristic of millions of years and temperatures of the order of 10^4 K. Complex phenomena occurring in the atmosphere of the star can be simulated by a numerical code. In recent decades, there have been developed sophisticated stellar atmosphere codes such as TLUSTY [1], FASTWIND [2, 3], CMFGEN [4], and the Potsdam Wolf–Rayet (PoWR) code [5–7]. As a result, significant advances have been achieved toward understanding the physical conditions prevailing in the atmospheres and winds of massive stars.

The number of models generated to study an object grows exponentially depending on the number of parameters included in the simulation, with the consequent microprocessor time consumption. A strategy to address this problem is to generate a grid of

© Springer Nature Switzerland AG 2019
M. Torres and J. Klapp (Eds.): ISUM 2019, CCIS 1151, pp. 163–170, 2019.
https://doi.org/10.1007/978-3-030-38043-4_14

models, covering characteristic values for each parameter, which can be used as a tool to study not only one, but an infinity of objects. With the use of the ABACUS-I supercomputer of the ABACUS Centre for Applied Mathematics and High Performance Computing of CINVESTAV (Mexico), it has recently been generated a grid with such characteristics [8]. This grid covers a six-dimensional space with different values of the main parameters of the star, wind, and chemical composition. Currently the grid has 40,000 models of stellar atmospheres, and hence it would be impossible to compare *by eye* the observed spectrum of a star with all models in the database.

In particular, the FIT*spec* code [9] is a tool for the automatic fitting of synthetic stellar spectra. To adjust the effective temperature, FIT*spec* requires as input the equivalent width (EW) of five helium lines: He II $\lambda\lambda 4541, 4200$; He I $\lambda\lambda 4471, 4387, 4144$; and He I + He II 4026. Additionally, to adjust the surface gravity, the program requires the EW of six Balmer lines: H_β, H_γ, H_δ, H_ϵ, H_ζ, and H_η. In order to achieve a good fit, it is important that the measurement of the EWs be as accurate as possible. The EW measured automatically may differ from what a human being would measure manually. It is important to reduce the effect of the lines mixed with the main line, since it overestimates the EW. In this paper we present a numerical method that reduces the effect of the mixed lines on the EW values.

2 Measurement of the Equivalent Width by Elimination of Secondary Lines

The equivalent width (EW) is defined as the width of a rectangle with an area equal to the spectral line and a height equal to the continuum. For an experienced astronomer it is easy to identify by eye the initial (w_i) and final (w_f) wavelengths, as well as the continuous wavelength in order to measure the area of the spectral line and establish the EW (Fig. 1). However, a computer cannot identify these values directly, and to determine them we analyze a sample of 20 spectra of the database. The selection was made using random numbers, corresponding to the spectrum number.

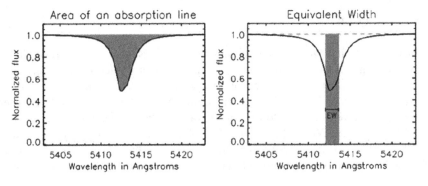

Fig. 1. Equivalent width of a spectral line.

For each spectrum of the sample, the w_i and w_f values of the six Balmer lines considered were established by simply analyzing the spectrum *by eye*. We calculated the mean and the standard deviation. The values of w_i and w_f were established as the mean plus the standard deviation (Table 1). The value of the continuum was fixed at 1.0 since it corresponds to the normalized spectra.

Table 1. The λ_i and λ_f assumed are given by the sum of the mean plus the standard deviation from the 20 spectra of the sample.

Line	λ_0	λ_i (Å)			λ_f (Å)		
		μ	σ	Assumed	μ	σ	Assumed
H_β	4861.28	4847.55	4.61	4842.94	4877.60	4.51	4882.11
H_γ	4349.47	4326.53	3.47	4323.06	4356.51	4.05	4360.56
H_δ	4101.71	4086.11	5.30	4080.81	4119.21	6.00	4125.22
H_ε	3970.08	3959.26	2.82	3956.44	3983.07	4.31	3987.37
H_ζ	3889.02	3878.75	3.00	3875.75	3902.25	3.49	3905.74
H_η	3835.40	3825.29	2.71	3822.58	3847.60	3.08	3850.68

To determine if there are more than one spectral line between w_i and w_f, we use Bolzano's theorem:

Let f be a continuous real function in a closed interval [a, b] with f (a) and f (b) of opposite signs. Then there is at least one point c of the open interval (a, b) with f (c) = 0.

This implies that when $f(a)$ and $f(b)$ have opposite signs, the function crosses the horizontal axis. We take advantage of this property to determine how many secondary lines are mixed with the main line that we want to measure. When the horizontal axis is arbitrarily set between the continuum and the depth of the spectral line (Fig. 2), we can express the modified flux as:

$$fm = f - rl, \tag{1}$$

where f is the normalized flow, and rl is the reference level, which can take any value between the continuum and the depth of the line. The modified flow, *fm*, is a function of the wavelength (w) in the interval $[w_i, w_f]$, while a and b are two subsequent values of w. For continuous functions, it is true that, if *fm(a)* and *fm(b)* have opposite signs, there is a point c where *fm(c)* = 0. In the case that concerns us, *fm* is a vector of discrete values, however, we can assume that *fm* crosses the reference level when *fm(a)* and *fm(b)* have opposite signs. In Fig. 2, it is seen that the number of spectral lines within the interval is given by the number of times (nc) that fm crosses rl divided by two. Considering that there is a main line and the rest are secondary lines, the number of secondary lines, nsl is given by

$$nsl = \frac{nc - 2}{2}. \tag{2}$$

3 Algorithm

For a given reference level, the algorithm identifies the interval [w_c, w_d] in which there is a secondary line. Next, the fm values for this range are replaced by the value of the rl, which is equivalent to removing the secondary line. For each Balmer line, we established iteratively 25 reference levels between the continuum and the depth of the line. We show the simplified version of the algorithm for a spectral line, however, the process was repeated for the six Balmer lines used by FITspec.

---

input: f = normalized flux, float type array.
  w = wavelength, float type array.
  lc = central wavelength of the spectral line, float.
Output: fm = normalized flux with secondary lines removed.

Begin
    fc = flux in the central wavelength of the spectral line
    step = (1 - fc)/25.0)
    level = 1
    while level less or equal to 25
        rl = 1.0 − step * level
        n = number of elements of fm
        $fm = f - rl$
        for i = 1 to n - 1
            sign = fm[i] * fm[i+1]
        end for
        nl = (number of elements of sign < 0)/2
        if nl less or equal to 1 then there are not secondary lines
        if nl > 1 then there are nl - 1 secondary lines
            for i=1 to nl -1
                fm in secondary line[i] = average flux of the rl
            end for
        end if
        level = level + 1
    end while
    $fm = fm + rl$
    return fm
end

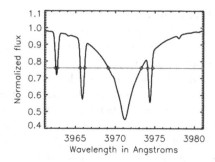

Fig. 2. The number of times that *fm* crosses the reference line (*rl*) in the interval [w_i, w_f] divided by two corresponds to the number of spectral lines crossing the reference level.

4   Errors

The purpose of the algorithm is to measure the equivalent width of the Balmer lines automatically, replacing the work of an experienced astronomer. Ideally, the algorithm should obtain the same EW values as the astronomer. Assuming that the error is the difference between both values and that the *true value* is the one that is measured manually, we can calculate the error as:

$$error = \frac{EW_{auto} - EW_{man}}{EW_{man}}, \tag{3}$$

where EW_{auto} is the equivalent width measured by the program, and EW_{man} is the EW measured by an astronomer.

The FIT*spec* code calculates which models fit an observed spectrum. This adjustment relies on the values of the EWs, therefore, it is important to reduce the errors in EW as much as possible. To verify the reliability of automatic EWs, Eq. 3 was applied to two sets of EWs: those that were measured after eliminating the secondary lines and those that had been measured in a previous job [9] without eliminating those lines. Both sets were compared with the same set of EW_{auto} measured by an astronomer. Finally, the errors generated in both sets of EW were compared.

5   Results and Discussion

Figure 3 shows a spectrum in which the secondary lines were removed with the use of the algorithm. It is clearly seen that the program has identified and eliminated the secondary lines properly. An astronomer can identify at first sight whether a spectral line is isolated or there are several lines mixed. However, this is not a trivial task for a computer. The term artificial intelligence is applied when a machine imitates some cognitive functions of human beings [10]. In this case, the algorithm mimics the process of perceiving the spectral lines through the sense of sight.

Using Eq. (3), we calculate the errors for the six Balmer lines in the twenty spectra of the sample. Subsequently, the standard deviation and the average of the errors in each line are calculated, considering two cases when the secondary lines are preserved or removed. The results are summarized in Table 2, Additionally, Fig. 4 shows a comparison between the errors produced for each line in both cases.

It would be expected that when the EW is calculated by preserving the secondary lines, its values would be overestimated. On the other hand, when the secondary lines are removed, the overestimation will decrease, and even so the EWs would be underestimated. However, Table 2 shows that in both cases, the EWs are underestimated in all the lines, except in H_η. This behavior is due to the λ_i and λ_f values having been considered in each case.

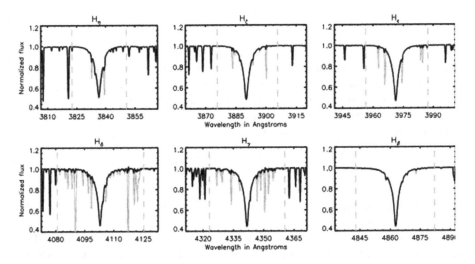

Fig. 3. Secondary lines removed (continuous gray line) before measuring the EW of the Balmer lines. Dashed gray lines indicate the λ_i and λ_f assumed when measuring the EW in all the spectra of the database.

Table 2. Average error and standard deviation of the EWs errors in the spectra of the sample using Eq. (3).

Line	λ_0	With secondary lines		Without secondary lines	
		Average error	σ	Average error	σ
H_β	4861.28	−0.0920	0.0838	−0.0402	0.0415
H_γ	4349.47	−0.1147	0.1694	−0.0953	0.2484
H_δ	4101.71	−0.1833	0.1881	−0.1560	0.1549
H_ε	3970.08	−0.0837	0.0560	−0.0577	0.0299
H_ζ	3889.02	0.0525	0.1230	−0.0022	0.0886
H_η	3835.40	0.1183	0.3405	0.0427	0.1364

When the EWs are measured by keeping the secondary lines, the values of λ_i and λ_f are established closer to the central wavelength to avoid the effect of such lines. This method underestimates the EWs, especially in those spectra where the Balmer lines are broadened by gravitational effects. On the other hand, the algorithm that suppresses the secondary lines, allowed to fix the values of λ_i and λ_f more realistically, from the spectra of the sample. This algorithm obtains values closer to those that an astronomer would measure regardless of whether the Balmer lines are narrow or broadened.

Figure 4 shows that when measuring the EWs while retaining the secondary lines, the average errors are 10%, while when eliminating the secondary lines, the average errors are reduced to 5%. Only for H_δ the EW could be underestimate as far as 25%, improving the underestimation of 40% obtained by the other method. As it can be seen in Fig. 3, H_δ presents a large number of mixed lines, this seem to influence the dispersion of errors. For this, we should consider H_δ as the least reliable line for the adjustment, with an average error of 15%.

Properly measuring the EWs of a spectrum is a task that requires an experienced astronomer. In a database with 40,000 synthetic spectra, the total time needed to measure the lines is dominated by the number of spectra, more than by the time needed to measure the lines in a spectrum. We estimated that measuring six spectral lines could come between 10 and 30 min, in function of the number of secondary lines in each spectrum, but, determine precisely the time required by the astronomer to measure a set of lines, is not relevant to the problem. The task of measuring six lines in a database with 40,000 spectra consume thousands of astronomer hours, due to this, it is not reasonable to perform such task manually.

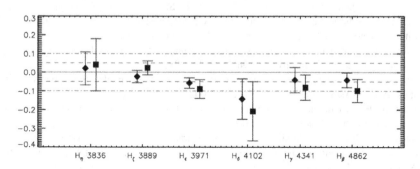

Fig. 4. Comparison of errors. The squares correspond to the errors in the EWs with secondary lines, while the diamonds are the errors when the secondary lines are eliminated before measuring the EWs.

6   Conclusions

In this work, we have presented an algorithm, which has the ability to perform a realistic measurement of EWs, identify the secondary lines mixed with the Balmer lines, and then eliminate them before calculating the EW, in a way similar to what an experienced astronomer would do.

The algorithm improves the results obtained in the previous version of FIT*spec,* reducing the average error from 10 to 5% in five Balmer lines, except for H_δ, whose average error was 15%. By improving the value of EWs, the algorithm also allows to increase the quality of the automatic adjustment of spectra made by FIT*spec.* The qualitative evaluation of the spectra before and after applying the program, shows that mimics the work of an astronomer in terms of eliminating secondary spectral lines mixed with the Balmer lines, behaving like an artificial intelligence program.

Acknowledgment. The authors acknowledge the use of the ABACUS-I supercomputer at the Laboratory of Applied Mathematics and High-Performance Computing of the Mathematics Department of CINVESTAV-IPN, where this work was performed. J. Zsargó acknowledges CONACyT CB-2011-01 No. 168632 grant for support. J. K. acknowledges financial support by the Consejo Nacional de Ciencia y Tecnología (CONACyT), Mexico, under grant 283151. The research leading to these results has received funding from the European Union's Horizon 2020 Programme under the ENERXICO Project, grant agreement no 828947 and under the Mexican CONACYT-SENER-Hidrocarburos grant agreement B-S-69926.

References

1. Hubeny, I., Lanz, T.: Non-LTE line-blanketed model atmospheres of hot stars. 1: hybrid complete linearization/accelerated lambda iteration method. Astrophys. J. **439**, 875–904 (1995)
2. Santolaya-Rey, A.E., Puls, J., Herrero, A.: Atmospheric NLTE-models for the spectroscopic analysis of luminous blue stars with winds. Astron. Astrophys. **323**, 488–512 (1997)
3. Puls, J., Urbaneja, M.A., Venero, R., Repolust, T., Springmann, U., Jokuthy, A., Mokiem, M.R.: Atmospheric NLTE-models for the spectroscopic analysis of blue stars with winds-II. Line-blanketed models. Astron. Astrophys. **435**(2), 669–698 (2005)
4. Hillier, D.J., Miller, D.L.: The treatment of non-LTE line blanketing in spherically expanding outflows. Astrophys. J. **496**(1), 407 (1998)
5. Gräfener, G., Koesterke, L., Hamann, W.R.: Line-blanketed model atmospheres for WR stars. Astron. Astrophys. **387**(1), 244–257 (2002)
6. Hamann, W.R., Gräfener, G.: A temperature correction method for expanding atmospheres. Astron. Astrophys. **410**(3), 993–1000 (2003)
7. Sander, A., Shenar, T., Hainich, R., Gímenez-García, A., Todt, H., Hamann, W.R.: On the consistent treatment of the quasi-hydrostatic layers in hot star atmospheres. Astron. Astrophys. **577**, A13 (2015)
8. Zsargó, J., Fierro, C.R., Klapp, J., Arrieta, A., Arias, L., John Hillier, D.: Database of CMFGEN models in a 6-dimensional space. In: Barrios Hernández, C.J., Gitler, I., Klapp, J. (eds.) CARLA 2016. CCIS, vol. 697, pp. 387–392. Springer, Cham (2017). https://doi.org/10.1007/978-3-319-57972-6_29
9. Fierro-Santillán, C.R., et al.: FITspec: a new algorithm for the automated fit of synthetic stellar spectra for OB stars. Astrophys. J. Suppl. Ser. **236**(2), 38 (2018)
10. Russell, S.J., Norvig, P.: Artificial Intelligence: A Modern Approach. Pearson Education Limited, Kuala Lumpur (2016)

HPC Architecture

Multi GPU Implementation to Accelerate the CFD Simulation of a 3D Turbo-Machinery Benchmark Using the RapidCFD Library

Daniel Molinero[1(✉)], Sergio Galván[1], Jesús Pacheco[1], and Nicolás Herrera[2]

[1] Universidad Michoacana de San Nicolás de Hidalgo, 58030 Morelia, Mexico
molherd@gmail.com
[2] Instituto Tecnológico de Morelia, 58120 Morelia, Mexico

Abstract. Recently, several research groups have demonstrated significant speedups of scientific computations using General Purpose Graphics Processor Units (GPGPU) as massively-parallel "co-processors" to the Central Processing Unit (CPU). However, the tremendous computational power of GPGPUs has come with a high price since their implementation to Computational Fluids Dynamics (CFD) solvers is still a challenge. To achieve this implementation, the RapidCFD library was developed from the Open Field Operation and Manipulation (OpenFOAM) CFD software to let that the multi-GPGPU were able of running almost the entire simulation in parallel. The parallel performance, as fixed-size speed-up, efficiency and parallel fraction, according to the Amdahl's law, were compared in two massively parallel multi-GPGPU architectures using Nvidia Tesla C1060 and M2090 units. The simulations were executed on a 3D turbo-machinery benchmark which consist of a structured grid domain of 1 million cells. The results obtained from the implementation of the new library on different software and hardware layouts show that by transferring directly all the computations executed by the linear system solvers to the GPGPU, is possible to make a typical CFD simulation until 9 times faster. Additionally a grid convergence analysis and pressure recovery measurements were executed over scaled computational domains. Thus, it is expected to obtain an affordable low computational cost when the domain be scaled in order to achieve a high flow resolution.

Keywords: GPGPU · CFD · Draft tube

1 Introduction

Computational Fluids Dynamics has a history of seeking and requiring ever higher computational performance because it uses numerical methods and algorithms to solve and analyze problems that involve fluid flow. In the High Performance Computing (HPC), the parallelism is being considered the future of computing since the efforts in the microprocessor development are concentrated on adding cores rather than increasing single-thread performance.

© Springer Nature Switzerland AG 2019
M. Torres and J. Klapp (Eds.): ISUM 2019, CCIS 1151, pp. 173–187, 2019.
https://doi.org/10.1007/978-3-030-38043-4_15

Using parallel computing techniques, GPGPUs have emerged as a major paradigm for solving complex computational problems because the GPGPU's design features result in computational power and memory bandwidth which exceeds the features of the fastest multi-core CPUs by almost an order of magnitude. Indeed, they are now an equivalent to a small HPC cluster and even just a single GPGPU is faster than a multicore CPU [1].

While GPGPUs are specialized to perform large amounts of arithmetic and have a large theoretical performance advantage over CPUs for many problems of interest to the CFD community, there are a number of barriers to their adoption in real world CFD codes and their implementation is still a challenge [2–4].

However, in order to GPGPUs take advantage of this large theoretical performance over CPUs their adoption requires a CFD parallelizable code and an intermediate low-level interface that can transfer data between the CPU and GPGPU and perform the required computation on the GPGPU. Nvidia's Compute Unified Device Architecture (CUDA) is one such interface. Thus, to complete this implementation, a CFD code compatible with CUDA Nvidia Language is needed [5].

The OpenFOAM code is an option since it provides a flexible simulation platform by mimicking the form of Partial Differential Equations (PDE) and it runs in parallel using automatic/manual domain decomposition. Furthermore, the best attractive characteristic of this CFD tool is that as open-source code it is free of charge, what makes it a true competitor to both commercial tools and in-house research codes being of interest to the international community researchers of CFD.

In recent years several libraries have been implemented to accelerate OpenFOAM through GPGPUs (e.g. Cufflink, ofgpu, speed IT) without modifying the original code and applied as a simple plug-in, these implementations have been very attractive. However some discordances and contradicting performance have been reported [6].

The aim of this paper is to estimate a plausible GPGPU acceleration for a new application library. RapidCFD is an open-source OpenFOAM implementation capable of running almost entire simulations on Nvidia GPGPUs. Introducing parallelism for multi-GPGPUs, this implementation should leads to a very promising performance improvement in certain CFD applications, such as the possibility of its implementation to solve scaled problems.

The simulations were run on a 3D turbo-machinery well-known benchmark with a structured grid of one million cells. In order to evaluate the parallel performance of the RapidCFD library, several parameters as fixed-size speed-up, efficiency and parallel fraction were compared in two massively parallel multi-GPGPU architecture using Nvidia Tesla C1060 and M2090 units.

The results suggest that the more the domain is decomposed the more speedup and parallelism fall, at least for this fixed-size problem. It seems that, porting too many parts of computational domain to multi-GPGPUs lead to significant des-acceleration in computation. For all that, when the domain have to be scaled, using different grid size, looking for achieving a high flow resolution, it is expected an efficient program execution which should result in an affordable low computational cost.

2 Methodology

2.1 Benchmark Description

The benchmark studied is the numerical model of the Hölleforsen Kaplan draft tube 1:11 which was previously used in three European Research Community on Flow Turbulence and Combustion (ERCOFTAC) workshops [7–9]. Allocated after the runner, the draft tube is part of a hydraulic turbine and its function is to convert the kinetic energy of the fluid leaving the runner into pressure energy with a minimum of losses. In reference [10] was validated and verified the numerical model to obtain reliable numerical data during the computation process. Figure 1 presents the computational model of the turbine T-99 used as benchmark.

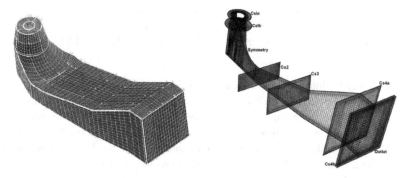

Fig. 1. Multi-block and structured mesh of the T-99 draft tube used as benchmark.

2.2 Acceleration Method

Using the same boundary conditions as [10], the numerical model was represented by the Navier-Stokes PDE and solved in steady state using OpenFOAM and RapidCFD.

For accelerating the time required to solve the case in CFD a hybrid parallel environment was established in two different hardware architectures:

- CPU parallelization with Message Passing Interface (MPI) library
- Multi-GPGPU parallelization with MPI and CUDA.

To port the solvers to the CPUs, OpenFOAM v1706 uses MPI which provide parallel multi-processor functionality. A decomposition of the computational domain is essential for the parallelization since every processor contributes to the solution of the simulation by solving a part of the computational domain. Besides, it scales well on homogeneous systems but do not fully utilize potential per-node performance on hybrid systems.

Equally, to port OpenFOAM solvers to multi-GPGPUs a new open-source implementation was used. According to [11, 12], RapidCFD can be capable of running almost the entire simulation on Nvidia GPGPUs which can lead in certain applications to a very promising performance improvements.

Table 1 shows the hardware architectures used in this research. Both work stations (WS) have two CPU with eight and six cores (twelve threads). However the massive parallelization should occur in one thousand CUDA cores distributed in two and four GPGPUs.

Table 1. Workstation specifications.

Workstation WSPAC	Workstation WSGAL
CPU	
2 x Intel Xeon E5504, 2.0 GHz	2 x Intel Xeon L5639, 2.13 GHz
4 cores per processor/4 threads	6 cores per processor/12 threads
12 GB Memory DDR3, 1060 Hz	24 GB Memory DDR3, 1060 Hz
GPGPU	
4 x Nvidia Tesla C1060	2 x Nvidia Tesla M2090
240 CUDA cores, 1.296 GHz	512 CUDA cores, 1.3 GHz
4 GB Memory GDDR3, 800 MHz	6 GB Memory GDDR5, 1.85 GHz

To get better scaling results using multi-GPGPUs [13] recommends that one CPU core needs to be devoted to each active GPGPU. RapidCFD enables the use of one CPU core (or thread depending on architecture) with one GPGPU enhancing better performance. When only CPUs were used, the domain was proportionally decomposed according to the number of cores/threads available in the WSs. However when using GPGPUs, the domain was decomposed according to the number of GPGPUs.

2.3 Numerical Considerations

The computational domain was solved with double floating precision using the application solver *simpleFoam* recommended for incompressible flow and setting *ddtSchemes* (time discretization) as *steadyState*, which means the time derivatives are not solved. Since the general transport equation used in the Finite Volume Method (FVM) is second order, it is necessary that the order of discretization be at least second order accurate in space. Consequently, *gradSchemes* (gradient terms), *divSchemes* (convective terms), *laplacianSchemes* (laplacian terms), *interpolationSchemes* (point-to-point interpolations) and *snGradSchemes* (component of gradient normal to a cell face) used second order discretization schemes.

The linear solver used for the pressure p discretized equation was PCG (Preconditioned Conjugate Gradient) and for the velocity U the Preconditioned Bi-conjugate Gradient (PBiCG) was used. There are a range of options for preconditioning of matrices in the conjugate gradient solvers. In this work diagonal preconditioning (*diagonal*) was selected. The term linear solver refers to the method of number-crunching to solve the set of linear equations, as opposed to application solver which describes the set of equations and algorithms to solve a particular problem [14].

The sparse matrix solvers are iterative, i.e. they are based on reducing the equation residual over a succession of solutions. The residual is an error measure in the solution so that the smaller it is, the more accurate the solution. For this reason the solver tolerance for each time step was settled to 10e-12 for all equations.

The Semi-Implicit Method for Pressure-Linked Equations (SIMPLE) algorithm was used to couple the *p-U* equation system. This algorithm is an iterative procedure for solving equations of velocity and pressure and is based on evaluating some initial solutions and then correcting them to reach a target residual, in this case 10e-03 [14].

The computational domain was decomposed using the *decomposePar* utility with the *scoth* decomposition method which does not require geometric input from the user and attempts to minimize the number of processor boundaries.

In many studies, the goal of fluid simulations on supercomputers that use many GPGPUs is typically to study turbulence, not complex geometries [15]. However, this study involves both of them and the viscous effect of the fluid flow. Thus, the *k-e* standard turbulence model was used in all the simulations since the experimental data given by [7–9] provide information at inlet related to the turbulent kinetic energy *k* and turbulent eddy dissipation rate *e*. The PBiCG linear solver was used to solve the turbulent scalar quantities *k* and *e*.

2.4 Study Cases

Using the same previously detailed setup, each simulation was run nine times using different hardware architecture as is shown in Table 2. In each WS one homogeneous and one heterogeneous parallel system were tested. In the homogeneous system only the parallelization of eight and twelve domains on CPU cores was evaluated. In the heterogeneous system (CPU+GPGPU) two and four domains were assigned to the GPGPU cores.

Table 2. Domain decomposition.

Workstation WSPAC			Workstation WSGAL		
Configuration	Cores	Domains	Configuration	Cores	Domains
1 cpu	1	1	1 cpu	1	1
2 cpu	2	2	2 cpu	2	2
4 cpu	4	4	4 cpu	4	4
6 cpu	6	6	6 cpu	6	6
8 cpu	8	8	8 cpu	8	8
1 cpu + 1 gpu	240	1	10 cpu	10	10
2 cpu + 2 gpu	480	2	12 cpu	12	12
3 cpu + 3 gpu	720	3	1 cpu + 1 gpu	512	1
4 cpu + 4 gpu	960	4	2 cpu + 2 gpu	1024	2

3 Results

The first part of this section details the CFD convergence solution for the one million cells benchmark. In the second part, the acceleration metrics for each WS are analyzed. In the third section, a grid convergence analysis and a comparison of the CFD against the experimental result are developed.

3.1   CFD Solution Convergence

In all cases studied in this first two sections, the same setup (boundary conditions and discretization schemes) was used for the computational model in which the residuals reached the convergence criteria of 10e-03 for momentum and continuity equations as follows: using OpenFOAM v1706 with CPUs 557 iterations were necessary (Fig. 2), and 599 iterations when the RapidCFD library linked the GPGPUs (Fig. 3).

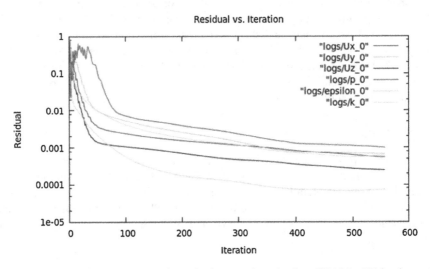

Fig. 2. Residuals of momentum and continuity equations in OpenFOAM v1706 using only CPUs.

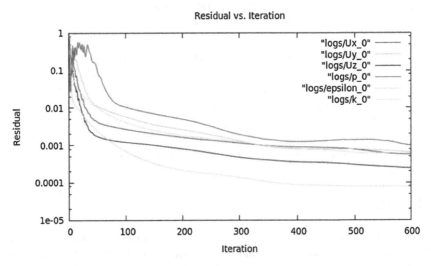

Fig. 3. Residuals of momentum and continuity equations in OpenFOAM using RapidCFD library and GPGPUs.

This difference in the number of iterations required to reach convergence could be related to RapidCFD was developed from OpenFOAM 2.3.1 and some upgrades regarding algorithms and discretization schemes have been included since then in OpenFOAM v1706.

Independently of the domain decomposition, the number of iterations required to reach the convergence criteria was the same. Surprisingly, just the time required to reach the convergence criteria was different. This difference between both libraries will be analyzed in further research towards a better solution of the numerical model.

3.2   Acceleration Metrics

A set of metrics quantified the performance of the architectures which found the solution to the matrix obtained from the discretization of the governing equations of fluid flow and mass transfer.

Figures 4 and 5 presents the results for the computational time registered for the WSPAC and WSGAL through the execution time and the wall clock time. The execution time measures only the time during which the processor is actively working on a certain task and the wall clock time is the time elapsed between the start of the process till end it. If wall clock time is smaller than execution time, the program was executed perfectly in parallel. If wall clock time is greater than execution time, the system will be waiting e.g. for disk, network or other devices between iterations. As can be observed, WSGAL is faster in both execution time and wall clock time mainly due to GPGPUs in it have more computing power per unit (512 CUDA cores vs. 240 CUDA cores) and also faster RAM (GDDR5 1.85 MHz vs. GDDR3 800 MHz). This has direct impact in the metrics measured further.

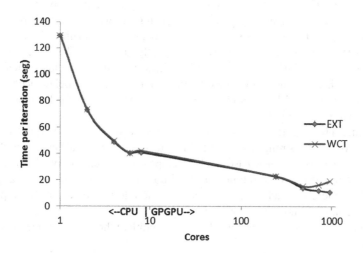

Fig. 4. Time comparison in the WSPAC.

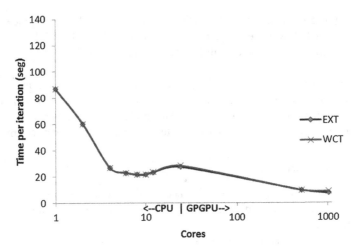

Fig. 5. Time comparison in the WSGAL.

Speed up is one of the most important actions in parallel computing and it actually measure how much faster a parallel algorithm runs with respect to the best sequential one. In our research, the speed up was compared through (1) [2]. For a problem of size n, the expression for speedup is:

$$S_p = T_s(n, 1)/T(n, N) \tag{1}$$

Where $T_s(n;1)$ is the time of the best sequential algorithm and $T(n;N)$ is the time of the parallel algorithm with N processors, both solving the same problem.

Figure 6 shows the speed up given by (1) using the wall clock time per iteration obtained from the CFD simulations of the draft tube flow field. With both machines, the GPGPUs were significantly faster. However, only using the WSGAL this metric reached up to a maximum of 9.32. WSPAC has a suddenly decline when a third GPGPU is used. This denotes that the GPGPU is a massively parallel device that needs an important quantity of threads to be filled with a huge number of cell elements for an efficient program execution.

Reference [16] reports until 4.29 times of speed up simulating Magneto Hydro Dynamics flow under strong magnetic field in fusion liquid metal blanket with structured or unstructured meshes. Also [17] developed the simulation of blood flow in a cardiac system reaching until 6 times of speed up. In many cases, obtaining a speedup of 5 or 10 is more than adequate, especially if the effort involved in developing the parallel program was not very large [18].

Amdahl's law [2] states that for a fixed size problem the expected overall speedup is given by:

$$S_p = 1/[(1 - c) + c/N] \tag{2}$$

Where c is the fraction of a program that is parallel, $(1 - c)$ is the fraction that runs sequential and N is the number of processors. But if the computer has a large number of processors, $N \approx \infty$, then the maximum speedup is limited by the sequential part of the algorithm $(1 - c)$.

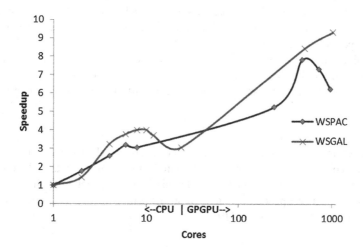

Fig. 6. Speedup for the T-99 draft tube model benchmark.

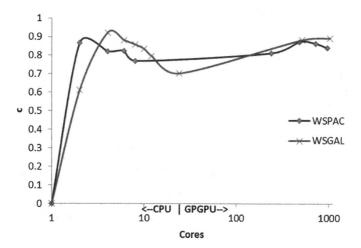

Fig. 7. Fraction of parallelism reached by the benchmark.

Figure 7 compares the fraction of parallelism c achieved by the hardware in both machines according to (2). The higher parallelism achieved was 0.92 and depends on the number of cores used (CPU and GPGPU). Then, we may consider this problem as strong scaling because using more cores it is possible to achieve a better fraction of parallelism and performance when the size of the problem is fixed.

As shown in Figs. 6 and 7, using around 500 CUDA cores, the speedup and parallelism are quite similar in both machines; however, the more the domain is decomposed the more speedup and parallelism fall in the WSPAC. When both machines work close to 1000 CUDA cores, the speedup in WSPAC is 6.32 while in WSGAL speedup continues growing up to 9.32. This reflected that parallel programming, especially using GPGPU acceleration, is much suitable for processing large number of calculations [16], since each time the domain is decomposed, the number of unknowns per subdomain that the GPGPU should process decreases.

In addition to the speedup, efficiency evaluation is necessary for studying the implementation of the new library in different hardware resources. The efficiency E tells how well the processors are being used according the following expression:

$$E = S_p/N \tag{3}$$

As shown in Fig. 8, the maximum efficiency value 1, which will mean an optimal usage of the computational resources, is difficult to maintain. In fact, as the number of cores increases, the efficiency tends to fall. This is a consequence of the difficulty to reach a perfect linear speedup in spite of its growing, however speedup is usually advertised for parallel computers [19].

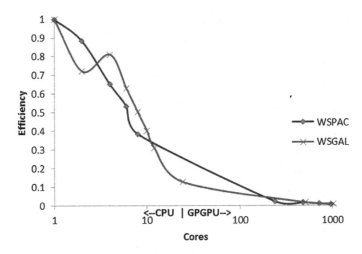

Fig. 8. Efficiency measurement for the benchmark workload.

Thus, the results obtained in this study show an important difference in parallelization between machines no matter if CPUs or GPGPUs were used. The GPGPU's memory and the combination of core types played a key role on multi-GPGPU implementations.

It is worth to mention that the GPGPUs deployed in this work have compute capability 1.3 (Nvidia Tesla C1060) and 2.0 (Nvidia Tesla M2090), the first ones to support double precision and ECC memory, also that RapidCFD was developed for

Nvidia compute capability 3.0 and above, which make them almost archaic and useless compared with newer Kepler, Maxwell, Pascal and Volta architectures from Nvidia with thousands of CUDA cores, so some changes were made at compilation time in CUDA 6.5 in order to get the library running in Ubuntu 16.04 with the available GPGPUs. Even so the results obtained are quite stoning since in some cases a speedup near 10 was reached compared to CPUs. This give a chance in the research and learning for coupling CFD and GPGPUs using old second hand and cheaper GPGPUs.

3.3   Accuracy of the CFD Simulations

Theoretically, a greater number of cells enhance accuracy of the results and convergence of the solution. Since so far only a fixed problem size has been used for the analysis, two studies were developed to estimate the largest problem size to be solved in order to reach an acceptable accuracy level and flow resolution in CFD. In both studies five computational domains were solved, from coarsest to finest grid size: 0.5, 1, 2, 3 and 4 million cells.

The first study was developed to validate the CFD solution. The wall pressure recovery coefficient obtained by the different grid size was compared against the available experimental data. Detailed velocity and pressure measurements made in [20] were used to set the boundary conditions and to validate the computational results. Figure 9 presents the upper and lower centerline wall of the draft tube along which the static pressure recovery (Cp_{wall}) was experimental and computationally measured using (5).

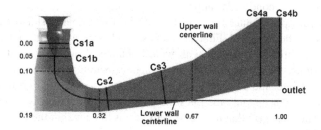

Fig. 9. Test measurement sections of the draft tube [9].

$$Cp_{wall} = P_{out} - P_{in}/0.5\rho U_{in}^2 \qquad (5)$$

Where P_{out} is the static wall pressure in different points along the wall centerline (0.0–1.0), P_{in} is the static wall pressure at CsIa (0.00), ρ is the density and U_{in} is the mean velocity at CsIa.

Figure 10 presents the approximation of the CFD solution over the entire computational domain as its grid size is increased. The pressure recovery factor indicates the degree of conversion of kinetic energy into static pressure where a higher value means higher efficiency for the draft tube. The exact value of the pressure recovery factor depends on the whole field solution and can be seen as an integral property of the solution.

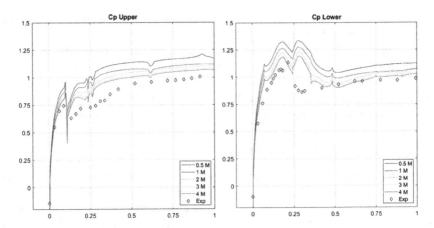

Fig. 10. Comparison of the pressure recovery at the lower and upper centerline of the draft tube with different grid sizes.

The second study was developed to verify the CFD solution. As described by [21], the values of performance variables, as Cp_{wall}, can be extrapolated based on initial values obtained through CFD from the solution of scaled grid size using Richardson extrapolation methods. Extrapolation values can be calculated by means of two approaches, first and second order, which depends on the method used in numerical methods to solve the problem studied, as mentioned before the FVM is a second order scheme, therefore a second order approach was be used.

In Fig. 11 for upper center line and Fig. 12 for lower line, results of the convergence analysis can be observed. First $\varphi(1)$ and second $\varphi(2)$ order extrapolations values of the total Cp_{wall} are shown along with values obtained from CFD solutions, φ, and punctual experimental values, $\varphi(E)$. In the graphics, α indicates the refinement level, the smaller the value, the finer the grid size, where a cero value corresponds to a continuous. For the Cp_{wall}, only the finest three grids are inside the asymptotic range of convergence. Thus, the grid that uses 2 M cells seems to be within the range that would minimize the CFD computations.

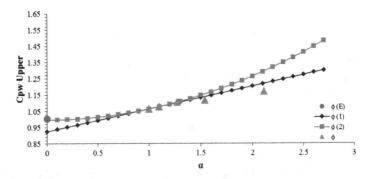

Fig. 11. Plots of the Cp: First $\varphi(1)$ and second $\varphi(2)$ order extrapolations, CFD solutions φ and experimental values $\varphi(E)$ for grid convergence analysis un the upper center line.

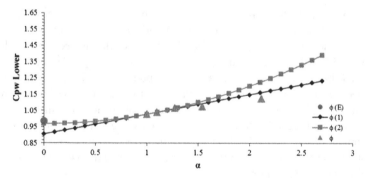

Fig. 12. Plots of the *Cp:* First $\varphi(1)$ and second $\varphi(2)$ order extrapolations, CFD solutions φ and experimental values $\varphi(E)$ for grid convergence analysis in the lower center line.

The error of the CFD and extrapolated values of Cp_{wall} against experimental ones is presented in Table 3.

Table 3. Error calculation against experimental values of Cp_{wall}.

Error %		
Source	Upper wall	Lower wall
0.5 M cells	14.36	12.28
1 M cells	10.21	8.34
2 M cells	9.25	7.51
3 M cells	6.83	5.12
4 M cells	5.62	4.01
1st Order	8.67	8.88
2nd Order	0.69	1.73

In conclusion, both studies are an example of accuracy in the quantitative results as the grid size grows up, which indicates that a mesh refinement will lead to a better solution, even without implement more robust turbulence models or accurate discretization schemes.

Further work will be focused on computational cost required to reach an acceptable accuracy and flow resolution, in terms of time and memory consumption in GPGPUs when it is given a fixed time and limited memory.

4   Conclusions

In this study, it has been investigated the acceleration of a turbo machinery numerical model adapting GPGPUs to the OpenFOAM CFD code. A major benefit of using this free CFD software instead of any commercial one has been that the full source code is open and available. This makes possible the development of new libraries as RapidCFD, which are out of reach in the CFD commercial software.

In consequence, the principal contribution of this work has been the implementation of two different GPGPUs to CFD computations through the new RapidCFD library, which have proved to accelerate the computational solution, even when their main characteristics are not the best compared to available hardware nowadays, demonstrating the advantage of using CUDA built in applications as the one deployed. The results obtained are very promising because they suggest that porting larger parts of CFD simulations to GPGPUs lead to significant acceleration in computation and could apply the CFD technology in very complexes industrial flows as the creation of a micro-turbine testing laboratory.

The parallelism efficiency was reduced significantly and a sub-linear speed up was presented in all the tested cases. This means that an alternative parallel model or changes in the benchmark domain decomposition could be needed.

Since the GPGPU is a massively parallel device, it should be necessary to know if the same number and distribution of cores will make better the performance computing of this benchmark with higher grid sizes.

Finally, another perspective of this work could be the change of CFD set-up using different turbulence models or discretization schemes in order to review not only computational cost but also the influence of the numerical concepts on the GPGPU accuracy.

References

1. Niemeyer, K.E., Sung, C.-J.: Recent progress and challenges in exploiting graphics processors in computational fluid dynamics. J. Supercomput. **67**(2), 528–564 (2014)
2. Navarro, C., Hitschfeld-Kahler, N., Mateu, L.: A survey on parallel computing and its applications in data-parallel problems using GPU architectures. Commun. Comput. Phys. **15**(2), 285–329 (2014)
3. Posey, S., See, S., Wang, M.: GPU progress and directions in applied CFD. In: Eleventh International Conference on CFD in the Minerals and Process Industries, Melbourne, Australia (2015)
4. AlOnazi, A.: Design and optimization of OpenFOAM-based CFD applications for modern hybrid and heterogeneous HPC platforms. Master thesis, King Abdullah University of Science and Technology, Thuwal, Kingdom of Saudi Arabia (2014)
5. NVIDIA Corporation, Cuda C Programming Guide v6.5 (2014)
6. Aissa, M.: GPU-accelerated CFD simulations for turbomachinery design optimization. Doctoral thesis, Delft University of Technology (2017)
7. Gebart, B., Gustavsson, L., Karlsson, R.: Proceedings of Turbine 99 Workshop on Draft Tube Flow in Porjus, Sweden, Luleå University of Technology (2000)
8. Engström, T., Gustavsson, L., Karlsson, R.: Turbine-99 workshop 2 on draft tube flow. In: Proceedings of 21st IAHR Symposium on Hydraulic Machinery and Systems, Lausanne, Switzerland (2005)
9. Cervantes, M., Engstöm, T., Gustavsson, L.: Proceedings of the Third IAHR/ERCOFTAC Workshop on Draft Tube Flows, Luleå University of Technology, Porjus, Sweden (2005)

10. Galván, S., Reggio, M., Guibault, F.: Assessment study of k-ε turbulence models and near-wall modeling for steady state swirling flow analysis in draft tube using fluent. Eng. Appl. Comput. Fluid Mech. **5**(4), 459–478 (2011)
11. Jasiński, D.: Adapting OpenFOAM for massively parallel GPU architecture. In: The 3rd OpenFOAM User Conference, Stuttgart, Germany (2015)
12. simFlow CFD software, Atizar/RapidCFD-dev, GitHub, Inc. https://github.com/Atizar/RapidCFD-dev
13. Afzal, A., Ansari, Z., Faizabadi, A.R., Ramis, M.K.: Parallelization strategies for computational fluid dynamics software: state of the art review. Arch. Comput. Methods Eng. **24**(2), 337–363 (2017)
14. OpenCFD Limited, OpenFOAM. The Open Source CFD Tool Box. User Guide v1706 (2017)
15. Khajeh-Saeed, A., Perot, J.B.: Computational fluid dynamics simulations using many graphics processors. Comput. Sci. Eng. **14**, 10–19 (2012)
16. He, Q., Hongli, C., Jingchao, F.: Acceleration of the OpenFOAM-based MHD solver using graphics processing units. Fusion Eng. Des. **101**, 88–93 (2015)
17. Malecha, Z., et al.: GPU-based simulation of 3D blood flow in abdominal aorta using OpenFOAM. Arch. Mech. **63**(2), 137–161 (2011)
18. Pacheco, P.: An Introduction to Parallel Programming. Elsevier, Amsterdam (2011)
19. McCool, M., Robison, A.D., Reinders, J.: Structured Parallel Programming: Patterns for Efficient Computation. Morgan Kaufmann Publishers, Waltham (2012)
20. Andersson, U.: Test case T- some news results and updates since workshop 1. In: Proceedings of Turbine 99-WS2, the Second ERCOFTAC Workshop on Draft Tubeflow, Alvkarleby, Sweden (2001)
21. Herrera, N., Galván, S., Camacho, J., Solorio, G., Aguilar, A.: Automatic shape optimization of a conical duct diffuser using a distributed computing algorithm. J. Braz. Soc. Mech. Sci. Eng. **39**(11), 4367–4378 (2017)

Cluster-UY: Collaborative Scientific High Performance Computing in Uruguay

Sergio Nesmachnow and Santiago Iturriaga[✉]

Universidad de la República, Montevideo, Uruguay
{sergion, siturria}@fing.edu.uy

Abstract. This article describes the national initiative for installing and operating a collaborative scientific HPC infrastructure in Uruguay (Cluster-UY). The project was conceived as a mean to foster research and innovation projects that face complex problems with high computing demands. The main ideas and motivations of the Cluster-UY project are described. The technological decisions to install the platform are explained and the collaborative operation model to guarantee sustainability is introduced. In addition, the perspectives of the national scientific HPC initiative are highlighted and sample current projects are presented.

Keywords: HPC · Scientific instrumentation systems

1 Introduction

Scientific instrumentation systems play a major role in the development of highquality research, especially in those areas of science and technology that heavily rely and emphasize on experimental studies. In this context, having platforms that implement scientific instrumentation services allows researchers to strengthen proposals, broaden the horizons of researches, and obtain high-impact results that are validated in practice [13, 24].

Nowadays, a specific and relevant case of scientific instrumentation systems are Supercomputing or high performance computing (HPC) systems. These systems allow solving complex problems that have large computing demands (e.g., because they deal with complex mathematical models, address very complex problem instances, and/or manages very large volumes of data). Parallel computing techniques [9] help researchers to face the aforementioned complex problems and solve them in reasonable computing times. However, specific high performance hardware is required to apply HPC and parallel computing techniques.

The reality of the scientific instrumentation systems in the world is diverse. There is a clear differentiation between developed countries and Latin American countries, from both the conceptual point of view and also from the methods applied for its implementation and operation. Regarding HPC systems, even within Latin America different situations are identified (e.g., between Brazil and other countries). HPC platforms are expensive and significant efforts are required to acquire, maintain, and operate the facilities.

© Springer Nature Switzerland AG 2019
M. Torres and J. Klapp (Eds.): ISUM 2019, CCIS 1151, pp. 188–202, 2019.
https://doi.org/10.1007/978-3-030-38043-4_16

This article describes a proposal for an HPC scientific instrumentation system to be installed and operated within the current reality of Latin American countries. The proposal was conceived as a mean to foster research and innovation projects with high computing demands, in a context where monetary resources are scarce. An approach based on ideas from collaborative economy is proposed for operation. The impact on science and technology is described and sample applications are briefly described.

The article is organized as follows. Next section describes scientific instrumentation systems and HPC facilities. Section 3 introduces the Cluster-UY project. Section 4 presents the details about the proposed self-managed business model. The impact and sample applications are described in Sect. 5. Finally, Sect. 6 formulates the main conclusions and current lines of work.

2   Scientific Instrumentation Systems and HPC Facilities

This section describes the main concepts about scientific instrumentation systems and HPC facilities.

2.1   Scientific Instrumentation Systems

Nowadays, most of scientific research, and all of experimental research, require using various equipment to address experimental analysis, simulation development, validation of prototypes, and other activities [24].

Scientific instrumentation services are structures for research and development that provide access to specialized and up-to-date equipment, and also to expert personnel in the methodologies for using the equipment. A specific objective of scientific instrumentation services is to diversify and expand the use of equipment by an increasing number of researchers, providing in turn the mechanisms, assistance, and training needed to take advantage of the systems. In universities, having sophisticated scientific instrumentation is vital to develop quality research. Scientific instrumentation services complement formation and research activities developed in groups and institutes [13].

A specific feature of modern scientific instrumentation systems, which is very relevant for the proposal introduced in this article, is their high economic cost and their very fast obsolescence. Having a well-planned and efficient service allows optimizing the resources allocated to the purchase of equipment. A centralized management of the infrastructure also allows reducing operating costs and improving the efficiency of operation/maintenance tasks by specialized technicians.

Due to the aforementioned reasons, the implementation of a scientific instrumentation service that provides various advisory services in the use of equipment is an efficient and rational alternative for research groups to make use of large and highly qualified equipment. In those institutions where there is no scientific instrumentation service, authorities must raise awareness in research groups that require the use of specific equipment to initiate the formation of multidisciplinary groups to gather critical mass and interest on a scientific instrumentation service.

Scientific instrumentation services also provides support to researchers for operating the equipment, advise on the design and planning of research methodologies and experimental analysis based on the computing infrastructure to use, and assistance on methodologies for processing results. The training of highly specialized technical personnel is fundamental for the correct operation of a scientific instrumentation service. Institutions must develop and strengthen a group trained to operate the service, including new personnel from those groups that gradually begin using the service. The most important lines for training include development and maintenance of tools, techniques to improve practice, scientific dissemination, design, analysis and adaptation of protocols for using the equipment, training in attention to users, etc. Likewise, institutions must provide or seek to obtain resources that complement the specific contributions of the research groups that use the infrastructure, to bring from other universities or foreign centers professors to train technicians, researchers, and students in situ, and facilitate the mobility of technicians to train and learn in other institutions.

2.2 Management Models of Scientific Instrumentation Services

A scientific instrumentation service requires applying management techniques to guarantee the effectiveness and efficiency of the service model offered.

The main aspects to be managed in a scientific instrumentation service correspond to: (i) the *availability of equipment, technicians, and methodologies* for using the infrastructure, considering the different models in which researchers can use the services according to your concrete needs; (ii) the *location and access to the infrastructure and services by the researchers*, considering the geographical location of the equipment, which can be centralized in a single installation of large dimensions or have different degrees of distribution in smaller and more dispersed facilities, and contemplating different policies and mechanisms for accessing equipment and services through local or remote interfaces; and (iii) the *maintenance and permanent updating of the equipment and the knowledge required for its efficient use*, including updating the infrastructure and equipment, considering the technological advances in products related to the discipline, and technical staff and researchers, contemplating the training in the methodological advances in operation and use and the possible future lines of work and application of the equipment for the scientific advance [13].

All the aforementioned aspects must be taken into account for a correct sizing, operation, operation and updating of the services, so that the scientific instrumentation system is an effective, agile, and dynamic tool adapted to the needs of researchers, which can provide an advantage to the development of quality scientific research. The management model must consider all these considerations to guarantee the success of the proposed system.

2.3 Large Computer Systems as Scientific Instrumentation Services

One of the technological transfer products recognized as the most spectacular, has been the development of computer systems.

In the last 50 years, large computer systems have become essential tools for scientific research, allowing calculations that would be impossible with other techniques.

Most of the modern scientific advances have been produced by applying systems that combine scientific instruments (microscopes, telescopes, etc.) and large computational systems that control the instruments, and process and analyze huge volumes of data from experiments. Through the application of new methodologies and techniques in the areas of mathematical methods, numerical simulations, computer science, software engineering, high-performance computing, distributed computing in grid and cloud environments, visualization, etc., computer platforms have been capable of providing researchers with the computational power necessary to solve problems involving complex systems, large-scale mathematical models, experimental analyzes that demand the processing of large volumes of data, and other problems of great difficulty [5, 9].

Turnkey-purchased computer systems (e.g., integrated supercomputers) have an extremely high cost that makes them prohibitive for small and medium-sized institutions. These systems are closed, practically do not allow modifications, and updating/maintenance is restricted to products and applications of a certain type. In addition, closed systems cover general needs that are sometimes different from the specific demands imposed by scientific research. These limitations are of especial relevance in our Latin American, and especially in universities. Usually, our institutions must develop their own computational systems, built with low cost components and applying knowledge of electronics and computers. These systems allow using the paradigm of open source software, based on freely developed and distributed products, which allow modifications and therefore the development of custom solutions, having a direct impact on the applicability of the instrumented system and expanding the target audience. Likewise, free software products allow reducing the operating costs of the platform, making possible the implementation of an inclusive model for a scientific HPC platform. The proposal presented in this article refers to a system of scientific instrumentation that is built on the ideas of an open platform built through the integration of low-cost components and the paradigm of open source software, as support for egalitarian research under the Developmental University model [3].

3   The Cluster-UY Project

This section presents the National Supercomputing Center of Uruguay and its technical details.

3.1   The Previous Project: Cluster-FING

Cluster FING [14] was the HPC infrastructure of Engineering Faculty, Universidad de la República, Uruguay, that provided support for solving complex problems that demand great computing power in science and engineering. The initial infrastructure for Cluster FING was funded by Sectoral Commission for Scientific Research, Universidad de la República, Uruguay, in 2008.

Cluster-FING began operating in March 2009. Previously, there were no centralized resources for scientific computing in the country with reliable, sustained, and growing capacity over time. Until that date, scientists acquired their own computing resources at their laboratories. Acquisitions were limited to the very limited resources available in specific projects (a few thousand dollars, which in general were only enough to acquire a conventional computer, not a powerful server). In addition, the acquired infrastructure did not include any type of update. Rapid obsolescence meant that at the end of the research project, the use of the computer was very limited. Researchers also faced the problem of the great inefficiency of the human resources required for the administration of the equipment and the energy costs (operation and thermal conditioning).

The limited capacity of computer equipment at laboratories limited the challenges that researchers could face, effectively cutting off the creativity of projects. Cluster-FING proposed a first step to change the paradigm of non-cooperative use of computing resources. Collaboration between different research groups was proposed to acquire a more powerful and shared computing platform. Instead of buying their own computing resources, i.e., spending valuable research funds, researchers had the opportunity of contributing to Cluster-FING and use their services. The contributions were significantly lower than in a non-cooperative model, as a result of savings due to centralized management of computing resources, equipment acquisition, operation, and energy costs.

Cluster-FING started to break down the barriers that had the computing capacity available individually in a laboratory as a limitation of the creativity of researchers. Gradually, the new paradigm had a significant impact on research in basic and applied sciences. As a result, researchers enhanced the quality of research and set new horizons and objectives, with application to the national reality. These more ambitious objectives have in turn implied a greater need for scientific computing resources. Likewise, the effectiveness of the Cluster-FING model caused that a greater number of research groups were interested in using the infrastructure. Cluster-FING progressively increased its computing capacity (from 8 servers with 64 computing cores in 2009, to 20 servers with more than 500 cores in 2017) and reached ten million hours of effective computing core in July, 2017, executing more than one million computing hours per semester.

3.2   National Supercomputing Center: Cluster-UY

The previous experience of the Cluster-FING project showed the viability of creating a HPC platform for HPC by applying a collaborative model. The new initiative described in this article proposed implementing a scientific HPC service at national level, based on an aggregation architecture (cluster) type, to create the National Supercomputing Center, Cluster-UY.

The main motivations of the Cluster-UY project include the success of the paradigm of use and centralized management of computing resources initiated by the Cluster-FING and its significant impact on national research in various areas of science, the need for greater resources of scientific computation, and the increase in research groups that use scientific and HPC techniques in Uruguay. The Cluster-FING project increased the demand of scientific applications, which exceeded the available computing capacities. To significantly improve the ability to address relevant scientific problems in the country, allow the resolution of larger problems, and promote better quality of research, the Cluster-UY project proposed scaling the dimension of the computing infrastructure and extending the service at national level. Cluster-UY provides support to research, development, and innovation activities of all scientific, technological, industrial, business and social communities, providing free and unrestricted access, focusing on the egalitarian paradigm proposed by the Developmental University model [3]. The main features of the proposed model are presented in Sect. 4, linking them with the installation, management, and administration of scientific instrumentation systems [13] and with relevant ideas of collaborative economy [1, 4].

3.3   Technical Description

Cluster-UY is comprised of 31 nodes: 28 computing nodes, 2 file-server nodes and 1 service node. Each computing node is comprised of two Intel Xeon Gold 6138 CPU with 20 cores each, 128 GB of RAM, a solid-state drive with a capacity of 400 GB, and one Nvidia Tesla P100 GPU. In total, Cluster-UY is comprised of 560 Xeon Gold computing cores delivering 35 trillion double precision floatingpoint operations per second (TFLOPS) and 28 T P100 devices delivering 131 double precision TFLOPS. Hence, its peak computing power is 166 TFLOPS.

Storage is served by two dedicated nodes: FS1 and FS2. FS1 hosts a RAID 1 + 0 storage with 60 TB of raw capacity (30 TB usable) and FS2 hosts a RAID 6 storage with 80 TB of raw capacity (60 TB usable). FS1 is used exclusively for storing user data since RAID 1 + 0 provides adequate fault tolerance levels while excelling at read and write performance, and it allows a rapid recovery upon failure. FS2 is dedicated for storing non-critical data such as intermediate computations, unprocessed raw data, initial conditions for experiments, etc. RAID 6 was chosen for FS2 because it increases the usable/raw capacity ratio when compared to FS1. However, RAID 6 provides much lower performance than RAID 1 + 0 for write operations and it may require heavy rebuilding operations when a failure is detected, so it is not advised to store critical data in FS2. On top FS1 and FS2, the high-speed SSD local storage of each computing node (11 TB) is used as scratch space for short-lived data. The available raw storage space was expanded by incorporating 144 additional TB in 2019.

Finally, the service node hosts three critical services isolated from each other in different virtual machines: a distributed resource manager, a front-end access to Cluster-UY and an application development environment for users. Virtualizing these services allows improving their provisioning, availability, and recovery. The Simple Linux Utility for Resource Management (SLURM) is used as distributed resource manager. SLURM is a well-known open-source utility for managing resources in Linux-based clusters [25]. The distributed resource manager is a key component of every HPC cluster. Its role consists in tracking which resources are in use and which are available, scheduling which job to execute first and in which resources, starting the actual processes of the scheduled job, and finally cleaning resources when the job finished its execution. SLURM also enables the accounting and report of resource usage for each user. The front-end access or *login VM* provides the entry point to the cluster to all users. This login VM is a stripped-down system with no development tools. However, the development environment or *dev VM* is a separate virtual machine with a full set of development libraries.

All nodes are interconnected by two separate networks. The administrative network is supported by a 1 GbE network and is used primarily for lights-out management of the nodes and for monitoring tasks. The general purpose network is supported by a

10 GbE network and is used for all other network traffic. User's homes are shared among all nodes using NFS over the general purpose network. Figure 1 shows the overall schema of Cluster-UY.

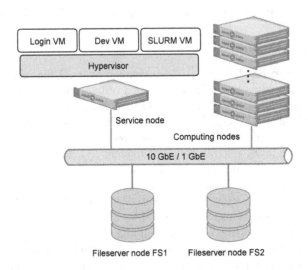

Fig. 1. Schema of the Cluster-UY infrastructure.

4   Installation, Operation, and Business Model

This section describes the main details about the operation and services of the National Supercomputing Center, Cluster-UY.

4.1   Geographical Location and Access to Services

A flexible centralized model is applied for Cluster-UY. The infrastructure is hosted in a large centralized installation, in datacenter "Ing. Josê Luis Massera" of the National Telecommunications Administration (ANTEL), a site that provides the necessary functionalities for the correct access, management and operation of the equipment, and to optimize the necessary energy resources.

A specific agreement between ANTEL and Universidad de la República allow both institutions to promote research in the related areas of knowledge (datacenters, mass data processing, data networks, etc.) and provide the services of the new platform in a reliable and efficient manner. Likewise, an agreement with the National Electricity Administration (UTE) was signed to receive support with operation costs (e.g., electric power for servers and thermal system). Cluster UY services are provided as a counterpart for research and initiatives carried out by both public companies. These partnerships are pillars of the proposed self-sustaining model. Interconnection with smaller computational infrastructures available in the country are also considered, as well as interconnection with computing platforms existing in the region, to share resources through the mechanism of voluntary peer networks [2]. This model establishes a paradigm of collaborative consumption, while promoting sustainable development and energy efficiency, as proposed by collaborative economy.

Access to the platform and its services is guaranteed 24 h a day, 365 days a year, from anywhere in the country and abroad. Cluster-UY services are accessible through Infrastructure as a Service, Software as a Service, and Platform as a Service models, operating at different levels according to the needs of each problem. Remote access and proper training are provided to allow users to gain a level of expertise to work autonomously and perform simple tasks without the assistance of experts. Two modalities are used: technicians in charge of solving specific problems in the infrastructure provide services on a permanent basis, as established in the hosting agreement of the infrastructure subscribed with ANTEL, and assistants scientists who support researchers using the infrastructure are available on a continuous schedule in working hours.

4.2   Services Provision and Potential Users

Services Provision. A mixed mechanism is applied for service provision, allowing two modalities. On the one hand, self-service utilization of the instrumentation by researchers is encouraged, mainly through assisted works, in which researchers with more experience contribute to guide less experienced researchers and students. On the other hand, continuous training is implemented by academic technicians to expand the base of users with knowledge of HPC techniques. New users will be requested, once they acquire the necessary knowledge to autonomously operate the platform and take advantage of their services, to collaborate with training/mentoring of new users.

This way, group work is encouraged, users are linked to each other and to the platform, and a cooperative training mechanism is established to overcome the lack of funds to develop formal training strategies through courses. A model of open knowledge and mutual assistance, two relevant postulates of collaborative economy, is then configured.

Cluster-UY services reach to a wide range of users, both internal and external to the research groups that proposed the project. Internal users are students, professors, and researchers of Universidad de la Repu´blica, and professionals/technicians of companies that support the project. All internal users have guaranteed free access to the services, disregarding money or work contributions. External users include technicians and researchers from institutions that use the Center through specific agreements to develop scientific-technological or social research activities. Peer networks are encouraged for technical/scientific assistance and to rationalize contributions. Services offered to external users are not for obtaining an income, but to allow the largest use of the platform and solidarily collaborate to the maintenance, administration, and updating of the infrastructure. Contributions from external groups are via agreements that establish the commitment of collaboration and clearly defines the contributions to be made (economic, if research funds are available, or work, in case of having experience for guiding/training other researchers, etc.) and their counterparts.

Users. All researchers can use Cluster-UY, even if they do not have funds. Foreign users also can use the Center when they work in collaboration with national groups, have research agreements, or propose a socially interesting research for our country. The agreements must establish the commitment of collaboration and clearly define the contributions to be made and their counterparts.

Assisted works, through the solidary collaboration of experienced researchers, are strongly promoted. These models can be applied due to the simplicity of use of computer services, i.e., delegating to users basic operative tasks that can be performed in a restricted environment, while technicians carry out heavier tasks (e.g., installation of libraries and frequent used software packages). Restricting the tasks enabled to users allows minimizing problems associated with installation/configuration of software products, especially considering the number of potential users of the Center (500–1000), thus impacting on the quality of service. Technicians work jointly with researchers and students and courses are organized to train users in the use of HPC techniques. The service focuses on frequent and very frequent users, with different levels of knowledge of the equipment, but knowing the specific techniques to be used in their research.

4.3 Organizational Structure

An autonomous ad-hoc Commission, including representatives of scientists, researchers, agencies, and companies that support the Center, is responsible for making relevant decisions. The commission also advise in the preparation of bids for purchasing equipment, to plan a useful platform, according to the needs of researchers. The Commission meet periodically with authorities from Universidad de la República, National Research and Innovation Agency, and other institutions to guarantee a proper relationship with the research community.

A Manager is in charge of coordinating the daily activities of the technical work team, of analyzing technological alternatives for the expansion and updating of the infrastructure, and of interacting with the engineers of the data center where the platform is located. The Manager is the visible face of the Center acting as main promoter of the services offer in order to attract a greater number of users. The Manager position is occupied by a researcher with high technical profile, appropriate knowledge of HPC, and experience in infrastructure management. The position is financed with part of the contributions of the research groups and the companies associated with the initiative.

4.4 Benefits, Contributions and Responsibilities

The Center applies an egalitarian model for access to services. Identical features are offered to all users, who in turn have the same responsibilities regarding the correct use, maintenance, and updating of the platform and services.

Contributions for Operation. Voluntary collaborations of research groups, organizations, and companies that use the Center contribute to self-finance the constant updating of equipment and knowledge (maintenance, administration, expansion, etc.).

The model is based on the previous experience of the ClusterFING project, but including other universities, institutions, and companies.

Taking into account the financing difficulties for science in Uruguay, contributions are not mandatory, but voluntary and according to the projects. A low amount is suggested, allowing the Center to be attractive to researchers without affecting the development of other project activities. This way, a more equitable work mechanism is established, without requiring the economic contribution of smaller research groups. Furthermore, funding agencies can appreciate the advantages of the cooperative model to rationalize the use of resources.

Training courses, seminars, and self-study groups are used to gain expertise for the correct use of the Center, taking advantage of peer networks to acquire and share knowledge at national, regional, and international level. Members of the scientific/technical group that operates the Center took courses on management of HPC systems at Universidad de Buenos Aires, Argentina. Through a specific agreement, the participants did not pay for the courses registration.

Contributions for maintenance and updating are not obligatory, but users are provided with guides on the amounts to be quoted in their project proposals. The proposed business model considers the costs of amortization, maintenance, management, and updating of the infrastructure, to obtain a reference value of 0.01 USD for computing resource/hour. This value is *ten times lower* than the cost of computing services in the cloud. The contribution comparable to acquiring an isolated server, without HPC capabilities, allows using more than 600,000 computing hours in the Center. Even with the cost of buying a desktop computer, not useful for solving complex problems, a researcher can use 100,000 computing hours. Researchers must not pay additional costs for server administration, software management, network use, power consumption, or cooling. Furthermore, by providing a minimum contribution, researchers access to a number of computing resources a thousand times greater than on an isolated server. These advantages show the convenience of the proposed collaborative and self-financing model.

A greater reference value is considered for agreements signed with organizations and companies that obtain an economic benefit from their activities. Projects that are validated as social interest and non-profit can use the infrastructure without requiring financial contributions.

Undergraduate and graduate students do not contribute for using the platform. Specific agreements are established with higher education institutions and the Center in included into those systems available for use and qualifiable for the applications for competitive funds for maintenance and expansion.

Agreements. Work and support agreements are signed with institutions, organizations, and companies. Partnerships are established to consolidate the collaborative model and open the Center to a wide variety of users, to promote research, innovation, and development. The Center makes special emphasis on promoting inclusive development in areas with social impact (health, education, research for development, etc.), under the University of Development model.

Agreements allow consolidating a clear self-financing and self-management model, and a work method with real social impact, allowing organizations and companies to justify investments to support of the Center. All information, indicators, agreements, contributions, and utilization from the Center are publicly open. The management is also open to external audits by agencies that support the initiative. This approach encourages and consolidate an open data model, closely linked to the ideal of collaborative systems.

Responsabilities. The project is based on clearly defining the relationships between the participants, defining an egalitarian collaborative model. Participants are considered as peers with the same rights and obligations, building a network for collaboration to improve and make equitable access to the infrastructure and services of the Center. Work is proposed in a mutual assistance regime to access self-sustaining resources and services, which would be very difficult to access in a non-collaborative model. The impact of the proposed model is of great relevance for national research and helps develop and consolidate incipient research groups, promoting equity in access to resources, diversity and equal opportunities, following the ideals of University for Development.

5   Impact on Science and Innovation, and Sample Projects

This section describes the impact of Cluster-UY and sample lines of research.

5.1   Impact on Science and Innovation

Cluster-UY has had a direct impact on science and innovation, significantly increasing the goals and horizons of research activities within the country. The list of application areas include Astronomy, Bioinformatics, Biology, Computer graphics, Computer Sciences, Data analysis, Energy, Engineering, Geoinformatics, Mathematics, Optimization, Physics, Social Sciences, Statistics, and others. Industry and public organizations are also using Cluster-UY. UTE is developing research related to the analysis of domestic power consumption patterns, load curve classification, energy efficiency, and other subjects. ANTEL is developing research on big data analysis, datacenter performance analysis, mobility of users, and other subjects. Other organizations and administrations are using Cluster-UY too, including: the National Administration for the Electric Market, for supporting the power generation investment and energy export planning for Uruguay, the Ministry of Industry and Mining, for energy-related research, and the Pasteur Institute, for research on bioinformatics and biotechnology.

Figure 2 summarizes the main areas of research using Cluster-UY.

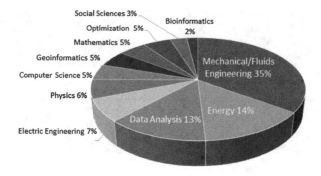

Fig. 2. Main areas of research using Cluster-UY.

5.2 Sample Projects and Researches

Many research and innovation projects have used Cluster-UY to improve its capabilities and results. Three relevant examples are presented next.

Weather Prediction Models Applied to Wind Turbines. This project studies wind velocity focusing on measurements at wind turbine heights (around 100 m). Using experimental measurements and through extensive numerical simulations using different planetary boundary layer schemes and mesoscale grid resolutions, a gust parametrization was proposed for wind forecasting in Uruguay. This gust parametrization provides gust factors to be applied to predicted turbine-level winds, achieving higher accuracy at coarser resolution than an algorithm based on surface layer data alone [11]. Figure 3 shows a forecast example of wind velocity values at wind turbine height. Red dots show considered the wind farms and each subfigure shows a possible atmospheric state, that is, a possible wind generation scenario in the forecast.

Analysis of Mobility Data from Intelligent Transportation Systems (ITS) in Smart Cities. ITS allow collecting large volumes of data that can be processed to extract valuable information for understanding mobility in smart cities [8]. The information can be offered to citizens planners, and decision makers, in order to improve the quality of service and user experience. This is a very important issue for Latin American cities, where the information can help improving public services. Our research group at Universidad de la República has applied data analysis, data processing, and computational intelligence for improving transportation systems and other public services [15–20].

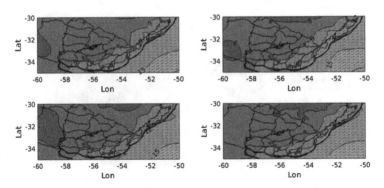

Fig. 3. Forecast example of wind velocity values at wind turbine height.

By applying a parallel-distributed approach for massive data analysis, the computing power of Cluster-UY has been applied to analyze data from the ITS in Montevideo (e.g., GPS location data from buses, ticket sales and smart card transaction data) and obtain valuable information to improve the access to the transportation system, quality of service, socio-economic implicances, etc. A general diagram of the proposed approach is presented in Fig. 4. The approach has proven to be very efficient, achieving significantly large speedup values [7, 15], and also very valuable for citizens and administrator. A sample analysis is presented in Fig. 5, showing a heatmap of ticket sales (smart card transactions) in the center of Montevideo in May 2015. Bright (white) pixels in indicate high concentration of ticket sales while dark (red) areas indicate low ticket sales.

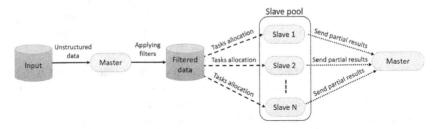

Fig. 4. Parallel-distributed model for mobility data analysis from ITS [15].

Fig. 5. Heatmap of ticket sales (smart card transactions) in the center of Montevideo

Other Projects. Cluster-UY has also been applied to many other research efforts in several areas, including Astronomy [10], Biomedicine [6], Energy [21], Fluid dynamics [23], Statistics [12], Telecommunications [22], and others.

6 Summary and Conclusions

This article presented the National Supercomputing Center, Uruguay (ClusterUY), a national initiative for installing and operating a scientific HPC infrastructure following a collaborative operation model.

The Cluster-UY project was described and the self-funded collaborative operation model involving scientific institutions, academia, and public/private companies, to guarantee sustainability was clearly explained.

The perspectives of Cluster-UY as a mean to foster research and innovation projects that face complex problems with high computing demands were highlighted and sample projects developed in the Center were briefly presented. The main lines for future work are related to continue developing and improving the infrastructure and services of Cluster-UY, as a key tool for improving scientific research in the country.

References

1. Algar, R.: Collaborative consumption. Leisure report, April 2007 (2007)
2. Andrade, N., Brasileiro, F., Cirne, W., Mowbray, M.: Automatic grid assembly by promoting collaboration in peer-to-peer grids. J. Parallel Distrib. Comput. **67**(8), 957–966 (2007)
3. Arocena, R., Goransson, B., Sutz, J.: Knowledge policies and universities in developing countries: Inclusive development and the developmental university. Technol. Soc. **41**, 10–20 (2015)
4. Botsman, R., Rogers, R.: What's Mine is Yours: The Rise of Collaborative Consumption. Collins Business, New York (2010)
5. Chapman, D., Joshi, K., Yesha, Y., Halem, M., Yesha, Y., Nguyen, P.: Scientific services on the cloud. In: Furht, B., Escalante, A. (eds.) Handbook of Cloud Computing, pp. 379–405. Springer, Boston (2010). https://doi.org/10.1007/978-1-4419-6524-0_16
6. Curi, M.E., et al.: Single and multiobjective evolutionary algorithms for clustering biomedical information with unknown number of clusters. In: Korošec, P., Melab, N., Talbi, E.-G. (eds.) BIOMA 2018. LNCS, vol. 10835, pp. 100–112. Springer, Cham (2018). https://doi.org/10.1007/978-3-319-91641-5_9
7. Denis, J., Massobrio, R., Nesmachnow, S., Cristóbal, A., Tchernykh, A., Meneses, E.: Parallel computing for processing data from intelligent transportation systems. In: International Supercomputing Conference in Mexico (2018)
8. Figueiredo, L., Jesus, I., Tenreiro, J., Rui Ferreira, J., Carvalho, J.: Towards the development of intelligent transportation systems. In: IEEE Intelligent Transportation Systems, pp. 1206–1211 (2001)
9. Foster, I.: Designing and Building Parallel Programs. Addison-Wesley, Boston (1995)
10. Frascarelli, D., Nesmachnow, S., Tancredi, G.: High-performance computing of self-gravity for small solar system bodies. IEEE Comput. **47**(9), 34–39 (2014)

11. Gutiérrez, A., Fovell, R.: A new gust parameterization for weather prediction models. J. Wind Eng. Ind. Aerodyn. **177**, 45–59 (2018)
12. López-Vázquez, C., Hochsztain, E.: Extended and updated tables for the Friedman rank test. Commun. Stat. Theory Methods **48**, 1–14 (2017)
13. Navarro, C.: Los servicios de instrumentaciôn científica. In: Master de Política y Gestion Universitaria, Universidad de Barcelona, pp. 73–127 (2017)
14. Nesmachnow, S.: Computaciôn científica de alto desempenô en la Facultad de Ingeniería, Universidad de la Repûblica. Revista de la Asociaciôn de Ingenieros del Uruguay, **61**(1), 12–15 (2010)
15. Nesmachnow, S., Baña, S., Massobrio, R.: A distributed platform for big data analysis in smart cities: combining Intelligent Transportation Systems and socioeconomic data for Montevideo. Uruguay. EAI Endorsed Trans. Smart Cities **2**(5), 1–18 (2017)
16. Nesmachnow, S., et al.: Traffic lights synchronization for bus rapid transit using a parallel evolutionary algorithm. Int. J. Transp. Sci. Technol. **8**, 53–67 (2019). https://www.sciencedirect.com/science/article/pii/S2046043018300339
17. Nesmachnow, S., Massobrio, R., Cristôbal, A., Tchernykh, A.: Planificaciôn de transporte urbano en ciudades inteligentes. In: I Ibero-American Congress of Smart Cities, pp. 204–218 (2018)
18. Nesmachnow, S., Rossit, D., Toutouh, J.: Comparison of multiobjective evolutionary algorithms for prioritized urban waste collection in Montevideo, Uruguay. Electron. Notes in Discrete Math. **69**, 93–100 (2018)
19. Pena, D., et al.: Operating cost and quality of service optimization for multi-vehicle-type timetabling for urban bus systems. J. Parallel Distrib. Comput. **133**, 272–285 (2019). https://www.sciencedirect.com/science/article/pii/S0743731518300297
20. Péres, M., Ruiz, G., Nesmachnow, S., Olivera, C.: Multiobjective evolutionary optimization of traffic flow and pollution in Montevideo. Uruguay. Appl. Soft Comput. **70**, 472–485 (2018)
21. Porteiro, R., Garabediân, G., Nesmachnow, S.: Generation and classification of energy load curves using a distributed MapReduce approach. In: International Supercomputing in Mêxico, pp. 1–15 (2019)
22. Risso, C., Nesmachnow, S., Robledo, F.: Metaheuristic approaches for IP/MPLS network design. Int. Trans. Oper. Res. **25**(2), 599–625 (2018)
23. Sassi, P., Freiria, J., Paz, P.L., Mendina, M., Draper, M., Usera, G.: Coupled discrete element and finite volume methods for simulating loaded elastic fishnets in interaction with fluid. Comput. Fluids **156**, 200–208 (2017)
24. Wilson, E.: An Introduction to Scientific Research. Dover Publications, Mineola (1956)
25. Yoo, A.B., Jette, M.A., Grondona, M.: SLURM: simple linux utility for resource management. In: Feitelson, D., Rudolph, L., Schwiegelshohn, U. (eds.) JSSPP 2003. LNCS, vol. 2862, pp. 44–60. Springer, Heidelberg (2003). https://doi.org/10.1007/10968987_3

Demand Response and Ancillary Services for Supercomputing and Datacenters

Sergio Nesmachnow, Santiago Iturriaga[(✉)], Jonathan Muraña,
Sebastián Montes de Oca, Gonzalo Belcredi, Pablo Monzón,
Pablo Belzarena, and Juan Bazerque

Facultad de Ingeniería, Universidad de la República, Montevideo, Uruguay
{sergion, siturria, jmurana, smontes, gbelcredi, monzon,
belza, jbazerque}@fing.edu.uy

Abstract. This article describes a proposal for the participation of supercomputing platforms and datacenters in the electric market, by implementing demand response techniques and ancillary services. Supercomputing and datacenters are appropriate candidates to adjust their power consumption in order to help the electric network to fulfill specific goals, either by consuming available surplus of energy to execute complex tasks, or by deferring activities when energy is more expensive or generation is lower than normal. Their thermal/cooling infrastructures demand about half of the energy consumption and provide a large inertia that can be carefully used to interact with the power grid. These strategies allow implementing a smart management of the electric grid, achieving a rational utilization of renewable energy sources, and the correct utilization of information technologies to improve decision-making processes. A specific case study is presented: The National Supercomputing Center in Uruguay (Cluster-UY), for which strategies for optimal planning of the execution of tasks and energy utilization are proposed, taking into account the energy consumption, the Quality of Service provided to the users, and the thermal/cooling demands of the infrastructure. In addition, the business opportunities and business models for supercomputing and datacenters in the electric market are revisited. Results suggest the effectiveness of the proposed strategies to implement demand response techniques and provide ancillary services under the smart grid paradigm.

Keywords: Energy efficiency · Demand response · Datacenters

1 Introduction

In modern electricity markets, a large consumer with flexible consumption of active and reactive power can participate in the market in different ways. This concept is key to implementing strategies oriented to smart networks, associating consumers with the roles of active clients and market agents [18]. As an active client, the consumer can adapt his demand to peak hours, reducing consumption in these periods and contributing to flattening the demand curve of the system. Multi-hour tariffs can also be implemented, handling time blocks where it is preferable to consume. 'Day-ahead agreements' (based on price announced in advance) can be set, or even a dynamic

M. Torres and J. Klapp (Eds.): ISUM 2019, CCIS 1151, pp. 203–217, 2019.
https://doi.org/10.1007/978-3-030-38043-4_17

behavior can be stimulated, when the price of energy is available in real time. Acting as an agent, the consumer can participate in the electricity market and receive income by applying mechanisms that may be restricted or driven by regulations, e.g., by establishing bilateral agreements between a large consumer and a generation company (possible in the Uruguayan energy market) or by auctions, e.g., in a day-ahead market, offering a profile of hourly consumption and establishing maximum prices to pay [13] (not yet present in our country).

In this context, demand response planning strategies are needed to manage energy consumption and be able to participate in the market, on different roles. Specific techniques are needed to dimension the activities that consume energy, advance or defer their execution, analyze the impact on global energy efficiency, and the possible degradation of the Quality of Service (QoS) offered to users.

This article describes a proposal for developing and applying demand response strategies on large consumers allowing them to participate in the electric market and provide ancillary services. As a case study, the project proposes to address the planning of supercomputing and datacenters, conceived as an example of planned systems that have emerged in modern societies, linked to the smart grid paradigm (other relevant examples are fleets of electric cars, smart buildings, irrigation systems, etc.). Supercomputing and datacenters provide scenarios that allow the direct experimentation of demand response strategies in the academic and business environments. These platforms can adjust power consumption in order to help the electric network to fulfill specific goals, either by consuming available surplus of energy to execute complex tasks, or by deferring activities (i.e., tasks execution) when energy is more expensive or generation is lower than normal. Furthermore, their thermal/cooling infrastructures demand about half of the energy consumption and provide a large inertia, that can be used to interact with the power grid. The studied strategies allow implementing a smart management of the electric grid, achieving a rational utilization of renewable energy sources, and the correct utilization of information technologies to improve decision-making processes.

Strategies for optimal planning of the execution of tasks and energy utilization are proposed the National Supercomputing Center in Uruguay (Cluster-UY) [22], taking into account the energy consumption, the QoS provided to users, and the thermal/cooling demands of the infrastructure. In addition, the business opportunities and business models for supercomputing and datacenters in the electric market are revisited. Results suggest the effectiveness of the proposed strategies to implement demand response techniques and provide ancillary services under the smart grid paradigm.

The article is organized as follows. Next section describes the model applied to characterize the energy consumption on datacenters. Section 3 describes the opportunities for datacenters in the electric market. The proposed strategies for energy-aware planning of datacenters are summarized in Sect. 4, including some preliminary results for smart planning to follow a reference power profile. Finally, Sect. 5 formulates the main conclusions and current lines of work.

2 Modeling the Energy Consumption of Datacenters

This section presents an analysis of the power consumption of the main components of a datacenter. Since servers are a key part of the datacenter energy usage, a power model for servers is introduced and a case study is evaluated. Finally, a specific power model for high-end multicores is introduced.

2.1 Breakdown of the Power Consumption of Datacenters

Two main operational components account for most power consumption of datacenters: (i) operation of the technological infrastructure (servers, network, storage, etc.) and (ii) operation of the cooling system and other physical resources [23, 27]. Both sources of power consumption are related because more power is required for the cooling system when servers operate a full capacity. Servers represent a significant percentage of datacenter power consumption and the variability of their power consumption in different load levels allows implementing specific techniques for energy savings. Moreover, variability can be used for demand response under external changes related to energy prices, temperature, etc.

Power models are used for predicting the servers power consumption and evaluating the efficacy of energy aware policies. Due to the high complexity and cost, the quality of energy aware policies is evaluated with simulation tools. Power consumption of high-end servers found in datacenters is broadly described by Eq. 1, where P_{idle} is the server power consumption without load and P_{peak} is the server power consumption at full (100%) utilization. The variable u is the current utilization percentage of the server and function f describes the relationship between utilization and power consumption [1, 2].

$$P_{server} = P_{idle} + (P_{peak} - P_{idle})f(u) \tag{1}$$

Most of power consumption of servers corresponds to the CPU. However, power consumption of other computing resources (memory, disk, network) are not negligible. Through workload categorization by resource utilization highly precise power models can be built. Modeling power consumption considering resource utilization also allows taking advantage of task consolidation. Equation 2 shows a server power model where u_{CPU} is the percentage of server capacity executing workload categorized as CPU-intensive, u_{mem} is the percentage of server capacity executing workload categorized as memory-intensive, and so on for each resource in the model.

$$P_{server} = P_{idle} + (P_{peak} - P_{idle})f(u_{CPU}, u_{mem}, u_{disk}, u_{inet}, \ldots) \tag{2}$$

The empirical study of AMD and Intel multicores by Muraña et al. [20] showed that for CPU-intensive workloads, the server power consumption has a linear relationship with resource utilization. Furthermore, power consumption of memory-intensive workload decelerates as utilization increases. Power consumption of memory-intensive workload was greater than CPU-intensive workload.

Some works have proposed empirical energy models that consider types of computing resources, measuring power consumption using different benchmarks (intensive in one specific computing resource), such as Linpack [12, 17], Abinit [9], and or Namd [17, 25]. Power data can be collected through software tools that consult internal hardware counters–e.g., Running Average Power Limit (RAPL) interface on Intel servers–or by using an external power meter [8, 20, 28].

2.2   Empirical Analysis of Power Consumption of Servers in a Datacenter

Power characterization measurements were performed over a HP ProLiant DL380 G9 server (2 Intel Xeon Gold 6138 CPUs, 20 cores each, 128 GB RAM) from Cluster-UY. The experiment consisted in executing a CPU-intensive benchmark and measuring its power consumption using *likwid* [29], a software tool that allows access to RAPL interface counters to estimate the power consumption.

Algorithm 1 presents the procedure applied for energy measurement. The power consumption reported by *likwid* is logged while executing an increasing number of benchmark instances to consider different levels of server utilization.

Algorithm 1 Procedure for power consumption measurement

```
 1: process_per_level ← 5
 2: utilization_levels ← 8
 3: independent_executions ← 30
 4: for j = 1 to independent_executions do
 5:     likwid-power-meter -s 60s
 6: end for
 7: for i = 1 to utilization_levels do
 8:     instances_current_level ← process_per_level × i
 9:     for j = 1 to independent_executions do
10:         launch_benckmark_instances(instances_current_level,60)   ▷ launch in
        background the benchmark instances for 60 seconds
11:         likwid-power-meter -s 60s
12:     end for
13: end for
```

For the experiments, eight utilization levels (UL) were defined with five process per level. Utilization level zero corresponds to server without load. UL one corresponds to 12.5% of server utilization, UL two corresponds to 25% of server utilization, and so on. Power consumption of each level is measured 30 times to obtain statistically significant values. Measurements for each UL last 60 s. The CPU-intensive benchmark utilized for experiment belongs to the Sysbench toolkit [16]. The benchmark is a procedure written in language c to calculate the prime number counting function using a backtracking technique.

Figure 1 reports the results of power consumption measurements of the CPU-intensive benchmark. The independent variable u corresponds to the percentage of server utilization and PC is the power consumption (in Watts) reported by *likwid* by consulting the RAPL interface. A significant difference in power consumption is measured between utilization zero and the following levels. This difference is explained by the internal power management of Intel chip (decreasing voltage of inactive resources).

u	PC (W)
0 %	30.06± 3.91
12.5 %	120.38 ± 0.51
25 %	142.36 ± 0.72
37.5 %	162.83 ± 0.90
50 %	176.17 ± 0.46
62.5%	180.03 ± 1.02
75 %	192.63 ± 1.01
87.5%	194.09 ±0.50
100%	208.17± 0.44

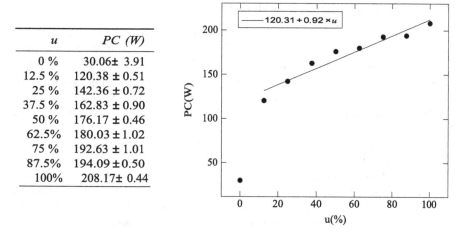

Fig. 1. Power consumption of CPU-intensive benchmark over Cluster-UY multicore

If utilization zero is not considered, the power consumption can be adjusted to a linear function, for example, using least squares. The derivative of the function (0.92) is coherent to the one reported in [20] (0.82), where the same benchmark was measured using a Power Distribution Unit over a similar high-end server. The same work also reports experimental result of memory-intensive benchmark in similar high-end servers. Equation 3, introduced in [20], presents a linear combination of models of CPU-intensive and memory-intensive workload. Equation 3, u_{CPU} is the server utilization corresponding to CPU-intensive workload and u_{mem} is the server utilization corresponding to memory-intensive workload. The variable u'_{CPU} is zero when u_{CPU} is less than 50% and $u_{CPU} - 50$ otherwise. An analog model can be built for the specific hardware of the case study.

$$P_{server} = 0.802 \times u_{CPU} + 0.042 \times u'_{CPU} + 2.902 \times u_{mem}$$
$$- 0.02107 \times u_{mem}^2 + 7.644 \times 10^{-5} \times u_{mem}^3 + \frac{56.36 + 36.89}{2} + 57.0 \quad (3)$$

Since the downside of energy savings is the degradation of system performance, the energy model must be complemented with a performance model. To empirically model the performance, similar experiments should be performed considering execution times instead of power consumption.

3 Opportunities for Datacenters in the Electric Market

This section describes the different ways a datacenter may participate in demand response and ancillary services mechanisms and introduces the particular case of multi-tenants datacenters.

3.1   Participation in the Electric Market

A flexible consumer needs planning techniques to ensure a proper use of its energy resources and to response to the energy market signals. In a datacenter, the energy is used evenly distributed into two particular sectors: the operative hardware that provides the services required by the datacenter clients and the thermal/cooling infrastructure. These are the knobs that may be adjusted according some time-varying power consumption profile. In this way, the datacenter can participate as an active agent in the electric market.

A relative simple way is to implement a mechanism of demand response, using the thermal inertia of the building to increase or decrease the power consumption, letting move the building temperature between acceptable levels. In order to define the limits of an electric power band that the datacenter can offer to the system operator, a proper model of the building temperature dynamics must be used. The more accurate the model, the more wide the offered power band and the more profit can be obtained. Of course, the model that describes the temperature evolution should include the impact of the servers activity, and this fact leads to the inclusion of the tasks execution profile into the datacenter demand response strategy. As explained in Sect. 2, the execution of the tasks directly consumes electric power and also affects the building temperature. Maintaining that temperature within prescribed limits implies the utilization of the thermal/cooling units, that also consume electric power. In this way, an appropriate demand-response strategy should combine the flexibility of the thermal behavior and the tasks allocation.

3.2   Demand Response in Multi-tenants Datacenters

Over the two main actions of a datacenter, new variants can be devised. This section focuses on a pricing mechanism for multi-tenant datacenter that allows the operator to obtain load shedding among tenants. Following the ideas of our previous work [19], a responsive scheme for the clients is proposed. Clients may choose to postpone or lose a task in exchange of some kind of economical reward provided by the datacenter, which is an active agent in the electric market.

We pay special attention on multi-tenants collocation datacenter, since the tenants deploy and keep full control of their own physical servers, while the datacenter operator provides facility support. Tenant's workloads in collocation datacenter are highly heterogeneous, and many tenants run non-critical workloads, with high scheduling flexibility, different delay sensitivities, different service level agreements with peak loads periods. This type of datacenters are often located in metropolitan areas, where demand response calls are most needed. They can participate actively in the energy market by modulating their power profile and helping maximize distribution grid resources. The main disadvantage is that each tenant manage its own servers independently and has very different incentives to cooperate with the operator during a demand response event.

In an electricity market with uncertainty in supply or price volatility, supply function as a strategic variable allows to adapt better to changing market conditions than a simple commitment to a fixed price or quantity does [15]. This is one reason why we propose to use supply function bidding, creating a market mechanism which fixed a uniform market clearing price. Other motivation is to respect practical informational constraints in the power network. A customer might not want to reveal its cost function because of incentive or security concerns, or the cost function may require a high description complexity, which means more communication. A properly chosen parameterized supply function *controls* information revelation while demands less communication.

Chen et al. [3] considered two abstract market models for designing demand response to match the supply and shape the demand, respectively. In the modeled situation, there is an inelastic supply deficit on electricity, and study a supply function bidding scheme for allocating load shedding among different users to match the supply. Each customer submits a linear parameterized supply function to the agent aggregator (i.e., the datacenter operator). In a competitive market where customers are price taking, the system achieves an efficient equilibrium that maximizes the social welfare. In an oligopolistic market where customers are price anticipating and strategic, the system achieves a unique Nash equilibrium that maximizes another additive, global objective function.

Montes de Oca et al. [19] proposed a distributed algorithm to optimize social welfare over a distribution network considering AC physical constraints over the grid but with several users aggregators. However, these forms of parameterized supply function do not admit treatable analysis. Johari and Tsitsiklis [14] considered an alternative supply function model (Eq. 4) where a finite number of producers compete to meet an infinitely divisible but inelastic demand reduce δ. Each user (or tenant) is characterized by a production cost, convex in the output produced, and the customers act as profit maximizers. The mechanism yields bounded efficiency loss at a Nash equilibrium and also characterize the problem of finding the Nash equilibrium as the solution of a collocation problem.

$$S_n(b_n, p) = \delta - \frac{bn}{p} \qquad (4)$$

Chen et al. [4] extended the previous work by proposing a uniform pricing mechanism for collocation datacenters where the operator can extract load shedding from tenants, without using the backup generator. The goal is to effectively provide incentives for tenants to reduce energy consumption during emergency demand response events. When an emergency demand response arrives, tenants bid using a parameterized supply function (Eq. 4), and then the datacenter operator announces a market clearing price which when plugged into the bids, specifies how much energy tenants will reduce and how much they will be paid. The main advantage of this mechanism is that for the tenants is very easy to participate in the market since they are only asked to bid a parameter but keeping the integrity of the private information. The authors propose a market mechanism and prove existence and uniqueness of the best strategy for each tenant. In addition, they characterize the Nash optima of the non-cooperative game as an optimization problem, which can be solved in a distributed manner between participants, preserving private information. A mathematical model for this approach is presented in Sect. 4.2.

4   Smart Strategies for Effective Planning of Datacenters

This section describes strategies for datacenter planning and operation and a proposal for a demand response scheme in a multi-tenant datacenter.

4.1   Datacenter Planning and Operation

One of the key issues related with energy-aware datacenter planning refers to the problem of following a reference power profile for energy consumption. The main goal is to appropriately plan the execution of tasks and the operation of the cooling system to minimize the deviation with respect to the reference power profile. This way, the datacenter can adapt its operation and participate in the energy market as an agent with the capabilities of fulfilling specific goals.

Our group has developed research on the holistic energy-aware planning of datacenters, and also including the use of renewable energy sources [7, 10, 11, 22–24]. The general approach consists in applying computational intelligence methods [21] to solve the underlying optimization problem that proposes determine the tasks scheduling and the energy consumption of both infrastructure and cooling systems, subject to QoS and operation (e.g., temperature) constraints.

Figure 2 presents an overview of the proposed system model, including their two key components: the computing infrastructure and the cooling system.

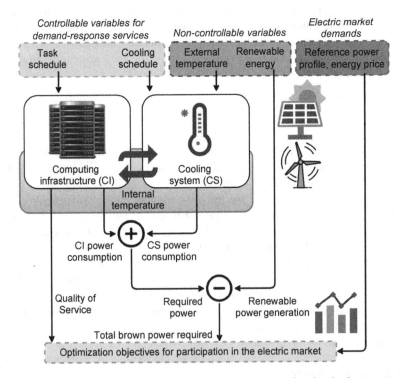

Fig. 2. Schema of the proposed model for energy-aware planning in datacenters

A realistic energy consumption model is considered for the computing infrastructure in which each computing resource may be executing, idle, or asleep. On the one hand, when a computing resource is executing a task, it is considered to be at its peak performance. On the other hand, when a computing resource is idle it is considered to be consuming the minimum amount of energy required of its operation. Finally, when asleep, a computing resource considered to be consuming a marginal amount of energy.

The objective are controlled by two input variables, the task schedule and the cooling schedule. The task schedule determines the execution of tasks on the computing infrastructure for the scheduling horizon. Likewise, the cooling schedule determines the on/off of the cooling system for the scheduling horizon. Three non-controllable input variables are considered: external temperature (the air temperature outside the datacenter), renewable energy generation (amount of available energy generated by renewable energy source such as solar panels, wind turbines, etc.), and power reference profile of the electric market, used by the datacenter to provide ancillary services and to consider demand response to match the supply and shape the demand. These variables are not controllable by the system and have uncertainty.

The optimization objectives and constraints are defined as follows. The maximization of the QoS is related to the number of tasks with unmet due dates. The total brown energy required by the datacenter and the reference power profile requested by the electric market for maximizing the profit. The internal temperature of the datacenter is constrained to a maximum operating value.

We proposed a number of exact methods, stochastic and deterministic heuristics, and single- and multi-objective metaheuristics for addressing several variants of this optimization problem with promising results [10, 11, 21, 23, 24]. As an example, our previous work [24] proposed the following mathematical model.

Controllable Variables. Cooling schedule (c_k), controls the operation of the cooling system; and the *power schedule* (s_k), controls the computing infrastructure power consumption. It controls the number of servers running, load constraints, and specific user requirements.

Non-controllable Variables. External temperature (α_k), air temperature outside the datacenter; *target reference power profile* (R_k), the desired total power consumption for each time step; and the *target reference temperature profile* (T_{ref}), the desired internal temperature of the datacenter for each time step.

Other Variables. The internal temperature (T_k) in the datacenter; the power consumption of the cooling system (C_k); the *power consumption of the computing infrastructure* (I_k); and the *total power consumption of the datacenter* (P_k).

The total computing infrastructure power is defined by $I_k = S_k^{max} + S_k^{idle} + S_k^{sleep}$. Where S_k^{max}, S_k^{idle} and S_k^{sleep} are the total power of all servers that are executing, idle, and sleep at time k, respectively.

The datacenter must execute a set of n tasks in a simulation period of K time steps. Each task i must finish before a deadline $D(i)$. The actual finishing time of a task FT (i) and its deadline $D(i)$ define whether a deadline is satisfied or violated and contributes to the QoS of the schedule.

The main goal is to schedule the operation of a datacenter in order to follow as closely as possible a predefined power and temperature reference while simultaneously minimizing its impact on the QoS of the system. Formally, this means to minimize the deviation from the reference power profile (Eq. (5)) and the deviation from the reference temperature profile (Eq. (6)), while simultaneously minimizing the total exceeding time of deadline violations (Eq. (7)).

$$\sum_{k=1}^{K} \frac{|P_k - R_k|}{\max(R_k)} \tag{5}$$

$$\sum_{k=1}^{K} |T_{ref} - T_k| \tag{6}$$

$$\sum_{i=1}^{K} \max(0, FT(i) - D(i)) \tag{7}$$

Our previous work [24] proposed a multiobjective evolutionary approach for solving the proposed problem. The experimental results show the proposed approach computes accurate schedules for all objectives as well as competitive trade-off schedules. Figure 3 show the computed solution for the reference power profile objective. It shows the power consumption closely follows the reference power, enabling the datacenter to potentially reduce electricity costs, maximize renewable energy use, or participate in the electricity market.

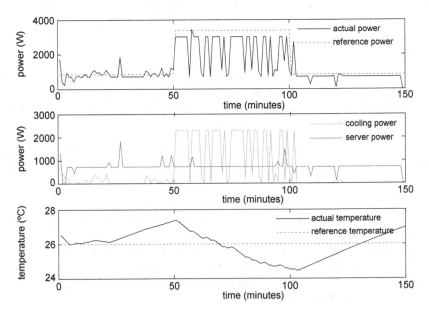

Fig. 3. Best computed solution for the reference power profile objective

4.2   Proposal for a Demand Response Scheme in a Multi-tenant Datacenter

This section proposes an optimization model for the demand response scheme described in Sect. 3.2.

A simple model of the cooling infrastructure and the thermal inertia of the building to increase or decrease the power consumption is proposed, letting move the temperature into the room between acceptable levels. For that, a multistage setting is considered. The proposal is based on a simple mechanism under which each consumer submits a single bid that reflects the willingness to adjust the consumer's demand over the entire T stages. Such mechanisms are easy to implement with a parameterized supply function, and would require the minimum effort from the tenants. In this line of word, results must be established on equilibrium characterization and bounded efficiency loss, analogous to those derived in related works [4, 14].

Overview of Market Mechanism. Amarket mechanism was conceived, where tenants bid for the next T stages using parameterized supply functions (Eq. 4) and then, given the bids, the operator decides how much load to shed via tenants and how much to shed via on-site generation and cooling system.

The operation of the market is summarized below:

- The datacenter operator receives an emergency demand response event for a reduction target $\delta := \{\delta^1, \ldots, \delta^T\}$ and broadcasts the supply function $S(\ , \mathbf{p})$, specified by Eq. 4, to tenants;
- Participating tenants respond by placing their bids $b_n := \{b_n^1, \ldots, b_n^T\}$;
- The operator decides the amount of on-site generation an the temperature scheduling and calculate market clearing price $\mathbf{p}$ to minimize its cost for T stages, using Eq. 8 to set the market clearing price p and Eq. 9 to set $\mathbf{y}$ and $\Delta \mathbf{P}_c$, minimizing the cost of the operation during the demand response event;
- Demand response event is exercised. Tenant n sheds $S_n(b_n, \mathbf{p})$, and receives $S_n(b_n, \mathbf{p}) \cdot \mathbf{p}^t$ as a reward.

The clearing market price is given by Eq. 8. This mechanism is illustrated in Fig. 4.

$$p^t(b_n^t, y^t, \Delta \mathbf{P}_c^t) = \frac{\sum_n b_n^t}{(N-1)\delta^t + y^t + \Delta \mathbf{P}_c^t} \tag{8}$$

To determine the vector of local generation amount $\mathbf{y}$ and power cooling reduction $\Delta \mathbf{P}_c$, the operator minimizes the cost of the three load-reduction options, given by Eq. 9.

$$(\mathbf{y}, \Delta \mathbf{P}_c) = \arg\min(\delta + \mathbf{y} + \Delta \mathbf{P}_c) \cdot \mathbf{p}(b_n, \mathbf{y}, \Delta \mathbf{P}_c)^T + \alpha \cdot \mathbf{y}^T + C(\Delta \mathbf{P}_c; t) \tag{9}$$

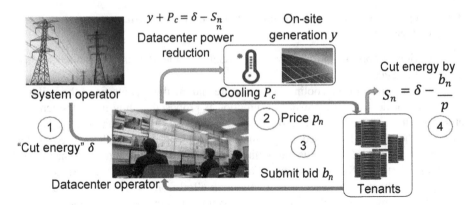

$$y + P_c = \delta - \underset{n}{S_n}$$

Datacenter power reduction

On-site generation y

Cut energy by $\dfrac{b_n}{p}$

$$S_n = \delta - \frac{b_n}{p}$$

System operator

Cooling P_c

(1)

"Cut energy" δ

(2) Price p_n

(3)

Submit bid b_n

(4)

Datacenter operator

Tenants

Fig. 4. Market mechanism for the proposed demand response scheme

Modeling Cooling Power. A simple temperature model can be considered as a function of the power for cooling P_c and the outdoor temperature T_{out} (Eq. 10).

$$\dot{T}(t) = a_1[T(t) - T_{out}(t)] + a_2 P_c(t) \tag{10}$$

The model needs to penalize the misalignment between the actual temperature T_{in} and a set-point temperature T_{set}. The cost function in Eq. 11 is considered, where $\Delta P_c(t)$ is the power difference between the power consumption at time t and the reference power for cooling before demand response takes place.

$$C(\Delta \mathbf{P}_c; t) = \kappa \| T(\Delta \mathbf{P}_c; t) - \mathbf{T}_{set}(t) \| \tag{11}$$

Cost Function $c_n(s)$. Chen et al. [4] proposed a cost function $c_n(.)$ that captures the effect of switching off m computers in a M/G/1/Processor-sharing queue, let's first consider an auxiliary function $\bar{c}_n(\cdot)$ defined as: $\bar{c}_n(m) = \frac{\beta T}{\frac{1}{vm} - \frac{1}{M-m}}$, where λ is the workload arrival rate, $v = \frac{\lambda}{\mu M}$ is the normalized workload arrival, μ is the service rate, β is a cost parameter (\$/time unit/job), T is the duration of the power reduction event, M is the total of available servers and m the number of switched off servers for tenant n. The power reduction model is considered linear in m, so that $S_n = \theta m$. Then the cost function for a tenant's energy reduction is written as: $c_n(S_n) = \bar{c}_n(S_n/\theta) - \bar{c}_n(0)$ and 0 otherwise.

Efficiency Analysis. The next step is to characterize the efficiency of the mechanism. There are two potential causes of inefficiency: the cost minimizing behavior of the operator and the strategic behavior of the tenants. In particular, since the forms of the tenant's cost functions are likely more complex than the supply function bids, tenants cannot bid their true cost function even if they wanted to. This means that evaluating the equilibrium outcome is crucial to understanding the efficiency of the mechanism. The equilibrium outcome depends highly on the behavior of the tenants whether they are price-taking or price-anticipating. The key to our analysis is the observation that the equilibrium can be characterized by an optimization problem. Once we have this optimization, we can use it to characterize the efficiency of the equilibrium outcome. This approach parallels the one proposed by Chen et al. [4] and Johari and Tsitsiklis [14].

Adding Uncertainty. The task arrivals could introduce uncertainty that would be better captured by probabilistic models. We are interested in deriving these models for the uncertainty in the costs and prices from the queuing theory modelling arrivals. Previous work relating workloads with prices and power resource allocation can be found in [5]. Another line of research is the negotiation of the power reduction levels (δ) between the grid and the datacenter operators. Under uncertainty of random effects, and constraints in the power level provided by the diesel generators, this δ may not be accommodated and should be negotiated taking into account its conditional value at risk [6, 26].

5 Conclusions and Future Work

This article introduced a proposal for supercomputing platforms and datacenters to participate in the electric market, by implementing demand response techniques and ancillary services.

A methodology was introduced for supercomputing and datacenters to adjust their power consumption in order to help the electric network to fulfill specific goals, either by consuming available surplus of energy to execute complex tasks, or by deferring activities when energy is more expensive or generation is lower than normal.

Smart strategies for effective energy-aware planning of datacenters were described, including a methodology applying computational intelligence for the problem of following a reference power profile, subject to QoS and temperature constraints, considering the power consumption of computing infrastructure and thermal/cooling system. A specific model is introduced for demand response in a multi-tenant datacenter applying a multistage procedure.

Preliminary results demonstrate that the proposed strategies allow implementing a smart management of the electric grid, achieving a rational utilization of renewable energy sources, and the correct utilization of information technologies to improve decision-making processes.

The main lines for current and future work are related to develop the proposed model and apply it to a relevant case study: The National Supercomputing Center in Uruguay (Cluster-UY), for which preliminary studies on evaluation and characterization of the power consumption of the computing infrastructure were also presented. The proposed models should be further improved to capture the reality of the case studies. Furthermore, more complex strategies are being studied to implement demand response techniques and provide ancillary services under the smart grid paradigm, including the application of single-objective and multi-objective computational intelligence methods.

References

1. Beloglazov, A., Buyya, R., Choon Lee, Y., Zomaya, A.: A taxonomy and survey of energy-efficient data centers and cloud computing systems. Adv. Comput. **82**, 47–111 (2010)
2. Chen, F., Grundy, J., Yang, Y., Schneider, J.G., He, Q.: Experimental analysis of task-based energy consumption in cloud computing systems. In: 4th ACM/SPEC International Conference on Performance Engineering, pp. 295–306 (2013)
3. Chen, L., Li, N., Low, S., Doyle, J.: Two market models for demand response in power networks. In: First IEEE International Conference on Smart Grid Communications (2010)
4. Chen, N., Ren, X., Ren, S., Wierman, A.: Greening multi-tenant data center demand response. Perform. Eval. **91**, 229–254 (2015)
5. Chen, T., Marques, A., Giannakis, G.: DGLB: distributed stochastic geographical load balancing over cloud networks. IEEE Trans. Parallel Distrib. Syst. **7**, 1866–1880 (2017)
6. DallAnese, E., Baker, K., Summers, T.: Chance-constrained ac optimal power flow for distribution systems with renewables. IEEE Trans. Power Syst. **32**(5), 3427–3438 (2017)
7. Dorronsoro, B., Nesmachnow, S., Taheri, J., Zomaya, A.Y., Talbi, E.G., Bouvry, P.: A hierarchical approach for energy-efficient scheduling of large workloads in multicore distributed systems. Sustain. Comput.: Inf. Syst. **4**(4), 252–261 (2014)
8. Du Bois, K., Schaeps, T., Polfliet, S., Ryckbosch, F., Eeckhout, L.: Sweep: evaluating computer system energy efficiency using synthetic workloads. In: 6th International Conference on High Performance and Embedded Architectures and Compilers, pp. 159–166 (2011)
9. Gonze, X., et al.: ABINIT: first-principles approach to material and nanosystem properties. Comput. Phys. Commun. **180**(12), 2582–2615 (2009)
10. Iturriaga, S., Dorronsoro, B., Nesmachnow, S.: Multiobjective evolutionary algorithms for energy and service level scheduling in a federation of distributed datacenters. Int. Trans. Oper. Res. **24**(1–2), 199–228 (2017)
11. Iturriaga, S., Nesmachnow, S.: Scheduling energy efficient data centers using renewable energy. Electronics **5**(4), 71 (2016)
12. Iturriaga, S., García, S., Nesmachnow, S.: An empirical study of the robustness of energy-aware schedulers for high performance computing systems under uncertainty. In: Hernández, G., et al. (eds.) CARLA 2014. CCIS, vol. 485, pp. 143–157. Springer, Heidelberg (2014). https://doi.org/10.1007/978-3-662-45483-1_11
13. Jie, B., Tsuji, T.: An analysis of market mechanism and bidding strategy for power balancing market in micro-grid. In: China International Conference on Electricity Distribution (2016)
14. Johari, R., Tsitsiklis, J.N.: Parameterized supply function bidding: equilibrium and efficiency. Oper. Res. **59**(5), 1079–1089 (2011)
15. Klemper, P.D., Meyer, M.A.: Supply function equilibria in oligopoly under uncertainty. Econometrica **57**(6), 1243–1277 (1989)
16. Kopytov, A.: Sysbench repository. https://github.com/akopytov/sysbench. Accessed Jan 2019
17. Kurowski, K., Oleksiak, A., Piatek, W., Piontek, T., Przybyszewski, A., Weglarz, J.: Dcworms–a tool for simulation of energy efficiency in distributed computing infrastructures. Simul. Model. Pract. Theory **39**, 135–151 (2013)
18. Momoh, J.: Smart Grid: Fundamentals of Design and Analysis. Wiley-IEEE Press (2012)
19. Montes de Oca, S., Belzarena, P., Monzon, P.: Optimal demand response in distribution networks with several energy retail companies. In: IEEE Multi-Conference on Systems and Control, pp. 1092–1097 (2016)

20. Muraña, J., Nesmachnow, S., Armenta, F., Tchernykh, A.: Characterization, modeling and scheduling of power consumption of scientific computing applications in multicores. Cluster Computing (2019). https://doi.org/10.1007/s10586-018-2882-8. Accessed Jan 2019
21. Nesmachnow, S.: An overview of metaheuristics: accurate and efficient methods for optimisation. Int. J. Metaheuristics 3(4), 320–347 (2014)
22. Nesmachnow, S., Iturriaga, S.: Cluster-UY: scientific HPC in Uruguay. In: International Supercomputing in México, pp. 1–15 (2019)
23. Nesmachnow, S., Perfumo, C., Goiri, Í.: Multiobjective energy-aware datacenter planning accounting for power consumption profiles. In: Hernández, G., et al. (eds.) CARLA 2014. CCIS, vol. 485, pp. 128–142. Springer, Heidelberg (2014). https://doi.org/10.1007/978-3-662-45483-1_10
24. Nesmachnow, S., Perfumo, C., Goiri, Í.: Holistic multiobjective planning of datacenters powered by renewable energy. Cluster Comput. 18(4), 1379–1397 (2015)
25. Phillips, J., et al.: Scalable molecular dynamics with namd. J. Comput. Chem. 26(16), 1781–1802 (2005)
26. Rockafellar, R., Uryasev, S.: Optimization of conditional value-at-risk. J. Risk 2, 21–42 (2000)
27. Rong, H., Zhang, H., Xiao, S., Li, C., Hu, C.: Optimizing energy consumption for data centers. Renew. Sustain. Energy Rev. 58, 674–691 (2016)
28. Srikantaiah, S., Kansal, A., Zhao, F.: Energy aware consolidation for cloud computing. In: Conference on Power Aware Computing and Systems, pp. 1–5 (2008)
29. Treibig, J., Hager, G., Wellein, G.: LIKWID: a lightweight performance-oriented tool suite for x86 multicore environments. In: 39th International Conference on Parallel Processing Workshops, pp. 207–216 (2010)

Evaluation of GPUSPH Code for Simulations of Fluid Injection Through Submerged Entry Nozzle

Ruslan Gabbasov[✉], Jesús González-Trejo,
César Augusto Real-Ramírez, Mario Martínez Molina,
and Francisco Cervantes-de la Torre

Departamento de Sistemas, Universidad Autónoma Metropolitana,
San Pablo 180, Col. Reynosa Tamaulipas, México City 02200, Mexico
gabbasov@azc.uam.mx

Abstract. In computational fluid dynamics a lot of theoretical and numerical effort is made to have a method with the ability to correctly simulate fluid-structure interaction, free surfaces, as well as evolve multiple components and phases within a system. Traditionally, commercial and open source software is based on meshes where the implementation of open boundaries and interfaces is not trivial. A particle method, the Smooth Particle Hydrodynamics (SPH), has the advantage of being mesh free and the ability to treat open surfaces. This paper presents a study of the characteristics and capacity of the GPUSPH open source software to simulate a fluid injection through a fork injector submerged in a tank. The objective of this system is to study the formation of vortices and the oscillations of the free surface in the tank, an open problem in continuous metal casting industry. A system similar to that described by [3] and [12] has been simulated to study the velocity field inside the tank and compare with previous results. Our fiducial simulation reproduce the qualitative behavior observed in physical and numerical experiments [3–9, 12]. However, in order to reproduce the dynamics of water near the nozzle more than a million particles are required leading to somewhat higher computational cost in comparison to the mesh based methods.

Keywords: Smoothed particle hydrodynamics · Numerical simulations · Submerged Entry Nozzle

1 Introduction

The study of non-stationary hydrodynamic phenomena represents a very important area in both basic sciences and engineering. The technological development in the last two decades allowed to create experimental techniques and sophisticated numerical models to study and simulate complex processes in multiphase, turbulent and thermal flows. The SPH method is a Lagrangian method that has been applied to various problems in different areas of science and engineering thanks to the easy incorporation of various physical processes (conduction, diffusion, solidification, etc.), the possibility of implementation of boundary conditions for complex geometries and good numerical

© Springer Nature Switzerland AG 2019
M. Torres and J. Klapp (Eds.): ISUM 2019, CCIS 1151, pp. 218–226, 2019.
https://doi.org/10.1007/978-3-030-38043-4_18

scaling on graphic processing units (GPUs) [2]. Numerous comparisons of solutions given by other codes have been made, mainly based on meshes, validating the SPH method and identifying its weaknesses and advantages. Specifically, the problems in engineering include transport phenomena of fluids in pipelines, multiphase media and catalysis in petrochemical industry, simulation of the impact of waves on coastal and maritime structures, simulation of molding processes and precision casting among many other applications [1, 10, 11].

One specific problem encountered in metallurgy is the design of a Submerged Entry Nozzle (SEN) through which the liquid metal is injected into a continuous casting mold [3]. The injected metal forms vortices in the mold that can trap slag, air and other smelting byproducts causing permanent defects in the metal. There are numerous scale studies using water and particle tracking technique to determine the velocity and vorticity fields inside the tank that have allowed mitigating several of the problems. Numerical simulations, on the other hand, helped to improve the design of the SENs by tracing the entire velocity field and mitigating the vorticity [5, 8, 12]. However, as of the authors knowledge there are no such studies that use SPH method. The aim of this work is to reproduce qualitatively the results of other authors using a modern SPH formalism available in an open source code GPUSPH[1].

2 Methodology

The GPUSPH code developed by Rustico et al. [2] is a parallel open source code that includes the modern formalism of the SPH method and different algorithms for the treatment of boundary conditions suitable for simulations of confined and open fluids. The code developed for its execution on GPU cards has shown encouraging results thanks to its innovative semi-analytical method of treatment of boundary conditions that allows to preserve high accuracy for complex geometries [13, 14]. In this study GPUSPH version 4.1 was used with a change in the equation of state that now includes the background pressure (see Eq. (3) below).

The hydrodynamic is governed by the Navier-Stokes equations that are solved by the GPUSPH in their Lagrangian form:

$$\frac{d\rho}{dt} = -\rho \nabla \cdot u, \tag{1}$$

$$\frac{du}{dt} = -\frac{1}{\rho} \nabla p + \nabla \cdot \left[v \left(\nabla u + \nabla u^T \right) \right] + g, \tag{2}$$

$$p = \frac{c_0 \rho_0}{\xi} \left[\left(\frac{\rho}{\rho_0} \right)^{\xi} - 1 \right] + p_0. \tag{3}$$

---

[1] https://www.gpusph.org.

where u is the velocity vector, ρ is the density, p is the pressure and g the gravitational force. In order to simulate a quasi-compressible medium a Tait equation of state (3) is used with an exponent $\xi = 7$ and a reference density ρ_0. The numerical sound speed c_0, is chosen as being ten times the typical velocity of the fluid and a constant background pressure p_0 is an empirical parameter chosen according to the problem studied [1]. In addition, as the flow is turbulent the turbulent viscosity, $v_T = 0.09\,k^2/\varepsilon$, is included in the momentum Eq. (2) which is given by the set of equations for $k - \varepsilon$ standard turbulence model. This means that two more equations should be solved for kinetic turbulent energy k and turbulent dissipation ε coupled by smooth wall law [14]. A full set of equations is given in a theory guide provided with GPUSPH code. As a stabilization method against spurious pressure oscillations Ferrari's correction was used whose dampening parameter only depends on the typical scale of the problem. The SPH equations were discretized using fourth order Wendland kernel with 230 neighbours on average and integrated using first order "predictor-corrector" scheme with adaptive timesteps. A high order kernel together with the increased number of neighbours and novel method for boundaries treatment in GPUSPH guarantee the first order consistency [13, 15].

The study of the system similar to described in [3, 12] was performed with the SPH method in order to compare qualitatively with the results of previous simulations obtained with the Ansys Fluent commercial software that uses volume of fluid technique to track the open surface [16]. Since we are mainly interested in the dynamics of fluid around the SEN and close to the surface the tank size was significantly reduced. The geometry of the system is given in Fig. 1a. Water with density $\rho_0 = 1000\,\text{kg/m}^3$ and kinematic viscosity $v = 1.0 \times 10^{-6}\,\text{m}^2/\text{s}$ is injected with parabolic velocity profile adapted for square duct and maximum velocity of $u_{max} = 2.0$ m/s through the SEN entrance. The SEN is submerged at a depth of 0.05 m in the rectangular tank containing water up to 2/3 of its volume. The tank has dimensions $0.14 \times 0.07 \times 0.16$ m along x, y, z directions respectively, and a square hole at the bottom of 0.02×0.02 m for free flow discharge. The SEN has a length of 0.105 m and square cross-section of 0.025×0.025 m on the inside walls. The walls have thickness of 0.005 m. The exit ports have square shape with size of 0.02×0.02 m and an inclination of $15°$ with respect to the free surface of the tank (Fig. 1b).

The geometry of the system is modelled using an open source software SALOME v8.4 and meshed with Netgen 2D and 3D algorithm restricting maximum cell size. The mesh has a resolution of 0.001 m and is used for the generation of SPH particle distribution of walls, free surfaces, and inlet/outlet. The mesh is exported in binary STL format and converted to a cloud of points using the Crixus routine included with the GPUSPH. Information contained in the mesh is used to determine velocity directions and particle masses required by semi-analytical boundary conditions. The boundary conditions of the walls are of the non-slip type, those of the entrance are given by prescribed entry speed and at the exit the fluid falls freely by the force of gravity. The particles that leave the problem domain are removed from simulation.

3 Results

Our model was simulated for different values of the number of particles, the smoothing length, the inflow rate, sound speed and the Ferrari stabilization scale. The obtained results allowed to define the appropriate numerical parameters to perform a stable simulation with reliable results. First simulations indicated the formation of particle-free voids in regions of negative pressure (vortex centers) in the tank. This numerical phenomenon has been previously observed by different authors who have recommended adding a constant positive pressure to the equation of state to eliminate this instability. However, there is no know criterion for choosing its value and is rather problem dependent. In particular, after several experiments we determined that the value of the background pressure $p_0 = 5 \times 10^4$ Pa is necessary to avoid the formation of regions of negative pressure. This is roughly the half of mean fluid pressure. It is worth mentioning that greater values of p_0 require smaller integration time steps which in turn lengthens the simulation time.

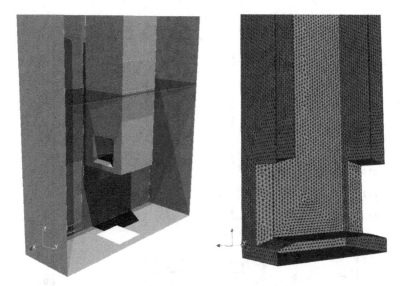

Fig. 1. (a) Left: SEN submerged into the tank filled with water (water level is shown in blue). (b) Right: geometry of the SEN and its mesh seen as longitudinal cut. (Color figure online)

Our fiducial simulation has 1,417,000 particles (1,044,270 of which represents the fluid and the rest are boundaries), the spatial resolution of 0.001 m, smoothing length of 0.0018 m, the Ferrari's coefficient 0.004 m, and ran up to $t = 1.0$ s. The simulation was performed on one node of GPU cluster of "Laboratory of Applied Mathematics and High-Performance Computing of the Mathematics Department of CINVESTAV-IPN ABACUS", containing two Tesla K40 m GPU cards and required one week with an average timestep of $\Delta t \approx 2.0 \times 10^{-6}$ s. After approximately $t = 0.6$ s the flow inside the SEN becomes developed and the water flow in the thank turns into a quasi-stationary state where the position and intensity of the main vortices does not change. Figure 2 shows the velocity field inside the tank for a final time $t = 1.0$ s, where one can clearly see four large vortices that have a mirror symmetry with respect to the z axis. These vortices are generated by water jets that impact the tank walls and they have been observed both in physical and numerical simulations [3–12].

In order to explore the velocity field in different regions of the tank, velocity vectors have been constructed in the xy plane at different values of $z = [0.13, 0.1, 0.06]$ m. These fields reveal complex dynamics inside the tank where the kinetic energy of the jets becomes convective movement of the fluid, contributing to the process of mixing the contents of the tank. In particular, four large vertical vortices are observed near the corners of the tank at the level of the exit ports (Fig. 3b). In the lower part of the tank there are vortices that are part of the vortices of the previous figure, but weaker and closer to $y = 0$ (Fig. 3c). A remarkable behavior can be observed near the exit hole of the tank, where two parallel flows converge around $x = 0$ before leaving the tank.

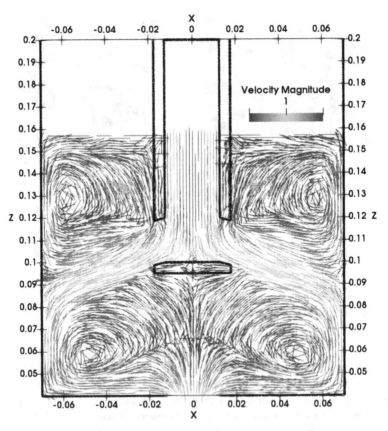

Fig. 2. Fluid velocity field along the plane $y = 0$ at time $t = 1.0$ s. The maximum velocity of 2 m/s shown in red. Note the formation of four vortexes at levels $z = 0.06$ and $z = 0.13$ m. (Color figure online)

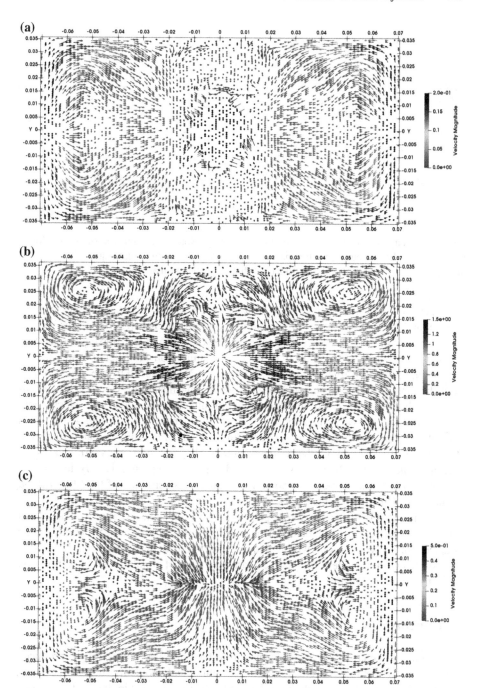

Fig. 3. Velocity vectors in the xy plane for: (a) $z = 0.13$ m, (b) $z = 0.1$ m, (c) $z = 0.06$ m. The arrows have the same length and their velocity magnitude is encoded by colour. Note also that scale of the colour bar is different in each panel. (Color figure online)

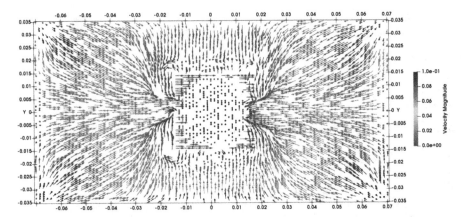

Fig. 4. Velocity vectors in the xy plane for $z = 0.15$ m. Note the asymmetric shape of velocity field near the SEN. Group of vectors parallel to the x axis that outline SEN square contour is an interpolation procedure artefact due to lack of fluid particles in that region.

Previous works [3–12] have shown the existence of irregular movements near the surface, and even the presence of oscillating flows around the SEN. The four vertical and four horizontal vortices coexist together interacting and transferring momentum between each other in a nonlinear manner. Our simulation indicates the presence of weak asymmetric movements near the surface (Fig. 3a) produced by the flows coming from the tank corners that impact the SEN generating instabilities observed as oscillations of the free surface. To further explore this situation, the additional velocity field was obtained very close to the surface, $z = 0.15$ m which is shown in Fig. 4. The flows that emerge from the four corners converge on the walls of the SEN and are submerged along the walls parallel to the x axis down to the exit ports. The irregularity of movement near the SEN walls is evident although its magnitude is very low and is possibly attributed to numerical errors. To ensure the consistency of the SPH method the number of neighbors must grow proportionally to the total number of particles in the domain [15]. It is necessary to repeat the simulation with a higher resolution that allows better accuracy of the behavior near the surface and for a longer period of time to detect surface oscillations whose frequency is found being a few hertz [12]. Next stage of this work includes quantitative characterization of simulations and comparison with physical experiments.

4 Conclusions

The qualitative behavior of vortex formation in the tank was successfully reproduced using the SPH method and allowed to detect numerical problems such as the penetration of fluid particles through the walls and formation of voids in the fluid. The main factor that determines the wall penetration is the numerical sound speed, c_0, which should be the highest possible. This however, leads to a decrease in the timestep which could reach the limit of single precision representation and the code will stop. On the other hand, for highly vortical flow a non-zero background pressure is necessary in the equation of state in order to inhibit the voids formation. The model considered in this work demands very tiny timesteps reaching in some cases machine single precision value. This leads to overall slow performance of the simulation. Finding a balance between the physical and numerical parameters represents a challenge and must be performed for each particular case studied.

Specifically, it is concluded that:

(i)   the meshing of the objects that represent the walls must have elements of a homogeneous size in order to reduce the velocity errors near the walls;

(ii)   The maximum flow rate (not the average) must be estimated before the simulation in order to avoid particle penetration through the walls.

(iii) It is necessary to add to the equation of state a background pressure more or equal to 10% of the typical problem pressure to avoid the formation of regions without particles (voids);

(iv)   The increase in simulation resolution reduces oscillations in the pressure field due to convergence with the type of kernel used (Wendland).

(v)   The GPUSPH code was able to reproduce the formation of the eight vortices and showed to be robust although with a high computational cost due to the techniques and the numerical parameters selected.

Future investigation will be focused on the increasing order of time integration together with the increased accuracy of SPH equations.

Acknowledgment. The authors gratefully acknowledge the developers of GPUSPH code for making it publicly available, as well as the facilities of the "Laboratory of Applied Mathematics and High-Performance Computing (ABACUS)" of the Mathematics Department of CINVESTAV-IPN where simulations were performed.

References

1. Monaghan, J.J.: Smoothed particle hydrodynamics and its diverse applications. Ann. Rev. Fluid Mech. **44**, 323–346 (2012)
2. Rustico, E., Bilotta, G., Hérault, A., Del Negro, C., Gallo, G.: Advances in multi-GPU smoothed particle hydrodynamics simulations. IEEE Trans. Parallel Distrib. Syst. **25**, 43–52 (2014)
3. Real-Ramirez, C.A., Gonzalez-Trejo, Jesus I.: Analysis of three-dimensional vortexes below the free surface in a continuous casting mold. Int. J. Miner. Metall. Mater. **18**, 397–407 (2011)
4. Gonzalez-Trejo, J., Real-Ramirez, C.A., Miranda-Tello, R., Rivera-Perez, F., Cervantes-De-La-Torre, F.: Numerical and physical parametric analysis of a SEN with flow conditioners in slab continuous casting mold. Arch. Metall. Materi. **62**(2), 927–946 (2017)
5. Real-Ramirez, C., Miranda, R., Vilchis, C., Barron, M., Hoyos, L., Gonzalez, J.: Transient internal flow characterization of a bifurcated submerged entry nozzle. ISIJ Int. **46**(8), 1183–1191 (2006)

6. Real-Ramirez, C.A., Gonzalez-Trejo, J.I.: Analysis of three-dimensional vortexes below the free surface in a continuous casting mold. Int. J. Miner. Metall. Mater. **18**(4), 397–407 (2011)
7. Real-Ramirez, C.A., Carvajal-Mariscal, I., Sanchez-Silva, F., Cervantes-de-la-Torre, F., Diaz-Montes, J., Gonzalez-Trejo, J.: Three-dimensional flow behavior inside the submerged entry nozzle. Metall. Mater. Trans. B Process Metall. Mater. Process. Sci. **49**(4), 1644–1657 (2018)
8. Real-Ramirez, C.A., Miranda-Tello, R., Carvajal-Mariscal, I., Sanchez-Silva, F., Gonzalez-Trejo, J.: Hydrodynamic study of a submerged entry nozzle with flow modifiers. Metall. Mater. Trans. B Process Metall. Mater. Process. Sci. **48**(2), 1358–1375 (2017)
9. Real-Ramirez, C.A., Miranda-Tello, R., Hoyos-Reyes, L., Reyes, M., Gonzalez-Trejo, J.I.: Numerical evaluation of a submerged entry nozzle for continuous casting of steel. Indian J. Eng. Mater. Sci. **19**(3), 179–188 (2012)
10. Real-Ramirez, C.A., Palomar-Pardave, M., Rodriguez-Torres, I., Hoyos-Reyes, L., Gonzalez-Trejo, J.: Biphasic numerical simulation of a rotating disc electrochemical cell. ECS Trans. **20**, 51–61 (2009)
11. Real-Ramírez, C.A., Orduna-Martínez, R., Huerta Velázquez, V.: Notas para el curso taller Diseño Aerodinámico Experimental, vol. 1. Universidad Autónoma Metropolitana, México (2011)
12. Kalter, R., Tummers, M.J., Kenjereš, S., Righolt, B.W., Kleijn, C.R.: Oscillations of the fluid flow and the free surface in a cavity with a submerged bifurcated nozzle. Int. J. Heat Fluid Flow **44**, 365–374 (2013)
13. Ferrand, M., Laurence, D., Rogers, B.D., Violeau, D., Kassiotis, Ch.: Unified semi-analytical wall boundary conditions for inviscid, laminar or turbulent flows in the meshless SPH method. Int. J. Numer. Methods Fluids **71**(4), 446–472 (2012)
14. Leroy, A., Violeau, D., Ferrand, M., Kassiotis, C.: Unified semi-analytical wall boundary conditions applied to 2-D incompressible SPH. J. Comput. Phys. **261**, 106–129 (2014)
15. Gabbasov, R., Sigalotti, L.D., Cruz, F., Klapp, J., Ramirez-Velasquez, J.M.: Consistent SPH simulations of protostellar collapse and fragmentation. Astrophys. J. **835**, 287 (2017)
16. Ansys Software (2010). https://www.ansys.com/products/fluids/ansys-fluent. Accessed 4 Mar 2019

Creating and Using Large Grids of Pre-calculated Model Atmospheres for Rapid Analysis of Stellar Spectra

Janos Zsargó[1(✉)], Celia Rosa Fierro-Santillán[2], Jaime Klapp[2],
Anabel Arrieta[3], Lorena Arias[3], Jurij Mendoza Valencia[1],
and Leonardo Di G. Sigalotti[4]

[1] Departamento de Física, Escuela Superior de Física y Matemáticas,
Instituto Politécnico Nacional, Mexico City, Mexico
jzsargo@esfm.ipn.mx, jurijmev@gmail.com
[2] Instituto Nacional de Investigaciones Nucleares (ININ),
La Marquesa, Estado de México, Mexico
celia.fierro.estrellas@gmail.com,
jaime.klapp@inin.gob.mx
[3] Universidad Iberoamericana, Mexico City, Mexico
{anabel.arrieta,lorena.arias}@uia.mx
[4] Área de Física de Procesos Irreversibles, Departamento de Ciencias Básicas,
Universidad Autónoma Metropolitana-Azcapotzalco (UAM-A),
Mexico City, Mexico
leonardo.sigalotti@gmail.com

Abstract. We present a database of 45,000 atmospheric models (which will become 80,000 models by the end of the project) with stellar masses between 9 and 120 $M_\odot$, covering the region of the OB main sequence and W-R stars in the H–R diagram. The models were calculated using the ABACUS I supercomputer and the stellar atmosphere code CMFGEN. The parameter space has 6 dimensions: the effective temperature T_{eff}, the luminosity L, the metallicity Z, and three stellar wind parameters, namely the exponent β, the terminal velocity V_∞, and the volume filling factor F_{cl}. For each model, we also calculate synthetic spectra in the UV (900–2000 Å), optical (3500–7000 Å), and near IR (10000–30000 Å) regions. To facilitate comparison with observations, the synthetic spectra were rotationally broaden using ROTIN3, by covering v sin i velocities between 10 and 350 km/s^{-1} with steps of 10 km/s^{-1}, resulting in a library of 1 575 000 synthetic spectra. In order to demonstrate the benefits of employing the databases of pre-calculated models, we also present the results of the re-analysis of ε Ori by using our grid.

Keywords: Astronomical databases: miscellaneous · Methods: data analysis · Stars: atmospheres

1 Introduction

Thanks to the fertile combination of the large amount of public data and the availability of sophisticated stellar atmosphere codes such as CMFGEN [14], TLUSTY [15], FASTWIND [19, 20], and the Potsdam Wolf-Rayet code (PoWR) [9, 10] self-consistent

M. Torres and J. Klapp (Eds.): ISUM 2019, CCIS 1151, pp. 227–236, 2019.
https://doi.org/10.1007/978-3-030-38043-4_19

analysis of spectral regions from the UV to the IR is now possible. As a result of this we have made significant advances in the understanding of the physical conditions in the atmospheres and winds of massive stars.

For example, early far-UV observations showed that there were inconsistencies between the optical effective temperature scale and that implied by the observed wind ionization [8]. Studies by Martins et al. [16], and others, have shown that the neglect of line blanketing in the models leads to a systematic overestimate of the effective temperature when derived from optical H and He lines. On the other hand, Crowther et al. [4], Bouret et al. [2], and Hillier et al. [13] simultaneously analyzed the *FUSE*, the *HST*, and the optical spectra of O stars and were able to derive consistent effective temperatures using a wide variety of diagnostics.

Another crucial result was the recognition of the important effect of wind inhomogeneities (clumping) on the spectral analyses of O stars. For instance, Crowther et al. [4] and Hillier et al. [13] could not reproduce the observed P V $\lambda\lambda$ 1118–1128 profiles when using mass-loss rates derived from the analysis of Hα lines. The only ways the P V and the Hα profile discrepancies could be resolved were either by assuming substantial clumping or using unrealistically low phosphorus abundances. As a consequence of clumping, the mass-loss rates have been lowered by significant factors (i.e., from 3 to 10). However, the possibility of optically thick clumping was raised recently which would change this conclusion (see, e.g., Ref. [21] and references therein).

Unfortunately, performing such investigations by using any of the above mentioned stellar atmosphere codes is not an easy task! To run these codes and perform a reliable analysis requires a lot of experience; something that many investigators do not have the time to gain. Therefore, it is useful to develop databases of pre-calculated models. Such databases will free up valuable time for astronomers, who could study stellar atmospheres with reasonable accuracy but without the need of running time consuming simulations. Furthermore, these databases will also accelerate the studies of large numbers of observed spectra that are in line for analysis.

The basic parameters of such databases of pre-calculated models are: the surface temperature (T_{eff}), the stellar mass (M), and the surface chemical composition. An adequate analysis of massive stars also has to take into account the parameters associated with the stellar wind, such as the terminal velocity (V_∞), the mass-loss rate ($\dot{M}$), and the clumping. If one takes into account the variations of all necessary parameters the number of pre-calculated models that are needed increases exponentially. Therefore, production of such databases is only possible by using supercomputing facilities.

There are already a few databases of synthetic stellar spectra available, but only with a few tens or hundreds of stellar models (see, for example, the atlas of CMFGEN models for OB massive stars by Fierro et al. [6], the grid of W-R stars by Hamann and Gräfener [10], and the POLLUX database by Palacios et al. [17]). On the other hand, we are generating a database with tens of thousands of models [22], which will be publicly available in a year or so. Obviously, it will be impossible to manually compare an observed spectrum with such an amount of model calculations. Therefore, it is imperative to develop tools that allow the automation of this process but without compromising the quality of the fit. In particular, in Ref. [7] we have presented

FIT*spec*, a program that searches our database for a model that better fits the observed spectrum in the optical region. It uses the Balmer lines to measure the surface gravity (log(g)) and the equivalent width ratios of He II and He I lines to estimate T_{eff}.

In this article we describe the state of our grid of pre-calculated models and the results of a test analysis to verify the usefulness of the grid. In Sects. 2 and 2.1, we briefly describe the stellar atmosphere code (CMFGEN) which we use to produce our models. In Sect. 3, we describe our model grid and in Sect. 4 we describe a simple test analysis to demonstrate the benefits of using our grid. Finally, in Sect. 5 we summarize the relevant conclusions.

2 CMFGEN

CMFGEN is a sophisticated and widely-used non-LTE stellar atmosphere code [13, 14]. It models the full spectrum and has been used successfully to model O & B stars, W-R stars, luminous blue variables, and even supernovae. The code determines the temperature, ionization structure, and level populations for all elements in the stellar atmosphere and wind. It solves the spherical radiative transfer equation in the co-moving frame in conjunction with the statistical equilibrium equations and radiative equilibrium equation. The hydrostatic structure can be computed below the sonic point, thereby allowing the simultaneous treatment of spectral lines formed in the atmosphere, the stellar wind, and the transition region between the two. Such features make it particularly well suited for the study of massive OB stars with winds. However, there is a price for such sophistication, a CMFGEN simulation takes any where between 24 and 36 h of microprocessor time to be completed.

For atomic models, CMFGEN utilizes the concept of "super levels" by which levels of similar energies are grouped together and treated as a single level in the statistical equilibrium equations (see, Ref. [14] and references therein for more details). The stellar models in this project include 28 explicit ions of the different elements as function of their T_{eff}. Table 1 summarizes the levels and super levels included in the models. The atomic data references are given by Herald and Bianchi [11].

Table 1. Super levels/levels for the different ionization stages included in the models.

Element	I	II	III	IV	V	VI	VII	VIII
H	20/30	1/1	...	...	...	...	...	...
He	45/69	22/30	1/1	...	...	...	...	...
C	...	40/92	51/84	59/64	1/1	...	...	...
N	...	45/85	41/82	44/76	41/49	1/1	...	...
O	...	54/123	88/170	38/78	32/56	25/31	1/1	...
Si	...	...	33/33	22/33	1/1	...	...	...
P	...	...	...	30/90	16/62	1/1	...	...
S	...	...	24/44	51/142	31/98	28/58	1/1	...
Fe	...	...	104/1433	74/540	50/220	44/433	29/153	1/1

To model the stellar wind, CMFGEN requires values for the mass loss rate ($\dot{M}$), terminal velocity (V_∞), β parameter, and the *volume filling factor* of the wind (F_{cl}). The profile of wind speed is modeled by a beta-type law [3]

$$\mathbf{v(r)} = v_\infty \left(1 - \frac{r}{R_*}\right)^\beta , \tag{1}$$

The β parameter controls how the stellar wind is accelerated to reach the terminal velocity (see Fig. 1), while the volume filling factor F_{cl} is used to introduce the effects of optically thin clumping in the wind (see Ref. [21] and references therein).

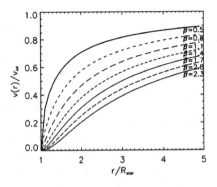

Fig. 1. Examples of beta-type velocity laws.

2.1   Synthetic Spectra

The auxiliary program CMF FLUX of the CMFGEN package computes the synthetic observed spectrum in the observer's frame which is one of the most important output of our models [12]. To simulate the effects of rotation on the spectral lines, the synthetic spectra are also rotationally broadened using the program ROTIN3, which is part of the TLUSTY package [15].

For each model in the grid, we calculate the normalized spectra in the UV (900–3500 Å), optical (3500–7000 Å), and IR (7000–40 000 Å) range; then, we apply rotation by sampling the range between 10 and 350 km/s^{-1} with steps of 10 km/s^{-1}. This process results in a library with a total of 1 575 000 synthetic spectra.

3   The Model Grid

The main parameters of a model atmosphere are the luminosity (L) and the effective temperature (T_{eff}), whose values allow to place the star in the H-R diagram. In order to constrain appropriately the input parameters, we use the evolutionary tracks of Ekström et al. [5] calculated with solar metallicity (Z = 0.014) at the zero age main sequence (ZAMS). For any track, each point corresponds to a star with specific values of T_{eff}, luminosity (L), and stellar mass (M). We calculated several models along each track with the approximate steps of 2 500 K in T_{eff}, while the stellar radius and the surface gravity $\log(g)$ were calculated to get the luminosity L and the stellar mass M corresponding to the track.

The elements included in our models are H, He, C, N, O, Si, P, S, and Fe. The values of H, He, C, N, and O were taken from the tables of Ekström et al. [5]. For consistency, we assumed solar metallicity as reported by Asplund et al. [1] for Si, P, S, and Fe in all models.

The grid is organized as a hypercube data in dimensions which correspond to T_{eff}, L, V_∞, β, Fcl, and the metallicity. The plane generated by T_{eff} and L is the H-R diagram (see upper part of Fig. 2); the values of these variables are restricted by evolutionary tracks. For V_∞ we use two values, a low ($V_\infty = 1.3 V_{esc}$) and a high ($V_\infty = 2.1 V_{esc}$) velocity model, where the escape velocity (V_{esc}) has the usual meaning. The fourth dimension is the β parameter of the stellar wind for which we use the values of $\beta = 0.5$, 0.8, 1.1, 1.4, 1.7, 2.0, and 2.3 (see bottom left of Fig. 2). Models with different values of Teff, L, and F_{cl} populate a data cube. Each value of $F_{cl} = 0.05, 0.30, 0.60$, and 1.0 generates a similar cube, all of which are aligned one after another in a fifth dimension. Finally, we have two values of metallicity: solar and solar enhanced by rotation. This 6-dimensional arrangement generates a plane populated with data cubes (see bottom right of Fig. 2).

This arrangement only populates regions of the H-R diagram where nature forms stars, and does not produce non-physical models. If needed, we can interpolate between models to achieve better fits to the observed spectra.

4   A Simple Test to Demonstrate the Usefulness of Our Grid

We demonstrate the benefits of having a mega-grid by a re-analysis of ε Ori. This O9/B0 supergiant was studied by Puebla et al. [18] by using CMFGEN in the traditional way (i.e., by producing every model that was needed). They reported $T_{eff} = 27,000$ K, $\log g = 3$, a mass-loss rate $\dot{M} \sim 10^{-7} M_\odot \, \mathrm{yr}^{-1}$, and a highly clumped and slowly accelerating wind ($F_{cl} = 0.01$, $\beta > 2.0$) for this star. Figure 3 shows a comparison of selected models from the grid with the optical He I and He II lines observed for ε Ori. We tried to select models which only differ in the effective temperature and have a low mass-loss rate to avoid complications. Obviously, our grid is still not fine enough to be able to do that.

The He lines are normally used to estimate the effective temperature of O stars. Although, the He II lines are very weak for ε Ori since this star is on the borderline between type O and B, the comparison still shows that T_{eff} has to be around 25,000 K.

Moreover, Fig. 4 shows models from the grid which vary in $\log g$ in comparison with the observed H Balmer series. Unfortunately, the H Balmer lines are also affected by mass-loss, namely the absorption is filled in by the emission in the base of the wind. For example, Fig. 4 shows that Hα and Hβ are basically useless as $\log g$ indicator even at relatively low $\dot{M}$. Nevertheless, the higher order members of the Balmer series are not affected by mass-loss and they support the published value of $\log g \sim 3$.

The most useful spectral region to estimate the mass-loss rate ($\dot{M}$) and terminal velocity (V_∞) is the ultraviolet one. Here, we encounter strong resonance lines of the dominant ionization states of various elements in the winds of massive stars. These lines normally show P-Cygnii profiles which are particularly useful to measure $\dot{M}$ and V_∞; see e.g., the C IV doublet around 1550 Å or the Si IV doublet around 1400 Å in Fig. 5. However, these lines are not useful to estimate F_{cl} and, if saturated, they are also useless to measure β. The comparison of models with the observations in Fig. 5 shows a somewhat contradictory situation, while the Si IV λλ 1400 doublet suggests a low $\dot{M}$. To fit the C IV λλ 1552 profile we would need much higher mass-loss rates. However, $\dot{M} \sim 10^{-6}\,M_\odot\,\mathrm{yr}^{-1}$ would result in Hα emission which is not observed. Therefore, we conclude that $\dot{M} \sim 10^{-7}\,M_\odot\,\mathrm{yr}^{-1}$ is the best estimate we can have.

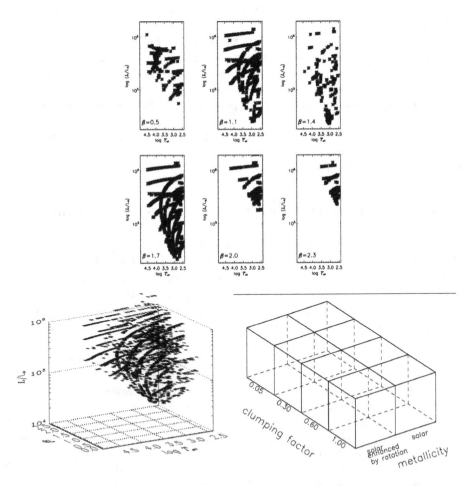

Fig. 2. Organization of the grid as a 5-dimensional hypercube. Top: T_{eff}-Luminosity planes with different values of β parameter. *Bottom Left*: Data cube with the models contained in the six planes. *Bottom Right*: Plane formed by cubes similar to that shown on the left, the dimensions of these are different values of the volume *filling factor* with two different metallicities.

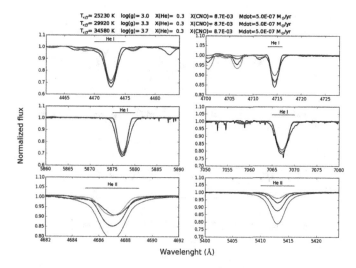

Fig. 3. Comparison of selected models (coloured lines) with the observed He I and He II lines for ε Ori (black curves) to estimate the T_{eff} of the star. The parameters of the models are colour-coded above the figure. (Color figure online)

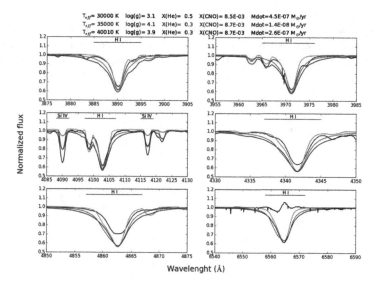

Fig. 4. Comparison of selected models (coloured lines) with the observed H I Balmer series for ε Ori (black curves) to estimate the surface gravity (log *g*) of the star. The parameters of the models are colour-coded above the figure. (Color figure online)

Estimations of F_{cl} and β are very difficult because we do not have many diagnostics and those that we have, like Hα, are affected by a combination of parameters. Nevertheless, the comparison of selected models with the observed Hα lines in Fig. 6 indicates that the values reported in Ref. [18] are plausible.

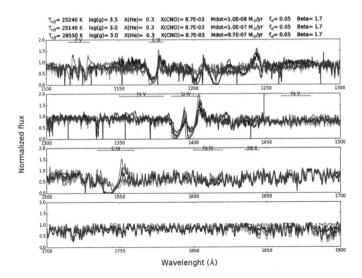

Fig. 5. Comparison of selected models (coloured lines) with the observed UV spectra (*IUE*) for ε Ori (black curves) to estimate the mass-loss rate ($\dot{M}$) of the star. The parameters of the models are colour-coded above the figure. (Color figure online)

As expected, the re-analysis of ε Ori supported the values that were published in Ref. [18]. Obviously, the analysis by using the grid is much cruder, but also much faster. We needed only an afternoon to perform the analysis presented here, while several months of work was necessary to achieve the results presented by Puebla et al. [18].

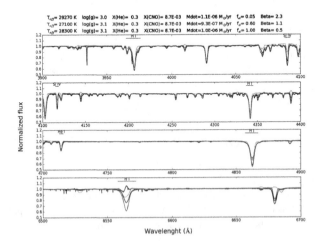

Fig. 6. Comparison of selected models (coloured lines) with the optical spectrum observed for ε Ori (black curves). We can estimate the F_{cl} and β (see Sect. 2 for an explanation) using Hα. The parameters of the models are colour-coded above the figure. (Color figure online)

5 Summary

We present a mega grid of 45,000 (which will soon becomes more than 80,000) stellar atmospheric models calculated by the CMFGEN package. These models cover the region of the H-R diagram populated by OB main sequence and W-R stars with masses between 9 and 120 $M \odot$. The grid provides UV, visual, and IR spectra for each model. We use T_{eff} and luminosity values that correspond to the evolutionary tracks of Ekström et al. [5]. Furthermore, we sample seven values of β, four values of clumping factor, and two different metallicities and terminal velocities. This generates a 6-dimensional hypercube of stellar atmospheric models, which we intend to release to the general astronomical community as a free tool for analyzing OB stars.

We have also demonstrated the usefulness of our mega-grid by the re-analysis of ε Ori. Our somewhat crude but very rapid analysis supported the stellar an wind parameters reported by Puebla et al. [18]. The re-analysis has demonstrated the benefits of having a large grid of pre-calculated models. This way we can perform rapid and reliable estimates of the stellar and wind parameters for a star; and if needed, a more detailed study can be performed but by starting with good initial values. This significantly shortens the time that is needed to complete the spectral analysis.

Acknowledgments. The authors acknowledge the use of the ABACUS-I supercomputer at the Laboratory of Applied Mathematics and High-Performance Computing of the Mathematics Department of CINVESTAV-IPN, where this work was performed. J. Zsargo acknowledges CONACyT CB-2011-01 No. 168632 grant for support. The research leading to these results has received funding from the European Union's Horizon 2020 Programme under the ENERXICO Project, grant agreement no 828947 and under the Mexican CONACYT-SENER-Hidrocarburos grant agreement B-S-69926. J.K. acknowledges financial support by the Consejo Nacional de Ciencia y Tecnología (CONACyT), Mexico, under grant 283151.

References

1. Asplund, M., Grevesse, N., Sauval, A.J., Scott, P.: The chemical composition of the sun. ARA&A **47**, 481–522 (2009)
2. Bouret, J.C., et al.: Quantitative spectroscopy of O stars at low metallicity: O dwarfs in NGC 346. Astrophys. J. **595**, 1182–1205 (2003)
3. Castor, J.I., Abbott, D.C., Klein, R.I.: Radiation-driven winds in of stars. Astrophys. J. **195**, 157–174 (1975)
4. Crowther, P.A., Hillier, D.J., Evans, C.J., Fullerton, A.W., De Marco, O., Willis, A.J.: Revised stellar temperatures of Magellanic cloud O supergiants from far ultraviolet spectroscopic explorer and Very Large Telescope UV- Visual Echelle Spectrograph spectroscopy. Astrophys. J. **579**, 774–799 (2002)
5. Ekström, S., et al.: Grids of stellar models with rotation. I. Models from 0.8 to 120 M⊙ at solar metallicity (Z = 0.014). A&A 537, A146 (2012)
6. Fierro, C.R., et al.: Atlas of CMFGEN models for OB massive stars. PASP **127**, 428–436 (2015)
7. Fierro-Santillán, C.R., et al.: FITspec: a new algorithm for the automated fit of synthetic stellar spectra for OB stars. Astrophys. J. **236**, 38 (2018)

8. Fullerton, A.W., et al.: Far ultraviolet spectroscopic explorer observations of the stellar winds of two O7 supergiants in the Magellanic clouds. Astrophys. J. **538**, L43–L46 (2000)

9. Gräfener, G., Koesterke, L., Hamann, W.R.: Line-blanketed model atmospheres for WR stars. Astron. Astrophys. **387**, 244–257 (2002)

10. Hamann, W.R., Gräfener, G.: Grids of model spectra for WN stars, ready for use. Astron. Astrophys. **427**, 697–704 (2004)

11. Herald, J.E., Bianchi, L.: A far-ultraviolet spectroscopic analysis of the central star of the planetary nebula Longmore 1. Astron. Soc. Pacific **116**, 391–396 (2004)

12. Hillier, D.J.: CMFGEN manual (2013)

13. Hillier, D.J., et al.: A tale of two stars: the extreme O7 Iaf+supergiant AV 83 and the OC7.5III((f)) star AV 69. Astrophys. J. **588**, 1039–1063 (2003)

14. Hillier, D.J., Miller, D.L.: The treatment of non-LTE line blanketing in spherically expanding outflows. Astrophys. J. **496**, 407–427 (1998)

15. Lanz, T., Hubeny, I.: Non-LTE line-blanketed model atmospheres of hot stars. II. Hot, metal-rich white dwarfs. Astrophys. J. **439**, 905–916 (1995)

16. Martins, F., Schaerer, D., Hillier, D.J.: On the effective temperature scale of O stars. Astron. Astrophys. **382**, 999–1004 (2002)

17. Palacios, A., et al.: POLLUX: a database of synthetic stellar spectra. Astron. Astrophys. **516**, A13 (2010)

18. Puebla, R.E., Hillier, D.J., Zsargó, J., Cohen, D.H., Leutenegger, M.A.: X-ray, UV and optical analysis of supergiants: ε Ori. MNRAS **456**, 2907–2936 (2016)

19. Puls, J., et al.: Atmospheric NLTE-models for the spectroscopic analysis of blue stars with winds II. Line-blanketed models. Astron. Astrophys. **435**, 669–698 (2005)

20. Santolaya-Rey, A.E., Puls, J., Herrero, A.: Atmospheric NLTE-models for the spectroscopic analysis of luminous blue stars with winds. Astron. Astrophys. **323**, 488–512 (1997)

21. Sundqvist, J.O., Puls, J., Owocki, S.P.: Mass loss from inhomogeneous hot star winds. III. An effective-opacity formalism for line radiative transfer in accelerating, clumped two-component media, and first results on theory and diagnostics. Astron. Astrophys. **568**, A59 (2014)

22. Zsargo, J., et al.: A mega-grid of CMFGEN model atmospheres for rapid analysis of stellar spectra. In: Miroshnichenko, A., Zharikov, S., Korcáková, D., Wolf, M. (eds.) The B[e] Phenomenon: Forty Years of Studies. Astronomical Society of the Pacific Conference Series, vol. 508, p. 407, February 2017

Lagarto I RISC-V Multi-core: Research Challenges to Build and Integrate a Network-on-Chip

Neiel I. Leyva-Santes[1]([⊠]), Ivan Pérez[2]([⊠]),
César A. Hernández-Calderón[1]([⊠]), Enrique Vallejo[2]([⊠]),
Miquel Moretó[3]([⊠]), Ramón Beivide[2]([⊠]),
Marco A. Ramírez-Salinas[1]([⊠]), and Luis A. Villa-Vargas[1]([⊠])

[1] Computing Research Center,
National Polytechnic Institute, Mexico City, Mexico
Israel.leyva.santes@gmail.com, hdzces@gmail.com,
{mars,lvilla}@cic.ipn.mx
[2] University of Cantabria, Santander, Spain
{ivan.perezgallardo,enrique.vallejo,
ramon.beivide}@unican.es
[3] Barcelona Supercomputing Center, Barcelona, Spain
miquel.moreto@bsc.es

Abstract. Current compute-intensive applications largely exceed the resources of single-core processors. To face this problem, multi-core processors along with parallel computing techniques have become a solution to increase the computational performance. Likewise, multi-processors are fundamental to support new technologies and new science applications challenges. A specific objective of the Lagarto project developed at the National Polytechnic Institute of Mexico is to generate an ecosystem of high-performance processors for the industry and HPC in Mexico, supporting new technologies and scientific applications. This work presents the first approach of the Lagarto project to the design of multi-core processors and the research challenges to build an infrastructure that allows the flagship core of the Lagarto project to scale to multi- and many-cores. Using the OpenPiton platform with the Ariane RISC-V core, a functional tile has been built, integrating a Lagarto I core with memory coherence that executes atomic instructions, and a NoC that allows scaling the project to many-core versions. This work represents the initial state of the design of mexican multi-and many-cores processors.

Keywords: Multi- and many-core · Multiprocessors RISC-V · Interconnection networks

1 Introduction

The "Lagarto" project [1], developed by the Computer Architecture research team at the Computing Research Center of the National Polytechnic Institute of Mexico, aims to generate an open computing platform for academia and research to ease the

© Springer Nature Switzerland AG 2019
M. Torres and J. Klapp (Eds.): ISUM 2019, CCIS 1151, pp. 237–248, 2019.
https://doi.org/10.1007/978-3-030-38043-4_20

understanding of fundamental concepts of Computer Architecture and Operating Systems. The project has two main branches of development: the first one is focused on the educational area, and the second one on the development of a high-performance processors ecosystem, targeting both industry and HPC.

Around 2006, multi-core processors appeared in the market to overcome the "power wall". Multi-core processors increase compute power via parallelism, which rises dramatically the complexity of microprocessors design and programming.

Considering the HPC segment, nowadays all systems rely on multi-core processors, often coupled with highly-parallel accelerators. The use of multiple interconnected compute nodes, each of them with several multi-core processors, allows to build supercomputers with high performance. HPC systems have been built with more than 10 million cores (for example, the Sunway TaihuLight of the National Supercomputing Center in Wuxi) and peak performance above 100,000 TFLOPs (for example The Summit of the Oak Ridge National Laboratory). Relevant information can be found in the Top500 list [3].

The first core designed in the Lagarto project is denoted Lagarto I. The Lagarto I core design supports different ISAs, including RISC-V [2]. RISC-V is an instruction set architecture (ISA) that is completely open and freely available to industry, license-free and royalty-free. RISC-V is a RISC-based architecture; RISC-based processors lead the mobile and embedded markets, partially because of their characteristics of low energy consumption and small area. By contrast, the HPC market is nowadays dominated by traditional x86 processors. However, a growing share of HPC systems rely on the use of RISC designs. Some examples are the BlueGene systems, the Mont-Blanc project and the Tibidabo cluster prototype, to name a few [4–7].

In the Lagarto project, the main challenge to overcome in the second branch (industry and HPC) is to design and develop an infrastructure that allows our processors to scale to multi- and many-cores. Such infrastructure is required to optimize and develop multi-core processors for the industry segment and many-core processors for HPC. The Lagarto project currently has two different core designs: the Lagarto I, which is a scalar core, and the Lagarto II, which is a superscalar core, both with a memory system that allows them to function as mono-core processors. To implement the parallelism required for HPC systems, it is necessary that the cores of Lagarto project can operate as multi-core system, this is, multiples core running multiple coordinated tasks in the same memory space. Scaling to many-cores requires to have a Network-on-Chip (NoC) that allows to transport messages and data between the cores and the memory system. The first objective of this stage of the Lagarto project is to develop the infrastructure required to implement many-cores processors, integrating a NoC into the memory system of Lagarto I core to allow scale to many-core.

This work shows the initial process to integrate the Lagarto I core (the educational version) into a multi-core system based on a Network-on-Chip. The design relies on a RISC-V development framework. We analyze the current RISC-V open-source ecosystem and discuss the selection of one of the available development frameworks, in order to select the most compatible with the Lagarto I core. The analysis of previous works between RISC-V and these platforms with NoCs were fundamentals to select a platform; Also, we show the final design of "Lagarto I" tile that we will use in our versions of multi and many cores.

The rest of the work is organized as follows. Section 2 presents the required background, including Atomic instructions, Cache coherence protocols, interconnection networks and relevant development tools. Section 3 presents an overview of the Lagarto Project and the architecture of the educational core "Lagarto I". Section 4 discusses the selection of the tools to integrate and design the Lagarto I tile. Section 5 presents the fundamental modules of the architecture of Lagarto I tile. Section 6 discusses the advantages and disadvantages of Lagarto I tile final design, possible optimizations and the future work.

2   Background

This section presents the required background to understand the paper. First, the main fundamentals related to the design of multi-core processors are presented. Next, it discusses relevant development tools, covering both simulation tools and hardware development frameworks.

Shared-memory multi-core CPU design mainly involves three aspects:

(a) Atomic instructions: used to atomically access data that is shared between cores. They are required to build synchronization mechanisms like mutex, semaphores or locks.
(b) Cache coherence protocols and memory consistency: essential to maintain coherence and consistency among shared data hosted in the private caches of each core.
(c) The interconnection network: to transport control messages and data between cores and the memory system.

Despite dealing with different aspects of the design, they must be considered as a whole when designing the complete system. These aspects are discussed next.

(a) *Atomic instructions*

During multithreaded execution, it is essential to synchronize the running subprocesses on the different threads. This is usually solved by executing "read-modify-write" (RMW) atomic operations. An atomic operation refers to the execution of RMW in a single apparent step. This is implemented by carrying out the read and write operations consecutively, blocking the interruptions to prevent the interleaving of any other memory access with these read and write operations. This guarantees the atomicity of the memory access [8], without interleaving other accesses.

The "A" extension of the RISC-V ISA is the subset of the architecture that describes atomic instructions. RMW atomic instructions are defined in this extension to support the synchronization of multiple RISC-V hardware threads running in the same memory space. It contains two sets of atomic instructions: load-reserved/store-conditional and atomic fetch-and-op memory instructions.

RISC-V supports several consistency models such as: unordered, acquire, release and sequential consistency (SC). SC is a highly intuitive consistency model introduced by Lamport [9], who formulated that a multiprocessor is sequential consistent if it complies with the following: (a) the result of any execution distributed in multiple cores must be the same as when all the executed instructions are run in a certain sequential order, and (b) operations assigned to a specific kernel must maintain the sequence specified by the program. However, this simplicity significantly restricts the implementation of memory units and hinders performance. More relaxed memory models allow to reorder memory accesses and to implement less restrictions in the load/store units of the cores. This often translates into higher performance, at the cost of memory access rules which are harder to reason about and the requirement of explicit fences to delimit synchronization accesses.

(b) *Cache coherence protocols*

The cache coherence protocol distributes the updates performed on each memory location to all the private caches in the system, guaranteeing that all the cores observe, at a given point in time, the updates to shared data.

Snoopy based cache coherence protocols typically rely on broadcast mediums like buses or crossbars, where every connected element listens to all the traffic. This kind of design offers a global vision of the memory accesses to every element interconnected, easing the implementation of the coherence protocol. However it becomes a bottleneck when it interconnects several cores, as all of them share the same network resources. This is the most common solution when the processor has a low number of cores, typically less than 10.

By contrast, directory based cache coherence protocols are typically used with distributed cache memories and NoCs. This type of design follows a distributed philosophy, in which each of several directory controllers tracks the state of the data assigned to it. In other words, each directory acts as a server to data requests that belongs to its domain. This scheme, supports parallel requests to different directories, with the NoC transporting the messages with the result of these requests. Building a distributed cache memory system implies more complexity due to the lack of global information, requiring more complex coherence protocol implementations. However, it is a more scalable solution.

(c) *Interconnection networks*

The system networks are used in supercomputer and datacenters to interconnect multiple servers, each server with multiple cores. For each server (node) to communicate with other nodes, it can use electrical or optical cables to transfer the data packets.

Similarly, the processor internal cores, memory controllers and peripheral controllers communicate through an on-chip interconnect. Typically, when cores work in parallel, they share data in the different shared-memory levels. The interconnection serves as a communication channel to transfer data between the levels of the memory hierarchy and to maintain coherence between different copies of the same data.

Buses and crossbars are frequently employed in the interconnections in multi-core CPUs. They are simple to design and perform well for a low amount of cores. Nevertheless, they do not scale well, and alternative solutions have been used when interconnecting tens of cores, which is typical in the HPC market. These alternatives are denoted Networks on Chip (NoC).

NoC are scalable interconnects that typically rely on tile-based CPUs. Commonly, each tile has one or more cores with their private caches, plus a bank of a shared and distributed cache. Some of them have memory and peripheral controllers too. Such basic block is replicated multiple times to build a processor of the required size, including one router in each tile. Typical topologies for NoCs include rings and meshes.

Rings have been used widely, for example by Intel in their Xeon processors. More recently, Intel has included meshes in their 72-core Xeon Phi Knights Landing accelerator [10] and the newest Xeon processors. ARM also offers a mesh interconnect that supports up to 128 cores [11]. Meshes are gaining ground in the market as they are more scalable than rings, thought large designs might introduce more scalable topologies in the future, like torus or Flattened Butterflies.

(d) *Development tools*

There are platforms dedicated to the design and simulation of multicore systems and interconnection networks. Standalone NoC simulators, such as Booksim or Garnet, typically employ traffic generators to create random requests to feed the network. However, some platforms allow to perform whole-system functional simulation at the software level, such as Spike and Gem5.

Alternatively, there are platforms that perform RTL simulations with specific cores and synthesize multicore processor designs in FPGAs, supporting parameter configuration such as number of threads and cores, cache size, interconnection type, processor, etc.

Table 1 shows some of the most popular platforms available. Some platforms offer processor designs for free, but the tools needed to work with the design are proprietary and require a license. This is the case of the Bluespec company, which offers a platform with two freely available RISC-V processors called Piccolo and Flute. These processors are designed with the high-level language Bluespec (same as the company name), and it is necessary to acquire a Bluespec license to compile the processor codes. In addition, it offers commercial platforms such as RISC-V Verification Factory and RISC-V Acceleration Factory dedicated to the integration, verification and debugging of integrated systems and FPGAs.

Other platforms are open source designs, but their tools can be open source or not and they can be part of their own platform or not. Both Pulp and OpenPiton are open source designs. They rely on a set of open source tools such as Icarus Verilog and other proprietary tools as Mentor Graphics QuestaSim. Specifically, the users can decide between the compatible tools to design, simulate and implement their system.

While some platforms are completely dedicated to RISC-V processors, some others also support other processor ISAs, such as Gem5 and OpenPiton platforms. In the case of Gem5, it employs a generic processor model which is configured with the parameters of the target processor. By contrast, OpenPiton gives some options about the processors to integrate into its platform, for example OpenSparc T1, PicoRV32 and Ariane processors.

OpenSPARC T1 was the default core of the OpenPiton processor from the OpenPiton platform. Given the potential of the NoC and the protocols of coherency implemented in the cache hierarchy of the OpenPiton processor, in recent years, projects have emerged with the main goal of incorporating RISC-V cores into the OpenPiton processor. Some examples are Juxtapiton [18], where the PicoRV32 core was integrated with the OpenPiton platform and inherited all the capabilities of the infrastructure, and the integration of Ariane core into the OpenPiton processor [19], started in 2019 by the ETH Zürich and the Wentzlaff Parallel Research Group.

Table 1. Popular platforms to simulation and implementation of multicore processors.

Platform	Simulation		FPGA implementation	Processor		Open source
	Functional	RTL		RISC-V	Other	
Spike simulator [12]	✓	–	–	✓	–	✓
Gem5 simulator [13]	✓	–	–	✓	✓	✓
Bluespec [14]	–	✓	✓	✓	–	–
LowRisc [15]	–	✓	✓	✓	–	✓
Pulp [16]	–	✓	✓	✓	–	✓
OpenPiton [17]	–	✓	✓	✓	✓	✓

3   Lagarto I RISC-V Architecture

The computer architecture design team of the Microelectronic and Embedded System Laboratory of the Computing Research Center of the National Polytechnic Institute of Mexico has developed the Lagarto I core. Its main goal is to provide its users with a scalable low-cost development platform for hardware and software systems. These users could come from the academic field as well as the industry sector. For the academic field, it will be possible for the students to understand the tradeoffs and challenges related to the microarchitecture design process; for the industry sector, it will grant the opportunity to use a customizable development platform.

Lagarto I core is a scalar 64 bit RISC-V based processor, that supports the RV64I instruction set, the M extension for multiplication and division, and the A extension for atomic operations, the minimum requirements to support an embedded Linux booting process. Additionally, Lagarto I supports the RISC-V Privileged Architecture Version 1.7.

Lagarto I core has been developed in Verilog, taking advantage of the hardware description language tools for designing, testing and verifying digital systems as robust as a SoC. The microarchitecture implements a six-stage pipeline and includes optimized modules for instruction processing. Additionally, Lagarto I includes a Memory Management Unit looking to allow not only the flow of data through the different memory levels, but also the implementation of multicore systems, establishing the guideline to explore massive processing systems for High Performance Computing.

4   Design Proposal for Lagarto Multi-core

Currently, tiled architectures have gained ground in the design of multicores. They provide communication using shared memory and direct communication networks, allowing the flow of data and messages from one tile to another without the need to use system software [20].

The minimum requirements of a tile are the processor, L1 cache memory (including coherence support), private or shared L2 memory and an interconnection network. In order to have an infrastructure that allows the Lagarto I processor to scale to a large number of cores, its current design needs to be transformed to a tile implementation, which we denote the Lagarto tile. Starting from the single-core Lagarto I design, it requires a coherence protocol in the L1 cache memory, an interconnection network and a shared memory level. Likewise, it requires a chipset that hosts the memory controllers and the OS boot. It is also essential to incorporate the atomic instructions, a feature already implemented in the Lagarto I processor.

The available open-source multi-core processor design platforms have been analyzed to determine if they can be used to facilitate the design of multi-core Lagarto processors. Three open-source platforms have been chosen for the analysis: Lowrisc, PULP and OpenPiton. Table 2 shows a summary of the analysis of the three platforms under the following headings: (a) HDL language, which should be compatible with that used in Lagarto I core, (b) interconnection network used, (c) coherence protocol support, (d) compatible with RISC-V and (e) OS boot support.

The chosen platforms are suitable to be integrated into this work thanks to the fact that they have been developed with HDL, as well as Lagarto I core. LowRisc, in particular, has been developed in the high-level language Chisel. With respect to the interconnection network, only OpenPiton implements a NoC. The Pulp platform does not support a coherence protocol, since its designs are focused on hardware acceleration. The three platforms integrate at least one RISC-V processor and implement atomic instructions, although Pulp only implements atomic fetch-and-op memory instructions.

OpenPiton has been selected as the most suitable platform for this work, mainly for its ability to scale the number of cores thanks to the implemented NoC. It is completely free, fully configurable (cache size, interconnection network, processor) and modular, exploiting the use of the Verilog language. It is a platform developed mainly in Verilog for hardware description and Perl + Python to integrate tools and build designs. In the most recent version, released in 2019, it supports three different processors: OpenSPARC T1 and two RISC-V based processors, PicoRV32 and Ariane, integrated from the PULP framework.

Table 2. Analysis of development platforms to be used with Lagarto I

| Platform | Developers | Language | Interconnect | | Coherence protocol | Memory levels | Processor | | Linux boot | |
			Crossbar	Noc			RISC-V	Others	Mono core	Multi core
LowRisc	University of Berkeley and Cambridge	Chisel	✓	–	✓	2	✓	–	✓	–
Pulp	ETH Zürich	System Verilog	✓	–	–	2	✓	–	✓	–
OpenPiton	Princeton University	Verilog	✓	✓	✓	3	✓	✓	✓	–

5 Lagarto I Multi-core

This section presents the design decisions for the Lagarto Multi-core system. It first details the recent integration of OpenPiton with the Ariane processor. Next, it presents the implementation details required for Lagarto I.

The most recent OpenPiton release integrates the OpenPiton project with the Ariane processor. This design has been used as a reference to build and design the Lagarto I tile. This design upgrades the RISC-V privileged extension from 1.7 to 1.10; this is required to support more stable OS execution and boot, offers more support to physical-memory protection (PMP) and Virtual-memory page faults. This upgrade has been analyzed to obtain enough experience to identify, recognize and adapt the required modifications for the upgrade. This design will be considered a reference to compare the execution of instructions and the flow of control messages within the NoCs, simplifying the debug process of the design.

The original version of OpenPiton leveraged an OpenSPARC core to build a tiled NoC design. The OpenSPARC T1 processor implements 8 cores connected through a crossbar, using a write-through policy to guarantee cache coherency. However, such design does not scale to large core counts, since it relies on the centralized crossbar to serialize memory accesses and invalidate sharers.

In order to scale the system, the OpenPiton approach implements an additional cache level between the private L1 and the shared L2. This new private memory level is denoted L1.5 cache, because it sits between the original L1 and the L2. Therefore, the design employs two private cache levels per core. The first level is called L1 and is part of the OpenSPARC T1 processor, operating with its write-through policy. The second level is the L1.5, which is a write-back private data cache that implements a MESI coherence protocol, allowing larger scalability. With this approach, the OpenSPARC T1 RTL is not modified and the L1.5 operates as a higher cache level above the L1. In scalable multicores, write-back caches operate more efficiently than write-through since the high write-bandwidth required by the write-through caches produces data congestion into the NoC and the memory hierarchy [21]. The OpenPiton L1.5 cache only has one input port, where both instruction and data requests are received. Both requests can be generated simultaneously in the same processor cycle, so the design requires an arbiter to determine the priority to send each request to the L1.5. In the design, instruction fetch requests always receive higher priority.

The OpenPiton project has integrated two different processor cores with different approaches with respect to the coherence protocol. In [18] the PicoRV32 processor replaces the OpenSparc T1 in OpenPiton. In this case, the processor is directly connected to the L1.5 cache from OpenPiton, removing its original L1 cache. This represents a relevant improvement at the hardware level, because it avoids the duplication of caches, with the corresponding increase in area and latency. However, it only operates with virtual memory accesses since the L1.5 cache in OpenPiton doesn't include an MMU. In [23] the Ariane processor was integrated with OpenPiton. The implementation turns its L1 write-back cache into a write-through cache similar to the one in OpenSparc T1 L1, and adapts the interfaces between Ariane L1 write-through cache and OpenPiton L1.5 cache using an arbiter. With this change, the Ariane cache system become similar to the one used by OpenSparc T1.

Our work adapts the Lagarto I core to the OpenPiton project following a similar approach. The basic building blocks employed in our project are shown in Fig. 1. Figure 1(a) shows the design of the Lagarto tile. Each tile has a Lagarto I core, the L1 cache from the Ariane processor and the related modules. Figure 1(b) shows the OpenPiton structure, including caches, NoC routers and chipset.

Lagarto I core interacts with the L1 cache in its Fetch Stage (FS) to request instructions, and in its Memory Access stage (MA) to load/stores data in memory. It also interfaces with the Control and Status Registers (CSR) which are read or written by privileged instructions. The upgrade of the privilege extension to version 1.10 requires to add and discard some registers within the CSR module, as well as adding hardware support for new instructions into the Lagarto core microarchitecture.

Originally, the Lagarto I processor implements a Memory Management Unit (MMU) that includes L1 caches for data and instructions, with the L1 data cache operating with a write-back policy. Considering the alternative approaches in previous works, the approach followed to merge with OpenPiton was similar to the most recent case of Ariane. The Lagarto MMU is preserved, to access the L1 caches using physical addresses. The L1 data cache is converted to write-through and connected to the L1.5 from OpenPiton. When adapting the interfaces, the alternatives are to adapt the L1 interface from Lagarto to the L1.5, or employ the caches from Ariane. We decided to employ the L1 caches from Ariane because they are already adapted to the bus arbiter interface and the L1.5. This design is suboptimal because it almost replicates the caches in levels L1 and L1.5, with the corresponding increase in area and latency. However, it allows for a faster design and a simpler integration with the other modules from OpenPiton, leaving the integration of both cache levels for future work.

The final design of L1 cache system of the Lagarto tile integrates an instruction and data cache, MMU and an arbiter. The instruction cache has 16 KB size and 4-way associativity, and the data cache has 8 KB, 4-way associativity and a write-through policy for compatibility with OpenPiton. The main purpose of the MMU is to implement address translation and monitor memory accesses, to detect memory access faults. The MMU hosts the instruction and data Translation Lookaside Buffers (TLBs) and the Page Table Walker (PTW). The PTW is a hardware used to handle page faults: it listens to all incoming translation requests on both iTLB and dTLB, and in case of fault page on the TLB it will use the virtual address to start the search for its page translation in a table walk.

The module Arbiter has two main goals; first, it arbitrates between requests from the FS or MA processor stages, with FS requests always receiving more priority; second, it generates and manages the request signals, as well as packages the request to be sent to the L1.5, using an interface that is compatible with OpenPiton L1.5 cache. Likewise, the arbiter attends all responses from the L1.5 cache to the L1 cache system.

The L1.5, L2 cache and NoC router are reused from the OpenPiton project [21]. The remainder of the chipset has been modified, only reusing the bootrom module and a fake memory DRAM controller. The bootrom module contains a minimal boot of the linux code and the fake DRAM controller simulates the operation of a DRAM controller. This fake controller simulates that the operating system loads the program code into the DRAM to be executed by the cores, but the program is actually loaded

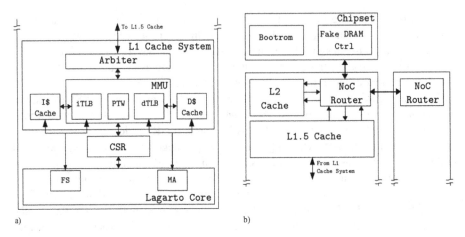

Fig. 1. Lagarto tile (a) Lagarto core connect to system cache of Ariane processor. (b) Cache system, NoC, routers and chipset from Open Piton.

manually in this fake DRAM. In the current status of the design, the program code is placed into this module to be executed after loading the boot.

Figure 2 shows the block diagram of a multi-core architecture where the Lagarto tile is interconnected to others tiles through NoC routers in the P-Mesh by OpenPiton. OpenPiton provides scalable meshes of tiles on a single chip using, what they have called, a P-Mesh cache coherence system, which is capable to connect together up to 8192 chips [22]. The NoC routers are also used to interconnect the Lagarto tiles to a chipset to access the bootrom and the fake DRAM controller.

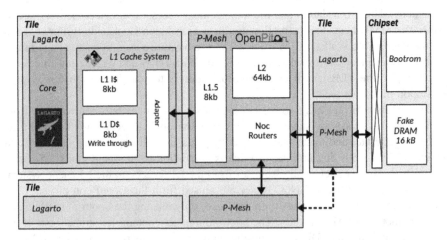

Fig. 2. Block diagram of a multi-core architecture with Lagarto tiles (based on [18])

6 Conclusions and Future Work

This work describes the initial process of adapting the Lagarto I core to a multicore system using a NoC. The Lagarto project wants to generate a high-performance ecosystem based on RISC processors for the industry and the academic field in Mexico. For this goal, is necessary to develop an infrastructure that allows the Lagarto I processor to scale to multi- and many-cores. It has been decided to take advantage of several previous developments on multicore, which has led to perform various analysis of compatibility with the Lagarto I processor, as well as requirements for its adaptation. Consequently, the OpenPiton platform has been chosen to employ the NoC it integrates as well as the MESI protocol implemented in its memory system.

For this first approach, it has been decided to follow the process of development of previous projects carried out with processors based on RISC-V and the OpenPiton platform, which involves modifying the L1 cache to operate as a write-through cache and connect it directly with the OpenPiton L1.5 cache and thus be able to exploit the MESI protocol and access the NoC.

While effective and simpler to develop, this results in a suboptimal design because of the redundant modules. To achieve the main objective of the Lagarto project, it is desired to eventually get rid of the L1.5 memory and implement the MESI protocol in the L1 write-back memory integrated in the MMU of the Lagarto I processor. This will establish direct communication between the interface of the OpenPiton NoC to the Lagarto L1 cache, allowing direct access from the L1 cache to the L2 cache and the Chipset, as well as reducing the latency and area of the tile. An additional advantage is to be able to process instruction requests and data accesses in parallel. Finally, it will be necessary to perform tests to guarantee memory consistency and to successfully execute a SMP Linux boot.

References

1. Ramírez, C., Hernández, C., Morales, C.R., García, G.M., Villa, L.A., Ramírez, M.A.: Lagarto I - Una plataforma hardware/software de arquitectura de computadoras para la academia e investigación. Res. Comput. Sci. **137**, 19–28 (2017)
2. Waterman, A., Asanović, K. (eds.): The RISC-V Instruction Set Manual, Volume I: User-Level ISA, Document Version 2.2. RISC-V Foundation, May 2017
3. TOP500 List: November 2018|TOP500 Supercomputer Sites (2019). https://www.top500.org/list/2018/11/
4. Adiga, N.R., et al.: An overview of the BlueGene/L supercomputer. In: Proceedings of the 2002 ACM/IEEE Conference on Supercomputing, SC 2002, Baltimore, MD, USA, p. 60 (2002). https://doi.org/10.1109/sc.2002.10017
5. IBM100: Blue Gene. (2012). https://www.ibm.com/ibm/history/ibm100/us/en/icons/bluegene/
6. Rajovic, N., et al.: The Mont-Blanc prototype: an alternative approach for HPC systems. In: Proceedings of the International Conference for High Performance Computing, Networking, Storage and Analysis, SC 2016, Salt Lake City, UT, pp. 444–455 (2016). https://doi.org/10.1109/sc.2016.37

7. Rajovic, N., Rico, A., Puzovic, N., Adeniyi-Jones, C., Ramirez, A.: Tibidabo: making the case for an ARM-based HPC system. Futur. Gener. Comput. Syst. **36**, 322–334 (2014). https://doi.org/10.1016/j.future.2013.07.013

8. Sorin, D.J., Hill, M.D., Wood, D.A.: A Primer on Memory Consistency and Cache Coherence, 1st edn. Morgan & Claypool Publishers, San Rafael (2011)

9. Lamport, L.: How to make a multiprocessor computer that correctly executes multiprocess programs. IEEE Trans. Comput. **C-28**(9), 690–691 (1979). https://doi.org/10.1109/TC.1979.1675439

10. Sodani, A., et al.: Knights landing: second-generation Intel Xeon Phi product. IEEE Micro **36**(2), 34–46 (2016). https://doi.org/10.1109/MM.2016.25

11. Arm System IP Ltd.: CoreLink CMN-600: Arm developer. https://developer.arm.com/ip-products/system-ip/corelink-interconnect/corelink-coherent-mesh-network-family/corelink-cmn-600

12. riscv/riscv-isa-sim (2017). https://github.com/riscv/riscv-isa-sim

13. gem5. http://gem5.org/Main_Page

14. RISC-V Processor IP & Tools for Cores & Subsystems: Bluespec (2019). https://bluespec.com/

15. lowRISC. https://www.lowrisc.org/

16. PULP platform: Open-source efficient RISC-V architecture. https://www.pulp-platform.org/

17. Princeton Parallel Group: OpenPiton open source research processor (2017). http://parallel.princeton.edu/openpiton/index.html

18. Lim, K., Balkind, J., Wentzlaff, D.: JuxtaPiton: enabling heterogeneous-ISA research with RISC-V and SPARC FPGA soft-cores. CoRR, abs/1811.08091 (2018)

19. PrincetonUniversity: Openpiton + ariane - preliminary support for ariane rv64imac core. https://github.com/PrincetonUniversity/openpiton/tree/openpiton-dev#preliminary-support-for-ariane-rv64imac-core

20. Wentzlaff, D., et al.: On-chip interconnection architecture of the tile processor. IEEE Micro **27**(5), 15–31 (2007). https://doi.org/10.1109/MM.2007.4378780

21. Balkind, J., et al.: OpenPiton: an open source manycore research framework. In: Proceedings of the Twenty-First International Conference on Architectural Support for Programming Languages and Operating Systems, ASPLOS 2016 (2016). https://doi.org/10.1145/2872362.2872414

22. Balkind, J., et al.: OpenPiton: an emerging standard for open-source EDA tool development

23. Schaffner, M., Balkind, J.: OpenPiton + Ariane Tutorial. Presentation, HiPEAC 2019, Valencia (2019). https://www.pulp-platform.org/docs/hipeac/openpiton_ariane_hipeac_tutorial.pdf

Parallel Computing

Discretization of the Convection-Diffusion Equation Using Discrete Exterior Calculus

Marco A. Noguez[(⊠)], Salvador Botello, and Rafael Herrera

Centro de Investigación en Matemáticas, A.C. (CIMAT), Guanajuato, Mexico
{marco.noguez,botello}@cimat.mx,
rherrera.cimat@gmail.com

Abstract. A discretization of the Convection-Diffusion equation is developed based on Discrete Exterior Calculus (DEC). While DEC discretization of the diffusive term in the equation is well understood, the convective part (with non-constant convective flow) had not been DEC discretized. In this study, we develop such discretization of the convective term using geometric arguments. We can discretize the convective term for both compressible and incompressible flow. Moreover, since the Finite Element Method with linear interpolation functions (FEML) and DEC local matrix formulations are similar, this numerical scheme is well suited for parallel computing. Using this feature, numerical tests are carried out on simple domains with coarse and fine meshes to compare DEC and FEML and show numerical convergence for stationary problems.

1 Introduction

Discrete Exterior Calculus (DEC) is a recent numerical method for solving partial differential equations (PDE's), based on the discretization of the theory of Exterior Calculus [3]. It was first proposed by Hirani in his PHD thesis [5]. Since then, DEC has been successfully applied to solve Darcy's equation [4], Navier-Stokes and Poisson's equations [2], and the transport equation with incompressible flow for advection-dominated problems [1]. In this latter work, the authors showed that, in simple cases, the system of equations resulting from DEC are equivalent to other numerical methods such as Finite Differences and Finite Volume methods, leading to a stable upwind DEC variation.

The transport equation, or Convection-Diffusion equation, is a PDE which models the transport of a scalar field (*e.g.* mass, heat or momentum), due to transport mechanisms known as *convection*, which occurs whenever a fluid is in motion, and *diffusion*. This equation arises in several engineering problems like air pollution and groundwater contamination, where the solute is transported by *advection* due to the particle velocity field, which usually depends on time and spatial coordinates. Commonly, this type of problems are advection-dominated problems, leading to numerical instabilities for most of the mesh-based numerical methods for solving PDE's. In such cases, stabilization techniques such as [6–8] are employed, but are not well suited for some problems, and refining the mesh may lead to a numerical stabilization, but also to a higher computational cost. Thus, the importance of an efficient implementation and parallel computing of the numerical methods becomes evident.

© Springer Nature Switzerland AG 2019
M. Torres and J. Klapp (Eds.): ISUM 2019, CCIS 1151, pp. 251–265, 2019.
https://doi.org/10.1007/978-3-030-38043-4_21

In this paper, we propose a local DEC discretization of the Convection-Diffusion equation, for compressible and incompressible flow using geometric arguments, which is described in Sect. 2. Since this is a local discretization of the Exterior Calculus operators, the matrix formulation is similar to that of Finite Element Method (FEM), and is well suited for parallel computing. Using this feature, numerical tests are carried out to show numerical convergence and a comparison between the Finite Element Method with linear interpolation functions (FEML) and our DEC discretization of the differential equation, for coarse and fine meshes. These numerical tests are explained in Sect. 3.

2 The Convection – Diffusion Equation Dec Discretization

Recall the 2D isotropic, homogeneous and stationary Convection-Diffusion equation,

$$\nabla \cdot (\underline{v}u) = k\nabla^2 u + q, \tag{2.1}$$

where $\underline{v}$ is the particle velocity, k is the heat diffusion coefficient, and q is the external source. It is an elliptic equation which describes the transport of a scalar quantity due to transport processes known as convection, which is modeled by the left-hand side of Eq. (2.1), and diffusion for mass transport, or heat conduction, which in turn, is modeled by the right-hand side of Eq. (2.1). An alternative expression of Eq. (2.1) is

$$\underline{v} \cdot \nabla u + u\nabla \cdot \underline{v} = k\nabla^2 u + q, \tag{2.2}$$

and, when the fluid is incompressible ($\nabla \cdot \underline{v} = 0$), one has:

$$\underline{v} \cdot \nabla u = k\nabla^2 u + q. \tag{2.3}$$

In order to develop a DEC discretization of Eq. (2.2), we first rewrite the differential equation in Exterior Calculus notation, and then we discretize the involved operators in matrix form [2].

2.1 The Diffusive Term

The discretization with DEC of the diffusive term of the equation, which is equivalent to the Poisson's Equation, is well understood and reported in [2] and [3]. The Laplacian operator, as described in mentioned works, can be expressed using Exterior Calculus notation as

$$\nabla^2 u = *\nabla \wedge *\nabla u, \tag{2.4}$$

where $*$ is the Hodge Star and $\wedge$ is the wedge product operators. If we use d, to denote the exterior derivative, one has

$$\nabla^2 u = *d * du, \tag{2.5}$$

thus, Eq. (2.2) can be rewritten using Eq. (2.5) as

$$\underline{v} \cdot \nabla u + u \nabla \cdot \underline{v} = k * d * du + q. \tag{2.6}$$

Next, we discretize these operators locally. Consider the single, counterclockwise oriented triangle mesh, shown in Fig. 1, formed by the vertices $V1, V2$ and $V3$. The boundary operator ∂ for oriented triangles $([V1, V2, V3])$, edges $([V1, V2], [V2, V3], [V3, V1])$ and vertices $([V1], [V2], [V3])$, as described in [3], can be expressed as a matrix operator by considering each triangle, edge and vertex as an element of a basis of a vector space. Then, for the mesh shown in Fig. 1, the boundary matrix operator sending oriented triangles to a sum of its oriented edges is

$$\partial_{2,1} = \begin{pmatrix} 1 \\ 1 \\ -1 \end{pmatrix}, \tag{2.7}$$

where the subscript $\partial_{2,1}$ means we are sending the boundary of a 2-dimensional element to the boundary of a 1-dimensional one. Similarly, the boundary operator sending oriented edges to a sum of its oriented vertices is

$$\partial_{1,0} = \begin{pmatrix} -1 & 0 & 1 \\ 1 & -1 & 0 \\ 0 & 1 & -1 \end{pmatrix}. \tag{2.8}$$

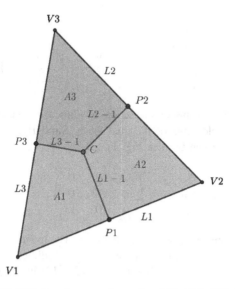

Fig. 1. Triangle [V1, V2, V3]. Its edges are denoted as [V1, V2], [V2, V3] and [V3, V1]. Its vertices are denoted as [V1], [V2] and [V3].

Then, due to the duality in *Green's Theorem*, the discretization of the exterior derivative is given by

$$d = (\partial)^T. \tag{2.9}$$

For instance, the discretization of the operator $d_{1,0}$ is

$$d_{1,0} = \begin{pmatrix} -1 & 1 & 0 \\ 0 & -1 & 1 \\ 1 & 0 & -1 \end{pmatrix}. \tag{2.10}$$

Now, to discretize the Hodge Star operator, we define the dual mesh for a triangle as follows (See Fig. 1):

- The dual of the 2-dimensional triangle [V1, V2, V3] is the 0-dimensional circumcenter point C of the triangle.
- The dual of the 1-dimensional edges of the triangle is the 1-dimensional straight segment joining the center of the edge and the triangle's circumcenter (Segments $L1 - 1, L2 - 1$ and $L3 - 1$ in Fig. 1).
- The dual of the 0-dimensional vertices of the triangle is the 2-dimensional quadrilateral formed by the two mid-points of its adjacent edges and the circumcenter (*E.g.* The dual of the vertex [V1] is the quadrilateral [V1, P1, C, P3]).

Therefore, we need two matrices to discretize de Hodge Star operator, one relating the original and dual edges, and another one relating vertices and dual cells. The first one is defined as follows (see Fig. 1.)

$$M_{1,1} = \begin{pmatrix} \frac{lenght(L1-1)}{lenght(L1)} & 0 & 0 \\ 0 & \frac{lenght(L2-1)}{lenght(L2)} & 0 \\ 0 & 0 & \frac{lenght(L3-1)}{lenght(L3)} \end{pmatrix}, \tag{2.11}$$

where the subscripts $M_{1,1}$ means we are sending 1-dimensional elements of the original mesh to 1-dimensional elements of the dual mesh. Similarly, the second Hodge Star matrix discretization is given by (see Fig. 1).

$$M_{0,2} = \begin{pmatrix} A1 & 0 & 0 \\ 0 & A2 & 0 \\ 0 & 0 & A3 \end{pmatrix}, \tag{2.12}$$

where $A1, A2$ and $A3$, are the areas of the dual cells. The inverse of $M_{0,2}$, $M_{2,0}$ will then send 2-dimensional elements of the dual mesh to 0-dimensional elements of the original mesh. Substituting Eqs. (2.10), (2.11) and (2.12) in (2.6) one has

$$\underline{v} \cdot \nabla u + u \nabla \cdot \underline{v} = k M_{2,0} D_{1,2}^{dual} M_{1,1} D_{0,1} u + q, \tag{2.13}$$

where $D_{1,2}^{dual} = -D_{0,1}^T$.

2.2   The Convective Term

We first address the case of incompressible flow, Eq. (2.3). We develop the discretization of this term locally, by means of geometric arguments. Consider a scalar function u, discretized by its values at the vertices of an oriented triangle $[V1, V2, V3]$, we can approximate the directional derivative of u at vertex $V1$, in the direction of the vector $V2 - V1$ as

$$du_{V1}(V2 - V1) \approx u_2 - u_1,$$

similarly

$$du_{V2}(V3 - V2) \approx u_3 - u_2,$$

$$du_{V3}(V3 - V1) \approx u_3 - u_1.$$

Thus, in order to find the discrete gradient vector $\underline{W_1}$ of u at vertex $V1$, we need to solve the following system of equations

$$\underline{W_1} \cdot (V2 - V1) = u_2 - u_1, \tag{2.14}$$

$$\underline{W_1} \cdot (V3 - V1) = u_3 - u_1, \tag{2.15}$$

where

$$V1 = (x_1, y_1),$$

$$V2 = (x_2, y_2),$$

$$V3 = (x_3, y_3),$$

which leads to

$$\underline{W_1} = \frac{1}{2A} \begin{bmatrix} u_1(y_2 - y_3) + u_2(y_3 - y_1) + u_3(y_1 - y_2) \\ -(u_1(x_2 - x_3) + u_2(x_3 - x_1) + u_3(x_1 - x_2)) \end{bmatrix}, \tag{2.16}$$

where A is the area of the triangle. Following the same procedure to find $\underline{W_2}$ and $\underline{W_3}$, it is seen that

$$\underline{W_1} = \underline{W_2} = \underline{W_3}, \tag{2.17}$$

moreover, Eq. (2.16) coincides with the gradient vector obtained with the Finite Element Method with linear interpolation functions. We then consider the particle velocity defined at each vertex of the triangle, *i.e.*

$$\underline{v_1} = (v_{1,1}, v_{1,2}),$$

$$\underline{v_2} = (v_{2,1}, v_{2,2}),$$

$$\underline{v_3} = (v_{3,1}, v_{3,2}).$$

By taking the inner product of the gradient vector and the particle velocity at each vertex, we obtain the local matrix discretization for the left hand-side of the Eq. (2.3)

$$V_e = \frac{1}{2A} \begin{bmatrix} V_{1,1} & V_{1,2} & V_{1,3} \\ V_{2,1} & V_{2,2} & V_{2,3} \\ V_{3,1} & V_{3,2} & V_{3,3} \end{bmatrix} \begin{bmatrix} u_1 \\ u_2 \\ u_3 \end{bmatrix}, \tag{2.18}$$

where

$$V_{1,1} = v_{1,1}(y_2 - y_3) + v_{1,2}(x_3 - x_2),$$

$$V_{1,2} = v_{1,1}(y_3 - y_1) + v_{1,2}(x_1 - x_3),$$

$$V_{1,3} = v_{1,1}(y_1 - y_2) + v_{1,2}(x_2 - x_1),$$

$$V_{2,1} = v_{2,1}(y_2 - y_3) + v_{2,2}(x_3 - x_2),$$

$$V_{2,2} = v_{2,1}(y_3 - y_1) + v_{2,2}(x_1 - x_3),$$

$$V_{2,3} = v_{2,1}(y_1 - y_2) + v_{2,2}(x_2 - x_1),$$

$$V_{3,1} = v_{3,1}(y_2 - y_3) + v_{3,2}(x_3 - x_2),$$

$$V_{3,2} = v_{3,1}(y_3 - y_1) + v_{3,2}(x_1 - x_3),$$

$$V_{3,3} = v_{3,1}(y_1 - y_2) + v_{3,2}(x_2 - x_1).$$

Next, we consider the case of compressible flow, Eq. (2.2). Recall the Laplacian operator written as

$$\nabla^2 u = \nabla \cdot (\nabla u), \tag{2.19}$$

as mentioned in [2], the divergence operator can be expressed with Exterior Calculus notation as

$$\nabla \cdot \underline{\phi} = *d * \underline{\phi}, \tag{2.20}$$

where vector $\underline{\phi}$ is a 1-form. Thus, in order to discretize the term $u\nabla \cdot \underline{v}$, we need to assign the values of $\underline{v}$ to the edges of the triangle. By taking into account the orientation of the triangle, we have the following vectors:

$$w_1 = V2 - V1,$$

$$w_2 = V3 - V2,$$

$$w_3 = V1 - V3.$$

As before, we consider the particle velocity v defined at each vertex. Therefore, we can take the inner product of the direction w_1 and $\frac{1}{2}(v_1 + v_2)$, i.e.

$$\phi_1 = \tfrac{1}{2}(v_1 + v_2) \cdot w_1, \tag{2.21}$$

where ϕ_1 is the value assigned to the edge $[V1, V2]$, similarly

$$\phi_2 = \tfrac{1}{2}(v_2 + v_3) \cdot w_2, \tag{2.22}$$

$$\phi_3 = \tfrac{1}{2}(v_3 + v_1) \cdot w_3. \tag{2.23}$$

Substituting the matrix discretization of the Hodge Star and the Exterior Derivative operators described previously, one has

$$u\nabla \cdot v = M_{2,0}D_{0,1}^T M_{1,1}\phi u. \tag{2.24}$$

Substituting Eqs. (2.18) and (2.24) in (2.13) we obtain the DEC discretization of Eq. (2.2):

$$\left[V_e - M_{2,0}D_{0,1}^T M_{1,1}\left(\phi + kD_0\right)\right]u = q, \tag{2.25}$$

Since Eq. (2.25) is a local discretization of the Convection-Diffusion equation, the processes of computing the local matrices (M_e) for every element in the mesh and the subsequent construction of the global system of equations are the most demanding in terms of computational requirements. Thus, introducing parallel computing in these stages leads to significant savings in both time and system resources. Fortunately, since the DEC construction of the global system of equations is similar to that of the Finite Element Method, known parallel algorithms for FEM can be used, such as [10, 11] and [12].

As described in [9], K parallel threads can be used to compute N/K elemental matrices, where N is the number of elements in the mesh (see Fig. 2). Therefore, the time to build the global system of equations using parallel computing can be estimated by

$$T_p = N\left(\tfrac{I}{K} + m\right) + K \cdot t_{\{thread\}}, \tag{2.26}$$

Where I is the CPU time for computing a local matrix, m is the time the CPU takes to assemble a local matrix in to the global matrix and $t_{\{thread\}}$ is the CPU time to create/destruct a thread. In this case, the assembly of the global matrix is non *thread-*

safe, therefore, access to the global matrix should be blocked whenever a thread is updating the global matrix.

Similarly to FEM, the global system matrix obtained with DEC is sparse, and a storage format is required. We have chosen the CSR format, and suitable parallel matrix-vector multiplication algorithm.

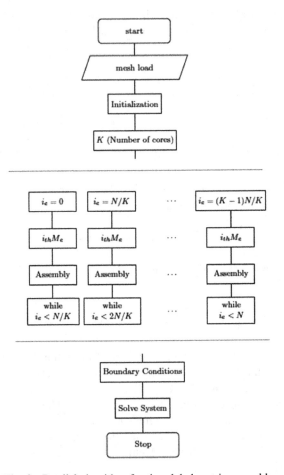

Fig. 2. Parallel algorithm for the global matrix assembly.

3   Numerical Experiments

For the numerical experiments we have used a computer with Intel Core i7-7700T (4 cores and 8 threads) 2.9 GHz CPU and 8 GB of RAM, with openMP for thread management.

Consider a rectangular domain with dimensions 10×5, under the following conditions (see Fig. 3):

- Heat diffusion constant $k = 1$
- Source term $q = 1$, over disk of radius 0.4, and center in $(1, 2.5)$
- Dirichlet boundary condition $u = 0.0$ over left, upper and bottom boundaries
- Right boundary with no condition

The meshes used vary from coarse to fine meshes, some of them are shown in Fig. 4.

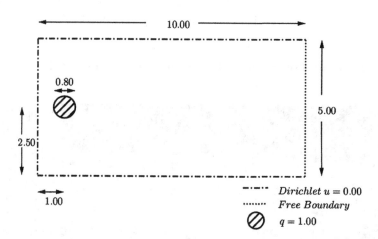

Fig. 3. Domain with diffusion constant k = 1, source q = 1 over disk of radius 0.4 and center in (1, 2.5)

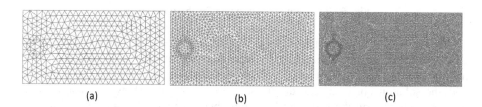

(a)   (b)   (c)

Fig. 4. Examples of meshes used in numerical experiments

3.1 Constant Particle Velocity

In this example, we consider the problem with constant particle velocity in x direction, of magnitude $v = (10, 0)$. Table 1 summarizes numerical results for maximum temperature value, and a comparison with results obtained with the Finite Element Method with linear interpolation functions (FEML) is also shown.

Table 1. Maximum temperature values obtained in the numerical simulation.

Mesh	# Elements	# Nodes	Max. temperature value	
			DEC	FEML
Figure 4(a)	722	703	0.11114	0.10638
Figure 4(b)	2900	1526	0.088065	0.087268
Figure 4(c)	11574	5938	0.080251	0.080145
	18078	9228	0.07931	0.07937
	1152106	577554	0.076914	0.076914

The temperature distribution for the finest mesh is shown in Fig. 5.

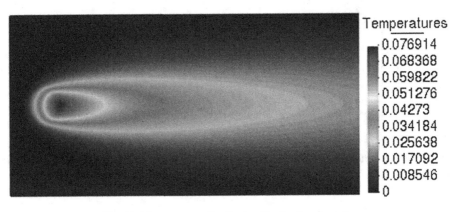

Fig. 5. Temperature distribution for the finest mesh.

Figures 6(a), (b), (c) and (d) shows graphs of the temperature values obtained with DEC and FEML, along a horizontal cross section at the centerline of the domain for the meshes in Figs. 4(a), (b), (c) and for the second finest mesh, respectively, compared with the solution obtained with the finest mesh. Figure 6(e) shows a graph of temperature values along the same cross section obtained with DEC and FEML for the finest mesh.

As can be seen from Table 1 and Fig. 6, DEC and FEML behaves in a similar fashion with coarse meshes, and converges to the same value with finer meshes, as expected. In Fig. 6(a), oscillations in the temperature values can be seen on the coarsest mesh, as a result of numerical instability present in convection dominated problems.

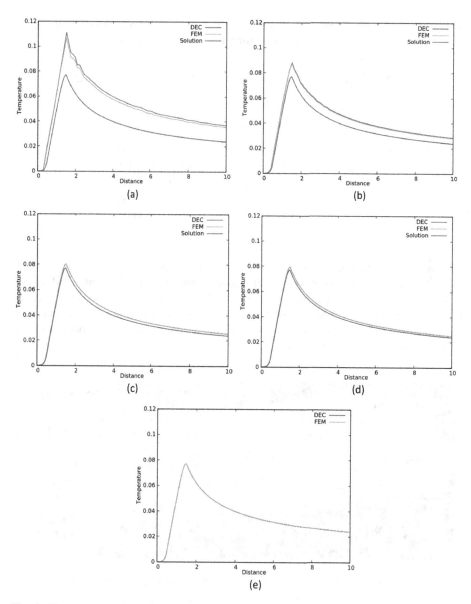

Fig. 6. Temperature values along a cross horizontal section at the centerline of the domain for different meshes. (a) Graph for the mesh in Fig. 3(a). (b) Graph for the mesh in Fig. 3(b). (c) Graph for the mesh in Fig. 3(c). (d) Graph for the second finest mesh. (e) Graph for the finest mesh.

3.2 Variable Particle Velocity

In this example, we consider a variable in space particle velocity $v = (x, sin(x))$ and heat diffusion constant $k = 0.5$, over the same domain with the same boundary conditions and source term. As before, Table 2 shows the maximum temperature values obtained with DEC and FEML, using the same set of meshes.

Table 2. Maximum temperature values obtained in the numerical simulation.

Mesh	# Elements	# Nodes	Max. temperature value	
			DEC	FEML
Figure 4(a)	722	703	0.54571	0.52831
Figure 4(b)	2900	1526	0.43644	0.43356
Figure 4(c)	11574	5938	0.40118	0.4012
	18078	9228	0.39562	0.39717
	1152106	577554	0.3833	0.3833

Temperature distribution for the finest mesh is shown in Fig. 7. As before, Fig. 8 (a), (b), (c) and (d) shows the temperature values obtained with DEC and FEML along a horizontal cross section at the centerline of the domain for the meshes shown in Figs. 4(a), (b), (c) and for the second finest mesh, compared with the solution obtained with the finest mesh. Figure 8(e) shows the graph of temperature values obtained with DEC and FEML for the finest mesh.

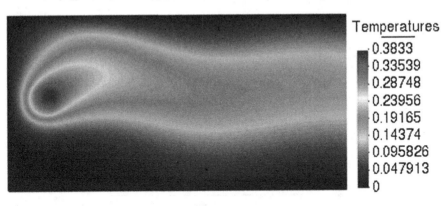

Fig. 7. Temperature distribution for variable in space particle velocity.

As can be seen from Table 2 and Fig. 8, FEML and DEC behaves similarly for coarse meshes and both converge to the same value with fine meshes. In Fig. 8(a), oscillations of the temperature values can be seen for the coarsest mesh, due to numerical instability.

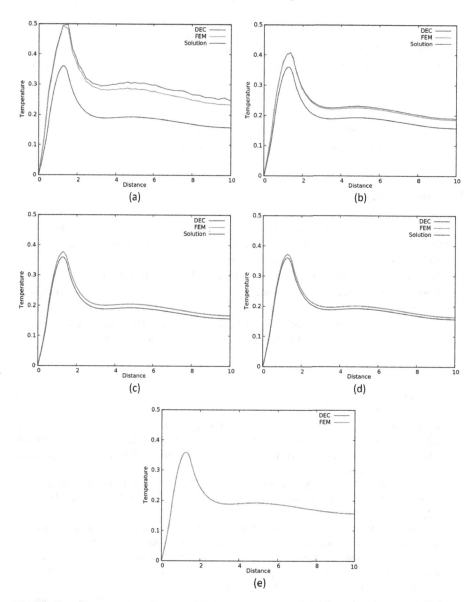

Fig. 8. Temperature values along a cross horizontal section at the centerline of the domain for different meshes. (a) Graph for the mesh in Fig. 4(a). (b) Graph for the mesh in Fig. 4(b). (c) Graph for the mesh in Fig. 4(c). (d) Graph for the second finest. (e) Graph for the finest mesh.

The execution time for the finest mesh is shown in Table 3.

Table 3. Execution time for finest mesh.

Finest mesh (1152106 elements and 577554 nodes)

Number of threads	System assembly time in seconds	Solution of linear system of equations time in seconds
2	1.762037	16.63890
4	1.312588	16.472596
6	1.139405	16.447437
8	1.015354	16.311359

4 Conclusions

1. We have proposed a discretization for the convective term of the Convection-Diffusion equation, which was developed using geometric arguments and known DEC discretization for the divergence operator.
2. Since DEC can be formulated locally, like FEML, DEC is well suited for parallel computing. Using this feature, numerical experiments were carried out on coarse and fine meshes.
3. Our results shows a similar behavior between DEC and FEML for coarse meshes. For finer meshes, DEC and FEML converges to the same solution.

References

1. Griebel, M., Rieger, C., Schier, A.: Upwind schemes for scalar advection-dominated problems in the discrete exterior calculus. In: Bothe, D., Reusken, A. (eds.) Transport Processes at Fluidic Interfaces. AMFM, pp. 145–175. Springer, Cham (2017). https://doi.org/10.1007/978-3-319-56602-3_6
2. Mohamed, M.S., Hirani, A.N., Samtaney, R.: Discrete exterior calculus discretization of incompressible Navier-Stokes equations over surface simplicial meshes. J. Comput. Phys. **312**, 175–191 (2016)
3. Esqueda, H., Herrera, R., Botello, S., Moreles, M.A.: A geometric description of discrete exterior calculus for general triangulations. arXiv preprint arXiv:1802.01158 (2018)
4. Hirani, A.N., Nakshatrala, K.B., Chaudhry, J.H.: Numerical method for darcy flow derived using discrete exterior calculus. Int. J. Comput. Methods Eng. Sci. Mech. **16**(3), 151–169 (2015). https://doi.org/10.1080/15502287.2014.977500
5. Hirani, A.N.: Discrete exterior calculus. Dissertation, California Institute of Technology (2003)
6. Brooks, A.N., Hughes, T.J.R.: Streamline upwind/Petrov-Galerkin formulations for convection dominated flows with particular emphasis on the incompressible Navier-Stokes equations. Comput. Methods Appl. Mech. Eng. **32**, 199–259 (1982)
7. Franca, L.P., Frey, S.L., Hughes, T.J.R.: Stabilized finite element methods: I. Application to the advective-diffusive model. Comput. Methods Appl. Mech.
8. Hughes, T.J.R., Franca, L.P., Hulbert, G.: A new finite element formulation for computational fluid dynamics: VIII. The Galerkin/least-squares method for advective-diffusive equations. Comput. Methods Appl. Mech. Eng. **73**, 173–189 (1989)

9. Choporov, S.: Parallel computing technologies in the finite element method. In: 3th International Conference on HPC-UA 2013 (2013)
10. Vollaire, C., Nicolas, L., Nicolas, A.: Parallel computing for the finite element method. Eur. Phys. J. Appl. Phys. **1**(3), 305–314 (1998)
11. Savic, S.V., Ilic, A.Z., Notaros, B.M., Ilic, M.M.: Acceleration of higher order FEM matrix filling by OpenMP parallelization of volume integrations. In: Telecommunications Forum (TELFOR), pp. 1183–1184 (2012)
12. Mahinthakumar, G., Saied, F.: A hybrid MPI-OpenMP implementation of an implicit finite-element code on parallel architectures. Int. J. High Perform. Comput. Appl. **16**(4), 371–393 (2002)

Parallel Computing for Processing Data from Intelligent Transportation Systems

Jonathan Denis[1], Renzo Massobrio[1], Sergio Nesmachnow[1(✉)],
Alfredo Cristóbal[2], Andrei Tchernykh[3], and Esteban Meneses[4,5]

[1] Universidad de la República, Montevideo, Uruguay
{jonathan.denis,renzom,sergion}@fing.edu.uy
[2] Universidad Veracruzana, Heroica Veracruz, Mexico
acristobal@uv.mx
[3] Centro de Investigación Científica y Educación Superior de Ensenada,
Ensenada, Mexico
chernykh@cicese.mx
[4] Centro Nacional de Alta Tecnología, San José, Costa Rica
emeneses@cenat.ac.cr
[5] Instituto Tecnológico de Costa Rica, Cartago, Costa Rica

Abstract. This article describes the application of parallel computing techniques for efficiently processing large volumes of data from ITS. This is a relevant problem in nowadays societies, especially when working under the novel paradigm of smart cities. The proposed approach applies parallel multithreading computing for processing Global Positioning System records for a case study on the Intelligent Transportation System in Montevideo, Uruguay. The experimental analysis is performed on a high performance computing platform, considering a large volume of data and different computing resources. The main results indicate that the proposed approach allows achieving good speedup values, thus reducing the execution time to process more than 120 GB of data from 921 to 77 min, when using 32 threads. In addition, a web application to illustrate the results of the proposed approach for computing the average speed of public transportation in Montevideo, Uruguay, is described.

Keywords: Parallel computing · Intelligent Transportation Systems

1 Introduction

The paradigm of *smart cities* proposes incorporating information and communication technologies to improve the quality and efficiency of urban services [2]. Smart cities allow the responsible use of resources and encourage the active participation of citizens in decision-making processes, in order to achieve a sustainable and inclusive city.

Intelligent Transportation Systems (ITS) are an important component in smart cities. These systems allow collecting large volumes of data about the mobility in cities, which can be processed in order to extract valuable information about the mobility of citizens [6]. The obtained information can be offered to citizens that use the transport system as well as to planners and decision in order to improve the Quality of Service and user experience.

© Springer Nature Switzerland AG 2019
M. Torres and J. Klapp (Eds.): ISUM 2019, CCIS 1151, pp. 266–281, 2019.
https://doi.org/10.1007/978-3-030-38043-4_22

One of the main sources of information for smart cities is about mobility of citizens. Our research group has developed research on applying computational intelligence methods in smart cities [14, 16, 18, 19]. This article reports a research developed within the project 'Urban transport planning in smart cities' [15], funded by Fondo Conjunto de Cooperación Uruguay–México (AUCI–AMEXCID). The research proposes developing methodologies to support decision-making related to mobility and urban transport in smart cities.

This article describes the design and implementation of a system applying parallel computing for processing large volumes of data from ITS. The system applies parallel collections from the Scala programming language to build an efficient and portable solution applying multithreading parallel computing. A specific case study is presented for computing a relevant metric (average speed of buses) for the ITS in Montevideo, Uruguay, by efficiently processing Global Positioning System (GPS) data. The main results of the experimental evaluation indicate that the proposed approach achieves good speedup values, reducing the execution time to process more than 120 GB of data from 921 to 77 min, when using 32 threads. A web application is developed for the proper visualization of the information from the processing of GPS data to compute the average speed of public transportation in Montevideo, Uruguay. The visualization makes use of an important feature of data, i.e., georeferencing. Several libraries and services are used in the developed visualization tool, including a geographical database, a geographical web service, and a service for maps creation.

The article is organized as follows. The next section describes the main concepts related to ITS and parallel computing, and reviews related works. Section 3 describes the ITS in Montevideo, Uruguay and the problem of computing the average speed of buses. The details about the proposed solution to process large volumes of mobility data applying parallel computing are presented in Sect. 4. The experimental evaluation of the proposed approach is reported in Sect. 5. Finally, Sect. 6 formulates the main conclusions and current lines of work.

2 Intelligent Transportation and Parallel Computing

This section describes ITS, parallel computing, the software library applied in the research, and reviews related works.

2.1 Intelligent Transportation Systems

ITS are one of the most valuable components to understand and manage mobility under the paradigm of smart cities. By including transportation and traffic models and using synergistic technologies, ITS aim at improving transportation safety and urban mobility [6]. Modern ITS incorporate a plethora of sensors into vehicles and roadside infrastructure, which allow gathering large volumes of data that can be analyzed to understand mobility in the city and assess the quality of service offered to the users. The technology used as a source of urban data in this research is Automatic Vehicle Location (AVL).

AVL systems allow automatically determining and communicating the geographic location of a moving vehicle [23]. The information can be collected at a central server to overview and control a fleet of vehicles. GPS is the most common technology to determine the location of vehicles in AVL, mainly due to its widespread availability, low cost, and precision. AVL technology is frequently incorporated in ITS and constitutes a rich source of data, as it helps to monitor and control the quality of service provided by the transportation system to users.

2.2 Parallel Computing and Scala Parallel Collections

This subsection describes the paradigm of parallel computing and the tool for supporting parallel computing applied in this work.

Parallel Computing. Parallel computing is a paradigm of computation that applies concurrent processes that execute sentences simultaneously, in order to address complex problems using several computing units at the same time. In this way, it is possible to solve problems that are inherently difficult, because of the complexity of calculations and/or because the amount of data they handle [7].

The strategy applied by parallel computing is to divide the initial problem into subproblems of smaller size, which can be solved in parallel, managing communications with a concurrent programming scheme to maintain the consistency of the data. The different processes that work with each of the parts of the problem to be solved must apply synchronization mechanisms, which consist of the use of shared resources, such as shared memory, or the passage of messages using distributed memory. The computer systems that support this type of programming are called parallel computers.

Scala Parallel Collections and Parallel Arrays. Scala is a programming language that proposes an integration between object-oriented programming and functional programming, with the main goal of taking advantage of the main features of these paradigms [17]. The Scala syntax is similar to the one used by Java, but including some simplifications and new components. The programs developed in Scala are executed on the Java Virtual Machine (JVM) and are compatible with applications and libraries implemented in the Java language. Scala supports parallel programming through Parallel Collections [20].

Parallel Collections are specific implementations of Scala to simplify the development of parallel applications. Parallel Collections generate an abstraction of low level details, allowing users to work at a high level in a simple and intuitive way and bringing parallel programming closer to non-expert users. Scala proposes using collections, which allow managing and processing elements in a parallel, independent way. The parallel work performed by a Parallel Collection consists in recursively dividing a given set of elements, applying a requested operation in parallel on each partition of the collection, and recombining the results at the end of the processing. Executions occur concurrently and out of order, so they should be used with caution when applying non-associative operations.

The type of collection used in this work is Scala Parallel Arrays [1]. A Parallel Array is a sequence of linear contiguous elements that allows accessing and updating the elements efficiently, by modifying the underlying structure (an array). The iteration on ITS elements is also efficient for this same reason. The main characteristic of the Parallel Arrays is that they have a constant size, like sequential arrays. To perform the processing of a Parallel Array, Scala internally uses *splitters* that divide the original Array and create new splitters with updated indexes. When all elements are processed, *combiners* are used to group the results. Combiners usually perform heavier tasks than splitters, as the number of output elements is not known in advance, so each combiner works as a buffer array where splitters add elements in a parallel and concurrent way.

2.3   Related Works

ITS Data Generation and Utilization. Seguí and Martínez [21] described the main issues of public transportation systems in large cities, including pollution, downgraded quality of service, delays on schedules, etc. The European initiative Civitas was also described, as an effort to develop and implement good practices to improve urban transportation. The role of information and communication systems was highlighted, and the use of GPS data was presented as one of the means to improve quality of service and safety of public transportation. The role of data on planning and operating ITS was also pointed out and commented, in order to help decision makers to manage and improve public transportation. A specific case studied was presented, describing the data transmission from buses using an on-board computer and a central server on the transportation company, where data analysis is performed to solve bus bunching and bus delay problems. Weiland and Purser [22] analyzed the key points for the application of technologies to ITS in order to reduce costs and improving the user experience. The main lines for research, including the processing and using of large volumes of data to improve the quality of service were also described.

Demoraes et al. [3] described technology improvements applied to the public transportation system in Quito, Ecuador. Data analysis was proposed as a mean to improve the service. A semi-automatic system was introduced to gather data about the position of buses through GPS records and also to determine the number of passengers that board and alight via manual surveys on buses. A system with four stages was proposed For processing the collected data: (i) data transcription and data cleansing using datasheets and storing the results in a database; (ii) calculation of short segments from the data obtained in the previous stage; (iii) assigning geographic information to the defined segments, and (iv) expand the sample, taking into account the number of buses operating in each hour. Valuable information was obtained, including the total demand and the rush hours. This work is similar to the one proposed in our research, as it deals with generating and processing large volumes of geo-referenced data from ITS. However, a relevant difference is that in the case study presented in this article (ITS on Montevideo) data is generated online and a data streaming approach can be applied to address specific problems as soon as they arise.

Parallel Computing for Processing ITS Data. Several previous articles from our group have proposed the calculation of different ITS metrics and indicators. The general approach of a framework for distributed big data analysis for smart cities was introduced in our previous work [13]. The proposed framework allows combining ITS and socioeconomic data for the city of Montevideo, Uruguay. The efficiency of the proposed framework was studied over a distributed computing infrastructure, demonstrating that it scales properly for processing large volumes of data for both off-line and on-line scenarios. Applications of the proposed platform and case studies using real data were presented, as examples of the valuable information that can be offered to both citizens and authorities. Parallel and distributed big data were applied by our group of work to different problems related to extract and analyze information from the mobility of citizens in public transportation. A parallel distributed approach for extracting useful mobility information from large volumes of data was presented by Fabbiani et al. [5]. A specific solution was introduced for estimating demand and origin-destination matrices based on ticket sales and location of buses and two algorithms were described for the efficient processing of large mobility data from public transportation in Montevideo, Uruguay. Parallel versions of the proposed algorithms were proposed for distributed memory (e.g., cluster, grid, cloud) infrastructures and a cluster implementation was evaluated using realistic datasets, demonstrating the efficacy of the proposed approach.

Massobrio et al. [11] applied distributed computing to study GPS data from buses. A MapReduce approach was introduced to process historical data for studying QoS metrics of the transportation system in Montevideo, Uruguay. The proposed strategy was applied to calculate the arrival times of buses to each bus stop in Montevideo. Delays and deviations to arrive at each bus stop allow detecting specific problems in the public transportation system. The distributed approach was able to scale properly when processing large volumes of data.

Our recent article [4] studied mobility patterns of citizens using public transportation and relocation of bus stops in urban areas. A big-data approach was applied to process large volumes of information and obtain user demand and origin-destination matrices by analyzing the tickets sale information and the buses locations. The proposed parallel implementation was able to reach good execution time improvements. A multiobjective evolutionary algorithm was developed to solve the bus relocation problem, to minimize the travel time and bus operational costs. Results obtained for Montevideo, Uruguay, improved up to 16.7% in time and 33.9% in cost, compared to the current bus planning.

In this line of work, this article contributes with a proposal for processing large volumes of data from ITS using parallel computing. A specific case study is presented, to compute the average speed of buses in Montevideo, Uruguay.

3   Problem Description

This section introduces the ITS in Montevideo, Uruguay, describes the available data, and presents the problem of computing the average speed of buses.

3.1   The Intelligent Transportation System in Montevideo, Uruguay

The government of Montevideo, Uruguay, introduced the *Urban Mobility Plan* in 2010, for redesigning and modernizing public transportation [9]. The Metropolitan

Transportation System (STM) was implemented with the main goal of centralizing all the components of the public transportation system in the city.

One of the first actions of the new STM consisted in installing on each bus a GPS. Several other advances such as a smart card to pay for tickets and new mobile applications for users, allowed the system to improve the user experience. All the IoT devices included in the STM allow collecting huge volumes of data, about the location of buses, ticket sales, transfers between lines, among others.

GPS data from buses in the STM are stored in files that describe the mobility of buses. Table 1 describes each trip performed for each vehicle within a specific bus line variant. A line is a trajectory that connects two locations in the city (departure and destination). There are 145 lines in STM. Each bus line has different variants, accounting for outward and return trips, as well as shorter versions of the same line. The total number of line variants is 1383.

Table 1. Fields on the GPS records input files.

Field	Description
line number	bus line for the trip
timestamp	date and time of the record
latitude	coordinate (latitude) of the record
longitude	coordinate (longitude) of the record
trip id.	identifier of the trip
instant speed	bus speed at the moment of taking the record
variant code	code of the variant of the line for the corresponding trip
bus stop	indicates whether the record was taken in a bus stop or not
bus stop code	bus stop code, if the record was taken in a bus stop

Data on Table 1 allow reconstructing each trip and computing different metrics by studying the positions and travel times of each bus. Data of bus lines and variants are available from the National Catalog of Open Data [8]. Table 2 presents the information available on the bus lines input files. The dataset for each line includes a shapefile with the trajectory of each line, defined as a polygonal chain (a connected series of segments or *polyline*).

Table 2. Fields on the bus lines input files.

Name	Description
gid	identifier (internal use)
cod_linea	line code
desc_linea	line number/description
ordina_subline	correlative number of subline in a line
cod_sublinea	subline code
desc_sublinea	subline description
cod_variant	code of line variant
desc_variant	description of line variant

Another relevant dataset describes the bus stops in the STM. Table 3 presents the available information, including bus stops location, lines, variants, and other data for each bus stop. Names and codes are according to the official nomenclator of Montevideo. Coordinates X_coord and Y_coord correspond to Geocentric Reference System for America (SIRGAS2000 UTM 21s). A shapefile and other supplementary files are also available for proper visualization.

Table 3. Fields on the bus stops input file.

Name	Description
bus stop location code	code of the location of the bus stop
cod_variant	code of the line variant
ordinal	correlative number of the bus stop on the line trajectory
street	name of the street where the bus stop is located
cod_street	code of the street where the bus stop is located
corner	name of the nearest corner
cod_corner	code of the nearest corner
X_coord	coordinate on the X axis of the bus stop location
Y_coord	coordinate on the Y axis of the bus stop location

3.2   Average Speed of Buses

This article focuses on studying a relevant metric related to the quality of service offered to citizens: the average speed of vehicles from the public transportation system. The analysis of the average speed is a valuable input for decision makers to improve quality of service and travel experience for users. Different problems and situations, e.g. troublesome locations in the city, can be identified from the analysis and specific actions can be taken to solve or mitigate their impact.

A preliminary study of the average speed of the public transportation system in Montevideo was presented in our previous article [13]. The analysis was performed for 18 de Julio, one of the main avenues in Montevideo, where a significantly large number of lines travel through [10]. The aforementioned study was proposed as a first step to determine the capabilities of the average speed calculation from GPS data analysis to provide a useful input for authorities. The preliminary study had several limitations, including: (i) the analysis was performed only for seven bus lines; (ii) only one month of GPS data was processed; (iii) just three large segments (each one of about 1500 m) were considered. Anyway, the preliminary analysis proved to be an important tool for authorities. In this line of work, this article extends the case study proposed in the previous work by considering all avenues, roads, and streets where buses travel through, considering the 145 lines and 1383 variants of the STM in Montevideo, and the whole database of GPS records for the year 2015. The computed speed data are organized and grouped taking into account different time ranges (morning, afternoon, and night) and also rush hours. Furthermore, a different granularity is considered in the analysis: the speed calculation and estimations are performed in segments defined by consecutive bus stops in the city, thus providing a significantly more precise information for both citizens and authorities.

4 The Proposed Solution

This section describes the proposed approach to process data and present the results to final users.

4.1 General Design Approach

The research involved two phases: developing algorithms for data processing and designing a web interface for results visualization. Parallel/distributed approaches were applied in each phase. The main details are presented next.

Data Processing. Data processing is divided in three stages: data preparation, parallel processing, and post-processing.

Stage 1: Data Preparation. This stage involves performing data partition, configuring segments, and generating separate files for the processing. Data partition implies splitting the input CSV file containing GPS records for each bus, ordered by timestamp. The applied criteria splits the records by trips, generating one data block per trip, considering the trip identifier in each line. Simultaneously, a trips log is created for each line variant. This log is used to relate the trips with the line variants in the next stage of processing. After that, the segments where speed, time, and distance will be computed are prepared, and data from bus stops are defined and organized, according to the path of each line variant. One segment is the stretch between two consecutive bus stops in a given line variant. As a result, one CSV file is generated for each line variant. Each text line of this CSV file contains the information of each segment for the line variant.

Stage 2: Parallel Processing. This stage performs the search of timestamps for the points that define each segment and the calculation of the speed in each segment. This stage uses as input the CSV files from the previous stage: trips for each line variant, GPS records for each trip, and segments defined for each line variant. Considering that the calculations for each line variant are independent from each other, a simple data-parallel approach can be applied to take full advantage of parallel processing. Following a parallel multithreading programming approach, one execution threads is assigned to each line variant. Since all trips are already split, it is guaranteed that the different execution threads do not compete for using the same input data files (both for GPS data and segments data). This way, a complete partition is obtained, assuring that no concurrency issues occur during the processing. The result of this stage is one CSV file for each line variant and for each month. Each record (line) on each file include the fixed data of each segment and the metrics computed for it (average travel time, average speed, and number of GPS records considered in the calculation).

Stage 3: Post-processing. This stage collects the data from the parallel processing, by applying a sequential procedure that reduces all the information obtained in the previous stage. The result of this stage is a single CSV file with all the computed data for the year.

Data Visualization. A multi-tier architecture is applied, using distributed servers. All components work independently, making easier to extend the approach, share data, or connect with additional tools for data visualization.

Database Layer. A geographic database is used to store geo-referenced data, represented in a coordinates system. The database stores the data for each segment defined for each line variant, according to the geographic coordinates of each bus stop, which constitutes the lower layer of the proposed data architecture. The database used is PostgreSQL, which is open source and includes an specific add-on for managing geographic information: PostGIS. PostGIS allows storing and handling geographic information following standards by the Open Geospatial Consortium. The designed solution applies an open source paradigm, using a well-documented database, assuring the applicability of the system.

Services Layer. A thin service layer is proposed, providing two services that execute separated: web server and geographic server. The web server handles the website that allows users to access and visualize information. The geographic server exposes geographic data using web services. The geographic server used is Geoserver, one of the most used open source servers for sharing geospatial data.

Presentation Layer. The upper layer exposes the main results of the processing over a map of Montevideo, including all the relevant data layers (bus lines, bus stops, segments, etc.) and the values computed for each segment. A rich client is proposed, incorporating all the logic needed to handle geographic data, The presentation layer is developed in Javascript, using the OpenLayers library.

Figure 1 shows a diagram of the architecture of the proposed system.

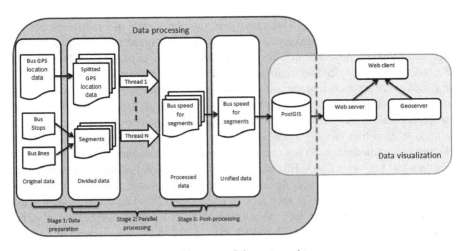

Fig. 1. Architecture of the proposed system.

4.2   Implementation Details

Data Processing. Data processing is divided in three stages: data preparation, parallel processing, and post-processing.

Stage 1: Data Preparation. Python scripts are used to split records for each line variant and bus. A script processes CSV files with several million lines (more than 10 GB) each. The data parallel approach is implemented by an extraction procedure that split the file according to each trip, identified by the trip id field, taking advantage of the structured format of CSV files. All records of the same trip id are written to a different file, named as the line variant.

Three CSV files (line variants, line paths, and bus stops) are processed by a Scala program that generates the segments for each line variant. All data are stored in memory and segments are defined according to the information in the bus stops file, following an ascending order. The coordinates of each generated segment are obtained and the distance is computed. Since the coordinates of the bus stops are expressed in UTM format and segments have short length, Pitagoras' theorem can be applied to compute the distance in meters. All data is stored in order in output CSV files whose name is the line variant id.

Stage 2: Parallel Processing. A Scala program is used to compute the travel time and the average sped for each segment. The program takes as input a time range (defined by initial and final time) and the number of threads to use for the parallel processing. A sequential load is performed for each line variant and the sequential list is converted to a parallel list, whose elements are processed in parallel. GPS records for all trips for each line variant are extracted, the closest records to the two points that define the segment are located and used to compute the travel time and average speed. A transformation is needed since coordinates of GPS records and bus stop locations are expressed in different systems. A threshold (30 m) is used to avoid considering locations that are far from the bus stops that defines each segment. The average period for GPS records is 15 s and the average speed of buses according to the theoretical timetable is 15 km/h. The average distance between consecutive measurements is 60 m, so a bus stop is located 30 m from each measurement. This calculation is conservative; in a real scenario, the bus speed is lower than 15 km/h and there are several valid measurements in a radius of 30 m from each bus stop. The processing algorithm identifies those measurements and uses the closest one for the calculations. The average speed is computed after applying a reduction phase and the results are stored in output CSV files, one for each line variant.

Stage 3: Post-processing. The post-processing gathers all the results, summarizes a set of statistics about the processing, and outputs warning and error messages if needed (for example, segments with few or no data). All data are exported to the PostGIS database using QGIS, to be used for data visualization.

Data Visualization. Visualization is offered by a web application, which is a specific product developed in the research. The application makes use of the database and services layers, already described in the previous section. Three filters are available for data visualization: time ranges (including peak hours in the morning and in the afternoon), date, and line variant. All computed values are available in the visualization, including: travel time, average speed, distance, number of measurements considered in the calculation, bus stops that define segments and their coordinates, date, time range, and line variant.

Furthermore, specific geographic web servers were implemented to obtain and visualize the data layers used in the research (bus lines, bus stops, segments, and speed) with all the information properly sanitized. These web services can be used to design more powerful tools and applications for ITS characterization.

OpenGIS Styled Layer Descriptors (SLD) are used to modify the visualization criteria for the segment layer. Five speed ranges are defined for visualization; red: less than 10 km/h, orange: between 10 and 15 km/h, yellow: between 15 and 20 km/h, light green: between 20 and 25 km/h, and dark green: more than 25 km/h. SLDs are used via a XML file with the standard format and a style layer with the custom style defined by a set of rules (one rule per category or speed range). For each rule, two labels are defined: PointSymbolizer, which states how to represent the points, and TextSymbolizer, that defines the attributes of the text shown near each point. The web application is shown in Figs. 2 and 3.

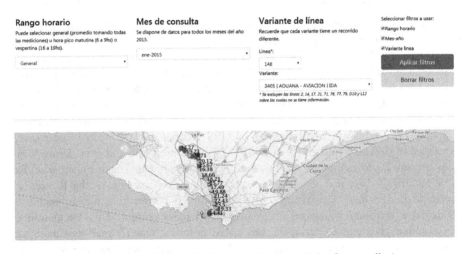

Fig. 2. Web application for data visualization. (Color figure online)

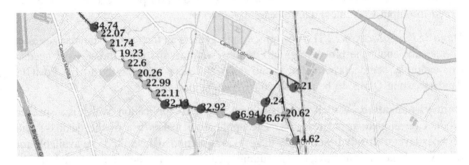

Fig. 3. Web application: map detail. (Color figure online)

5 Experimental Evaluation

This section reports the experimental evaluation of the parallel algorithm.

5.1 Methodology of the Experimental Evaluation

The main goal of the research is to determine the capabilities of the proposed approach to process large volumes of mobility data in reasonable execution times, by exploiting the available computing resources. A standard methodology was applied, varying the number of threads (partitions) and evaluating the execution time, speedup, and efficiency of the parallel algorithm. Experiments were performed in a HP Proliant DL385 G7 (2 AMD Opteron 6172 CPUs, 12 cores each, 72 GB RAM) from Cluster FING [12], Universidad de la República, Uruguay.

5.2 Performance Analysis

Execution Time. Table 4 reports the execution time of the parallel algorithm for processing GPS records using different number of computing units (threads). Five independent executions were performed to reduce deviations due to non-determinist execution.

Table 4. Execution time of the parallel algorithm using different computing units

# execution		Execution time (minutes)						
		Parallel algorithm: computing units						
Sequential algorithm		1	2	4	8	16	24	32
1	921	821	579	265	143	115	94	83
2	917	920	581	255	140	119	82	77
3	925	918	564	266	141	100	85	109
4	931	924	588	288	152	118	149	89
5	910	931	554	260	143	116	81	99
Average	920.8	922.8	573.2	266.8	143.8	113.6	98.2	91.4

Results in Table 4 show a fast reduction in execution times when using up to 8 threads. Beyond that number of threads, reductions are less significant. When using 32 threads, a reduction of 10 is achieved in the execution time. Computations that require 15 h to perform sequentially can be performed in one hour and a half using the proposed parallel model. Results are graphically reported in Fig. 4.

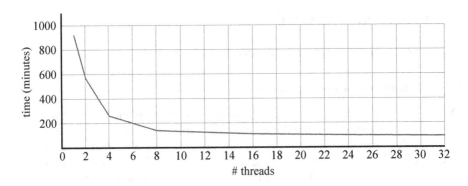

Fig. 4. Execution time

Speedup and Computational Efficiency. Table 5 reports the values for the speedup and the computational efficiency of the parallel algorithm when using different computing resources.

Table 5. speedup and computational efficiency

Computing units	Speedup	Computational efficiency
1	1	1
2	1.61	0.80
4	3.46	0.86
8	6.42	0.80
16	8.12	0.51
24	9.40	0.39
32	10.10	0.32

Results in Table 5 clearly show that accurate speedup and computational efficiency values are computed for up to eight computing units (e.g., speedup 6.42, computational efficiency 0.80). However, values significantly decreases when using 16 to 32 computing resource. The computational efficiency when using more threads than the cores available in the server (24) is significantly lower, i.e., using 32 computing units it is rather low (0.32), suggesting that hyperthreading is not useful for the proposed parallel GPS data processing. These results are graphically presented in Figs. 5 and 6.

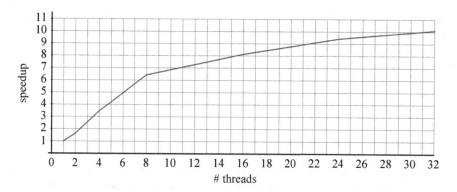

Fig. 5. Speedup of the proposed parallel algorithm

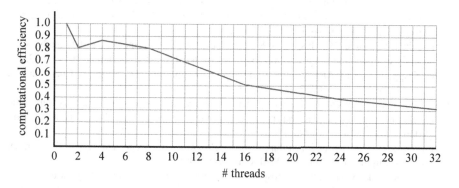

Fig. 6. Computational efficiency of the proposed parallel algorithm

6 Conclusions and Future Work

This article presented a proposal applying parallel computing techniques for efficiently processing massive data from ITS. This is a relevant problem within the novel paradigm of smart cities, where ITS generate large volumes of data that must be properly analyzed to contribute to improve the quality of service of public transportation.

A parallel multithreading algorithm was proposed for processing GPS records from the ITS in Montevideo, Uruguay. An implementation combining Python scripts and programs in the Scala language was developed.

Scala Parallel Collections were useful to effectively parallelize the processing, without a significant development effort. The proposed workflow allow easily adapting the approach to work with other data and/or visualization tools.

Results from the experimental analysis performed on a high performance computing platform indicate that the proposed approach achieves good speedup values when using up to 16 threads for the processing. The overall execution time to process more than 120 GB of data was reduced from 921 to 77 min, when using 32 threads. A web application was also designed to properly present the result of the mobility analysis to end users and administrators. The proposed approach can be directly applied for the processing of other data from ITS or even to analyze data from other sources. The main lines for future work include extending the approach to process streaming data, in order to compute useful information in real time.

References

1. Blanvillain, O., Miller, H.: Concrete parallel collection classes. https://docs.scala-lang.org/overviews/parallel-collections/concrete-parallel-collections.html. Accessed 2 Jan 2019
2. Deakin, M., Al Waer, H.: From intelligent to smart cities. Intell. Buil. Int. **3**, 133–139 (2011)
3. Demoraes, F., Bondoux, F., Souris, M., Núñez, H.: Innovaciones tecnológicas aplicadas al transporte colectivo en Quito. Optimización en la evaluación de la demanda con GPS y SIG. Bull. de l'Institut français d'études andines **33**(1), 193–212 (2004)
4. Fabbiani, E., Nesmachnow, S., Toutouh, J., Tchernykh, A., Avetisyan, A., Radchenko, G.: Analysis of mobility patterns for public transportation and bus stops relocation. Program. Comput. Softw. **45**(1), 34–51 (2019)
5. Fabbiani, E., Vidal, P., Massobrio, R., Nesmachnow, S.: Distributed big data analysis for mobility estimation in intelligent transportation systems. In: Barrios Hernández, C.J., Gitler, I., Klapp, J. (eds.) CARLA 2016. CCIS, vol. 697, pp. 146–160. Springer, Cham (2017). https://doi.org/10.1007/978-3-319-57972-6_11
6. Figueiredo, L., Jesus, I., Machado, J.T., Ferreira, J.R., Carvalho, J.L.: Towards the development of intelligent transportation systems. In: IEEE Intelligent Transportation Systems, pp. 1206–1211 (2001)
7. Foster, I.: Designing and Building Parallel Programs: Concepts and Tools for Parallel Software Engineering. Addison-Wesley, Boston (1995)
8. Intendencia de Montevideo: Transporte colectivo: paradas y puntos de control. https://catalogodatos.gub.uy/dataset/transporte-colectivo-paradas-y-puntos-de-control. Accessed 9 Jan 2019
9. Intendencia de Montevideo: Plan de movilidad urbana: hacia un sistema de movilidad accesible, democratico y eficiente (2010). http://www.montevideo.gub.uy/sites/default/files/plan_de_movilidad.pdf Accessed 07 Jan 2019
10. Massobrio, R.: M.Sc. thesis, Universidad de la República, Uruguay (2018). www.fing.edu.uy/~renzom/msc. Accessed 24 Feb 2019
11. Massobrio, R., Pias, A., Vázquez, N., Nesmachnow, S.: Map-reduce for processing GPS data from public transport in Montevideo, Uruguay. In: 2nd Argentinian Symposium on Big Data, pp. 41–54 (2016)
12. Nesmachnow, S.: Computación científica de alto desempeñõ en la Facultad de Ingeniería, Universidad de la República. Rev. la Asociación de Ingenieros del Uruguay **61**(1), 12–15 (2010)
13. Nesmachnow, S., Banã, S., Massobrio, R.: A distributed platform for big data analysis in smart cities: combining intelligent transportation systems and socioeconomic data for Montevideo, Uruguay. EAI Endorsed Trans. Smart Cities **2**(5), 1–18 (2017)
14. Nesmachnow, S., et al.: Traffic lights synchronization for Bus Rapid Transit using a parallel evolutionary algorithm. Int. J. Transp. Sci. Technol. (2018). https://www.sciencedirect.com/science/article/pii/S2046043018300339
15. Nesmachnow, S., Massobrio, R., Cristóbal, A., Tchernykh. A.: Planificación detransporte urbano en ciudades inteligentes. In: I Ibero-American Congress of Smart Cities, pp. 204–218 (2018)

16. Nesmachnow, S., Rossit, D., Toutouh, J.: Comparison of multiobjective evolutionary algorithms for prioritized urban waste collection in Montevideo, Uruguay. Electron. Notes Discret. Math. **69**, 93–100 (2018)
17. Odersky, M., Spoon, L., Venners, B.: Programming in Scala: A Comprehensive Step-by-Step Guide. Artima Incorporation, Mountain View (2011)
18. Penã, D., et al.: Operating cost and quality of service optimization for multi-vehicle-type timetabling for urban bus systems. J. Parallel Distrib. Comput. (2018). https://www.sciencedirect.com/science/article/pii/S0743731518300297
19. Péres, M., Ruiz, G., Nesmachnow, S., Olivera, C.: Multiobjective evolutionary optimization of traffic flow and pollution in Montevideo, Uruguay. Appl. Soft Comput. **70**, 472–485 (2018)
20. Prokopec, A., Miller, H.: Parallel collections. http://docs.scala-lang.org/overviews/parallel-collections/overview.html. Accessed 2 Jan 2019
21. Seguí, J., Martńez, M.: Los sistemas inteligentes de transporte y sus efectos en la movilidad urbana e interurbana. Scripta Nova, Revista electrnica de geografa y ciencias sociales, Universidad de Barcelona **6**(170) 2004
22. Weiland, R., Purser, L.: Intelligent transportation systems. Transportation Research Board, Washington, DC (2000)
23. Zhao, Y.: Vehicle Location and Navigation Systems. Artech House, Norwood (1997)

Multiphase Flows Simulation with the Smoothed Particle Hydrodynamics Method

Carlos E. Alvarado-Rodríguez[1]([⊠]), Jaime Klapp[2], J. M. Domínguez[3],
A. R. Uribe-Ramírez[1], J. J. Ramírez-Minguela[1],
and M. Gómez-Gesteira[3]

[1] División de Ciencias Naturales y Exactas, CONACYT-Universidad
de Guanajuato, Col. Noria Alta s/n, 36050 Guanajuato, Guanajuato, Mexico
ce.alvarado@ugto.mx
[2] Instituto Nacional de Investigaciones Nucleares (ININ), Km. 36.5 Carretera
México-Toluca, 52750 La Marquesa, Estado de México, Mexico
[3] Environmental Physics Laboratory (EPHYSLAB),
University of Vigo, Ourense, Spain

Abstract. This work presents a new multiphase SPH model that includes the shifting algorithm and a variable smoothing length formalism to simulate multiphase flows with accuracy and proper interphase management. The implementation was performed in the DualSPHysics code, and validated for different canonical experiments, such as the single-phase and multiphase Poiseuille and Couette test cases. The method is accurate even for the multiphase case for which two phases are simulated. The shifting algorithm and the variable smoothing length formalism has been applied in the multiphase SPH model to improve the numerical results at the interphase even when it is highly deformed and non-linear effects become important. The obtained accuracy in the validation tests and the good interphase definition in the instability cases, indicate an important improvement in the numerical results compared with single-phase and multiphase models where the shifting algorithm and the variable smoothing length formalism are not applied.

Keywords: Multiphase flow · SPH method · Parallel code

1 Introduction

Multiphase flow is an important area of study in many industrial practices such as chemical engineering, environmental analysis and oil recovery processes. Nowadays, there exist two main approaches to analyze this kind of phenomena: laboratory experiments and numerical models. In many cases, laboratory experiments are difficult to perform or very expensive for some of the processes mentioned through this article because of the complex processes involved and the irregular boundary conditions necessary to accurately represent these phenomena.

Computational Fluid Dynamics (CFD) has become a useful tool in science and engineering. The recent advances in computer hardware have increased the applicability,

© Springer Nature Switzerland AG 2019
M. Torres and J. Klapp (Eds.): ISUM 2019, CCIS 1151, pp. 282–301, 2019.
https://doi.org/10.1007/978-3-030-38043-4_23

range, and resolution of simulations that CFD methods can properly solve. There are two main approaches to solve the CFD equations, the Eulerian and the Lagrangian formalism. Usually the Eulerian formalism is linked to the use of a mesh to discretize the domain, for example, the finite elements, finite differences, and finite volume methods. These mesh-based methods have been used to simulate multiphase flows but one of their drawbacks is their inability to describe large deformation flows, which can be properly modelled by the meshless Smoothed Particle Hydrodynamics (SPH) method. The SPH method present some advantages comparing with Eulerian methods as: easy to model complex geometries, good representation for mobile boundaries and free surfaces, easy to follow the evolution of the continuous medium, and others.

This method has a simple physical interpretation that allows including sophisticate physics, thus presenting an advantage for new developments. Several SPH multiphase methods have been proposed to simulate flows with different viscosity and density ratios. For example, [1] developed an original SPH model to treat two-dimensional multiphase flows with low density ratios, where the main contribution of their model was a new implementation of the particle evolution according to [2]. Tartakovsky and Meakin [3] developed a model that combines particle density number based equations and inter-particle forces, this last implementation prevents the presence of artificial surface tension at the interphase between fluids that is a common issue of the standard SPH formulation. Monaghan [4] proposed a variation in the viscous term of the standard SPH, the modification consists of a small increase in the pressure term when the interaction is among particles from different phases.

Among the available options, due to the advantages with respect to other SPH models, DualSPHysics has been chosen as the platform to implement the multiphase model. DualSPHysics is an open-source code developed at the University of Vigo (Spain) and the University of Manchester (UK) that can be freely downloaded from www.dual.sphysics.org [5]. DualSPHysics is implemented in C++ and CUDA and is designed to perform simulations either on multiple CPU's or on GPU's. Due to the SPH method has a high computational cost, the DualSPHysics code presents the advantage to perform the mathematical calculus in a parallel way using all unit processors in a CPU or GPU device, furthermore, the code has tools to perform simulations with irregular boundary conditions easily. The code is performed by duplicate, one version for CPU and the other for GPU devices, this presents some advantages to implement new physical models starting in CPU version and then export the new model to the GPU version.

The implemented optimizations in DualSPHysics allows performing high-resolution simulations in reasonable computational times due to its high level of parallelization in both CPUs and GPUs [6]. The main objective of this work is to present a multiphase model that consists of a combination of different approaches, mainly the shifting algorithm and the variable smoothing length formalism, to improve the treatment for cases with high non-linear deformations at the interphase. Several validation cases are presented, Poiseuille flow and Couette flow, comparing the results provided by the new implementation and the analytical solution. Also three applications cases were conducted, namely, the Rayleigh-Taylor and Kelvin-Helmholtz instabilities, and the oil-water two phase flow in a pipe where the numerical results are compared with the experimental data in the literature.

2 The SPH Method

In the SPH method, the fluid is discretized as a set of points or fluid elements called particles. The integral equations that govern the fluid dynamics are transformed to a discrete description. This new set of equations is solved in the Lagrangian formalism. The values of the main physical variables (position, velocity, density and pressure) for each particle are obtained as the interpolation of the values of the neighboring particles. A function called kernel is used to transform the continuous medium (fluid) to a discrete description (particles). For a more detailed description of the method the reader is referred to [4, 7–10].

$$A(r) = \int A(r')W(r - r', h)dr', \tag{1}$$

where r is the position vector, W the kernel, and h the smoothing length which is a distance larger than the initial particle spacing. The previous equation can be rewritten in discrete notation as

$$A(r) = \sum_j m_j \frac{A_j}{\rho_j} W(r - r_j, h), \tag{2}$$

where the subscript j represents all the neighbouring particles inside the kernel function domain; these are the particles whose contribution cannot be neglected. The derivative of a function can be rewritten in discrete notation as

$$\nabla A(r) = \int A(r')\nabla W(r - r', h)dr' \approx \sum_j m_j \frac{A_j}{\rho_j} \nabla W(r - r_j, h). \tag{3}$$

The kernel function is a key parameter in the SPH method. There is a wide range of functions that can be used as kernel [11–13] but all of them must satisfy certain conditions: positivity, compact support and normalization. In addition, $W(r,h)$ must have a delta function behaviour when h goes to zero, and be monotonically decreasing with the distance between particles. For this work we use the kernel function proposed by [13] which can be written as:

$$W(r, h) = \alpha_D \left(1 - \frac{q}{2}\right)^4 (2q + 1) \qquad 0 \le q \le 2, \tag{4}$$

where $\alpha_D = 7/(4\pi h^2)$ in 2D and $\alpha_D = 21/(16\pi h^2)$ in 3D, $q = r/h$ with r being the distance between particles i and j.

According with [11], this kernel provide a high order of interpolation at a moderate computational cost.

The equations that govern the fluid are presented in the following sections. In Sect. 2.1 the standard SPH formulation implemented in DualSPHysics is introduced. Since the aim of this work is to properly represent multiphase flows, the standard formulation falls short and additional formulations and approximations are required. All changes performed are presented in Sect. 2.2.

2.1 The Standard SPH Model

The momentum and continuity equations used in this work can be expressed as a continuous field as follows:

$$\frac{dv}{dt} = -\frac{1}{\rho}\nabla P + g + \Gamma, \tag{5}$$

$$\frac{d\rho}{dt} = -\rho\nabla v, \tag{6}$$

where v is velocity, t is time, P is pressure, ρ represents the density, g the gravitational acceleration, and Γ refers to dissipative terms.

The governing equations in the standard SPH formulation (continuity and momentum) referred to particle i are

$$\frac{d\rho_i}{dt} = \sum_j m_j v_{ij} \nabla_i W_{ij}, \tag{7}$$

$$\frac{dv_i}{dt} = -\sum_j m_j \left(\frac{P_j}{\rho_j^2} + \frac{P_i}{\rho_i^2} + \Gamma \right) \nabla_j W_{ij} + g, \tag{8}$$

where P_j and ρ_j denote the pressure and density of neighbouring particles, respectively.

The dissipative term Γ is implemented in two different ways in DualSPHysics, namely, the artificial viscosity proposed by [4], and the laminar viscosity plus sub-particle scale (SPS) turbulence [14, 15, 16, 34].

Artificial viscosity is frequently used due to its stability and simplicity. The viscosity term Γ in Eq. (8) can be written for artificial viscosity as:

$$\Gamma = \begin{cases} \frac{-\alpha \bar{c}_{ij}\mu_{ij}}{\rho_{ij}} & v_{ij}\cdot r_{ij} < 0 \\ 0 & v_{ij}\cdot r_{ij} > 0 \end{cases}, \tag{9}$$

where $r_{ij} = r_i - r_j$, $v_{ij} = v_i - v_j$, $\mu_{ij} = h v_{ij}\cdot r_{ij}/\left(r_{ij}^2 + \eta^2\right)$, $\bar{c}_{ij} = 0.5\left(c_i + c_j\right)$ is the mean speed of sound, $\eta^2 = 0.01 h^2$, and α is a free parameter that must be tuned depending on the problem configuration.

When the laminar + SPS turbulence is used to represent the viscous stresses, the momentum Eq. (8) can be expressed as:

$$\frac{dv_i}{dt} = -\sum_j m_j \left(\frac{P_j}{\rho_j^2} + \frac{P_i}{\rho_i^2} \right) \nabla_j W_{ij} + g + \sum_j m_j \left(\frac{4 v_0 r_{ij} \cdot \nabla_i W_{ij}}{(\rho_i + \rho_j)\left(r_{ij}^2 + \eta^2\right)} \right) v_{ij}, \qquad (10)$$

where v_0 is kinetic viscosity (10^{-6} m^{2}s in the case of water).

Laminar viscosity was used for the validation cases and artificial viscosity for the instability cases, the different selection helps to adequately represent non-linear effects at the interphase in the application cases. These non-linear effects could be smoothed or disturbed by the viscosity laminar treatment.

In the SPH formalism the fluid is considered as weakly incompressible and pressure is calculated as a function of density. Following [17], Tait's equation is used to relate pressure and density. This equation provides high pressure variations at small density oscillations and is written in the form

$$P = B \left[\left(\frac{\rho}{\rho_0} \right)^{\gamma} - 1 \right], \qquad (11)$$

where $B = c_0^2 \rho_0 / \gamma$, ρ_0 is the reference density, γ is the polytropic constant which is set to 7, and $c_0 = c(\rho_0)$ the speed of sound at the reference density. B also provides a limit for the maximum change that the density can experience. The speed of sound (c_0) is an artificial value that must be, at least, 10 times bigger than the highest fluid velocity estimated for the physical problem under study. This condition only allows a density oscillation of 1% around the reference density (ρ_0).

2.2   The Multiphase SPH Model

Different approaches and methods have been proposed to simulate multiphase flows [3, 12, 18]. In this work several new approaches are added to the standard formalism. These features permit to properly simulate multiphase flows, where the main contribution lies in the improved management to interphase with highly nonlinear deformations.

2.2.1   The Momentum Equation for the Multiphase Model

The instability and artificial surface tension produced in a multiphase flow using the standard SPH has been reported by [1] and [19]. For this work we have replaced the Eq. (8) used in the standard SPH formulation by the expression (12) which to permit that higher density ratios in simulations avoiding the artificial surface tension [1]. The method is rather robust, even for large free-surface fragmentation and folding, efficient and relatively easy-to-code and results stable and capable to easily treat a variety of density ratios [1].

$$\frac{dv_i}{dt} = -\sum_j m_j \left(\frac{P_i + P_j}{\rho_i \rho_j} + \Gamma \right) \nabla_i W_{ij} + g. \tag{12}$$

Higher density ratios can be simulated with the use of this expression avoiding the artificial surface tension.

2.2.2   The Equation of the State for the Multiphase Model

According to [1] the pressure of each phase is calculated using the equation of state (11), which is calculated using appropriate parameters according to each phase reference density. So, the equation of state (11) is calculated for each phase using:

$$P_H = B_H \left[\left(\frac{\rho}{\rho_{0H}} \right)^{\gamma_H} - 1 \right], \qquad P_L = B_L \left[\left(\frac{\rho}{\rho_{0L}} \right)^{\gamma_L} - 1 \right], \tag{13}$$

where the subscripts H and L denote the fluid with higher and lower density, respectively.

The constant B_H is chosen to permit a small compressibility of the higher density fluid, that is $v_{maxH}/c_H \ll 1$, where v_{maxH} is the maximum velocity of the fluid with higher density expected in the considered problem. Then B_L is matched to B_H in the equation of state for the fluid with lower density to create a stable pressure at the interphase. Moreover this formalism ensures that the fluid stays at rest when $\rho = \rho_H$ or $\rho = \rho_L$ and the pressure is zero. This formulation allows the simulation of high density ratios (e.g. 1:1000, which is similar to the air-water ratio). For the water-air interaction typical values are $\gamma_H = 7$ and $\gamma_L = 1.4$. However, only simulations with lower densities ratios (1:2) and a value of $\gamma = 7$ are considered for the cases presented in this work.

2.2.3   The Shifting Algorithm

The shifting algorithm, henceforth *shifting*, is a new implementation in DualSPHysics. This algorithm was proposed by [20] and it is used to keep a better distribution of particles. This algorithm shifts the position of particles slightly after their normal interaction, due to pressure and velocity and is applied in this work to prevent voids in the particle distribution formed by the interaction between particles with different densities. The magnitude and direction of the position shift is governed by Fick's law, which slightly moves particles from higher to lower particle concentration regions. The displacement is calculated assuming that the flux of particles is proportional to the velocity. So, according to Fick's law the shifting displacement of a particle can be written as:

$$\delta r_s = -K \nabla C, \tag{14}$$

where $K = -2$ is considered and the shift, δr_s, is added to the equation of particle displacement as follow

$$r_i^{n+1} = r_i^n + \Delta t v_i^n + 0.5 \Delta t^2 F_i^n + \delta r_s. \tag{15}$$

Then, the particle concentration is calculated at each time step from the summation of the kernel function and the concentration gradient in the usual way by

$$C_i = \sum_j V_j W_{ij}, \qquad \nabla C_i = \sum_j V_j \nabla W_{ij}, \tag{16}$$

where V_j means particle volume and C_i is the concentration of the neighbour particles.

2.2.4 The Variable Smoothing Length Formalism

The variable smoothing length formalism, henceforth h_{var}, was proposed by [21] and [22] to properly describe shock waves and the interphase between two fluids where the density changes by a significant amount. The basic idea is to allow the smoothing length to change from particle to particle through a series of kernels. The h_{var} is calculated from an initial density $(\hat{\rho})$ and smoothing length (h_0) as:

$$\hat{\rho}_i = \sum_{j=1}^{N\_n} m_j W \left(\left| r_i - r_j \right|, h_0 \right), \tag{17}$$

where N_n means the number of neighbors.

Then local bandwidth factors, λ_i, are constructed according to

$$\lambda_i = k \left(\frac{\hat{\rho}_i}{\bar{g}} \right)^{-\epsilon}, \tag{18}$$

$$\log \bar{g} = \frac{1}{N} \sum_{j=1}^{N\_n} \log \hat{\rho}_j, \tag{19}$$

where k is a constant ($k \approx 1$), and ϵ is a sensitive parameter that ranges from 0 to 1.

Then, the h_{var} is calculated according to

$$h_{var} = \lambda_i h_0. \tag{20}$$

The kernel is symmetrized to conserve linear momentum using the following average for each pair of particles

$$h_{varij} = \frac{h_{vari} + h_{varj}}{2}. \tag{21}$$

So, the kernel with the new smoothing length will replace the previous version:

$$W_{ij} = W \left(\left| r_i - r_j \right|, h_{varij} \right). \tag{22}$$

2.3 Parallel Structure in the Code

The DualsSPHysics code presents a parallel structure using the OpenMP and CUDA tools. The code is write by duplicate, one version is write in the C++ computational language for CPU processors where all unit processor are used by default using OpenMP and other version is write in CUDA computational language for use the internal CUDA cores in one GPU processor.

In the SPH method the main computational time for simulations is during the particle interaction, so the calculus in the interaction is processed in parallel, then the results are processed in a serial way. For the GPU version, only the interaction are calculated in the CUDA cores and the preprocessing and post-processing are handled by the CPU processor. The mean characteristics of the DualSPHysics code can be consulted in [5]. The advantage of the use parallel codes are describe in [23, 24].

3 Validation

Several improvements to the numerical method have been mentioned in previous sections. All of them focused on the multiphase treatment and aimed to increase the accuracy of the model. This section provides four test cases that highlight the accuracy of our multiphase model implemented in DualSPHysics. The case 3.1 evidences the accuracy in the evolution of the velocity profile within a duct for the Poiseuille flow test case with two densities. The case 3.2 shows the accuracy in the evolution of the velocity profile when the velocity of the fluid is induce by a boundary simulating a Couette flow with two densities. The results from SPH simulations are compared with the analytical solution for all cases.

3.1 Poiseuille Flow with Two Densities

The plane Poiseuille flow consists of a laminar flow produced by a constant pressure gradient between two parallel infinite plates. The plane Poiseuille flow test on SPH has already been performed by [25–27]. This case tests out the accuracy of the evolution in the velocity profile when the numerical results are compared with the analytical solution. In this case a Plane Poiseuille flow is conducted for two fluids with different densities and viscosities. The test is simulated in the XY plane (2-D), neglecting the gravitational acceleration, the distance between the plates is 1 mm. The test was performed using periodic conditions in X direction at $x = -0.5$ mm and $x = 0.5$ mm. The laminar viscosity model is used to calculate de momentum equation, but as mentioned before with different density and viscosity values. The initial condition of simulation is shown in Fig. 1 and the set-up configuration is summarized in Table 1.

This case evidences the accuracy of the evolution in the velocity profile in multiphase simulations using de multiphase model coupling h_{var} and *shifting*, where the accuracy of the SPH simulations is determined by comparing the numerical and analytical solutions.

Table 1. Set-up configuration for the Poiseuille flow test case with two densities.

Parameter	Value
Total particles	700; 1,188; 2,600
Initial inter-particle spacing	$4 \times 10^{-5}, 3 \times 10^{-5}, 2 \times 10^{-5}$ m
Lower density (ρ^I)	500 kg/m^3
Higher density (ρ^{II})	1000 kg/m^3
Body force parallel to X-axis (F)	10^{-4} m/s^2
Viscosity for lower density (μ^I)	0.5×10^{-6} m^2/s
Viscosity for higher density (μ^{II})	1×10^{-6} m^2/s

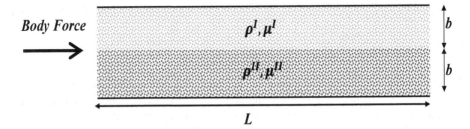

Fig. 1. Initial condition for the Poiseuille test case with two densities.

The analytical solution for the steady state was presented in [28] and compared here with the SPH simulation results. The pressure difference used in the analytical solutions is $\Delta P = 1.83x10^{-7} Pa$. The analytical solutions are

$$v_x^I = \frac{\Delta P b^2}{2\mu^I L} \left[\left(\frac{2\mu^I}{\mu^I + \mu^{II}} \right) + \left(\frac{\mu^I - \mu^{II}}{\mu^I + \mu^{II}} \right) \left(\frac{y}{b} \right) - \left(\frac{y}{b} \right)^2 \right], \tag{23}$$

$$v_x^{II} = \frac{\Delta P b^2}{2\mu^{II} L} \left[\left(\frac{2\mu^{II}}{\mu^I + \mu^{II}} \right) + \left(\frac{\mu^I - \mu^{II}}{\mu^I + \mu^{II}} \right) \left(\frac{y}{b} \right) - \left(\frac{y}{b} \right)^2 \right], \tag{24}$$

where $b = 0.5$ mm is the height of each fluid, μ^I and μ^{II} are the viscosities of fluids I and II, respectively, and $L = 1$ mm the length of the container.

Figure 2 shows the velocity (v_x) profile at 0.5 s once the steady state has been attained for three different resolutions. Velocity was calculated at 21 points located at the same X position and varying the Y position every 0.05 mm.

Numerical and analytical results show good agreement. The convergence test was carried out using three different resolutions corresponding to 700; 1,188 and 2,600 particles, for the same case. The relative error was calculated using Eq. (25).

$$\%RMSE = 100 \times \sqrt{\frac{1}{N_d} \sum \left(u_{SPH} - u_{analytical} \right)^2}, \tag{25}$$

where %RMSE is the relative mean square error, u_{SPH} the SPH velocity, $u_{analytical}$ the analytical velocity and N_d is the number of data points.

The velocity profile corresponding to the steady state shown in Fig. 2 is asymmetric due to the different viscosity values. In this case the top velocity value is located at the low viscosity part of the fluid. These results are in good agreement with theory since the stress tensor decreases when the viscosity decreases.

Results of the convergence test are shown in Table 2 where the relative error (% RMSE) decreases when the resolution increases.

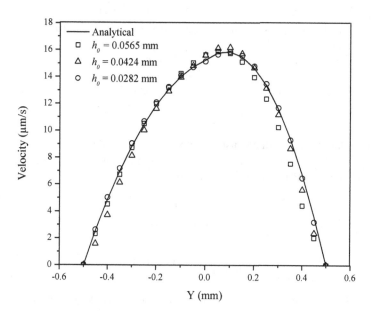

Fig. 2. Numerical and analytical solution for the Poiseuille test case with two densities at t = 0.5 s, when the steady state has been attained.

Table 2. Numerical parameters and errors for SPH velocity profiles shown in Fig. 2.

Np	Dp (mm)	h_0 (mm)	%RMSE at the steady state
700	0.04	0.0565	8.44×10^{-5}
1,188	0.03	0.0424	6.01×10^{-5}
2,600	0.02	0.0282	3.55×10^{-5}

3.2 Couette Flow with Two Densities

The second validation case is a Couette flow. Numerical SPH calculations of Couette flow has also been performed in [27] and [25]. This test consists of a laminar flow between two parallel infinite plates produced by the displacement of the top plate with constant velocity. As in previous cases, the infinite plates are represented using periodic boundary conditions and the case is simulated in XY plane (2-D). In this case a Couette flow validation is conducted using two fluids with different densities and viscosities. The set-up configuration is summarized in Table 3 and the initial configuration is depicted in Fig. 3. This case tests the accuracy of the evolution in the velocity profile when the motion of the fluid is induced by a boundary and the simulation is performed with two densities.

Table 3. Set-up configuration for the Couette flow test case with two-densities.

Parameter	Value
Total particles	2,277; 5,976; 12,948
Initial inter-particle spacing	$5 \times 10^{-5}, 4 \times 10^{-5}, 2 \times 10^{-5}$ m
Lower density (ρ_1)	1000 kg/m^3
Higher density (ρ_2)	2000 kg/m^3
Viscosity for lower density (μ_1)	0.5×10^{-6} m^2/s
Viscosity for higher density (μ_2)	1×10^{-6} m^2/s

The top plate moves with a constant velocity $V_p = 1x10^{-3}$ m/s in X-direction. The analytical solution for a steady state was presented in [29] and compared here with the results provided by SPH simulations. The analytical solution is

$$v_{\rho 1} = \frac{\mu_1 V_p}{\mu_2 b_1 + \mu_1 b_2} y, \tag{26}$$

$$v_{\rho 2} = \frac{V_p}{\mu_2 b_1 + \mu_1 b_2} (\mu_1 (y - b_1) + \mu_2 b_1), \tag{27}$$

where $b_1 = b_2 = 0.5$ mm and μ_1 and μ_2 are indicated in Table 3.

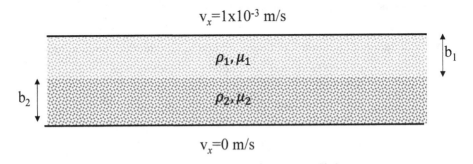

Fig. 3. Initial configuration for the Couette flow with two densities.

Figure 4 shows the comparison between SPH calculations and the analytical solution for the Couette flow with two densities. In this case, the velocity profile at the steady state is not linear as in Fig. 4 due to the different viscosity and density values.

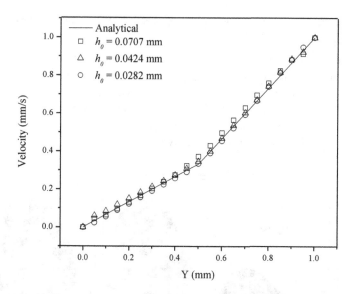

Fig. 4. Numerical and analytical solutions for the Couette test case with two densities.

The agreement between numerical results and the analytical solution for the Couette flow with two densities is good and the accuracy increases with the resolution. The relative error was calculated using Eq. (25). Results from the convergence test are shown in Table 4.

Table 4. Numerical parameters and errors for SPH velocity profiles shown in Fig. 4.

Np	Dp (mm)	h_0 (mm)	%RMSE at the steady state
2,277	0.05	0.0707	10^{-6}
5,976	0.04	0.0424	1.31×10^{-6}
12,948	0.02	0.0282	9.63×10^{-7}

The results of the cases 3.1 and 3.2 prove the good accuracy in multiphase simulations using multiphase model coupling h_{var} and *shifting*.

3.3   Rayleigh-Taylor Instability

The Rayleigh-Taylor instability was numerically studied in [4, 30] and [31]. This test case presents two different challenges, namely, the proper reproduction of the interphase between two different fluids and the reproduction of non–linear effects involved in this evolution case. Thus the Rayleigh-Taylor instability is a perfect case to test the improvement of coupling h_{var} and *shifting* in the multiphase model.

The initial set-up is described here, two fluids are confined in a rectangular container and the interphase between them is set to be at $y = 0.15\sin(2\pi x)$ to create an initial perturbation. In order to be consistent with [30], the gravity acceleration is -1.0 m/s^2. The set-up configuration is summarized in Table 5 and shown in Fig. 5.

Table 5. Set-up configuration for the Rayleigh-Taylor instability test case.

Parameter	Value
Total particles (Np)	20,901; 81,801; 232,601
Initial inter-particle spacing (Dp)	10.0, 5.0, 0.9 mm
Lower density (ρ_1)	1,000 kg/m^3
Higher density (ρ_2)	1,800 kg/m^3
Artificial viscosity for lower density (α_1)	0.05
Artificial viscosity for higher density (α_2)	0.05

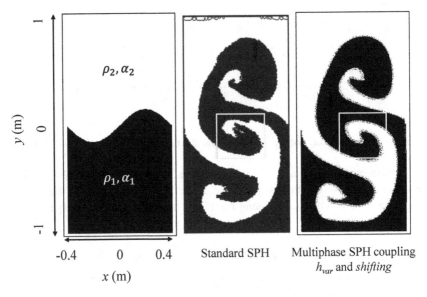

Fig. 5. Rayleigh-Taylor instability simulation. Left: Initial conditions. Middle: simulation with standard SPH. Right: Simulation with multiphase model coupling h_{var} and *shifting*.

A preliminary simulation was carried out with standard SPH, a second simulation was conducted with the multiphase model coupling h_{var} and *shifting*. Then, two numerical results were compared. Figure 5 presents the same instant (t = 5 s) for both simulations.

The general evolution of the system is similar in the both cases, however the definition and shape of the interphase is even better when the h_{var} is coupling with *shifting*, also the void that appear at the top of the simulation (second panel in Fig. 5) are prevented. These simulations show how the SPH model can handle non-linear effects and provide a proper interphase representation. The multiphase model using h_{var} and *shifting* presents better results than those reported by [30] for the Weakly Compressible SPH method and the SPH projection method, in both cases the instability is not totally formed. The reference [4] also reported the Rayleigh-Taylor instability using a simple SPH algorithm for fluids with high density ratios obtaining similar results. However, applying h_{var} and *shifting*, the interphase provides a better definition in zones with high deformation. The reference [31] reported a multiphase model where pressure is continuous at the interphase obtaining similar results.

3.4   Kelvin-Helmholtz Instability

The Kelvin-Helmholtz instability is a good test to probe that the implemented model can simulate instabilities created by the interaction between two fluids, more precisely the shear stress at the interphase. The test was performed in two dimensions using periodic conditions in X direction at $x = -0.5$ cm and $x = 0.5$ cm and limited by dynamic boundary layers proposed by [32] at $y = -0.125$ cm and $y = 0.125$ cm. In this case, the instability was simulated using artificial viscosity applying h_{var} and *shifting*. The set-up configuration is presented in Table 6.

Table 6. Set-up configuration for the Kelvin-Helmholtz instability test case.

Parameter	Value
Total particles	501,501
Initial inter-particle spacing	1.0 mm
Lower density (ρ_1)	1,000 kg/m^3
Higher density (ρ_2)	2,000 kg/m^3
Artificial viscosity for lower density (α_1)	0.05
Artificial viscosity for higher density (α_2)	0.1

The initial velocities in the X direction are 0.5 m/s and -0.5 m/s for ρ_1 and ρ_2, respectively. An initial perturbation at the interphase was set-up using an initial small velocity in the Y direction, $v_y = 0.025 \, sin(-2\pi(x+0.5)/\lambda$, where $\lambda = 1/6$. The initial conditions of the Kelvin-Helmholtz instability test are shown in Fig. 6.

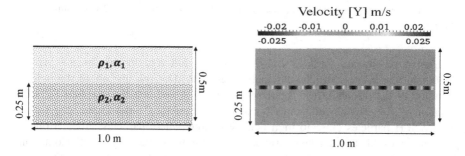

Fig. 6. Initial condition of the Kelvin-Helmholtz instability test. The left panel shows the positions of two fluids with different densities. The right panel shows the initial perturbation in velocity (v_y).

The Kelvin-Helmholtz instability is reproduced using artificial viscosity in standard SPH and the multiphase model, as is shown in the Fig. 7. However, results show

Standard SPH

Multiphase SPH coupling
h_{var} and *shifting*

Fig. 7. Results of the Kelvin-Helmholtz instability test.

particle voids and a strait shape at the interface in simulations with standard SPH. The results improve when h_{var} and *shifting* is applied, which prevents the formation of voids observed in previous simulations and the shape is continuous.

The characteristic growth timescale of the incompressible Kelvin-Helmholtz improve of the shape at the interface can be seen better with a zoom in each eddy of the instability as observed in Fig. 8. Accordingly, multiphase simulations between two fluids is improved when both h_{var} and *shifting* are applied.

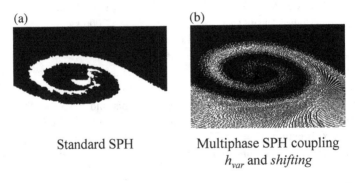

Standard SPH

Multiphase SPH coupling
h_{var} and *shifting*

Fig. 8. Comparison at the interface: (a) standard SPH, and (b) multiphase SPH coupling h_{var} and *shifting*.

Similar results are reported by [33] using a different model for the variable smoothing length and artificial dissipation terms to treat the interphase through the evolution of the discontinuity. Agertz et al. [34] reported that the standard SPH formulation is not capable of properly modelling dynamical instabilities due to low density SPH particles close to high density regions where particles suffer erroneous pressure forces due to the asymmetric density within the smoothing kernel. Comparing the numerical results reported by [33] and [34] with the results obtained with the model presented in this work, the shape of interface between fluids is improve and the internal vortex is formed clearly and in a continuous way. However, the numerical results should be review comparing with an analytical solution. Therefore, in order to establish an analytical value to validate the numerical results, the characteristic onset time of the Instability in the linear regime given by Eq. (28) was used to qualitatively compare the numerical values obtained with SPH

$$\tau = \frac{(\rho_1 + \rho_2)\lambda}{\sqrt{\rho_1\rho_2}|v_2 - v_1|} \tag{28}$$

For the above initial condition values the characteristic time is $\tau = 0.35$ s for $\lambda = 1/6$ m, and the numerical results gives e characteristic onset time $\tau = 0.375$.

3.5 Oil-Water Two Phase Flow in a Pipe

This test shows a very common application in engineering. The simulation is based following the experimental data reported by [35]. This test proves that the multiphase model coupling h_{var} and shifting can simulate the correct flow patterns of two phase oil-water flow in a horizontal pipe. The case was performed in 2D, water and oil are mixed together via a 45° T junction placed at the inlet of the pipe. The overall length and internal diameter of the test section are 2 m and 20 mm, respectively. At first, the flow conditions were determined and oil–water flow was allowed to reach equilibrium. This equilibrium was determined when the fluid velocities are constant, at this time the flow patterns are considered.

Four cases were performed with different inlet values to obtain diverse internal flow patterns in the pipe.

The inlet zone was performed with a constant Poiseuille velocity profile according to the Eq. (29) where v_i is the inlet velocity for each fluid. Inlet velocities of oil are 0.085, 0.25, 0.085 and 0.65 m/s for case 1, 2, 3 and 4 respectively. Inlet velocities of water are 0.16, 0.20, 1.0 and 0.16 m/s for case 1, 2, 3 and 4 respectively. The initial parameters used in the simulations are shown in the Table 7. The geometry and initial conditions are shown in the Fig. 9.

$$v_{inlet} = v_{o(w)}\left(1 - \left(\frac{r}{R}\right)^4\right). \tag{29}$$

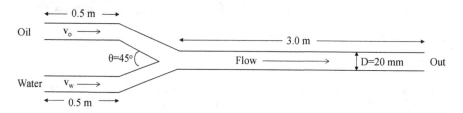

Fig. 9. Geometry and dimensions of the water-oil two phase flow in a pipe case. Water and oil are mixed together via a 45° T junction placed at the inlet of the pipe. The v_o and v_w are the inlet velocities of oil and water respectively.

The relation between superficial velocity and real velocity is $u_{sq} = u_q * \alpha_q$, where u_{sq} is superficial velocity of phase q, u_q is real velocity of phase q, and α_q is void fraction of phase q. Void fraction of phase q is $\alpha_q = A_q/A_{tot}$ where A_q is area of phase q, and A_{tot} is total area in a cross-section of the pipe. Generally, seven different types of flow patterns were observed at horizontal pipe, namely; bubbly, slug, smooth stratified, wavy stratified, churn, annular and dual continuous flow. In this work only the bubbly, smooth stratified, wavy stratified and dual continuous flow are simulated and compared visually with the captured photos of experimental flow patterns in a horizontal pipe reported in [35]. In the Fig. 10 are shown the patterns got by SPH simulations of the cases 1 to 4.

Table 7. Set-up configuration for the water-oil two phase flow in a pipe.

Parameter	Value
Total particles	124,533
Initial inter-particle spacing	0.65 mm
Oil density (ρ_1)	840 kg/m^3
Water density (ρ_2)	998 kg/m^3
Artificial viscosity for oil (α_1)	0.045
Artificial viscosity for water (α_2)	0.01

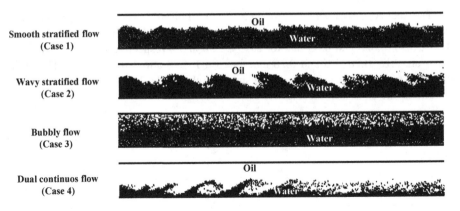

Fig. 10. Flow patterns got by SPH simulations using the multiphase model coupling the h_{var} and shifting.

At low inlet oil and water velocities, smooth stratified flow was identified in numerical results. If then inlet water velocity increases, wavy stratified flow was shaped. At high inlet water velocities stratified flow convert to bubbly flow. Conversely, at high inlet oil velocities, stratified flow converts to dual continuous flow. Patterns and their evolution obtained with SPH are in accordance with the experimental patterns reported by [35] and with the flow pattern maps in the literature [36, 37]. This results prove the application of multiphase model in a popular engineering application getting good fitting between simulation and experiments.

4 Conclusions

In this work, a numerical multiphase model coupling a variable smoothing length and the shifting algorithm based on Smoothed Particle Hydrodynamics (SPH) has been developed and implemented using the DualSPHysics code. The multiphase model implemented in the DualSPHysics code improve the numerical results in the interface between two-fluids for multiphase SPH simulations.

For evaluating the multiphase implementation, several numerical validation test were conducted. The Poiseuille and Couette test cases, for two-fluids with different densities and viscosities were simulated and compared with the analytical solution. Results obtained for the multiphase model implemented in DualSPHysics provide a relative mean square error in the range 9.63×10^{-7} to 3.16×10^{-4}. This result shows that our model that incorporate the shifting algorithm and the variable smoothing length formalism keeps good accuracy as compared with previous studies by [25–27]. The accuracy of our model was evaluated through a convergence test where all validation cases were simulated for three different resolutions. As expected, accuracy clearly increases with resolution.

The root mean square error (RMSE) for the Poiseuille and Couette test cases with two densities are reported in Tables 2 and 4, respectively. The low RMSE error indicates good accuracy of the model for multiphase simulations that are usually affected by the presence of voids close to the areas where the interface is highly deformed. The coupling of the variable smoothing length formalism and the shifting algorithm prevents the creation of voids since it provides a better interface definition while keeping the continuity of the fluid.

The multiphase model coupling the shifting algorithm and the variable smoothing length formalism is able to better represent highly deformed interfaces and non-lineal effects in typical numerical examples of instabilities such as Rayleigh-Taylor and Kelvin-Helmholtz, as compared with other multiphase models reported by [4, 30, 31].

The multiphase model is able to simulate properly the three forces that affect the dispersed phase in two-phase liquid-liquid flow; namely buoyancy, gravity and inertia force. The multiphase model coupling the variable smoothing length formalism and the shifting algorithm is able to generate numerical patterns of two phase flow for different superficial velocity ratios of fluids. Numerical results are comparable with real flows according to the flow pattern maps in the literature.

Acknowledgment. The authors thank the financial support by the Mexican CONACyT, as well as ABACUS: Laboratory of Applied Mathematics and High-Performance Computing of the Mathematics Department of CINVESTAV-IPN. Our institution provided the facilities to accomplish this work. The research leading to these results has received collaboration from the European Union's Horizon 2020 Programme under the ENERXICO Project, grant agreement no 828947 and under the Mexican CONACYT-SENER-Hidrocarburos grant agreement B-S-69926.

References

1. Colagrossi, A., Landrini, M.: Numerical simulation of interfacial flows by smoothed particle hydrodynamics. J. Comput. Phys. **191**, 448–475 (2003)
2. Bonet, J., Lok, T.S.L.: Variational and momentum preservation aspects of SPH formulations. Comput. Methods Appl. Mech. Eng. **180**, 97–115 (1999)
3. Tartakovsky, A., Meakin, P.: Pore scale modeling of immiscible and miscible fluid flows using smoothed particle hydrodynamics. Adv. Water Resour. **29**, 1464–1478 (2006)
4. Monaghan, J.J.: Smoothed particle hydrodynamics. Annu. Rev. Astron. Astr. **30**, 543–574 (1992)
5. Crespo, A.J.C., et al.: DualSPHysics: open-source parallel CFD solver based on Smoothed Particle Hydrodynamics (SPH). Comput. Phys. Comm. **187**, 204–216 (2015)
6. Dominguez, J.M., Crespo, A.J.C., Gómez-Gesteira, M.: Optimization strategies for CPU and GPU implementations of a smoothed particle hydrodynamics method. Comput. Phys. Comm. **184**(3), 617–627 (2013)
7. Monaghan, J.J.: Smoothed particle hydrodynamics. Rep. Prog. Phys. **68**, 1703–1759 (2005)
8. Liu, G.R.: Mesh Free Methods: Moving beyond the Finite Element Method, p. 692. CRC Press (2003)
9. Gómez-Gesteira, M., Rogers, B.D., Dalrymple, R.A., Crespo, A.J.C.: State of the art of classical SPH for free-surface flows. J. Hydrau. Res. **48**, 6–27 (2010). https://doi.org/10.3826/jhr.2010.0012
10. Gómez-Gesteira, M., Rogers, B.D., Crespo, A.J.C., Dalrymple, R.A., Narayanaswamy, M., Domínguez, J.M.: SPHysics—development of a free-surface fluid solver-Part 1: theory and formulations. Comput. Geosci. **48**, 289–299 (2012)
11. Natanson, I.P.: Theory of Functions of a Real Variable. New York Ungar (1960)
12. Monaghan, J.J., Kocharyan, A.: SPH simulation of multi-phase flow. Comput. Phys. Commun. **87**, 225–235 (1995)
13. Wendland, H.: Piecewiese polynomial, positive definite and compactly supported radial functions of minimal degree. Adv. Comput. Math. **4**, 389–396 (1995)
14. Lo, E.Y.M., Shao, S.: Simulation of near-shore solitary wave mechanics by an incompressible SPH method. Appl. Ocean Res. **24**, 275–286 (2002)
15. Gotoh, H., Shibihara, T., Hayashii, M.: Subparticle-scale model for the mps method-Lagrangian flow model for hydraulic engineering. Comput. Fluid Dyn. J. **9**, 339–347 (2001)
16. Dalrymple, R.A., Rogers, B.D.: Numerical modeling of water waves with the SPH method. Coast. Eng. **53**, 141–147 (2006)
17. Monaghan, J.J., Kos, A.: Solitary waves on a Cretan beach. J. Waterw. Port Coast. Ocean Eng. **125**, 145–154 (1999)
18. Sigalotti, L.D.G., Troconis, J., Sira, E., Peña-Polo, F., Klapp, J.: Diffuse-interface modeling of liquid-vapor coexistence in equilibrium drops using smoothed particle hydrodynamics. Phys. Rev. E **90**, 013021 (2014)
19. Hoover, W.G.: Isomorphism linking smooth particles and embedded atoms. Phys. A **260**, 244 (1998)
20. Xu, R., Stansby, P.K., Laurence, D.: Accuracy and stability in incompressible SPH (ISPH) based on the projection method and a new approach. J. Comput. Phys. **228**, 6703–6725 (2009)
21. Sigalotti, L.D.G., López, H., Donoso, A., Sira, E., Klapp, J.: A shock-capturing SPH scheme based on adaptive kernel estimation. J. Comput. Phys. **212**, 124–149 (2006)
22. Sigalotti, L.D.G., López, H.: Adaptive kernel estimation and SPH tensile instability. Comput. Math Appl. **55**, 23–50 (2008)

23. Domínguez, J.M., Crespo, A.J.C., Gómez-Gesteira, M.: Optimization strategies for CPU and GPU implementations of a smoothed particle hydrodynamics method. Comput. Phys. Commun. **184**(3), 617–627 (2013)
24. Mokos, A., Rogers, B.D., Stansby, P.K., Domínguez, J.M.: Multi-phase SPH modelling of violent hydrodynamics on GPUs. Comput. Phys. Commun. **196**, 304–316 (2015). https://doi.org/10.1016/j.cpc.2015.06.020
25. Morris, J.P., Fox, P.J., Zhu, Y.: Modeling low Reynolds number incompressible flows using SPH. J. Comput. Phys. **136**, 214–226 (1997)
26. Sigalotti, L.D.G., Klapp, J., Sira, E., Meleán, Y., Hasmy, A.: SPH simulations of time-dependent Poiseuille flow at low Reynolds numbers. J. Comput. Phys. **191**, 622–638 (2003)
27. Holmes, D.W., Williams, J.R., Tilke, P.: Smooth particle hydrodynamics simulations of low Reynolds number flows through porous media. Int. J. Numer. Anal. Meth. Geomech. **35**, 419–437 (2011)
28. Bird, R.B., Stewart, W.E., Lightfoot, E.N.: Fenómenos de transporte, 2nd edn. Editorial Limusa Wiley (2006)
29. Cengel, Y.A., Cimbala, J.M.: Mecánica de fluidos: fundamentos y aplicaciones, 1 edn. McGraw-Hill (2006)
30. Cummins, S.J., Rudman, M.: An SPH projection method. J. Comput. Phys. **152**, 584–607 (1999)
31. Chen, Z., Zong, Z., Liu, M.B., Zou, L., Li, H.T., Shu, C.: An SPH model for multiphase flows with complex interfaces and large density differences. J. Comput. Phys. **283**, 169–188 (2015)
32. Crespo, A.J.C., Gómez-Gesteira, M., Dalrymple, R.A.: Boundary conditions generated by dynamic particles in SPH methods. Comput. Mater. Continua **5**, 173–184 (2007)
33. Price, D.J.: Modelling discontinuities and Kelvin-Helmholts instabilities in SPH. J. Comput. Phys. **227**, 10040–10057 (2008)
34. Agertz, O., et al.: Fundamental differences between SPH and grid methods. MNRAS **380**, 963–978 (2007)
35. Hanafizadeh, P., Ghanbarzadeh, S., Saidi, M.H.: Visual technique for detection of gas–liquid two-phase flow regime in the airlift pump. J. Pet. Sci. Eng. **75**, 327–335 (2011)
36. Sotgia, G., Tartarini, P., Stalio, E.: Experimental analysis of flow regimes and pressure drop reduction in oil–water mixtures. Int. J. Multiph. Flow **34**, 1161–1174 (2008)
37. Edomwonyi-Out, L.C., Angeli, P.: Pressure drop and holdup predictions inhorizontal oil–water flows for curved and wavy interfaces. J. Chem. Eng. Res. Des. **93**, 55–65 (2014)

A Parallel Implementation for Solving the Fluid and Rigid Body Interaction

C. Samaniego$^{(\boxtimes)}$, G. Houzeaux, and M. Vázquez

Barcelona Supercomputing Center, Barcelona, Spain
cristobal.samaniego@gmail.com

Abstract. This work describes the implementation of a computational system to numerically simulate the interaction between a fluid and a rigid body. This implementation was performed in a distributed memory parallelization context, which makes the process and its description especially challenging.

An embedded boundary approach is proposed to solve the interaction. In such methods, the fluid is discretized using a non body conforming mesh and the boundary of the body is embedded inside this mesh. The force then that the fluid exerts on the rigid solid is determined. And the velocity of the solid is imposed as a Dirichlet boundary condition on the fluid.

The physics of the fluid is described by the incompressible Navier-Stokes equations. These equations are stabilized using a variational multiscale finite element method and solved using a fractional step like scheme at the algebraic level. The incompressible Navier-Stokes solver is a parallel solver based on a master-worker strategy.

The body can have an arbitrary shape and its motion is determined by the Newton-Euler equations. The data of the body is shared by all the subdomains.

1 Introduction

The numerical simulation of the interaction of a fluid and a rigid body in the context of high performance computing is still a challenging subject. Efficiency is tightly interlinked with a careful implementation. In this work, we tackle the problem by means of a new embedded boundary strategy that aims at being both accurate and computationally efficient.

Typically, in an embedded boundary method, the fluid is discretized using a non body-conforming mesh and described in an Eulerian frame of reference. The wet boundary of the body is embedded in this mesh and geometrically tracked by means of a moving polyhedral surface mesh.

The physical behavior of the fluid is mathematically modeled by the incompressible Navier-Stokes equations. The incompressible Navier-Stokes solver we use is a parallel solver based on a master-worker strategy, which can run on thousands of processors. It was implemented inside the Alya System [1], a parallel multiphysics code based on the Finite Element method. For this work, a rigid body solver together with a new embedded boundary interaction algorithm were implemented inside Alya.

M. Torres and J. Klapp (Eds.): ISUM 2019, CCIS 1151, pp. 302–317, 2019.
https://doi.org/10.1007/978-3-030-38043-4_24

For the interaction, on the one hand, the force that the fluid exerts on a body is determined from the residual of the momentum equations. On the other hand, the velocity of the solid is imposed as a Dirichlet boundary condition on the fluid.

To account for the fact that solid nodes can become fluid nodes due to the rigid body movement, we have adopted the FMALE approach [2, 3], which is based on the idea of a virtual movement of the fluid mesh at each time step.

Numerical examples will show that the proposed strategy is able to render very accurate simulations, especially, regarding the behavior of the velocity field on the interface.

The rest of the paper is structured as follows. First of all, some set definitions aiming at elucidating some important data structures used in our implementation are made. The Navier-Stokes solver is then described with some aspects about its parallelization. The rigid body solver is briefly described later. The next section is dedicated to the interaction. Details about the proposed scheme is then given. The performance of the proposed approach is then assessed by means of numerical simulations. The article ends by stating some concluding remarks.

2   Set Definitions

Let the spatial discretization of the continuous problem domain for a typically finite element implementation be defined as a set of elements $E = \{e_1, e_2, ...\}$ and a set of nodes $N = \{n_1, n_2, ...\}$, where each node $n \in N$ is defined by its position inside the problem domain and each element $e \in E$ is defined, for our purposes, by a subset of the set of nodes as $e = \{n_1^e, n_2^e, ...\} \subset N$.

These last definitions allow us to relate any node $n \in N$ with other nodes and elements of the mesh. Let these relations be called as the connectivity of a node n. They can be characterized by the following definitions:

- *Element connectivity of n.* Let $C_{ele}(n)$ denote the set of elements in E directly connected to the node n, the red elements in Fig. 1. Formally,

$$C_{ele}(n) = \{e \in \varepsilon : n \in e\}.$$

- *Node connectivity of n.* Let $C_{nod}(n)$ denote the set of nodes in N directly connected to n, the circles inscribed in squares in Fig. 1. Formally,

$$C_{nod}(n) = \{m \in \mathcal{N} : \exists e \in C_{ele}(n), m \in e\}\setminus\{n\}$$

3   Fluid

The physics of the fluid is described by the incompressible Navier-Stokes equations. Let μ be the viscosity of the fluid, and ρ its density. Let also σ and ε be the stress and the velocity rate of deformation tensors respectively, defined as:

$$\boldsymbol{\sigma} = -p\boldsymbol{I} + 2\mu\varepsilon(\boldsymbol{u}) \quad \text{and} \quad \varepsilon(\boldsymbol{u}) = \frac{1}{2}(\nabla\boldsymbol{u} + \nabla\boldsymbol{u}^t)$$

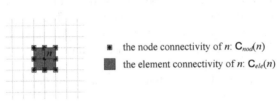

■ the node connectivity of n: $\mathbf{C}_{nod}(n)$

▪ the element connectivity of n: $\mathbf{C}_{ele}(n)$

Fig. 1. Connectivities of node n. (Color figure online)

The problem is then stated as follows. Find the velocity u and mechanical pressure p in a domain Ω such that they satisfy in a time interval $(0, T]$ that

$$\rho\frac{\partial u}{\partial t} + \rho[(\boldsymbol{u} - \boldsymbol{u}_{\mathrm{msh}}) \cdot \nabla]\boldsymbol{u} - \nabla \cdot [2\mu\varepsilon(\boldsymbol{u})] + \nabla p = \rho\boldsymbol{f} \quad \text{in } \Omega \times (0, T] \tag{1}$$

$$\text{and } \nabla \cdot \boldsymbol{u} = 0 \quad \text{in } \Omega \times (0, T] \tag{2}$$

together with initial and boundary conditions.

In the momentum equations, u_{msh} is the velocity of the fluid particles, which basically enables one to go locally from an Eulerian ($u_{\mathrm{msh}} = 0$) to a Lagrangian ($u_{\mathrm{msh}} = u$) description of the fluid motion. The reason of such description has to do with the fact that at some time step of the simulation a set of solid nodes can become fluid nodes due to the rigid body movement. Their fluid velocities will be then not determined. As a solution, we propose to obtain these values considering a hidden movement of the mesh equals to u_{msh} as will be described in Sect. 5.2.

The boundary conditions considered in this work are:

$$u = u_D \quad \text{on } \Gamma_D \times (0, T],$$
$$u = u_S \quad \text{on } \Gamma_S \times (0, T], \text{ and}$$
$$\boldsymbol{\sigma} \cdot \boldsymbol{n} = t \quad \text{on } \Gamma_N \times (0, T],$$

where Γ_D, Γ_S and Γ_N are the boundaries of Ω where Dirichlet, rigid body Dirichlet and Neumann boundary conditions are prescribed respectively, and $\partial\Omega = \Gamma_D \cup \Gamma_S \cup \Gamma_N$. Note that the wet boundary of the solid Γ_S, and the associated prescribed solid surface velocity u_S will change in time.

3.1 Numerical Formulation

The stabilization is based on the Variational MultiScale (VMS) method, see [4]. The formulation is obtained by splitting the unknown into a grid and a subgrid scale components. This method has been introduced in 1995 and sets a remarkable mathematical basis for understanding and developing stabilization methods [5].

The time discretization is based on second order BDF (Backward Differentiation) schemes and the linearization is carried out using the Picard's method. At each time step, the linearized velocity-pressure coupled algebraic system

$$
\begin{bmatrix} \mathbf{A}_{uu} & \mathbf{A}_{up} \\ \mathbf{A}_{pu} & \mathbf{A}_{pp} \end{bmatrix} \begin{bmatrix} \mathbf{u} \\ \mathbf{p} \end{bmatrix} = \begin{bmatrix} \mathbf{b}_u \\ \mathbf{b}_p \end{bmatrix}
$$

must be solved, where u and p are velocity and pressure unknowns. In order to solve efficiently this system on large supercomputers, we consider a split approach, see [6]. That is, we solve for the pressure Schur complement system. In its simplest form, this method can be understood as a fractional step technique. The advantage of this technique is this it leads to two decoupled algebraic systems: one for the velocity and one for the pressure. The Orthomin(1) method, explained in [7], is used to solve the pressure system.

The two algebraic systems resulting from the Orthomin(1) method applied to the pressure Schur complement must be solved. For the momentum equation, the GMRES method is considered. For the pressure system, a Deflated Conjugate Gradient (CG) method [8] with a linelet preconditioning when boundary layers are considered.

3.2 Parallelization

The parallelization is based on a master-worker strategy for distributed memory supercomputers, using MPI as the message-passing library [6, 9]. The master reads the mesh and performs the division of the mesh into mesh subdomains using METIS (an automatic graph partitioner). Each process will then be in charge of a subdomain, the workers. They build then the local element matrices and the local right-hand sides, and are in charge of finding the resulting system solution in parallel. In the elementary assembling tasks, no communication is needed between the workers.

During the execution of the iterative solvers, two main types of communications are required:

- global communications via MPI_AllReduce, to compute residual norms and scalar products and
- blocking point-to-point communications via MPI_Send and MPI_Recv, when matrix-vector products are calculated.

Fluid simulations have been tested on Blue Waters Supercomputer and Jugene Supercomputer with two viscous Navier-Stokes benchmarks, see Fig. 2.

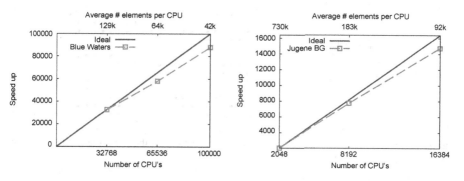

Fig. 2. Speedup of the incompressible Navier-Stokes solver for solving different physical problems.

4 Rigid Solid

The linear acceleration a(t) and angular acceleration α(t) of the body are related with the input force f_F (t) and input torque $\tau_F(t)$ by the Newton-Euler equations

$$f_F(t) = ma(t) \text{ and } \tau_F(t) = I(t) \cdot \alpha(t) + \omega(t) \times (I(t) \cdot \omega(t)), \quad (3)$$

where m is the total mass of the body and $I(t)$ is the inertia tensor. By integrating in time the Eqs. (3), the velocity and the position of the rigid body can be determined.

In general, we use Newmark as method of numerical integration together with the implementation of an iterative method in order to obtain the solution of the nonlinear Euler rotation equation in Eqs. (3).

5 Embedded Boundary Mesh Method

Let Ω_F and Ω_S be the fluid and solid domains. In an embedded boundary mesh method, at the beginning, $\Omega_F \cup \Omega_S$ is discretized without any particular regard to the rigid body. The movement of the boundary describes the movement of the solids inside the fluid. Then, at each time step of the simulation, the program identifies the elements in E, see Sect. 2, whose volumes of intersection with the rigid body domain are big enough to consider them as part of the solid; that is, the elements that belong to the set of hole elements E_{hol}, see Fig. 3 at the left. They are then excluded from the finite element assembly process. Let $\hat{\Gamma}_{S,h}$ be the internal boundary mesh generated in the fluid mesh once the hole elements have been excluded. In Fig. 3 at the left, the bold black line represents $\hat{\Gamma}_{S,h}$. In an embedded boundary mesh method, the velocity of the solid is imposed on the nodes that define $\hat{\Gamma}_{S,h}$. Let this set be called as the set of fringe nodes: N_{fri}. The set N_{fri} allow us to define other important sets of nodes: the set of free N_{fre} and the set of hole nodes N_{hol}. The set of free nodes belongs to the discretized fluid domain and the set of hole nodes belongs to the discretized solid domain, see Fig. 3 at the right. The implementation details of the embedded mesh boundary method described next in this work was previously published in [10, 11].

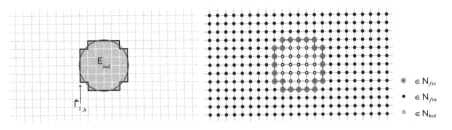

Fig. 3. At the left, the hole elements and $\hat{\Gamma}_{S,h}$ schematization. At the right, the resulting sets of fringe, free, and holes nodes.

The numerical schemes to solve the Navier-Stokes (NS) and the Newton-Euler (NE) equations need information from each other to account for the interaction. On the one hand, the variables that the fluid receives from the rigid body are enumerated below.

- The linear and angular velocities v^{n+1} and w^{n+1} of the rigid body.
- The definition of the internal boundary mesh $\hat{\Gamma}_{S,h}^{n+1}$.
- The total velocity u_s^{n+1} to be imposed on $\hat{\Gamma}_{S,h}^{n+1}$.

On the other hand, the set of variables that the solid requires from the fluid problem are enumerated below.

- The force f_F^{n+1} and torque τ_F^{n+1} that the fluid exerts on the rigid solid.

Taking into account all the coupling variables described above, a new coupling strategy is briefly described in Algorithm 1.

Note that the NS-NE system is a two-way coupled problem. Therefore, Algorithm 1 consists of a staggered approximation of the coupled solution at each time step, as no coupling loop has been introduced and variables Γ_S^{n+1}, u_S^{n+1}, f_F^{n+1}, τ_F^{n+1} are approximations of the actual values at time step $n + 1$. We thus expect the accuracy of the scheme to depend not only on the way the set of coupling variables is defined but also on the time step Δt. Let us now briefly describe the main steps of Algorithm 1.

5.1   Embedded Approach

A high order kriging interpolation algorithm was implemented. The idea is to impose the velocity of the body on each fringe node n_{fri} in an interpolating way. For this purpose, the program first has to consider a convenient subset of the set of free nodes N_{fre} that have a close connectivity with n_{fri}; denoted it as $N_{sel}(n_{fri})$. Then, the program imposes the velocity of the rigid body on the fringe node n_{fri} equation as

---

Algorithm 1 NS-NE Coupling strategy
_____
Initialize the variables
repeat
    1. Determine the time step Δt, see Subsection 5.3.
    2. Solve NE equations to obtain v^{n+1} and w^{n+1}, see Section 4.
    3. Define $\hat{\Gamma}_{S,h}^{n+1}$, which implies to determine $\mathcal{N}_{fri}^{n+1}$, see at the beginning of this section.
    4. Determine u^n and u_{msh}^n applying the FMALE method, see Subsection 5.2.
    5. Embedded approach. Impose u_S^{n+1} on $\mathcal{N}_{fri}^{n+1}$, see Subsection 5.1.
    6. Solve the NS equations to obtain u^{n+1} and p^{n+1}, see Section 3.
    7. Determine f_F^{n+1} and τ_F^{n+1} from u^{n+1} and p^{n+1}, see Subsection 5.4.
until the time of simulation is reached
_____

$$N_{fri}u_{fri} + \sum_{n_i \in \mathcal{N}_{sel}(n_{fri})} N_i u_i = u_S(x_S), \tag{4}$$

where u_i is the velocity of free node n_i, x_S is the projection point of the fringe node on the surface mesh of the body, and $u_S(x_S)$ is the velocity of the body at x_S. N_{fri} and N_i are the interpolation coefficients determined by solving the kriging system matrix.

The whole algorithm can be divided into three consecutive main steps. For each fringe node n in N_{fri} do:

- Select a convenient subset of free nodes that has a close connectivity with n to perform the interpolation: $N_{sel}(n) \subset N_{fre}$.
- Assemble the kriging system matrix to interpolate the body surface velocity. In particular, this velocity will correspond to the solid velocity at the projection point p of n on the body surface. The positions of the free nodes in $N_{sel}(n)$ and p will be used in the assembly.
- Invert the matrix of the kriging system by using the LU decomposition method in order to obtain the interpolation coefficients N_{fri} and N_i of Eq. (4).

Parallel Nodes Selection. The interpolation requires to previously select a subset of the set of free nodes N_{fre} with a close connectivity for each fringe node n. The idea is schematized in Fig. 4.

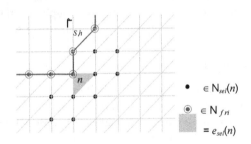

Fig. 4. Illustration of the selection algorithm. The gray square denotes $e_{sel}(n)$, the red concentric circles denote members of the set of fringe nodes, and the black circles are the free nodes that belong to set $N_{sel}(n)$. (Color figure online)

Considering an arbitrary fringe node n, the definition of the set $N_{sel}(n)$ can be carried out in an algorithmic fashion as follows:

- Select a convenient element $e_{sel}(n) \in C_{ele}(n)$, that is $n \in e_{sel}(n)$. In Fig. 4, the gray square denotes $e_{sel}(n)$.
- Then, define the set of nodes used to perform the interpolation as

$$\mathcal{N}_{sel}(n) = \bigcup_{m \in e_{sel}(n)} C_{nod}(m) \cap \mathcal{N}_{fre}$$

In Fig. 4, the black circles represent the free nodes that belong to set $N_{sel}(n)$.

Kriging Interpolation Algorithm. In particular, we use an approximation method known as the universal kriging. The concepts and implementation aspects are detailed in [12].

In the kriging approach, the unknown function $F(x)$ is the sum of a mean value $\mu(x)$ and an error term $\varrho(x)$,

$$F(x) = \mu(x) + \varrho(x),$$

where x is the position vector of the unknown function.

The approximation function $f(x)$ of $F(xt)$ is expressed as a linear combination of the data $\{F(x_i)\}_{i=1,n}$ as

$$f(x) = \sum_{i=1}^{n} N_i(x)F(x_i).$$

The weights N_i are chosen to minimize the squared variance of the error of prediction:

$$\mathrm{Var}(F(x) - f(x))^2 = \mathrm{Var}\left(F(x) - \sum_{i=1}^{n} N_i(x)F(x_i)\right)^2,$$

subject to the unbiasedness condition. This condition states that the mean of the unknown function is equal to the mean of its approximation, that is

$$\mu(x) = \sum_{i=1}^{n} N_i(x)\mu(x_i).$$

Our choice for the mean of the unknown function is a polynomial function. Some implementation aspects are taken from [13].

5.2   FMALE

As mentioned before, the proposed embedded boundary technique identifies a set of free nodes N_{fre}, a set of fringe nodes N_{fri}, and a set of hole nodes N_{hol} at each time step of the simulation. Then, only the nodes in N_{hol} are excluded from the finite element assembly process. Now, consider the nodes in $N_{fre} \cup N_{fri}$ at the current time step t^{n+1} that were hole nodes at the previous time step t^n. They are the new fluid nodes of the simulation at t^{n+1}. These nodes were therefore, for practical purposes, nonexistent at the previous time step. Then, one of the practical problems with these new fluid nodes consists in defining the velocities at the previous time step t^n, which are required by the Navier-Stokes equations to compute the time derivatives.

This problem can be solved by considering a hidden motion of the mesh from t^n to t^{n+1}, which can be explained and formulated using the FMALE framework [14].

In order to illustrate it, let us consider the one-dimensional example shown in Fig. 5. The dotted lines represent the solid body at t^n, which moves to the right, and depicted with continuous lines at t^{n+1}, see Fig. 5 (original mesh.) At time t^n, the fringe node is node n_3 and at time t^{n+1} we end up with a new free node n_4, and a new fringe node n_5. The procedure is described below:

- Prescribe a displacement for the new fringe node n_5 such that at t^n it falls into the fluid, and move it incrementally together with nodes n_3 and n_4. Nodes n_1 and n_2 are assumed to be sufficiently far to remain fixed. The resulting new mesh at t^n* is shown in Fig. 5(b).
- The values of the velocities for the moved nodes n_3, n_4 and n_5 are then interpolated from the solution obtained at time t^n. This interpolation is represented by the vertical arrows between Figs. 5(b) and (a).
- The mesh velocity is then computed from the positions obtained at time t^n* to recover the positions of the nodes on the original mesh t^{n+1}, Figs. 5(b) and (c) for nodes n_3, n_4 and n_5. The nodal mesh velocity is simply $u^i_{msh} = (x^{n+1}_i - x^{n^*}_i)/\Delta t$. The mesh velocity is represented by horizontal arrows.

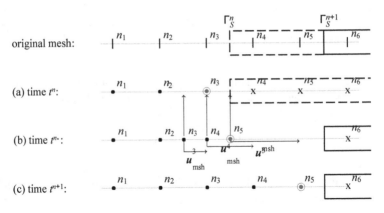

Fig. 5. Illustration of the FMALE framework. The dotted lines represent the body surface mesh at the previous time step t^n and the continuous lines represent the body surface mesh at the current time step t^{n+1}. The red concentric circles denote members of the set of fringe nodes, black circles members of the set of free nodes, and crosses members of the set of hole nodes. The plots (a) and (c) represent the fluid mesh in two consecutive time steps. (Color figure online)

5.3   Time Step ΔT

The strategy for the solid is to determine a time step Δt in such way that for each fringe node n, the set $N_{sel}(n) \neq \emptyset$, see Subsect. 5.1. That is, we have to assure that the kriging interpolation algorithm has enough data in order to impose the velocity of the solid on the fluid mesh for each fringe node n.

To this end, roughly speaking, we require that a rigid body do not cross more than two elements at each time step. Therefore, we define the time step of the NE solver as

$$\Delta t_{NE} = 2 \min_{n_f r_i \in \mathcal{N}_{fri}} \left(\frac{h_{fri}}{|u_{fri}|} \right),$$

where h_{fri} is the minimum edge length that connects n_{fri} with the set of nodes $C_{nod}(n_{fri})$ and u_{fri} is the velocity at n_{fri}.

To control the time accuracy of the NS equations, we use the CFL condition and define

$$\Delta t_{NS} = \alpha \min_{e_{fre} \in \mathcal{E}_{fre}} \left(\frac{4\mu}{\rho h_{fre}^2} + \frac{2|u_{fre}|}{h_{fre}} \right)^{-1},$$

where α is called the safety factor which, for an unconditionally stable implicit scheme, could take in principle a high range of values, depending on the physics of the problem. A typical range is [10, 1000]. One can alternatively prescribe a time step Δt_p which does not rely on the mesh but on the physics of the problem.

Thus, the time step of the simulation is computed as

$$\Delta t = \min(\Delta t_{NE}, \Delta t_{NS}) \text{ or } \Delta t = \min(\Delta t_{NE}, \Delta t_p).$$

5.4   The Force and Torque Exerted on the Solid Surface

In order to solve the Newton-Euler equations for the rigid body, we need the force f_F and the torque τ_F exerted by the fluid on the rigid body. In particular, we use the residual of the momentum equations in order to determine such forces. Considering only the fringe nodes, we can find the force as

$$f_F = \sum_{n_{fri} \in \mathcal{N}_{fri}} \left(b_u - A_{uu} u - A_{up} p \right) \Bigg|_{fri}$$

and the torque as

$$\tau_F = \sum_{n_{fri} \in \mathcal{N}_{fri}} \left(b_u - A_{uu} u - A_{up} p \right) \Bigg|_{fri} \times r_{fri}$$

The advantages of calculating the force in such way rather than other alternatives are detailed in [10].

6 Mass Conservation

To impose the velocity of a rigid body on the fluid by interpolation is a non-conservative strategy. As is shown in [15], the transmission of Dirichlet condition involves the necessity to ensure the conservation of the mass for the rigid body.

Thus, the idea is to obtain new velocities u^*_{fri} for the fringe nodes from the values u_{fri} obtained using a kriging interpolation algorithm by minimizing

$$\int_{\Gamma_S} \left| u^*_{fri} - u_{fri} \right|^2 d\Gamma_{S,h}$$

under the constraint

$$\int_{\Gamma_S} u^*_{fri} \cdot n \, d\Gamma_{S,h} = 0,$$

where $\Gamma_{S,h}$ is the wet boundary mesh of the rigid body and n is the normal vector. The restriction is derived in [15] and allows to conserve the mass going through the solid and therefore that of the whole system.

7 Results

This section is divided into three parts. In the first part, we will tackle a twodimensional test case of a fluid and rigid solid interacting. Its main purpose is to study mesh convergence for the approach described in the previous sections. In the second and third examples, we will solve a set of three-dimensional problems where the solutions can be analytically determined. The geometry is common to all of them. A spherical rigid body is immersed within a fluid. The simulation starts with the body at rest. The velocity of the body increases until the body moves with a constant velocity known as terminal velocity. Different Reynolds numbers will be considered. In the second part, a low Reynolds number will be considered. In the third part, moderate Reynolds numbers will be considered together with various mesh refinements in order to improve the performance of the results.

7.1 Mesh Convergence of a Manufactured Solution

The manufactured solution technique enables one, among other objectives, to easily carry out a mesh convergence of an implemented algorithm. Let us consider the Navier-Stokes operator $L_{NS}(u, p)$ represented by the LHS of Eqs. (1) and (2). Let u_{man} and p_{man} be some given target velocity and pressure, with a desired degree of smoothness. The manufactured solution technique consists in solving $L_{NS}(u, p) = L_{NS}(u_{man}, p_{man})$ together with $u = u_{man}$ as a Dirichlet boundary condition on the whole boundary of the computational domain, and $p = p_{man}$ on a unique node (indeed, when

$\Gamma_N = \emptyset$, the pressure is defined up to a constant and thus should be prescribed some-
where.) We consider the following manufactured solution:

$$u_{man} = [\sin(\pi x - 0.7)\sin(\pi y + 0.2), \cos(\pi x - 0.7)\cos(\pi y + 0.2)] \quad \text{and}$$
$$p_{man} = \sin(x)\cos(y),$$

to be sought in the computational domain depicted in Fig. 6. Note that the manufactured velocity field is divergence free.

We study the convergence of the solution as the mesh is refined. In particular, we
compare the L^2 convergence of our manufactured solution. The mesh convergence is
obtained using a linear and a quadratic kriging interpolations, as shown in Fig. 7. The
solid velocity is interpolated at each fringe node n so that it is equal to the manufactured velocity at the projection point of n on the body surface. We observe that the
convergence graphs for the quadratic kriging interpolation exhibits a quadratic convergence. It is also clear that the linear interpolation gives a linear mesh convergence.

7.2 Stokes Problem

Consider a spherical rigid body of radius $r = 1$ and density $\rho_s = 2$ immersed in fluid
with density $\rho_f = 1$ and viscosity $\mu = 10$. For low Reynolds numbers,

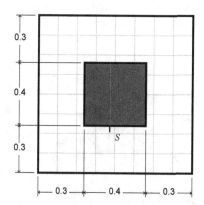

Fig. 6. Problem domain for the manufactured solution.

$Re \ll 1$, where the inertia effects are negligible, as in the problem just stated,
Stokes derived a simple equation to obtain the terminal velocity of a sphere:

$$v_s = \frac{2(\rho_s - \rho_f)r^2 g}{9\mu} = -0.222,$$

where g is the modulus of the gravity.

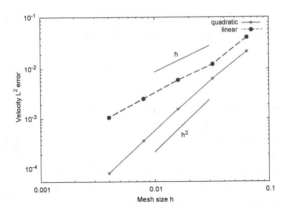

Fig. 7. Mesh convergence of the velocity field for the linear and quadratic kriging interpolations.

The geometry of the fluid domain is a cylinder with height equal to 60 and radius equal to 30. The initial position of the sphere is at 30 times the body radius from the sides of the cylinder and at 40 times the body radius from the bottom of the cylinder. The mesh is unstructured and composed of 400.000 tetrahedral elements. In Fig. 8, we can see the interior of the mesh, where the red elements represent the sphere inside the fluid mesh at the beginning of the simulation.

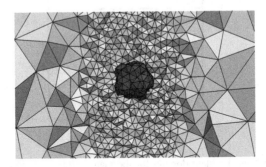

Fig. 8. Initial position of the sphere in the interior of the mesh. (Color figure online)

In Fig. 9, the terminal velocity is compared with the analytical solution. Clearly, the velocity tends to the analytical solution.

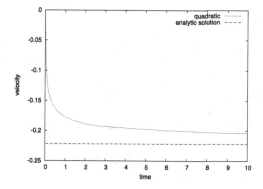

Fig. 9. Numerical and analytical Stokes terminal velocity for Re = 0.004.

7.3 Problems with Moderate Reynolds Numbers

Now, let us consider higher Reynolds numbers to solve the problem stated above. Also, a mesh refinement is carry out in order to improve the performance of the numerical results in order to reach the analytic ones. The details of how the analytic solution can be determined can be found in [16].

In Fig. 10, the difference between the velocities obtained with our approach and the analytic results becomes shorter and shorter as the mesh is refined. In particular, we use three different meshes of 400000, 3 million, and 23 million elements.

The solution reached is specially improved for the flow with a Reynolds number of 1647, as shown in Fig. 10 at the right. We start with a difference with respect to the analytic solution of 39.4% to finally obtain a difference of 13.5%. For the flow with a Reynolds number of 101 we have an initial difference of 21.6% and a final one of 7.6%.

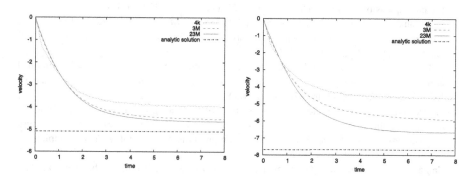

Fig. 10. Numerical and analytical terminal velocities for Re = 101, at the left, and Re = 1647, at the right, using different meshes considering only the quadratic kriging interpolation.

8 Conclusions

A non body-fitted approach to deal with the interaction of a fluid and a rigid body has been presented. It uses kriging as an interpolation method to impose the velocity of the rigid body on the fluid. A FMALE framework is considered in order to deal with the new fluid nodes appearing at each time step. Also, mass conservation is imposed by solving a minimization problem under a mass conservation constraint.

The approach has been tested by using numerical experiments and its accuracy has been studied. It is capable of closely reproducing the final velocity of the Stokes problem and other problems with moderate Reynolds numbers. In a general sense, the approach gives reasonably accurate results.

References

1. Owen, H., Houzeaux, G., Samaniego, C., Lesage, A.C., Vázquez, M.: Recent ship hydrodynamics developments in the parallel two-fluid flow solver alya. Comput. Fluids **80**, 168–177 (2013)
2. Codina, R., Houzeaux, G., Coppola-Owen, H., Baiges, J.: The fixed-mesh ale approach for the numerical approximation of flows in moving domains. J. Comput. Phys. **228**(5), 1591–1611 (2009)
3. Baiges, J., Codina, R., Owen, H.: The fixed-mesh ale approach for the numerical simulation of floating solids. Int. J. Numer. Methods Fluids **67**(8), 1004–1023 (2011)
4. Houzeaux, G., Príncipe, J.: A variational subgrid scale model for transient incompressible flows. Int. J. Comput. Fluid Dyn. **22**(3), 135–152 (2008)
5. Hughes, T.J.R.: Multiscale phenomena: Green's functions, the Dirichlet-to-Neumann formulation, subgrid scale models, bubbles and the origins of stabilized methods. Comput. Methods Appl. Mech. Eng. **127**, 387–401 (1995)
6. Houzeaux, G., Vázquez, M., Aubry, R., Cela, J.: A massively parallel fractional step solver for incompressible flows. J. Comput. Phys. **228**(17), 6316–6332 (2009)
7. Houzeaux, G., Aubry, R., Vázquez, M.: Extension of fractional step techniques for incompressible flows: the preconditioned orthomin(1) for the pressure schur complement. Comput. Fluids **44**, 297–313 (2011)
8. Löhner, R., Mut, F., Cebral, J.R., Aubry, R., Houzeaux, G.: Deflated preconditioned conjugate gradient solvers for the pressure-poisson equation: extensions and im- provements. Int. J. Numer. Methods Eng. **87**, 2–14 (2011)
9. Houzeaux, G., et al.: Developments in parallel, distributed, grid and cloud computing for engineering. In: Computational Science, Engineering and Technology Series, Saxe-Coburg Publications, 2013, Chapter 8: A Parallel Incompressible Navier-Stokes Solver: Implementation Issues, vol. 31, pp. 171–201 (2013)
10. Samaniego, C., Houzeaux, G., Samaniego, E., Vázquez, M.: Parallel embedded boundary methods for fluid and rigid-body interaction. Comput. Methods Appl. Mech. Eng. **290**, 387–419 (2015)
11. Houzeaux, G., Samaniego, C., Calmet, H., Aubry, R., Vázquez, M., Rem, P.: Simulation of magnetic fluid applied to plastic sorting. Open Waste Manage. J. **3**, 127–138 (2010)
12. Deutsch, C.V.: Geostatistical Reservoir Modeling. Oxford University Press, New York (2002)

13. Le Roux, D.Y., Lin, C.A., Staniforth, A.: An accurate interpolating scheme for semi-Lagragian advection on an unstructured mesh for ocean modelling. Tellus **49**, 119–138 (1997)
14. Houzeaux, G., Codina, R.: Finite element modeling of the lost foam casting process tackling back-pressure effects. Int. J. Heat Fluid Flow **16**(5), 573–589 (2005)
15. Houzeaux, G., Codina, R.: Transmission conditions with constraints in finite element domain decomposition method for flow problems. Commun. Numer. Methods Eng. **17**, 179–190 (2001)
16. Brown, P.P., Lawler, D.F.: Sphere drag and settling velocity revisited. J. Environ. Eng. **129**(3), 222–231 (2003)

Parallel High-Performance Computing Algorithm to Generate FEM-Compliant Volumetric Mesh Representations of Biomolecules at Atomic Scale

Jorge López[1]($\boxtimes$), Salvador Botello[1], Rafael Herrera[1],
and Mauricio Carrillo-Tripp[2]

[1] Center for Research in Mathematics, A.C.,
Computational Sciences Department, Jalisco S/N, Col. Valenciana,
36023 Guanajuato, Gto, Mexico
{jorge.lopez,botello,rherrera}@cimat.mx
[2] Biomolecular Diversity Laboratory, Centro de Investigación y de Estudios
Avanzados del Instituto Politecnico Nacional Unidad Monterrey, Vía del
Conocimiento 201, Parque PIIT, 66600 Apodaca, Nuevo León, Mexico
mauricio.carrillo@cinvestav.mx

Abstract. The computational study of biomolecules has been undermined by the lack of models that accurately represent the structure of big complexes at the atomic level. In this work, we report the development of an algorithm to generate a volumetric mesh of a biomolecule, of any size and shape, based on its atomic structure. Our mesh generation tool leverages the octree algorithm properties with parallel high-performance computing techniques to produce a discretized hexahedral model faster than previous methods. The reported algorithm is memory efficient and generates volumetric meshes suitable to be used directly in Finite Element Analysis. We tested the algorithm by producing mesh models of different biomolecule types and complex size, and also performed numerical simulations for the largest case. The Finite Element results show that our mesh models reproduce experimental data.

Keywords: Biomolecule · Parallel computing · Bitwise · Mesh · Octree · FEM · HPC

1 Introduction

A derivation of the central tenet of Molecular Biology states that the structure of a biomolecule determines its function. Many syndromes and diseases are caused by the incorrect structuring of a certain biomolecule. Hence, efforts have been made to study the structure of biomolecules, their physicochemical properties, and the effect of changes in their structure on their function. In particular, there are many studies based on computational methods that try to explain the molecular mechanisms governing cellular processes. Even though there has been progress in our understanding of how these biological systems work, current molecular *all-atom* models have come short when the studied system is of considerable size ($>10^5$ atoms).

© Springer Nature Switzerland AG 2019
M. Torres and J. Klapp (Eds.): ISUM 2019, CCIS 1151, pp. 318–333, 2019.
https://doi.org/10.1007/978-3-030-38043-4_25

Molecular *coarse-grain* models were introduced to allow the study of larger complexes (a group of two or more associated biomolecules). Nevertheless, these models also have upper limits given by the current computational technologies. It is desirable to come up with a computational model that, keeping an atomic representation, can describe very large biological systems, e.g., a virus, a cellular organelle (a specialized subunit within a cell that has a specific function), or even the whole cell.

Volumetric meshes are a potential candidate to overcome such a problem. Not only do they give an atomic-level description of a large system, but they are also compatible with numerical methods (e.g. the Finite Element Method or FEM) in order to perform simulations of a certain biophysical process. However, the generation of a volumetric mesh of *good quality* is not an easy task. Several factors have to be taken into account, namely, shape of the mesh elements, their size distribution, regularity, etc.

In this work, we describe the development of an algorithm designed to discretize the volume occupied by all the atoms of a given biomolecule or biocomplex. The discretization process generates an approximation to the original biosystem through space decomposition combined with parallel and highperformance computing techniques. This approach makes efficient use of memory, and the multi-platform multi-processing implementation reduces the execution time by several orders of magnitude in comparison to previous developments. The output is a volumetric mesh suitable for FEM analysis.

We applied the algorithm to generate a volumetric mesh of representative examples of all major categories of molecules relevant to biological systems. These categories are *carbohydrates*, *lipids*, *nucleic acids*, and *amino acids*. The specific systems chosen for our study are described in Table 1 and illustrated in Fig. 1. Given its importance in life as an organic solvent, bulk water in liquid state was also included. In this study, we have been careful to consider a large diversity of biomolecules regarding their size, shape, and function.

Table 1. Major categories of biomolecules considered in this study. Two representative systems were chosen in each case, either a single molecule or a complex, plus water. Number of atoms and characteristic size are shown.

Category	Name	Atoms	diameter	Å
Carbohydrate	(A) cellulose	43	12	
	(B) glycogen	87	16	
Lipid	(C) phospholipid	50	27	
	(D) membrane patch	3200	60	
Nucleic acid	(E) DNA	902	80	
	(F) tRNA	1652	90	
Amino acid	(G) transcription factor	3802	110	
	(H) viral capsid	227040	288	
Solvent	(I) water	10583	60	

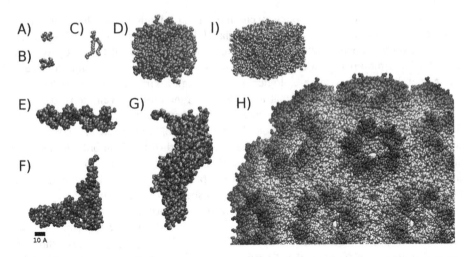

Fig. 1. Biomolecules considered in this study: (A) cellulose, (B) glycogen, (C) phospholipid, (D) small section of a biomembrane (64 phospholipids), (E) DNA (22 nt long), (F) tRNA, (G) transcription factor, (H) icosahedral viral capsid, (H) 1×10^{-19} ml of bulk liquid water. In all the cases, except for the viral capsid, colors correspond to the element type: Carbon in cyan, Hydrogen in white, Oxygen in red, and Nitrogen in blue. All biomolecules shown in the same scale. (Color figure online)

Furthermore, in order to test the compatibility of the mesh generator with FEM, we carried out numerical simulations of nanoindentation on the viral capsid. There are experimental results of Atomic Force Microscopy (AFM) where the authors *squeeze* the capsid while measuring the applied force and the produced deformation on the complex structure [Arkhipov2009, Roos2010, Michel2006]. We estimated the Young's modulus for the capsid by using the spring constant derived from the experimental force-indentation profile in the linear regime. We show that our model is able to reproduce experimental results and is in agreement with previous models.

2 Meshing

The state of the art in meshing techniques-methods can be summarized in three categories: Advancing Front (ADF), Delaunay Triangulation (DT), and Space Decomposition (SD). Each meshing technique presents advantages and drawbacks, so it is important to choose the correct technique in order to produce a mesh compliant for an accurate and fast FEM analysis. This work is focused on a particular SD method given by an octree algorithm due to its advantages in managing computational and memory complexity.

2.1 Delaunay Triangulation

This technique tackles the mesh generation problem by performing efficient geometric operations hence improving computation time. DT has been widely studied [Paul1990, Pascal2008, Siu2013, Paul1998]. DT methods are highly regarded by researchers and engineers since numerical methods for solving PDE models of real life problems require high quality triangulations. DT generates good 2D meshes. However, it presents a significant drawback in 3D, namely, it may generate elements with null volume that comply with the Delaunay properties. Some implementations try to solve this problem by relaxing the Delaunay condition [Paul1990].

DT takes a set of points P and creates a triangulated mesh called the convex hull [Pascal2008, Siu2013]. This mesh can be used to perform numerical simulations, but if some elements have a volume close to zero, the stability and accuracy of the numerical solution is affected. Thus, some modifications may be needed, such as removing collapsed elements and refining the mesh to improve the quality of the mesh. The method's main advantages are its high speed and robustness. On the other hand, the main drawback is that it does not preserve the meshing domain. Other algorithms can be applied to circumvent this problem but with the cost of losing efficiency and increasing computation time [Weatherill1992]. Also, it is difficult to parallelize this technique because the creation of elements requires the information of all the triangles contained in its circumscribing circle, causing concurrency problems. Nevertheless, some parallel implementations have been reported [Hardwick1997, Cigoni1993].

2.2 Advancing Front

This approach starts on the boundary and inserts new points inside the domain. These points are used to create triangles in 2D or tetrahedrons in 3D, but they can also be used to create quadrilateral or hexahedral elements by slight modifications. A well-known mesher based on ADF is NETGEN [Schöber1997]. It is customizable in the sense that the user sets parameters to determine the mesh size and the optimization steps to apply on the generated mesh. ADF consumes more time than other techniques due to its complexity. It could be said that this meshing technique generates triangles which are almost equilateral because of the tests performed before it creates a new element. This technique is based on local operations and, as a consequence, it is highly parallelizable.

2.3 Space Decomposition

A remarkable feature of the SD methods is the creation of meshes with acceptable quality in a short time using highly parallelizable methods. Thus, SD is widely used by researchers that use FEM in their work. Broadly speaking, there are two types of SD methods that create FEM-suitable meshes. One is the *bin method*, and the other one is the *octree technique*. Both are based on performing bisections over different dimensions depending on a maximum level of refinement determined by the user. Although these algorithms look the same, the octree technique performs bisections based on the domain to be meshed, whereas the bin technique divides the bounding box on cells of the same size over each dimension which causes excessive memory requirements. In octree, cells are represented as binary numbers, decreasing memory requirements and allowing to move through the tree by bitwise operations, thus accelerating search operations in contrast with other techniques. The octree algorithm can be used to easily generate tetrahedral or hexahedral meshes, unlike other techniques that need to be modified in either case.

One of the main drawbacks of SD techniques is the inability to preserve corners, usually known as sharp features, because the octree is based on quadrilateral elements. Complex domains cannot be well-fitted with these geometric forms. The problem can be tackled by performing some modifications on boundary elements to achieve the best possible approximation to the original domain. The main advantage of this method is that meshes can be created for most domains due to the spacial adaptability of the method. Another advantage is the possibility to develop efficient parallel implementations which lead to the fast generation of high quality meshes. Since all the mesh elements are equal, there are improvements in the numerical solutions.

Remark. The three techniques perform similar operations. For instance, DT and SD require a ray casting technique that can be carried out using computer graphic strategies. This could lead to an inefficient algorithm. However, since the octree nodes are aligned, the ray casting technique can be implemented taking advantage of its structure. Also, the three meshing techniques need to perform geometric tests in order to create the best possible triangulation. While SD methods have control over all the objects contained in the working space, the DT and ADF methods have difficulties controlling objects inside the domain. Furthermore, the number of geometric tests in SD is reduced due to its local operation.

3   Octree Mesher

The octree is an SD method which must be used in a delimited space. The overall efficiency of the algorithm can be increased considerably when the space is defined correctly. The best option is to work on a normalized domain such as the square $[0, 1] \times [0, 1]$ in 2D, or the cube $[0, 1] \times [0, 1] \times [0, 1]$ in 3D.

The first step is to scale the object Ω we wish to mesh to fit into the square or the cube, whose boundary is the bounding box (see Fig. 2). The next step is to subdivide the box progressively in order to choose only the smaller boxes (octree cells) that intersect Ω, and thus obtain a volume made up of small octree cells that closely approximates Ω.

The subdivision generates children from a given parent cell (see Fig. 2(b)). Cells to be bisectioned are selected based on some intersection tests. The traditional octree method performs intersection tests between cells and triangles.

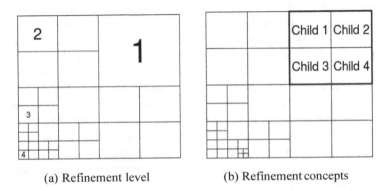

(a) Refinement level   (b) Refinement concepts

Fig. 2. Refinements generalities

The way to perform the test efficiently is by using computer graphics strategies which considerably reduce the calculation time. The octree subdivision generates octree cells with different sizes that are associated to the concept of *refinement level*. In Fig. 2(a) there are red numbers indicating the refinement level of each cell. The bounding box is considered as a zero refinement cell.

The octree can be used either to generate hexahedral or tetrahedral meshes. In order to create the tetrahedral meshes, it is required to accomplish the constraint 2:1, i.e., for each cell, all its neighbors in all directions must have a difference of at most one level of refinement. For example, the green square in Fig. 2(b) shows a cell which fulfills the constraint. On the other hand, the red cell does not fulfills the constraint because the right neighbor has two refinements levels below the tested cell. However, in our implementation, the constraint is not required because all the elements of the generated hexahedral meshes are of the same size.

The purpose of scaling Ω to the normalized square or box is to encode the order of the octree cells in binary numbers. This allows us to move through the complete octree using bitwise operations, which is faster than traditional arithmetic operations. This is, in fact, the main HPC feature of octree that reduces computing time, although its implementation may be challenging. The binary implementation to manage octree cells is based on a work previously reported [Frisken2002]. In that work, the authors explain how to move through the octree by binary codding and neighbour cells. In order to achieve a domain decomposition, the octree must be bisectioned.

Figure 3 shows how to work with the bisections and binary coding using a simplified 1D example. Panel 3(a) shows the root or initial line segment. This line lies in the domain [0, 1] and has the binary coding shown on top. The first bi-section generates what is shown in panel 3(b), where two segments have been created and two binary

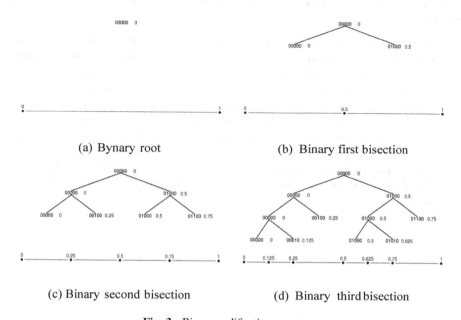

Fig. 3. Binary codification on octree

numbers represent them. Panel 3(c) shows one more partition. Here, there are four segments and their corresponding binary codes. Finally, adding two more bisections, as in panel 3(d), six line segments are generated, each one with a binary number associated to it (blue numbers). It is easy to convert from binary to decimal by using the line segment refinement level and binary codding.

The selection of cells belonging to the final mesh is naturally achieved during subdivision of the octree, keeping the elements that intersect Ω as the final mesh. The octree cells that become part of the final mesh must fulfill the following features:

- Two distinct elements must not overlap.
- In 2D, an edge is only shared by two adjacent elements. In 3D, a face is only shared by two adjacent elements.
- The elements must be positively oriented (correct node labeling in FEM).

The final step is to return Ω to its original scale together with the selected octree cells.

The time reduction when using the octree mesher is achieved by using parallel computing in some of the operations, as well as the use of some HPC techniques (binary codification). Using the parallel scheme, meshes are generated in one computer by using, concurrently, several cores. However, if the computer has a processor with more than one core and all the cores share the same RAM, all of them can modify the same variables at the same time. This must be avoided since it could lead to erroneous results or low parallel performance. Nevertheless, OpenMP is a paradigm suited for high-level parallelization in a simple manner with a low number of preprocessor instructions (shared memory parallel scheme [OpenMP2018]). In this work, our goal is to parallelize the implementation to achieve high efficiency. Hence, we must take care of concurrent operations and data synchronizations. Some of the parallel operations we propose are:

- **Octree refinement:** Since they are independent, several cells can be refined at the same time by using as many cores as available. This means that for every refinement level in the octree, all the cells can be subdivided into eight children without affecting cells in other levels. Details are described in Algorithm 1.
- **Cells nodes setting:** This operation adds all the coordinates to the octree cells. This operation is parallelized due to the independence of the information added on each cell, it is well controlled through the binary coding used in the cell nodes. See parallel loop on algorithm 2.
- **Intersection tests:** The independence of the cells means that various cells can be tested for intersection with spheres at the same time. The parallel loop is shown on algorithm 3.

Algorithm 1 Parallel Refinement

Require: $root, \Omega, r_{level}$
1: **for** i in $0, 1, ..., r_{level}$ **do**
2:     Get all octree leaves from $root$
3:     PARALLEL LOOP
4:     **for** j in $0, 1, ..., n_{leaves}$ **do**
5:         **if** j_{leaf} intersects Ω **then**
6:             Subdivide j_{leaf}
7:             Translate objects to sons
8:         **end if**
9:     **end for**
10: **end for**
11: **return** $root$ subdivided until r_{level}

Algorithm 2 Parallel nodes setting

Require: leaves from $root$
1: PARALLEL LOOP
2: **for** i in $0, 1, ..., n_{leaves}$ **do**
3:     Set coordinates on leaf i_{leaf}
4: **end for**

These parallel operations are used in our octree mesher. The input of the algorithm is a set of atoms forming a given biomolecule. Each atom is represented by a sphere, with the coordinates of its center and a type-specific radius. More details of the biomolecule meshing process are provided on the next sections.

Algorithm 3 Parallel intersection test

Require: $root, \Omega$
1: Get all octree leaves from $root$
2: PARALLEL LOOP
3: **for** i in $0, 1, ..., n_{leaves}$ **do**
4:     **for** j in $0, 1, ..., n_{objects}$ on Ω **do**
5:         **if** i_{leaf} intersects Ω_j **then**
6:             Set i_{leaf} as intersected
7:         **end if**
8:     **end for**
9: **end for**

3.1 Intersection Test for Meshing

In general, biomolecules are represented by clustered sets of spheres, one for each atom present. Thus, the intersection test of the octree method was modified to reduce the execution time. The algorithm only processes the spheres contained in the cell that is being subdivided, so the total number of intersection tests is reduced and, as a consequence, the total meshing time. It might seem that Algorithm 3 has concurrency problems because of the loop beginning on line 4. However, this does not happen because each core makes a copy of the Ω_j object. The data on memory is not modified.

One more advantage of our proposed mesher for biomolecules is that all the elements in the resulting mesh have the same shape and size and are FEM- compliant. This implies that the solution of any structural analysis through numerical methods will be carried out in an efficient way, saving memory and computing time.

3.2 Biomolecules

The meshing strategy we describe here can process biomolecules of any size and shape, even non-symmetrical structures, thus constituting an improvement over our previously reported methodology [Alonzo2018]. An example of the progressive enhancement in atomic detail achieved by increasing the mesh resolution is shown in Fig. 4 for the cellulose molecule. Higher resolution gives more detail on the shape of the molecule. We generated a mesh for all the biomolecules in the data set described earlier. Results are shown in Fig. 5 and their characteristics are given in Table 2. The mesh resolution is different for each biomolecule due to their different sizes.

The biggest biomolecule considered here, based on the number of atoms, is a viral capsid containing more than 200,000 atoms. In this case, the mesher performs the highest number of intersection tests, which grow for higher mesh resolutions, to

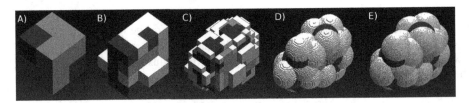

Fig. 4. Cellulose octree mesh generated using different resolutions: (A) 6.0 Å, (B) 3.0 Å, (C) 1.0 Å, (D) 0.1 Å, (E) 0.03 Å. The colors correspond to the atom type: Carbon in cyan, Hydrogen in white, and Oxygen in red. (Color figure online)

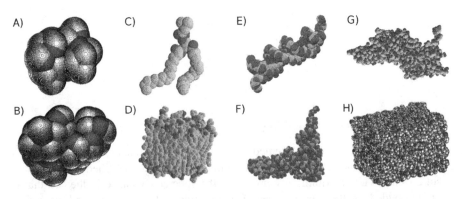

Fig. 5. Octree mesh representation of biomolecules considered in this study. (A) Cellulose, (B) glycogen, (C) phospholipid, (D) biomembrane patch (64 phospholipids), (E) DNA (22 nt long), (F) tRNA, (G) transcription factor, (H) 1×10^{-19} ml of bulk liquid water. The colors correspond to the atom type: Carbon in cyan, Hydrogen in white, Oxygen in red, and Nitrogen in blue. Not in the same scale. (Color figure online)

Table 2. Octree mesh features for the biomolecules considered in this study. Mesh resolution given in Å

Category	Name	Mesh resolution	Mesh elements	Time (s)
Carbohydrate	(A) cellulose	0.0375	8,862,661	200.92
	(B) glycogen	0.0450	9,069,479	220.12
Lipid	(C) phospholipid	0.0460	4,672,597	106.06
	(D) membrane	0.2250	3,934,749	95.74
Nucleic acid	(E) DNA	0.1300	8,790,359	246.40
	(F) tRNA	0.1530	4,973,299	122.32
Amino acid	(G) transcription factor	0.2100	5,272,603	133.26
	(H) viral capsid	5.0000	4,709,364	114.83
Solvent	(I) water	0.2400	6,405,468	160.16

generate a good representation. Since it is the extreme case in our dataset and there are FEM-analysis results previously reported using other meshers, in the following sections we focus on the capsid. We explain some generalities of the viral capsid and the simulations performed on it. The numerical simulations take the hexahedral mesh generated by the octree mesher and uses the Finite Element Method to produce a deformation when applying a force on the capsid. The results are then compared to experimental measurements.

4   Application of the Octree Mesher to a Viral Capsid

The protein shell encapsulating the genome material of a virus is known as its *capsid*. Its fundamental functions are the protection and transport of the viral genome, as well as helping recognize the host cell. Detailed knowledge about the physical properties that characterize the viral capsid have proved to be very important in structural biology, biotechnology, and medicine. On the one hand, the analysis of virus nanoindentation by AFM has been used as the standard way to study the mechanical response of capsids as well as to understand their molecular structure. On the other hand, numerical simulations of the nanoindentation process have allowed the estimation of physical parameters such as the Young's modulus. Various descriptions of this type of macromolecular complexes have been proposed at different scales for their study. Given the complexity of the viral capsid, most of the capsid meshers previously reported use a sphere as an approximation to an icosahedral capsid. Hence, they do not keep the internal structural features like tunnels and cavities. However, because the octree mesher does not make such approximations, the generated mesh is faithful to the true molecular shape.

4.1   Capsid Meshers

Only a few works address the problem of meshing a capsid to be used in numerical simulations, mainly due to their large size and geometrical complexity. In [Sanner1996], the authors present a surface meshing algorithm for the molecular complex. This algorithm was one of the first to avoid the self intersecting problem when the surface mesh was created. In [Yu2008], the authors introduced a new approach that could generate the surface and the volumentric mesh of a capsid, tackling for the first time "feature preservation". This algorithm generated quality meshes in a considerable amount of time. In [Cheng2009], the DT strategy was used to create surface meshes with thousands of elements in minutes. A recent proposal was focused on volumetric mesh generation, as opposed to surface mesh generation [Alonzo2018]. A volumetric mesh of the capsid was created using symmetry features, meshing a small geometric unit and rotating many copies to generate the full capsid. The main computational drawback of that method is the need to delete repeated overlapping nodes, which implies a cost increase for the creation of high resolution meshes. In contrast, octree mesh avoids such drawback by processing the full capsid in one step.

4.2   Nanoindentation

In an AFM experiment, the relation between the magnitude of an applied force and the capsid's indentation (biocomplex deformation) can be measured. As a result, a characteristic force-indentation graph is recorded. The slope of the curve in the linear regime is related to the capsid's spring constant.

The numerical simulation of an AFM experiment consists in aligning a particular capsid's symmetry axis with an applied force load (Fig. 6). Such force is directed over the top of the mesh, while the bottom is fixed on a base. We used the FEMT open source code [Vargas2012] to carry out the numerical simulation.

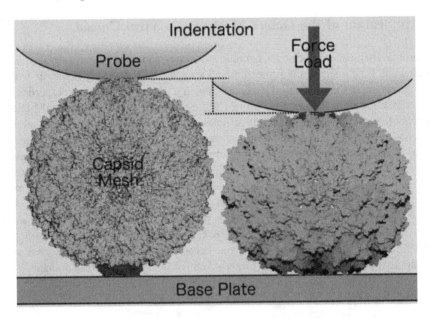

Fig. 6. Capsid nanoindentation simulation. Left: Initial conditions, where the mesh elements in blue are in direct contact to a base, and mesh elements in yellow are in direct contact with a probe. Right: A force load is applied on a given capsid's symmetry axis. The mesh deformation is quantified by the indentation produced (displacement measured in each mesh element). The color scale used represents minimum displacement in blue and maximum displacement in red. (Color figure online)

4.3   Numerical Simulations of Nanoindentation

Table 3 contains the information of nanoindentation and the force needed to produce it. The simulations were carried out using the same material properties and meshes of similar resolution.

The simulations results obtained with our octree mesh are comparable with the results obtained with the meshes of the CapsidMesh methodology, with the advantage of having a reduction in mesh generation time of more than 90%.

Table 3. Nanoindentation of a wild type empty capsid and mechanical properties of Cowpea chlorotic mottle virus (CCMV), using a mesh resolution of 1 Å. Shown: geometrical protein arrangement T, diameter d, capsid width w, nanoindentation I, displacement produced on simulation $disp$, Young's modulus used E, and experimental spring constant k_{exp} [Michel2006].

Mesher	Capsid name	T number	d Å	w Å	I Å	$Disp$ Å	E GPa	k_{exp} N/m
CapsidMesh	CCMV	3	288	50	46	3.9951	1.0	0.15
Octree	CCMV	3	288	50	46	3.8793	1.0	0.15

A summary of the results are shown in Table 3. The first column indicates the mesher used in the experiment, second column is the biocomplex name, T indicates the geometrical protein arrangement, d is the biocomplex diameter, w is the capsid width (outer radius minus inner radius), nanoindentation I (16% of d), $disp$ is the displacement produced after apply a force of 1 nN over 5-fold axis of capsid, Young's modulus E used in the simulation, and experimental spring constant k_{exp} [Michel2006]. In the results the displacement produced by both algorithms is equivalent considering that FEM simulations naturally generate numerical error.

We carried out numerical simulations of the nanoindentation of the viral capsid in our dataset using the volumetric mesh generated by the octree space decomposition method. The quality of the mesh produced by the algorithm reported here is validated by reproducing the nanoindentation simulations results presented in [Alonzo2018]. Results are shown in Fig. 7. The indentation, which is the maximum deformation produced on the mesh by the applied force as a function of mesh resolution, shows that both meshes respond almost identically. This implies that independently of the mesh generation strategy tested here, the FEM simulation produces the same deformation on the capsid mesh. This behaviour is the same in all values of mesh resolution. The stress analysis, measured by the von Misses, shows some differences in intermediate resolution values (2–5 Å), probably due to the shape of the mesh elements and the difference in the cavity shapes that are naturally present with these topologically faithful meshing methods. The CapsidMesh algorithm generates FEM elements with radial symmetry while the octree generates elements aligned to a canonical axis.

The most contrasting result is the meshing computing time. A significant difference is obtained between the two algorithms in terms of this measure. The CapsidMesh processing time tends to increase exponentially when the mesh resolution is increased (lower values) while the octree execution time increases linearly. The efficient and parallel implementation of the octree mesher plays an important role in reducing computing time. For instance, it takes 261 s to generate a mesh with resolution of 1 °A, while CapsidMesh needs 85, 598 s. Hence, octree spends 0.30% of the time that CapsidMesh requires to generate the mesh of the same biomolecule with the same resolution. The nanoindentation results were mapped into the capsid's mesh representations to illustrate the location of interesting structural features, shown in Fig. 8. Displacements, or deformations, are shown in Fig. 8(a) and (b), where the same displacement is produced by both simulations independently of the mesh used. The von Misses values are represented on Fig. 8(c) and (d). In this case, the maximum value is slightly different, but they are almost equivalent in the distribution over the viral capsid.

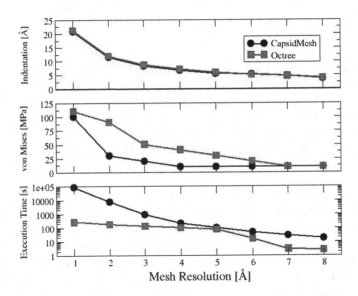

Fig. 7. Capsid meshing and nanoindentation results, comparison to previous method. From top to bottom: Indentation produced, structural stress analysis, and time spent to produce the mesh, as a function of mesh resolution.

The fact that both meshing algorithms produce meshes with different characteristics but that behave the same in the FEM numerical simulations is a positive result. Nonetheless, the octree mesher we present here reduces more than 99% of the meshing time.

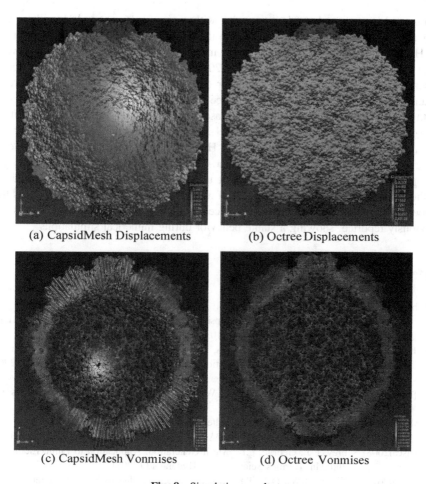

(a) CapsidMesh Displacements   (b) Octree Displacements

(c) CapsidMesh Vonmises   (d) Octree Vonmises

Fig. 8. Simulation results

5   Conclusion

In this work, we report the development of a computational algorithm to produce volumetric meshes of biomolecules based on the volume and position of their constituent atoms. Discretization of space is accomplished by the octree method. Parallelization in combination with HPC techniques allow for an efficient use of memory and fast execution times. Since the mesh elements have an hexahedral geometry, our algorithm can generate a volumetric mesh of any biomolecule or biocomplex, independent of its size, shape, or symmetry.

We built mesh models of representative examples of the four major categories of biomolecules, spanning a large diversity of biological structures and functions.

An important feature of these meshes is that they are FEM-compliant, i.e., they can be directly used to perform numerical simulations of a given biophysical process. To test this, we carried out the simulation of the nanoindentation of a full viral capsid represented by our mesh, and compared it with a previously reported algorithm. It is important to mention that viral capsids are the largest biocomplex in our dataset.

Hence, our results show that the octree mesh algorithm can be used to model very large biocomplexes, even with more than 200,000 atoms, and still keep atomic scale. When executed in a single-core computer (Intel Core i3-3120 2.5 GHz with architecture x86 64 and 4 cores available), octree mesh can generate volumetric meshes of up to 1×10^7 elements. This number increases to 1×10^8 or more when the algorithm is executed in a multi-core computer (Intel Xeon CPU E5-4627 2.6 GHz with architecture x86 64 with 40 available cores) or HPC cluster. Furthermore, it is possible to achieve mesh resolutions of 0.5 Å or higher. The algorithm can be executed in a single laptop PC or in an HPC having efficient use of the RAM. Compared to previous methods, the one reported here is orders of magnitude faster, faithfully reproduces the shape of the biological system, and produces meshes which respond the same as the previously reported, showing a stable behavior during numerical simulations.

References

[Gibbons2007]   Gibbons, M.M., Klug, W.S.: Nonlinear finite-element analysis of nanoindentation of viral capsids. Phys. Rev. E **75**(3), 031901:1–031901:11 (2007). https://doi.org/10.1103/PhysRevE.75.031901

[Arkhipov2009]   Anton, A., Wouter, R., Gijs, W., Klaus, S.: Elucidating the mechanism behind irreversible deformation of viral capsids. Biophys. J. **97**, 2061–2069 (2009)

[Roos2010]   Roos, W.H., Bruinsma, R., Wuite, G.J.L.: Physical virology. Nat. Phys. **6**, 733 (2010)

[Paul1990]   George, P.L., Hecht, F., Saltel, É.: Fully automatic mesh generator for 3D domains of any shape. IMPACT Comput. Sci. Eng. **2**, 187–218 (1990)

[Pascal2008]   Frey, P.J., George, P.L.: Mesh Generation: Application to Finite Elements, 2nd edn. Hermes Sciences ltd., Hyderabad (2008)

[Siu2013]   Cheng, S.W., Dey, T.K., Shewchuk, J.R.: Delaunay Mesh Generation. Chapman and HALL/CRC, Cambridge (2013)

[Paul1998]   Paul, G., Houman, B.: Delaunay Triangulation and Meshing. Application to Finite Elements. Hermes (1998). ISBN 2-86601-692-0

[Weatherill1992]   Weatherill, N.P.: Delaunay triangulation in computational fluid dynamics. Comput. Math Appl. **24**, 129–150 (1992)

[Hardwick1997]   Hardwick, J.C. Implementation and evaluation of an efficient 2D parallel Delaunay triangulation algorithm. In: Proceedings of the 9th Annual Symposium on Parallel Algorithms and Architectures (1997)

[Cigoni1993]   Cigoni, P., Montani, C., Perego, R., Scopigno, R.: Parallel 3D delaunay triangulation. Eurographics Association (1993)

[Schöber1997]   Joachim, S.: An advancing front 2D/3D mesh generator based on abstract rules. Comput. Vis. Sci. **1**, 41–52 (1997)

[Sanner1996]   Michael, S., Arthur, O., Juan-Claude, S.: Reduced surface: an efficient way to compute molecular surfaces. Biopolymers **38**, 305–320 (1996)

[Cheng2009]   Ho-Lun, C., Shi, X.: Quality mesh generation for molecular skin surface using restricted union of balls. J. Comput. Geom. Theory Appl. **42**, 196–206 (2009)

[Yu2008]   Yu, Z., Holst, M.J., Cheng, Y., McCammon, J.A.: Feature preserving adaptive mesh generation for molecular shape modeling and simulation. J. Mol. Graph. Modell. **26**, 1370–1380 (2008)

[Alonzo2018]   Alonzo-Velázquez, J., Botello Rionda, S., Herrera-Guzmán, R., Carrillo-Tripp, M.: CapsidMesh: atomic-detail structured mesh representation of icosahedral viral capsids and the study of their mechanical properties. Int. J. Numer. Methods Biomed. Eng. **34**, e2991 (2018)

[Vargas2012]   Vargas Felix, M., Botello-Rionda, S.: FEMT, open source tools for solving large systems of equations in parallel. Acta universitaria (2012)

[OpenMP2018]   OpenMP Architecture Review Board: OpenMP application programing interface OpenMP (2018)

[Frisken2002]   Frisken, S.F., Perry, R. N.: Simple and efficient traversal methods for quadtrees and octrees. Mitsubishi Electric Research Laboratories (2002)

[Michel2006]   Michel, J.P., et al.: Nanoindentation studies of full and empty viral capsids and the effects of capsid protein mutations on elasticity and strength. Proc. Nat. Acad. Sci. **103**, 6184–6189 (2006)

HPC Modelling

A Simple Model of the Flow in the Steam Chamber in SAGD Oil Recovery

F. J. Higuera[1(✉)] and A. Medina[1,2]

[1] ETSIAE, Universidad Politécnica de Madrid, Plaza Cardenal Cisneros 3,
28040 Madrid, Spain
fhiguera@aero.upm.es
[2] Instituto Politécnico Nacional, SEPI ESIME Azcapotzalco,
Av. de las Granjas 182, Col., 02519 Santa Catarina, CDMX, Mexico
amedinao@ipn.mx

Abstract. A theoretical model is proposed of the flow of steam and its condensation in the steam chamber that forms in an oil reservoir during steam assisted gravity drainage (SAGD). As usual in SAGD, it is assumed that the steam is injected through an upper horizontal pipe and liquid water is recovered through a lower parallel pipe. Numerical computations of the stream function and temperature are used to show that a realistic solution of the problem exists only when the injected mass flux of steam has a special value that depends on other parameters of the problem.

Keywords: Flows through porous media · General theory in fluid dynamics · Thermal convection

1 Introduction

Nearly two thirds of the world's current oil reserves are extra-heavy oil (API gravity less than 10°, density greater than 1000 kg/m³) [1], but the recovery of this unconventional oil, which typically is at low pressures and temperatures [2], requires that its viscosity be decreased by increasing its temperature. A successful method that allows high recovery efficiency is the steam assisted gravity drainage (SAGD) method, which involves injection of steam into the reservoir through a horizontal pipe and production of the mobilized oil through a parallel pipe beneath the injection pipe [3]; see sketch in Fig. 1.

The injected steam displaces the oil that initially saturated the reservoir, leading to the formation of a steam chamber partially depleted of oil around the injection pipe. The steam flows into this chamber through an array of orifices in the wall of the injection pipe, cools down by losing heat to the oil and the solid matrix while moving away from the pipe, and condenses at the boundary of the steam chamber. The latent heat that is released in the condensation is used to heat the oil around the chamber. The viscosity of the oil significantly decreases in a thin layer surrounding the chamber, which allows gravity to efficiently drain the oil in this layer, together with the condensed water, toward the underlying production pipe.

© Springer Nature Switzerland AG 2019
M. Torres and J. Klapp (Eds.): ISUM 2019, CCIS 1151, pp. 337–345, 2019.
https://doi.org/10.1007/978-3-030-38043-4_26

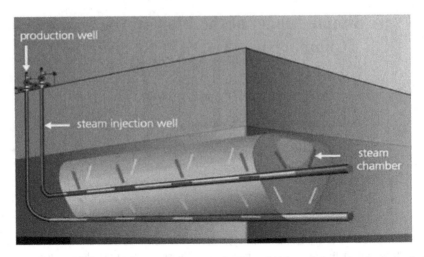

Fig. 1. Schematic of the SAGD method where the steam is injected through a horizontal pipe and the oil is produced through a parallel pipe below the injection pipe. The lower part of the steam chamber meets the production pipe.

In a first stage of growth, before the steam chamber reaches the production pipe, displacement of the cold oil requires a large overpressure. This stage is not considered here. Once the lower end of the chamber reaches the production pipe, the pressure in the chamber decreases to about the pressure in the production pipe, which is not very different from that of the reservoir [4]. The wall of the production pipe has small orifices designed to slowly recover oil and water while minimizing the inflow of sand to the pipe.

In this second stage, the spatial pressure variations in the steam chamber are small compared with the hydrostatic pressure variation in a distance of the order of the height of the steam chamber, which is the order of the pressure variation involved in the drainage of the mobilized oil. However, as we shall see, the small spatial pressure variations determine the flow of steam in the chamber and the distribution of condensation flux at its boundary.

Subsequent upward and sidewise growth of the steam chamber is determined by the rate of drainage of oil in the thin layer around its boundary, which frees space that is occupied by the steam [5–8].

The process in a real reservoir is complicated by additional factors. On the one hand, the boundary of the steam chamber need not be macroscopically smooth, because Saffman's instability may appear at the interface between steam and oil. On the other hand, the oil left in the chamber, and part of the oil mobilized near its boundary, may fall directly across the chamber rather than in the thin layer mentioned above. These important complexities are disregarded in the simple model introduced in the following section, which focuses on the steam flow and the steam condensation at the boundary of a stationary chamber of given size and shape.

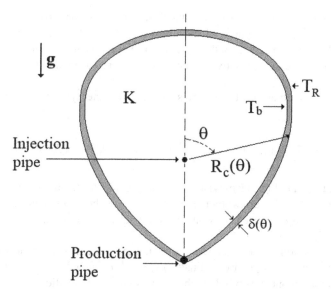

Fig. 2. Schematic of the steam chamber model with the injection and production pipes. The shape of the cross-section of the chamber is given by $R_c(\theta)$ and its wall is kept at the constant temperature T_R smaller than the boiling temperature T_b at the steam-liquid interface. The condensed water drains in the layer of thickness $\delta(\theta) \ll R_c(\theta)$, shaded in the figure.

2 A Model of the Steam Flow

To gain physical insight into the main mechanisms of heat and mass transfer in the steam chamber we consider the stationary, two-dimensional model problem sketched in Fig. 2. A chamber of given shape is filled with a homogeneous porous medium of permeability K. In the polar coordinates of the figure, the shape of the chamber is given by $r = R_c(\theta)$ with $R_c(-\theta) = R_c(\theta)$. A constant mass flux of steam, ϕ per unit length normal to the figure, is injected through the perforated wall of a horizontal pipe of radius small compared to the size of the chamber (which is seen as a steam source at the origin in Fig. 2). The inlet temperature of the steam is T_I, higher than its boiling temperature T_b at the mean pressure of the chamber. The wall of the chamber is impervious. To roughly account for the thermal effect of the rest of the oil reservoir (not included in the model), this wall is kept at a constant temperature T_R lower than T_b.

The steam flows out of the injection pipe, moves across the chamber, and condenses where its temperature decreases to T_b. The condensed water drains under gravity in a layer that extends between the condensation front to the wall of the chamber, and leaves the chamber through the perforated wall of a second horizontal pipe parallel to the injection pipe, at the lowest point of the chamber. The density ρ_w of the liquid water is large compared to the density of the steam, so that the effect of gravity on the steam can be neglected. The thickness $\delta(\theta)$ of the liquid layer is taken to be small compared to $R_c(\theta)$, so that the steam occupies most of the chamber. An estimation of δ is given below following Eq. (3).

The pressure variations associated to the flow of the steam are proportional to ϕ and are taken to be small compared to the mean pressure in the chamber, p_0. In these conditions, the equation of state of the steam can be simplified to $\rho T \approx$ constant $= p_0/R_g$, where ρ and T are the local density and temperature of the steam, and R_g is the steam gas constant.

The continuity equation, the Darcy's law and the energy equation for the steam are [9]

$$\nabla \cdot (\rho v) = 0, \quad v = -\frac{K}{\mu}\nabla p, \quad \rho c_p v \cdot \nabla T = k_e \nabla^2 T, \tag{1}$$

where μ and c_p are the steam viscosity and specific heat, and k_e is the effective conductivity of the medium, which is due mainly to the solid matrix. The thermal diffusivity $\alpha = k_e/\rho_b c_p$ is used in what follows, with ρ_b denoting the steam density at temperature T_b.

A stream function $\psi(r, \theta)$ exists for the stationary two-dimensional flow of steam in the chamber, such that in polar coordinates $\rho v_r = r^{-1}\partial\psi/\partial\theta$ and $\rho v_\theta = \partial\psi/\partial r$. Using the continuity equation and Darcy's law above, we obtain the equation

$$\frac{\partial}{\partial r}\left(Tr\frac{\partial\psi}{\partial r}\right) + \frac{\partial}{\partial\theta}\left(\frac{T}{r}\frac{\partial\psi}{\partial\theta}\right) = 0 \tag{2}$$

for the stream function. In what follows, $\psi_c(\theta)$ will denote the value of the stream function at the condensation front, with $\psi_c(0) = 0$ at the uppermost point of the front. This $\psi_c(\theta)$ is to be found as part of the solution.

Boundary conditions for this equation and the energy equation in (1) at the condensation front can be obtained from balances of mass and energy in the thin liquid layer that surrounds the steam. First, the mass flux of liquid across a section of this layer, characterized by a given value of θ, is equal to the mass flux of steam condensed between the uppermost point $\theta = 0$ and that section. Using Darcy's law for the liquid, of viscosity μ_w, the local draining velocity in a section of the layer is $\rho_w g K \sin \beta/\mu_w$, where $\beta(\theta)$ is the angle of the condensation front to the horizontal, and the local mass flux of liquid across this section of the layer is $\rho_w^2 g K \sin\beta\delta/\mu_w$, where $\delta(\theta)$ is the local thickness of the layer. The mass flux of steam that condenses between the uppermost point of the chamber boundary, $\theta = 0$, and the section considered is $\psi_c(\theta)$, from the definition of ψ_c. Therefore the balance of mass in the liquid layer reads

$$\frac{\rho_w^2 g K}{\mu_w}\sin\beta(\theta)\delta(\theta) = \psi_c(\theta). \tag{3}$$

Since $\psi_c \sim \phi$, the thickness of the liquid layer is $\delta \sim \mu_w\phi/\rho_w^2 g K$.

Second, the energy equation for the liquid reduces in first approximation to $\partial^2 T/\partial n^2 = 0$, where n is the direction normal to the condensation front. The solution of this equation with $T = T_b$ at the condensation front and $T = T_R$ at the wall of the chamber gives $-\partial T/\partial n = (T_b - T_R)/\delta$ in the liquid. Using this result, the energy balance across the condensation front is

$$k_e \frac{T_b - T_R}{\delta} = -k_e \frac{\partial T}{\partial n}\bigg|_{steam} + L\frac{d\psi_c}{ds}, \tag{4}$$

where the first term on the right-hand side is the heat flux reaching the condensation front by conduction in the steam, and the second term is the heat released by steam condensation per unit time and unit area of the condensation front. Here L is the latent heat of condensation, and $d\psi_c/ds$, with s the arc length along the front, is the local mass flux of steam condensing at the front.

In what follows, conditions (3) and (4) are applied at $r = R_c(\theta)$, which coincides in first approximation with the condensation front because $\delta \ll R_c$.

The problem can be written in dimensionless form scaling distances with the distance H between the injection and production pipes, the steam temperature with T_b, and the stream function and ψ_c with $k_e T_b/L$. Using the same symbols to denote the dimensionless variables and their dimensional counterparts, which will no longer appear, we have

$$\left. \begin{array}{l} 0 = \frac{\partial}{\partial r}\left(Tr\frac{\partial\psi}{\partial r}\right) + \frac{\partial}{\partial\theta}\left(\frac{T}{r}\frac{\partial\psi}{\partial\theta}\right), \\[2mm] \frac{S}{r}\left(\frac{\partial\psi}{\partial\theta}\frac{\partial T}{\partial r} - \frac{\partial\psi}{\partial r}\frac{\partial T}{\partial\theta}\right) = \frac{1}{r}\frac{\partial}{\partial r}\left(r\frac{\partial T}{\partial r}\right) + \frac{1}{r^2}\frac{\partial^2 T}{\partial\theta^2} \end{array} \right\} \tag{5}$$

with the boundary conditions

$$r = \epsilon : \psi = \phi\frac{\theta}{2\pi}, \quad T = T_I \tag{6}$$

$$r = R_c(\theta) : T = 1, \quad \Pi\frac{\sin\beta}{\psi_c} = -\frac{\partial T}{\partial n}\bigg|_{R_c} + \frac{d\psi_c}{ds} \tag{7}$$

$$\theta = 0 : \psi = 0, \quad \frac{\partial T}{\partial\theta} = 0, \quad \theta = \pi : \psi = \frac{\phi}{2}, \quad \frac{\partial T}{\partial\theta} = 0, \tag{8}$$

where $\psi_c(\theta) = \psi(R_c(\theta), \theta)$; $\phi = 2\psi_c$ is the dimensionless mass flux of steam injected into the chamber, scaled with $k_e T_b/L$; and $d\psi_c/ds = [R_c^2 + R_c'^2]^{-1/2}d\psi_c/d\theta$ and $\sin\beta = (R_c\sin\theta - R_c'\cos\theta)[R_c^2 + R_c'^2]^{-1/2}$, with $R_c' = dR_c/d\theta$. Conditions (6) state that the steam enters radially the chamber with temperature T_I. The first condition (7) says that the temperature at the condensation front is the boiling temperature of the liquid (equal to unity in dimensionless variables), while the second condition (7) is the dimensionless form of the energy balance (4) across the condensation front. Finally, conditions (8) are conditions of symmetry at the vertical center plane of the chamber.

The problem contains the four dimensionless parameters (in addition to ϕ)

$$S = \frac{c_p T_b}{L}, \quad \Pi = \frac{\rho_w^2 KgHL}{\mu_w k_e T_b}\frac{T_b - T_R}{T_b}, T_I, \quad \epsilon, \tag{9}$$

$\varepsilon \ll 1$ being the radius of the injection pipe scaled with H.

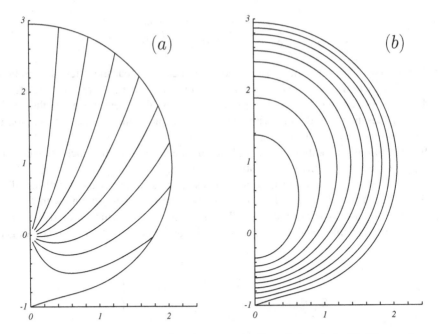

Fig. 3. (*a*) Ten equispaced streamlines between $\psi = 0$ and $\psi = \phi /2$. (*b*) Nine equispaced isotherms between $T = T_b$ and $T = T_I$. Values of other parameters are S = 0.469, Π = 43.6 and $\varepsilon = 0.1$.

3 Results

The formulation (5)–(8) is complete, but the two boundary conditions at $r = R_c(\theta)$ are atypical in that both involve the temperature. Consistency of these two conditions determines the stream function at the condensation front, $\psi_c(\theta)$. However, the solution of the problem, which must be computed numerically, turns out to be physically admissible only for a particular value of ϕ that depends on the dimensionless parameters (9). If the injected flow rate is larger than this value, then a fraction of the steam reaches the production pipe without condensing inside the chamber. If the injected flow rate is smaller, then the solution features additional influx of steam through the production pipe, which is not possible in a real reservoir. The value of ϕ that separates these undesirable or unrealistic conditions must be found as a function of the parameters (9).

For the numerical treatment, Eqs. (5) are rewritten in terms of the variables $\xi = (r - \varepsilon)/(R_c(\theta) - \varepsilon)$ and θ, and discretized using second order finite differences. An iterative scheme is used to solve the discretized problem which amounts to introducing an artificial time, adding time derivatives to the left-hand sides of (5) and the second condition (7) (so that, in particular, $\phi = 2\psi_c(\pi)$ depends on time), and marching in this time until the solution becomes stationary. Numerical solutions have been computed for $R_c(\theta) = 1 + \cos(1.1\ \theta) - \cos(1.1\ \pi)$, which resembles the shape of the steam chamber observed in some experiments [3, 6, 10].

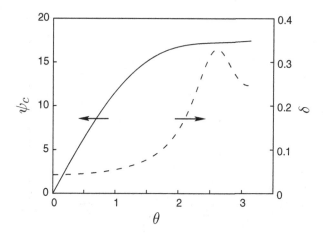

Fig. 4. Dimensionless stream function at the condensation front, $\psi_c(\theta)$ (solid), and thickness of the liquid layer, $\delta(\theta)$ (dashed, right-hand side scale), as functions of θ for S = 0.469, Π = 43.6, T_I = 1.2, T_R = 0.8 and ε = 0.1.

Figure 3 shows some streamlines and isotherms for S = 0.469, Π = 43.6, T_I = 1.2 and ε = 0.1. The value of Π is obtained for ρ_w = 1000 kg/m³, μ_w = 1 mPa s, H = 5 m, k_e = 4.5 W/m K, which are typical values for the Athabasca formation [11], for which p_0 = 15 atm (T_b = 473 K), and T_R/T_b = 0.8. This value of T_R/T_b amounts to a wall temperature of 377 K, which is higher than the reservoir temperature reported for this formation. The difference attempts to account for the fact that the reservoir temperature is attained in a real reservoir only at distances from the steam chamber large compared to the thickness of the layer of mobilized oil. The computed dimensionless mass flux of steam is ϕ = 34.88. The results show how the conditions (7) determine the distributions of temperature and velocity of the steam, whose streamlines are radial close to the injection pipe but bend upwards in the rest of the chamber, making the distribution of condensed flux $d\psi_c/ds$ nonuniform in order to simultaneously satisfy the balances of mass and energy (3) and (4). The distributions of ψ_c and the thickness δ of the liquid layer (scaled with H) are shown in Fig. 4.

Figure 5 illustrates the dependence of ϕ on the parameters Π and T_I. These results can be understood noticing that the heat flux across the liquid layer (the left-hand side of the second condition (7)) increases when Π is increased, be it by increasing $\widetilde{\Pi} = \rho_w^2 KgHL/\mu_w k_e T_b$ or by decreasing T_R/T_b. This leads to an increase of $d\psi_c/ds$ on the right-hand side of this equation, and thus of ϕ. Similarly, increasing T_I increases the heat flux that reaches the condensation front from the steam (the first term on the right-hand side of the second condition (7)), which leads to a decrease of $d\psi_c/ds$ and thus of ϕ.

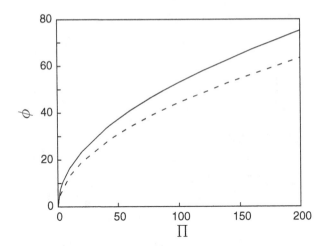

Fig. 5. Dimensionless mass flux of steam injected in the chamber as a function of Π for $T_l = 1.2$ (solid) and $T_f = 2$ (dashed). Values of other parameters are S = 0.469 and $\varepsilon = 0.1$.

4   Conclusions

A simple model of the flow in the steam chamber that forms during SAGD oil recovery has been proposed that accounts for the motion and cooling of the steam, its condensation at the boundary of the chamber, and the drainage of liquid water in a thin layer that surrounds the steam. The model consists of mass and energy conservation equations for a steam-saturated porous medium, supplemented with boundary conditions at the steam-liquid interface that express mass and energy balances across the interface and the layer of draining water. The flow of mobilized oil is not included in the model, which therefore cannot account for the growth of the steam chamber or predict the recovery factor. Heat transfer to the oil is modeled by keeping the temperature of a fictitious wall surrounding the chamber at a constant value smaller than the boiling temperature.

The pressure variations in the steam are small compared to the hydrostatics pressure variation in the reservoir over a distance of the order of the height of the chamber. However, these small pressure variations determine the pattern of the steam flow, whose stream lines are not radial from the injection pipe but bend upward in order for the local condensation rate at the steam-liquid interface to be consistent with the flux of water in the draining layer. Numerical solutions have been computed for realistic conditions. These solutions show that the mass flux of water leaving the chamber coincides with the mass flux of steam supplied through the injection pipe only for a special value of the latter that depends on the parameters of the problem.

Acknowledgments. AM acknowledges the support from IPN, CONACYT and UPM to the project *"Fundamental models for the thermal methods of steam injection in EOR"*. The work of FJH was supported by the Spanish MINECO through project DPI2017-86547-C2-2-P.

References

1. Reyes, M.G., Leon, A., López, G.: Nueva clasificación para yacimientos de aceites pesados y extrapesados de México. Ing. Petr. **57**, 421–436 (2017)
2. Meyer, R.F., Attanasi, E.D., Freeman, P.A.: Heavy oil and natural bitumen resources in geological basins of the world, Open File-Report 2007–1084, U.S. Geological Survey, Reston, Virginia (2007)
3. Butler, R.M.: Thermal Recovery of Oil and Bitumen. Prentice Hall, New Jersey (1991)
4. Fattahpour, V., et al.: Sand control testing for steam injection wells. In: SPE Canada Heavy Oil Technical Conference, Calgary, Alberta, Canada, Paper SPE-189766-MS, March 2018
5. Sasaki, K., Akibayashi, S., Yazawa, N., Doan, Q., Farouq Ali, S.M.: Experimental modelling of the SAGD process 3/4 enhancing SAGD performance with periodic stimulation of the horizontal producer, SPE-56544-MS. In: SPE Annual Technical Conference and Exhibition, Houston, Texas, October 1999
6. Sasaki, K., Akibayashi, S., Yasawa, N., Kaneko, F.: Microscopic visualization with high resolution optical-fiber scope at steam chamber interface on initial stage of SAGD process, SPE-75241. In: SPE/DOE Improved Oil Recovery Symposium, Tulsa, Oklahoma, April 2002
7. Mohammadzadeh, O., Rezaei, N., Chatzis, I.: Pore-level investigation of heavy oil and bitumen recovery using hybrid SAGD process. In: 2010 SPE Improved Oil Recovery Symposium, Tulsa, Oklahoma USA, Paper SPE 130011, April 2010
8. Mohammadzadeh, O., Rezaei, N., Chatzis, I.: Pore-scale performance evaluation and mechanistic studies of the solvent-aided SAGD (SA-SAGD) process using visualization experiments. Transp. Porous Med. **108**, 437–480 (2015)
9. Nield, D.A., Bejan, A.: Convection in porous media, 4th edn. Springer, New York (2013)
10. Butler, R.M., Stephens, D.J.: The gravity drainage of steam-heated heavy oil to parallel horizontal wells. J. Can. Pet. Technol. **20**, 90–96 (1981)
11. Gotawala, D.R., Gates, I.D.: Steam fingering at the edge of a steam chamber in a heavy oil reservoir. Can. J. Chem. Eng. **86**, 1011–1022 (2008)

Author Index

Printed in the United States
By Bookmasters